RESEARCHING SEX AND SEXUALITIES

RESEARCHING SEX AND SEXUALITIES

Edited by Charlotte Morris, Paul Boyce, Andrea Cornwall,
Hannah Frith, Laura Harvey and Yingying Huang

ZED

Researching Sex and Sexualities was first published in 2018 by Zed Books Ltd, The Foundry, 17 Oval Way, London SE11 5RR, UK.

www.zedbooks.net

Typeset in Plantin and Kievit by Swales & Willis Ltd, Exeter, Devon
Index by Rohan Bolton
Cover design by Kika Sroka-Miller
Cover photo © Jure Ahtik / EyeEm / Getty

A catalogue record for this book is available from the British Library

ISBN 978-1-78699-320-5 hb
ISBN 978-1-78699-319-9 pb
ISBN 978-1-78699-321-2 pdf
ISBN 978-1-78699-322-9 epub
ISBN 978-1-78699-323-6 mobi

Printed by CPI Group (UK) Ltd, Croydon, CR0 4YY

This book is dedicated to Ken Plummer in recognition of the inspiration he has provided and continues to provide to so many researchers in this field and his support and contribution to our conference and this publication.

CONTENTS

ACKNOWLEDGEMENTS

Thanks are due to all the contributors who have contributed such thoughtful and thought-provoking work to this volume, to all those who have given generously of their time to edit sections of the book and those who have supported the publication in so many ways. Particular thanks are due to Kim Walker from Zed Books for all the patience and support for the publication process and to Dr Beatrice Monaco for assistance with proofreading. Professor Ken Plummer has generously provided an interview, included in this volume, and provided a keynote at the Researching Sexualities conference which inspired the collection. Further keynote speakers included Dr Hannah Frith, Professor Rachel Thomson, Professor Yingying Huang, Dr Wei Wei, Professor Andrea Cornwall, Dr Laura Harvey and Professor Rachel Spronk, and all the attendees contributed so much to the ongoing discussions. Thanks are due to all those who helped to convene and organise the initial conference as well as the development of this publication, including Rachel Wood, Elsie Whittington, Emily Humphrey and Tianyang Zhou.

FOREWORD

Meg-John Barker

I was very excited indeed to be asked to write the foreword for this
excellent collection. That was not just because I sadly missed the
conference that it was based upon, having keynoted its precursor,
but also because the volume is utterly groundbreaking in the way
it captures both the pleasures and pains of working in this field.
Reading through the chapters is as emotional a journey as it is an
intellectual one. Also – appropriately – the erotic experience of
writer and reader is present, instead of strangely absent as it is in so
much work on sex and sexualities.

Researching Sex and Sexualities provides an ongoing meditation
on a set of themes that are very dear to my heart – and to the
hearts of many of us working in this area. It is great to see most
of the contributors explicitly attending to the importance of our
work having a tangible impact on the world, in terms of informing
practitioners, policy-makers and general publics, and challenging
taken-for-granted cultural assumptions. Also clearly present are
the tensions involved in achieving such an aim when sexualities
scholarship is so undervalued in the neoliberal academy. Within
this broader theme, the following interconnected threads weave
through many of the chapters:

- the related ethical questions which are raised whenever we coach
  sexual stories from individuals and communities, and disseminate them more widely, particularly stories which have previously
  been hidden or silenced;
- the power dynamics in play between researcher and researched,
  and the implications of these for the capacity to give and receive
  informed consent;

- the imperfections and messiness of the research process which mean that it is not always possible to predict the impact of what we are doing on participants, the wider world or ourselves;
- the engagement of our own erotic subjectivities in the process of research.

Given the latter point, it's fascinating to me how all the other threads regarding the research process echo what goes on in an erotic encounter. Indeed they are all key themes in the sex advice work that I have been doing with sex educator Justin Hancock, based on my own analyses of sex advice books, columns and websites (Barker and Hancock, 2017; Barker, Gill and Harvey, 2017).

Whenever we engage sexually with another person (or people) it is an imperfect, potentially messy, process in which it is not easy to predict the impact that what we do will have on the other person, on ourselves and beyond the encounter. Thus consensual engagement is vital, but this needs to be something far more nuanced and complex than the popular understanding of simply checking whether the other person is up for it, and then going for it if they are. Perhaps that standard way of navigating sexual consent could be seen as analogous to simply getting the go-ahead from the ethics committee and the participant signature on the consent form!

As Justin and I explore in our work, the process of consent needs to be ongoing throughout the encounter. It also needs to be done with awareness of the power imbalances between those involved, which means that some people are far more able than others to tune into their desires, to communicate them to others and to refuse what they don't want. Finally consent needs to be done in a way that is mindful for the dominant cultural scripts for sex which it is much harder to deviate from than it is to follow.

For this reason certain erotic interests, desires and orderings are far more sayable – and doable – than others. One or more person involved may endeavour to coax, from the other, a verbal and/or non-verbal sense of what their greatest delight would be in that moment. But how possible it is to admit that – to ourselves and/or to each other – depends a great deal on the wider cultural scripts, context and relationships in play. As Rachel Spronk rightly points out, sexual experiences are made possible – or impossible – by context. As in the research encounter, divulging the more hidden, secret or taboo sexual stories is a vulnerable business due to the potential reactions of the other people present at the time, and the other people with whom they may share those stories, all of which are unpredictable.

So sex – and research about sex – is messy, complex and unpredictable. It is shot through with power dynamics which may expand or contract the potential for consent. And it is potentially restricted by the existing culturally available scripts, the level of trust in the relationship and the ethical integrity of those involved, far beyond what a standard ethics committee procedure might understand by 'ethics'.

I think it is therefore incredibly helpful for those of us working in this area to take the lessons we learn from the process of research and apply them to sex, and to take the lessons we learn from the process of sex and apply them to research. Indeed that is something that my colleagues and I on the sex advice project (Justin Hancock, Laura Harvey and Rosalind Gill) have explicitly endeavoured to do in all our engagements. We reflect on this process in some depth in the book *Mediated Intimacy* (Barker, Gill and Harvey, forthcoming 2018) and on our ongoing podcast (megjohnandjustin.com).

In particular, the following practices, which are useful to apply to sex, were also useful to apply to the research and writing collaboration process. Again we see these themes appear several times over the chapters in this collection.

- Engaging critically with the wider culture in which we are embedded, in this case the academic research culture. This includes taken-for-granted assumptions about, for example, the speed at which research should be conducted and written up; the appropriate way to feedback on other people's writing; hierarchical assumptions about whose voices are more or less valuable; and the prioritising of deadlines, financial matters, and productivity over people.

- An ethos of self-consent where we tune into what excites and engages us rather than doing certain things in certain ways because we feel that we should, forcing our bodies and ourselves into non-consensual practices.
- An ethics of care and ongoing consent where we continually check in with each other about where we are at, and seek to focus on projects and areas where our passions overlap, rather than pushing people to research, write, or otherwise act in ways they're less comfortable with or keen on.
- This involves being present to ourselves and to each other, rather than being focused on a particular future goal or climax (e.g. funding, publication or praise).

Considering what we can learn about doing research from doing sex, and vice versa, takes us to a final vital theme that runs through this book which is the joy of (sex) research.

In Audre Lorde's essential (1984) essay, she argues that the erotic teaches us what we're capable of and how life can be. She uses a metaphor of the wartime blocks of margarine that were dull and pale but came with a pellet of golden colour that you worked through the block until it infused the whole thing bright yellow. She says that the erotic can be like that in our lives, making the whole thing more vibrant. We can allow the erotic to permeate our lives way beyond obviously sexual experiences, to everything that we do, whether that is building a bookcase or writing a poem (see Barker, 2017).

The authors who contribute to this volume provide excellent examples of infusing our research with the erotic in this way. Through their writing we get a real sense of the joy and excitement we experience as part of the research and writing process: through meeting participants; enjoying intimacies with them and with each other; making discoveries, connections and breakthroughs; and finding new ways to do things and to make a difference in spite of all the difficulties, emotional challenges and setbacks inherent in the process.

In Parts Three and Four of the book, Nicoletta Landi, Alba Barbé i Serra and Anna Madill all explicitly reflect on the importance of starting from the position of the researcher and researched as erotic beings whose subjectivities are present in the research encounter. Madill talks about the emotional intensities involved in writing about erotic content that she herself enjoys, for example, and Landi describes being seduced by her research topic.

In a similar way, we can be seduced by the kinds of theories and ways of knowing explored in the Part One of the book. Reading this section reminded me of Shannon and Willis's (2010) paper on theoretical polyamory. For example, we might have a regular primary relationship with one school of thought, while enjoying different kinds of engagement in a few secondary – theoretical – relationships. We might find ourselves flirting outrageously with a new perspective, or engaging in secret trysts with one that we are not supposed to find so attractive. Perhaps we might enjoy bringing our favourite theories together for a delightful – or awkward – threesome.

In the second section of the book on creative methodologies we get a clear sense of the way the erotic can infuse our research, as we engage with innovative techniques in ways which are playful, exciting and potentially deeply satisfying. Catherine Barrett's body mapping, Catherine Vulliamy's cultural patchworking, P.J. Macleod's poetry and Ester McGeeney and colleagues' cover versions all give a sense of the sensual possibilities of creative methods for engaging the erotic to capture something that is often intangible or elusive from participants, and to communicate that to an audience.

Finally the erotic runs through the wonderful interview with Ken Plummer that concludes this collection. As a long time fan I loved reading about the ways Ken's work has been driven by his personal/ political engagements, and about his playful and passionate encounters with the theories, values and methodologies he has been drawn to over the years. In considering how we can make the world a better place through what we do he rightly advises: 'be *passionate* about your research, your teaching, your work: make sure you have a good reason for doing it, find your values, make sure you know where you stand, not just in terms of why you are doing your research and where you want to take it but also in how you treat people'.

Meg-John Barker
October 2017

References

Barker, M.-J. (2017) 'Understanding Our Selves through Erotic Fiction', in Sky, A. (ed.) *Identity: An Eroticon Anthology*, London: Resonance Press, pp. 32–44.

Barker, M.-J. and Hancock, J. (2017) *Enjoy Sex (How, When and If You Want To): A Practical and Inclusive Guide*, London: Icon Books.

Barker, M.-J., Gill, R. and Harvey, L. (2017) 'Sex Advice Books and Self-Help', in Smith, C., Atwood, F., Egan, R.D. and McNair, B. (eds) *Routledge Companion to Media, Sex and Sexuality*, London: Routledge, pp. 202–213.

Barker, M.-J., Gill, R. and Harvey, L. (forthcoming, 2018) *Mediated Intimacy: Sex Advice in Media Culture*, London: Polity.

Lorde, A. (1984) 'The Uses of the Erotic: The Erotic as Power', in Lorde, A. (2012) *Sister Outsider: Essays and Speeches*, Berkeley, CA: Crossing Press.

Shannon, D. and Willis, A. (2010) 'Theoretical Polyamory: Some Thoughts on Loving, Thinking, and Queering Anarchism', *Sexualities*, 13(4), pp. 433–443.

EDITORIAL INTRODUCTION

Paul Boyce, Charlotte Morris and Andrea Cornwall

This book explores the creative, personal and contextual parameters of researching sex and sexualities. Building on conversations opened at an international conference held at the University of Sussex in 2015, the book extends out of the proposition that conceiving sexualities across epistemological and methodological perspectives is key to contemporary sexualities research. Such research transects formal disciplinary boundaries and flirts with theory versus application debates and divides in new and provocative ways. We hope that this collection might be read in concert with such transgressive aspirations.

Traversing disciplinary and global contexts, the contributors to the volume work from within varied fields, each employing different concepts and methods. Yet across this diversity, the authors share common concerns; mutual commitments to querying what research on sex and sexualities might entail, in the present moment and over time, and from within academic milieux and beyond. Intersectional in intent, a core aim of the volume is to open new critical considerations, based on close and reflexive research projects and innovative engagements on and in sexual life-worlds and of sexual practices and intimacies.

Sex and sexuality are complex concepts; they refer to bodily, situational and subjective experiences that resist ready categorisation. Naming sexualities as attributes of people's experience is an especially sensitive business in research. Part of the problem is that sexuality, as a term of analysis, may be bound up with both specific and universal terms of reference. On the one hand framing the sexual in research may be seen to adhere to a particular (Western) discourse that combines and claims certain attributes

2 | BOYCE ET AL.

of experience as sexualities. This may run counter to other contextual practices whereby 'sexuality', per se, may not exist as a domain term for conceiving certain configurations of embodied intimacies: what khanna (2016) terms sexualness, for instance. Nonetheless, comparability, and the capacity to conceive of sexualities across contexts and amidst global flows of political-economy, information technologies, legislation and so on, requires shared points of reference. Being sensitive to culture or context also risks falling into ontological specificity in a manner that closes down analysis, prevailing against any common site of concern that might be named as 'sexuality'.

On the other hand, in naming sexualities as experiential fields of study, researchers run the risk of stripping people's intimate and erotic encounters of the qualities that might make them affectively possible (Moore, 2012). In many scenes of life sexualities are typically not socially shown, claimed or cited. Even where sexualities are named and claimed, for example in the contexts of rights-based activism, intrinsic residues may remain, aspects of sexual life-worlds and experiences that might not fit into any given discourse aimed at recognition (Correa et al., 2008). Citing sexualities, then, might also be to inherently evoke experiences that may not be readily represented. Such qualities might be especially so in respect of stigmatised sexual practices and desires, but they also pertain more broadly. As social scientists we must be attendant to such ambiguities and representational deficiencies.

Amidst such concerns, much sexualities scholarship is typically informed by a will to know: to figure the sexual as a viable, yet problematic, research domain. A central proposition of the book is to bring such processes into question. The chapters each recognise sexualities as multifaceted performative fields. This in turn provokes reflection about how to explore sexual subjects, subjectivities and practices in empirical and experiential terms that are attendant to ambiguity. For many of the book's authors this has entailed the use of creative and experimental methods that explore what we can come to know – how, why and to what effect.

Against this background, a key aim of the book is to bring about innovative dialogues. The chapters, taken as a whole, engender cross-cutting questions pertaining to the conceptual and methodological framing of sex and sexualities. Some of the questions that interweave in and out of different chapters include: In what terms might sex and sexualities be studied as social, psychodynamic and bodily domains of experience? If we think of sexualities in the plural, as multiple and fractal, does this imply that they are not singularly evident empirically? And what do such concerns engender at the interface of theory, method and practice? Variations of such questions may be seen to have underscored the social scientific study of sexualities, from the emergence of the field of study to the present day. This is particularly so with respect to the promises presented by closely attentive commitments to sexualities research as opening out ongoing questions rather than presenting claims to any kind of holistic or total perspective. We consider such a sensibility as a critical orientation for work in this field. Work flowing out of such a standpoint may be tentative in terms of any aspirations to explain whole sexual life-worlds. Yet it may also embrace such an ethos as the basis for deeply reflexive, queer and querying research positionalities.

Sexualities, knowledge, power

Interpreting sexualities in relation to varying fields of meaning entails research registers that reach beyond purely subjective and interpersonal intent. Conceived of in these terms, sexualities are especially sensitive barometers of broader meanings and conditions. Such readings of sexualities have most often been put forward by contemporary students and scholars in conjunction with the emergence of constructivism as a dominant paradigm in the field of study, more than three decades ago (see, for example, Weeks, 1986; Epstein, 1987; Stein, 2013). Importantly, this emergence significantly contributed toward locating sexualities as a social scientific terrain within fields of power and politics, beyond biology and sexology. As Foucault wrote:

> The manifold sexualities – those which appear with the different ages (sexualities of the infant or the child), those which become fixated on particular tastes or practices (the sexuality of the invert, the gerontophile, the fetishist), those which, in a diffuse manner, invest relationships (the sexuality of doctor and patient, teacher and student, psychiatrist and mental patient), those which haunt spaces (the sexuality of the home, the school, the prison) – all form the correlate of exact procedures of power. (Foucault, 1978, p. 67)

This kind of analytical development, which settled sexualities amidst refracted regimes of knowledge/power also helped to dislocate sexualities too. The sexual was firmly disassociated from any assumptions of constancy, as if bodily fixed against socio-historical flows and temporalities. Rather, sexualities came to be understood as isomorphic with these. So too, in turn, the scope of sexualities research was magnified; pulled away from the orbit of micro-sociological perspectives bound up with the study of 'behaviour' (Gagnon and Parker, 1995). Rather 'sexual practices' entered the lexicon of sexualities scholarship, situating sexual and gendered intimacies within fields of wider signification.

We describe such processes equivocally. As we go on to consider, such a view of the effects of constructivism is inevitably partial and limited. Nonetheless analytical developments most associated with constructivist perspectives might be regarded as the most enduring in contemporary 'sex and sexualities' studies. In each of our varied experiences of teaching sexualities, for instance, scholars of the social sciences can still be seen as most compelled by constructivist legacies – with Foucault still rating highly in the incidence and frequency of student's citational practices. Such observations parse too into the prevalence of bio-politics and governance as prevailing paradigms in much contemporary sexualities research. Accordingly, we most often find sexualities conceived of at broadly macro-sociological scales.

Inevitably such analytics bring the sexual into view in certain kinds of ways; perhaps as discursive effects. Or as sites of necro-political pathologisation, structural violence and resistance, bio-medicalisation and/or in respect of legislative consequences (Haritaworn et al., 2014; Narrain and Gupta, 2011). Sexualities research, in these terms, has come to speak of wider life and death worlds, and the contemporary fragilities and futurities that might be born or foreclosed amidst divergent globalisms – perhaps especially amidst life-projects of sexual dissidence or patriarchal disempowerment.

Amidst such concerns, how, as researchers, do we traverse divides between attention to intimate moments within a wider pull to form interpretive meanings beyond the moment alone? One way of figuring such a question is to wonder about how we might reintegrate sex with sexuality in our research projects. By this we mean to evoke a view of sex as a domain of erotic encounter. Such encounters may be, for instance, pleasurable, violent, emotionally intimate and/or otherwise. They may empower and/or demean. They may bring life or hasten death. They may reproduce or undo gender norms. They may be figured with or against reproductive sexualities, and with or in variance to hetero- and homo-normative ways of being. Via what means, as researchers, might we telescope our projects across these conceptual and contextual parameters from one to the other, and over sites, subjectivities and systems? How might sensation and desire, for instance, reside within sexualities research at different scales of analysis – as experiential provinces that engender their own affects and effects? How might we figure the scope of contemporary sexualities research accordingly – inscribing the intimate with the global, and vice versa and all things in-between?

Such analytical concerns reside in the contemporary study of sex and sexualities in specific and vague ways. For some researchers, these may be directly defined domains of reflection.

For others, such queries may perform as a resonance field – a background reverberation, potentially felt but not always stated. For informants in research projects too, the inscribing of life-projects across intimate and macro scales of experiencing may be variously conceived. Rachel Spronk, who gave a keynote at the conference from which the book derives, has explored such concerns through her ethnographic work in contemporary Kenya. Engaging with young professionals in Nairobi she has addressed ways in which sexual sensations have come into being for her interlocutors in contexts of modernity (Spronk, 2012). Orgasm, for instance, might have become newly felt – or 'feelable' – among middle-class residents of Nairobi in a manner that speaks to changes in gendered, sexual and professional aspirations. But this is not to simply locate sexuality as a construct of economy of globalisation. Rather, for Spronk, an aim is to seek entry points into sexualities research that bring sex (touching, feeling, arousing) explicitly back into an ethnographic research register.

Such methodological concerns pertain to the present volume. This is so, for instance, in respect of contributing authors' methodological commitments to grounded, reflexive researcher orientations and felt intimacies. These may relate to the sexual experiences described in research processes and/or the erotics of the research moment. Landi, for example, emphasises the importance for her research of beginning from the standpoint of being a sexual person. Reflections on the intimate aspects of research – both in terms of approaching the subject matter and the intimacies which arise during the process – reverberate throughout this volume. For example, Barbé i Serra (Chapter 11) reflects deeply on the erotic subjectivities present but not always spoken in a research encounter. Vulliamy (Chapter 6) adopts a multi-layered research approach in order to capture the 'personal' realm of desires, fears and identities in relation to sex and love through collage; Barrett (Chapter 5) reflects on experiments with body mapping as a route to overcoming difficulties in articulation of complex feelings and sometimes painful experiences and Carter

(Chapter 4) emphasises the importance of challenging notions of 'disembodied research' in her field.

Authors in this volume raise issues about attending to the ethical dimensions of research which attempts to 'coach' (Plummer, 1995) participants into expressing aspects of their lives that have otherwise often remained hidden, taboo, silenced, elusive – indeed 'unthinkable' (Barbé i Serra, Chapter 11) or unspeakable (see for example Barrett, Chapter 5; McGeeney et al., Chapter 8; Morris, Chapter 15; Radoslovich, Chapter 14). Authors especially take up the personal and political implication of such research actions. And these reflections open questions about conceiving sexual identities and life-worlds creatively, and within erotic research stances.

A notable feature of the book, we feel, is the openness and candour from among the contributors concerning the imperfections of the research process – its messiness, failures, silences, and confusions; things left unexplored, unspoken, unknown and uncertain. See, for example, Day (Chapter 10) who discusses a first experience of conducting fieldwork and encountering multiple 'lost in translation' moments, thereby reminding us of the complex linguistic, cultural, social, political, organisational, erotic and legal terrains researchers need to navigate with varying degrees of success. Barrett (Chapter 5), Madill (Chapter 13), Morris (Chapter 15) and Radoslovich (Chapter 14) speak of the awkward moments, the silences and the shame, discomfort, guilt and embarrassment sometimes attached to talking about sex.

These are aspects of research that can so often be hidden in the academy, but which are especially germane to exploring sexual practices, identities and life-worlds in respect of their attendant opaque materialities and mysteries. In a special interview included in this volume, Ken Plummer reiterates, drawing on the symbolic interactionist perspective, the importance of working with ambiguity, complexity, contingency and flux. In concert with such thinking the book contains deep reflections on the complexities of understanding language, bodies and spaces and of capturing ostensibly personal emotional and embodied experiences in order to understand lived experiences of sexuality. Probing the lived experiences of researchers in this field raises questions of positionality; of situating ourselves as thinking, feeling, sexual, political beings – in the context of our research (as highlighted by Edelman in Chapter 3 and Landi in Chapter 16) while recognising that such positionalities, standpoints, perspectives and identities are in constant flux.

As researchers we often, perhaps inevitably, find ourselves in positions of privilege in relation to our participants and so power predictably comes into play in our encounters. This is noted by a number of contributors, including Judea Alhadeff (Chapter 1), Morris (Chapter 15), Radoslovich (Chapter 14) and Cornwall (Chapter 12). Indeed Plummer reminds us of the importance of attending to the care of, respect for, and dignity of research participants (in the interview, this volume). Researchers carry responsibility for ensuring the safety of participants, especially pertinent in a field where we are encouraging people to share aspects of their lives which may be deemed to be personal, even risky, potentially exposing non-normativities, vulnerabilities and desires. And as Plummer reminds us in his interview, there is the potential to change lives during the research process itself. Contributors have, in response to such ethical concerns, reflected on the importance of enabling participants to have ownership over the research process (Johnson, Chapter 9) and attending to issues of authorial voice (McGeeney et al., Chapter 8).

Researchers have also discussed ways of ensuring their work has a tangible impact in the world with the potential for contributing to social change by challenging assumptions and social myths (Barrett, Chapter 5), ensuring research paradigms enable meaningful data which reflects lived experiences (Edelman, Chapter 3), finding ways to bridge academic and practitioner contexts (Johnson, Chapter 9), reflecting on the implications and potentials for our own pedagogical practices and education more broadly (Landi, Chapter 16), committing to ethical and social justice concerns through art, writing, activism and teaching (Judea Alhadeff, Chapter 1) and identifying creative ways to reach and speak to diverse audiences (McGeeney et al., Chapter 8; Cornwall, Chapter 12).

Yet on taking up such requirements in our projects, within academic settings, as sexualities researchers we can often find ourselves relatively powerless. Our studies may be side-lined, not taken seriously or prioritised for funding – particularly in current challenging economic and political times. And so we may often be in a position of having to justify what we do and struggling to find the space, time and resources to think and develop our work. Taking up a career in sexualities research may in part be to orient toward a logos of professional restraint or failure – at least perhaps with respect to the aspirations of the mainstream neoliberal academy (Halberstam, 2011). (Landi, Chapter 16, reflects on being an insider/outsider with respect to the academy.) None of this is not to diminish the significance of the research projects presented in the present volume, or their successful outcomes. But it is to open reflections of the precarity of research careers in sex and sexualities. Some career paths in the field may point more readily toward 'success' as defined in monetary terms by the neoliberal academy, where the money earned by project funding may mean more than its achievement in other terms. Others, perhaps those more characterised by the kind of reflexive doubt and querying of much of the work in the present volume, may be necessarily and purposively marginal.

Such standpoints can be deeply connected to our own senses of self, as researchers and sexual beings, in terms that may be personally and professionally risky. Those of us drawn to sexualities research in the social sciences might most often come to such vocations out of felt senses of disidentification (Munoz, 1999). We might necessarily reproduce this in our work, especially where we seek to counter normative views on sexual and gendered experience. We are too in a position of potentially exposing our identities, emotions, sexualities and vulnerabilities as expressed so poignantly by Madill in Chapter 13. And yet the current academic environment, with its emphases on crudely measurable impact is not always conducive or sympathetic to such sensibilities. Especially for more junior researchers, orthodox research requirements can exacerbate professional, economic, emotional and academic precarity. It is not an easy environment in which to admit equivocation and feelings of not knowing. As Plummer suggests in the interview, the solidarity and support that can be offered in conferences (most often outside the mainstream) are vital. Moreover, while in the academy, sex and sexualities research can be peripheral and seen as apart from more 'serious research endeavours', within researchers' lives such research can be central to a sense of self and identity and to the profoundly important research agendas and ethics that emerge from such self-understandings. This is an important component of whom we may be as teachers, researchers and activists – people wanting to deeply understand human life, further social justice and create meaningful, enduring contributions to the world.

Telling stories

The work of Ken Plummer has been a notable orienting point for the present volume – cited by a number of the authors – as well as being a profound influence on many working in this field. Those who draw on Plummer's work in the present volume include Barrett (Chapter 5) who reflects on the importance of the concept of intimate citizenship (Plummer, 2003a) and the value of narratives as inviting empathy and enabling social change in the case of older people; Li (Chapter 2) who utilises Plummer's insights into the need to draw on sociology and queer theory in her exploration of ambiguity; Cornwall (Chapter 12) and Morris (Chapter 15) who revisit the notion of 'telling sexual stories' in relation to sex workers and single mothers respectively; and Barbé i Serra (Chapter 11) who acknowledges Plummer's assertion of the need to attend to the lusty, desiring body and erotic subjectivity of the researcher (Plummer, 2008).

More generally Plummer's presence might be said to perform as an overarching reverb within the book project as a whole – his having acted as keynote speaker at the conference from which this book derives. Plummer's critical contribution at the conference comprised what might be called a partial retrospective – charting a personal reflexive journey through the shifting terrains of sex and sexuality studies over the course of his career (spanning over five decades). As a way of locating a conference as a convergent moment in a wider span of time this was an especially salient intervention. What it means to research sex and sexualities now, we were reminded as attendees, is also to evoke past and imagined future trajectories together. Sex and sexualities are not simply empirical fields of study, but are refractions of conceptual lineages and projective concerns via which the sexual might appear or recede as object of analytical urgency. Within this, we were reminded to ask, how humanist stories of sex and sexualities might emerge into our research registers – at the confluence of theory, world and narrative.

Such thoughts were evoked early on in Plummer's work. As an advocate of symbolic interactionism, Plummer has long advanced research approaches grounded in everyday connections between people – for example, aiming to integrate hopes, desires and intimacies into what we pay attention to as researchers. Looking back on the contextual shaping of his doctoral research, for instance, Plummer has evoked the influence of symbolic interactionism as a conceptual tool – both vital to his early work, and in the present. Reflecting on working on the sociology of sexuality before the 'flood of constructivism perspectives', most often popularly parsed into the influence of Foucault, Plummer has grounded the importance of attending to people's interpretive processes, in iteration with the symbolic world around them (Plummer, 2003a). One might locate Plummer's critical humanism out of such an epistemological ethos. And this informs perspectives developed in the present book – helping to frame and figure the importance of close and affective relations and reflections in research processes.

Plummer has noted that a formative critique of constructivist theories was their tendency to abstract sexualities from sex (2003a). Such abstractions helped to locate a firm ground for understanding sexualities as within wider social/cultural parameters of study. Yet sexuality as a theoretical site in these terms might also be seen to have become divorced from sexual experiencing per se. Researching sex and/or sexualities, then, might be seen to have become divergent enterprises over-time – sex the province of sexology, and sexualities the domain of social sciences. Different theoretical commitments underscored these different paths as they took shape. Advocating for reintegration of sex with sexualities in sociological research, however, is not to seek to collapse research on sexualities into the symbolic minutiae of quotidian experience. Indeed, Plummer has especially argued that symbolic interactionist approaches are not about scaling research down, as if away from the macro scope offered by larger gauged theories and methods. Rather the challenge, and the promises, offered come about through the inscription of human stories within the wider domain and reach of sexualities scholarship.

Sexual stories, then, emerge not simply as narratives, for Plummer, but as ciphers for a humanist standpoint in relation to the abstractions and situated particularities of sexual experience and scholarship (1995). Stories do not just ground research, they open questions about people's created meanings via the symbolic inferences generated in everyday engagements in the world – with people, objects and other entities. Sexualities are an important locus for insight into such processes – because sexual experience is not fixed purely in mute bodily experience. The sexual is a symbolically interactive site – a field of intimacy at the interface of cultural, social and bodily infractions. Such an understanding opens conceptual entry points into the hope of cosmopolitanism, for instance. For Plummer, the cosmopolitan does not just stand for the effects of global flows on sexual life-worlds. Rather cosmopolitan sexualities are sites for locating and unfolding contemporary influences and resonances, across regional and transnational boundaries.

Towards a critical reflexivity

Plummer has long called for more critically reflexive methods, more recently informed by queer and other concerns (2003b). These might bring the sexual back in, for instance by admitting the sexuality of the researcher as a barometer for research engagement – sexuality, method and the reflexive subject as intimately intertwined (see, for example, Kulick and Willson, 1995; Hines and Taylor, 2012). Queer theory and method too helped to de-essentialise the sexual, to bring the sexual back into the frame but in a manner that might also query any seeming objective properties. Queer sexualities may be out of reach, not here yet – (always) elsewhere (Boyce et al., 2017). For research informed by such concerns we need methodologies that are sensitive to the importance of the indecipherable, to the conceiving of sexualities as out of reach even as we study them: methodologies of doubt and ambiguity, recognising that 'we can only ever be scraping the surface of a moment' (Plummer, interview, this volume). Such enquiries might not give rise to clear sexual subjects as an outcome of research, for instance, but might be best imagined as domains of reflexive wondering.

In the spirit of such questions, the book opens with Part One on 'knowability', raising a series of important epistemological questions: What is it possible to know about experiences, practices and understandings of sex and sexualities? What methodological approaches might help or hinder our efforts to probe, capture and conceive such experiences?

In Part Two the volume takes up creative, innovative ways of gathering, interpreting and disseminating research. In this part authors consider the kinds of knowledge about sexualities made possible by pushing and blurring conventional methodological boundaries.

In Part Three researchers share their experiences of working in contrasting contexts – globally and in terms of different research paradigms and practices. Authors reflect on research contexts to consider how constraints and opportunities may come together to enable novel, meaningful data collections and understandings.

Part Four explores researcher identities and experiences, viewing researchers as sexual beings with their own uncertainties and vulnerabilities as well as often being activists and teachers. This part is premised on querying who is a sex researcher. How do researcher identities and experiences in the realm of sex and sexualities relate to, inform and shape their choices, interpretations and research outcomes? Overall we hope that in this book readers will find an invitation to join and share the dialogues that its contributors seek to open up, and to further the pursuit of new questions in the study of sexualities.

References

Boyce, P., Engebretsen, E. and Posocco, S. (2017) 'Introduction: Anthropology's Queer Sensibilities' in *Anthropology's Queer Sensibilities*, Special Issue of the journal *Sexualities*, 21(1).

Correa, S., Petchesky, R. and Parker, R. (2008) *Sexuality, Health and Human Rights*, London: Routledge.

Epstein, S. (1987) 'Gay Politics, Ethnic Identity and the Limits of Social Constructionism', *Socialist Review*, 93/94 (May–August), pp. 9–54.

Foucault, M. (1978) *The History of Sexuality, Volume 1: An Introduction*, New York: Pantheon Books.

Gagnon, R. and Parker, R. (1995) 'Introduction' in Parker, R. and Gagnon, J. (eds) *Conceiving Sexualities: Approaches to Sex Research in a Postmodern World*, London: Routledge.

Halberstam, J. (2011) *The Queer Art of Failure*, Durham, NC: Duke University Press.

Haritaworn, J., Kuntsman, A. and Posocco, S. (eds) (2014) *Queer Necropolitics*, London: Routledge.

Hines, S. and Taylor, Y. (2012) *Sexualities: Past Reflections, Future Directions*, London: Palgrave Macmillan.

khanna, a. (2017) *Sexualness*, New Delhi: New Text.

Kulick, Don and Willson, Elizabeth (1995) *Taboo: Sex, Identity and Erotic Subjectivity in Anthropological Fieldwork*, London: Routledge.

Moore, H. (2012) 'Introduction' in Peter Aggleton, Paul Boyce, Henrietta Moore and Richard Parker (eds) *Understanding Global Sexualities: New Frontiers*, London: Routledge.

Munoz, J.E. (1999) *Disidentifications*, Minneapolis, MN: University of Minnesota Press.

Narrain, A. and Gupta, A. (2011) *Law Like Love: Queer Perspectives on Law*, New Delhi: Yoda Press.

Plummer, K. (1995) *Telling Sexual Stories: Power, Change and Social Worlds*, London Routledge.

Plummer, K. (2003a) *Intimate Citizenship: Private Decisions and Public Dialogues*, Washington, DC: University of Washington Press.

Plummer, K. (2003b) 'Queer Bodies and Postmodern Sexualities: A Note on Revisiting the "Sexual" in Symbolic Interactionism', *Qualitative Sociology*, 26(4), pp. 515–530.

Plummer, K. (2008) 'Studying Sexualities for a Better World? Ten Years of *Sexualities*', *Sexualities*, 11(1), pp. 7–22.

Spronk, R. (2012) *Ambiguous Pleasures: Sexuality and Middle Class Self Perceptions in Nairobi*, New York: Berghahn Books.

Stein, Edward (2013) *Forms of Desire: Sexual Orientation and the Social Constructionist Controversy*, London: Routledge.

Weeks, J. (1986) *Sexuality*, London: Routledge.

PART ONE

KNOWABILITY

INTRODUCTION

Paul Boyce

Questions pertaining to how sexualities might become knowable
are complexly interwoven with questions of methodology.
Sexualities enter the lexicons of any research project *with*
methodological commitments and orientations. These not only
offer insights into sexual life-worlds. They also vitally *frame what
counts as knowledge* about sexual experiencing – for instance as
performances, embodiments, subjectivities or other ways of being.
This is as opposed to an ontological view of 'the sexual' as an
extant attribute, as if potentially objectively retrievable, regardless
of whatever methodological approach is employed. Such concerns
open ontological questions; researching sexualities emerges as
investigations in knowledge making. How, as researchers, might
we compose versions of sexual life in a manner that is sensitive
to how people conceive of their own self-understandings of sexed
and gendered experience?

Thinking of the sexual in these terms signifies the mutual
inherence of sex, sexualities and research as complex sites of
mutual world making and as interconnected fields of power
and engagement. As Gayle Rubin (1984) alerted us, to *think
sex* must be to think about arrays of political investments, social
structures, moral authorities and so on, also. Sexualities perform
as extraordinarily sensitive conduits into where, for instance,
normative boundaries of conduct may be draw in any given
context or time. Moreover sexualities offer insight into how
such boundaries may be transgressed, wilfully or simply in acts
of everyday desire. Knowledge of sexualities is therefore also
knowledge of many other things too. Stories about sexualities are
stories of social change, transformation and resistance. And our

research methodologies, as social scientists, must be capacious enough to engage in such diverse terrains of meaning making and being.

Sexualities research also presents complex intransigencies. Shining a light onto sexual experiencing, as a researcher, might also render the sexual in unfamiliar forms. Sexual intimacies and feelings are often private affairs. Or where they are publically expressed this may not be so in any sense that can be conceived of as isomorphic with people's interior senses – commensurate with affect, feeling or desire. To research sexuality then is to confront boundaries – to query and push the extent of what, as social researchers, we might come to understand in our varied projects. Researching sexualities, consequently, might mean attending to the sexual as a domain of investigation but also letting go of aspirations to knowledge. It has for some time now been the province of queer theory, for example, to pose sexualities as experientially ambivalent and ontologically vague (Weiss, 2016). Sexual life-worlds are not just empirical facts in such terms, but are bound up with fantasies and (dis)satisfactions; with hopes for the future and narratives about the past; with things that may be 'known' and things that can only be conjectured or partially called to memory.

Such issues present challenges to theory and application alike, and the chapters in this section of the book each explore different aspects of salient critical and methodological concerns. Cara Judea Alhadeff's chapter seeks to open a space between public and private imaginaries of (women's) sexual bodies. Women's ejaculations, for instance, infer for Alhadeff a sexual embodiment that might disrupt the conceiving of the knowable. Alhadeff's initial experiences of ejaculation were greeted with surprise and even alarm by her lover – not expected of (normative) female sexuality. Reflecting on this opens desiring terrains of representation visually and textually in Alhadeff's research. And these displace locations of desire as points of evident knowledge.

The 'reclaiming' of female ejaculation by some feminists presents a problem for Alhadeff. With Grosz she is sympathetic to the idea that reifying female ejaculation might simply relocate women's sexualities within a hydraulic model of the sexual – with clearly demarcated bodily processes and orgasmic end points (and see Potts, 2002, for a similar discussion of Grosz). Grosz advocates for other ways of knowing. These might be more capacious and diffuse – conceiving knowledge of women's sexual experiencing in other terms and against phallocentric ejaculatory models. However for Alhadeff this is still a call toward knowledge. Alhadeff plots her research in other directions, so to speak, framing sexuality as more generally unknowable, and in these seeking to reconsider the logos of all gendered sexualness.

The implications for such forms of knowledge are explored across Alhadeff's chapter. For instance querying cultures of surveillance and their public iteration in conservative forms of public governance (Alhadeff is writing from the US at the inception of the Trump presidency). Alhadeff pushes us to go beyond such thinking in our research on sex and sexualities. Not to simply conceive of counter-discourses but to focus on moments of rupture, the uncanny and channels that traverse private and public conduits of sexual excess and containment. Boundaries might be re-scripted in these terms as knowledge of sexualities oscillates beyond definable contexts or moments.

Eva Cheuk-Yin Li approaches the subjects of her research indirectly – attendant to ambiguous ways of sexual and gendered being. *Zhongxing* is a concept term used in East Asian Chinese speaking contexts to denote 'non-normative' expressions of gender by some women. However, a key point is that the term is constructed negatively – as *neither* man nor woman and hence not a concept that is necessarily germane to any constructs of identity. In researching *zhongxing* therefore, Li has not been so much concerned with who might be defined by the term. Rather she has explored how women might employ *zhongxing* to navigate complex and subtle senses of gender and sexualities in their social worlds.

Imagined boundaries composed around the subjects of research are consequently continuously transgressed in Li's method. Secure subjectifications fall away, for example, through failure. Li's interviews led her to realise that ambiguous sexual and gendered self-understanding was likely not going to be evidently proclaimed by informants. At first finding interviewees who might be vague or distracted as a problem with her methodology Li came to realise that such encounters were helpful. They suggested the askance assemblages of *zhongxing* experiencing in which she was interested.

Natalie Edelman's chapter draws on her long-standing career as an applied sexual health researcher. She especially reflects on differentiations between quantitative and qualitative paradigms, and how these produce knowledge about sexualities in respect of often irreconcilable logics. And these divergences are further underpinned by the investigator's own life-worlds. Edelman reflects on her personal evolving understandings as a primarily quantitative researcher who has recently begun to engage more reflexively with her work. And this is a complex and intersectional process, because the ideas about 'self' that Edelman has found herself bringing to critical enquiry are connected and refracted across different values and experiences – as feminist and critical realist, among other variables.

Such thinking too draws Edelman up against a particular boundary in her professional practice – that between study-participant and/or sexual health patient as contrasted to the role of the research professional. Edelman works in a sector in which this is a normatively and relatively strictly demarcated border. Reflexively engaging her experiences at such conceptual and interactive limits has opened critical pathways for Edelman. She considers, for example, that even where epistemological objectivity may be valued in quantitative enquiry in sexual health many researchers in her experience draw on personal experience in hypothesis building, for example in relation to sexual risk data. Edelman calls for such thinking to be made conceptually explicit in her field – to somehow assimilate the sexual into analysis without ascribing it a coherence and containment.

Fran Carter's chapter orients toward sexuality in terms of objects, spaces and narratives – sex toys as conceived of by female identifying customer of women's sex shops. The relatively recent emergence of such shops on UK high streets might be read as a signifier of social change accompanied by shifting design aesthetics aimed at presenting such spaces as somehow both normative and transgressive sexually liberating. Values are typically conceived of within very particular (heteronormative) versions of female sexuality (Carter cites the stereotypically feminine décor of some the consumer spaces). Against this background, a central facet of Carter's research was to query her own assumptions.

Reflexive interviewing alerted Carter to some of her own biases. For instance, as a feminist researcher she uncovered a new awareness of how she might unconsciously react negatively toward women whose views ran counter to her own. And it was in transgressing the boundaries of her own assumptions that Carter located some of the most insightful aspects of her research. Such an incident occurred, for example, when Carter felt compelled, after one key interview, to think anew about women's sex shops as potentially therapeutic spaces of consumption (for some). Looking back on prior interviews Carter saw this as a salient theme that had always somehow been there in the narratives that she had gathered but which as researcher she had nonetheless somehow (subconsciously) refused. This experience might remind us that themes and objects of sexualities research may not be transparent. Such studies may deal in the taboo, the secreted and the resisted. And not just in the experiences of erstwhile research participants but across the mutuality of otherwise imagined researcher/ researched divides.

Overall the chapters in this section each compel thinking about what we might come to know about sexualities, and to what purpose and effect. Ambiguous bodies, consumer objects, epidemiological methods and scenes of public and private governance are among the domains (dis)located by Alhadeff, Li, Edelman and Carter. Each of these domains opens questions about the framing of the sexual as object of research, amidst divergence against easy conclusions. The chapters in this section plot journeys away from ready 'knowability' as a way to come back to sex and sexualities as ever querying sites of engagement. And it is in such journeys that uncertain figurations compel new research imperatives.

References

Potts, A. (2002) *The Science/Fiction of Sex: Feminist Deconstruction and the Vocabularies of Heterosex* (Women and Psychology), Hove: Routledge.

Rubin, G. (1984) 'Thinking Sex: Notes for a Radical Theory of the Politics of Sexuality' in Vance, C. (ed.) *Pleasure and Danger*, New York: Routledge.

Weiss, M. (2016) 'Always After: Desiring Queerness, Desiring Anthropology', *Cultural Anthropology*, 31(4), pp. 627–638.

1 | THE INSINUATING BODY

Cara Judea Alhadeff

Abstract

The Insinuating Body investigates how pornography, sex work and aberrant sexualities in the United States constitute an uncanny epistemological, ethical and aesthetic condition of the in-between – an oscillation between the private and the public. My theoretical-visual work[1] emerges from the intimacy of the 'I' as profoundly collaborative. Sexual justice actively seeks connections that may be saturated with irreducible differences. My choice to unapologetically implicate the 'I' is not a reaction to reductive vernacular, but a vital commitment to embodied thinking – an explicit integration of the private into the public. Protean sexualities, ranging from sex activism to female ejaculation, deconstruct patriarchal inscriptions on our bodies. In cultural production as in its reception, vulnerability becomes a vital intervention in public-private discourse. Since the private is construed as vulnerable and ambiguous, it 'requires' unquestioned taxonomies of regulation and normalisation. The sanctity of normalcy constitutes a hegemony of representation that colonises our relationships with our own bodies. In contrast, an uncanny erotic politics reorients our cultural notions of pleasure and vulnerability, and ultimately who has power, imagination and sovereignty over our bodies. Merging the private with the public – the ob-scene (off-stage) with the explicit – we can generate ethical individual and collective sexual justice.

> [V]oluptuous desire fragments and dissolves the unity and utility of the organic body and the stabilized body-image ... The voluptuous sense of disquiet engendered by and as lust

disarrays and segments the resolve of a certain purposiveness,
unhinging any determination of means and ends or goals.
Carnal experience is uncertain non-teleological, undirected.
(Grosz, 1995, p. 249)

Female ejaculation as social emancipation

1994. Happy Valley. The first time I ejaculated I revelled in
sharing the sensation. I felt free to inhabit my body's pleasures and
excesses – no judgement, no fear – until my partner expressed his
surprise. I had absolutely no idea it was considered abnormal for
women to ejaculate. Only then did my mind intervene. Tragically,
as we witness through hegemonic sex education programmes and
institutionalised misinformation in popular media, there is a cultural assumption that it is men, not women, who are capable of
ejaculation. The physiological reality is that both men and women
have active prostates, and millions of women do indeed ejaculate: in women, the prostate is identified as the para- or peri-ure-
thral glands. In 1998, I conducted the neurological research for
an instructional and diaristic video produced by Sundahl (1998)
(also known as Fanny Fatale), called *Tantric Journey to Female
Orgasm: Unveiling the G-Spot and Female Ejaculation* – a sequel to
her collaboration with Queen and Bell on their original female
ejaculation video *How to Female Ejaculate* (1992). My reference
to this phenomenon is not an attempt to replicate or usurp male
tendencies or to degrade women's bodies as a systematic functionality, thereby reifying hierarchical power relationships in which
sexuality is reduced to a generic hydraulic model: 'The fantasy
that binds sex to death so intimately is the fantasy of a hydraulic
sexuality, a biologically regulated need or instinct, a compulsion,
urge, or mode of physical release (the sneeze provides an analogue)' (Grosz, 1995, p. 204). Rather, my intention is to examine
the political potency of male and female ejaculation as deterritorialised sexualities, sites for infrastructural transformation.

Grosz critiques the current reclamation of female ejaculation
by some feminists (such as Bell) as an example of women being

absorbed into toxic mimicry – the homogenising, 'transcendental' patriarchy. Grosz invokes Irigaray 'for whom female sexuality is itself non-self-identical, non-enumerable, not made of distinct and separate parts, not one (but indeterminately more than one)' (1995, p. 222). If we do conceive of sexuality from within a dominant reference point, we maintain its invisibility – concretising male sexuality as the model of normalcy. Grosz underscores that '[i]nstead of assuming an inherent mystery, an indecipherable enigma, female sexuality must be assumed to be knowable, even if it must wait for other forms of knowledge, different modes of discourse, to provide a framework and the broad parameters of its understanding' (1995, p. 223).

Rather than refusing to call public attention to the reality of female ejaculation, I want to point out the dangers of seeking the knowable. I recognise that Grosz's call does not reflect Foucault's critique of *scientia sexualis*; she specifically seeks 'other forms of knowledge' (1995, p. 223). However, by focusing only on woman's corporeality, she may inadvertently be feeding into the historical elision of female sexual desires and pleasures – supporting the very psychological infrastructures she is determined to disentangle. I am proposing a shift from Grosz's entreaty for a 'knowable' female sexuality by combining Bristow's challenge to form a political project rooted in Deleuze's rhizomatic and schizo-analytic lines with Grosz's search for a reconceptualisation of female sexuality. Again, I am suggesting that we deterritorialise *both* sexes (recognising the limitations of a two-gender structure within this analysis).

We cannot afford to reassert another hegemony to replace or mimic existing normative paternal tyrannies. Such toxic mimicry would reinforce dichotomous habitual behaviour, while obliterating the potential for fertile vulnerability. In *The Temptation to Exist* (1956), the Romanian philosopher, Cioran, enlists Beckett: 'What is the good of passing from one untenable position to another, of seeking justification always on the same plane?' (Cioran, 1956). Like Grosz, I propose we re-examine the generic terms of sexuality: 'the relation *between* terms is what establishes a possibility of identity for each' (Grosz, 1994, p. 343). By reconceiving male sexuality as unknowable – we call into question the underpinnings of what it means to 'understand' any sexuality at all – whether biologically male or female.

The philosophical congruencies of Duden's (1991) distinction among incompatible meanings of knowledge that produce 'useful' citizenry, Spinoza's emphasis on questions not answers, and Arendt's embrace of herself as a 'conscious pariah' point to the urgency of vulnerability via uncertainty as a position of power. As a conscious pariah, Arendt chose to inhabit the liminality of openness: 'an absolute determination to be herself, with the toughness to carry it through in the face of great vulnerability' (Derwent, 1986, p. 26). We can exercise this receptivity when we begin to engage with a Spinozian ethological version of sexuality (Deleuze, 1989, p. 125). Deleuze writes about Spinoza's introduction of the concept of ethology – judging things as they relate to and with other things. Congruently, Grosz proposes an erotic politics: 'I am not suggesting a necessary reciprocity here, but rather a co-implication ... There is always equivocation and ambiguity in passion ... eroticism and sensuality tend to spread out over many things, infecting all sorts of other relations' (Grosz, 1995, p. 204).

As stated above, I am not looking for a substitute for male sexuality or to 'depict male sensibility in a female body' (Despuentes, 2010, p. 124) – such as representations of hospitalised birth and rape in film and the stereotypical ways in which women are represented in mainstream porn. Rather, I am driven toward Ronell's 'feminine intensity' – a sexual ethic that reconfigures how we experience sex and the erotic in the context of radical citizenship – *how* we inhabit our bodies in our everyday lives. Ronell questions ways in which women and men might internalise phallocentric discourses and systems of representation:

Could there be a feminine intensity or force that would not
be merely 'subversive'? Because subversion is a problem – it
implies a dependency on the program that is being critiqued
– therefore it's a parasite of that program. Is there a way to
produce a force or an intensity that isn't merely a reaction
(and a very bad and allergic reaction) to what is? (Ronell,
1991, p. 128)

By exaggerating, reorienting and cultivating vulnerability, conventionally designated 'private' expressions seep into the public
and expose the potential for collaborative-intuitive hysteria. In
this context, I am reappropriating this historically misogynis-
tic concept. Hysteria, like female ejaculation, ruptures clean-
cut categories and expectations. As a woman who ejaculates
without the need for specific physical stimulation, the socio-political
implications of what my body represents are vast: a rhizomatic,
molecular sexuality, without an endpoint; no arrival, no deriva-
tion. The closest physiological term 'representing' this experience
is *psychogenic* – an emotionally induced physical disorder. It is
not surprising that this ineffable experience is associated with a
dis-ease. A third type of orgasm, psychologically stimulated (here
I am not distinguishing between my orgasms and their corresponding ejaculations), 'is through mental (cortical) stimulation,
where the imagination stimulates the brain, which in turn stimulates the genital corpuscles of the glans [of the clitoris] to set off
an orgasm' (Ellman, 1968, p. 330). My body inhabits and produces haecceities and affects in a chiasmic dissolution of binary
codes and social expectations: 'infinite, open, and unlimited in
every direction; [they have] no top nor bottom nor center; [they
do] not assign fixed and mobile elements but rather distribute a
continuous variation' (Deleuze and Guattari, 1980, p. 476). I
am positioning myself within an intuitive reconfiguring of social-
ised sexuality. This Deleuze-Guattarian process of becoming-
different animates a biopolitical economy of subjectivity. The
chiasma of female ejaculation unfolds, thus 'in a becoming,

one is deterritorialised' (1980, p. 291). Massumi tells us, '[t]he heightening of energies is sustained long enough to leave a kind of afterimage of its dynamism that can be reactivated or injected into other activities, creating a fabric of intensive states between which any number of connecting routes could exist' (Massumi in Deleuze and Guattari, 1980, p. xiv).

This Taoist rhizome offers an irreducible difference among becomings. Both mindfulness and unpredictability play in perpetual disequilibrium – undergoing radical transformation that sheds the object while embracing the process. I am proposing a peripatetic sexual agency that engages sexual relations as both mobile and strategic positions – disrupting unchallenged assumptions of stratified, medicalised and demonised sexual practices and expressions. Grosz distinguishes between an Oedipal conceptual system of the citizen-via-family economy and a libidinal economy of an erotics of the unknown: 'Desire need not culminate in sexual intercourse, but may end in production. Not the production of a child or a relationship, but the production of sensations never felt, alignment never thought, energies never tapped, regions never known' (Grosz, 1995, p. 250). Whether I am exploring my own sexuality, a pedagogical imperative, or my photographic possibilities, my process incarnates a libidinal-somatic intensity. Such protean sexualities perform an erotics of the uncanny. My project both theorises and metabolises a conceptual shift away from a prescriptive project toward these deterritorialised sexualities. My performative practices and discursive self-portrait photographs and video pieces reconfigure patriarchal inscriptions on our bodies.

Grosz similarly describes how Lingis revels in the continual non-arrival of orgasm as a manifestation of deterritorialisation:

[Lingis] demonstrates that sexual passion is not reducible to the goal of sexual satiation, but lives and thrives on its own restless impetus. Orgasm need not be understood as the end of the sexual encounter, its final culmination and moment of conversion towards death and dissipation; instead it can be displaced to any and every region of the body, and in addition, seen as a mode of transubstantiation, a conversion from solid to liquid. (1995, p. 203)

Reinvention of the private ruptures the borders of the public. Using its own publicly designated excesses, my work eroticises and celebrates the private as excess: the monstrous, hysteria, mutation. Congruently, surrealist women artists/writers such as Mansour, Carrington, Agar, Toyen, Kahlo and Prassinos reorient the hybrid-monster-body: 'all are depictions of a grotesque body which call into question canonic representations, particularly those of the female body ... occupy either too much space or not enough, never just the right space. Their very disorganization defies the laws of anatomy and physics' (Caws, 1990, p. 392).

I am compelled to explore the terrain where logic and fragment converge and transform one another's meanings. Throughout this terrain, excessive unexpected juxtapositions cultivate the grotesque. These 'disorganized' relationships are nourished by an intuitive cohesive logic – the dreamworld of the discontinuous. '[I]n addition to this interpenetration of the exterior and interior of the body, an exchange of sexuality and an exchange between animal and human [organic and inorganic] also can be used to effect the grotesque and its corresponding sense of interchange and disorder' (Stewart, 1984, p. 105).

Both the disorder of the human body and health 'disorders' slip into the realm of the 'grotesque'. This insinuating body becoming-the-grotesque ruptures the order of official norms of representation. Similarly, I intend for my images to remind the viewer of shifting positions that require continual negotiations among expectations, desires and fears. It is the possibility of the viewer's visceral relationship to her/his interpretation of the images that titillates both the imagination and lived relations.

My visual and theoretical work is intended to evoke a sense of disorder and difference as potential erotic agency. I am critically interested in the corpo-social implications of an ejaculating woman. In contrast, the patriarchal fetishisation of female ejaculation positioned as a mechanical goal-oriented 'how to' creates a false hierarchy – an improvement or progression over non-ejaculatory orgasms. When physical proliferation gives way to theoretical excess and we delve into the embodied zone of *ars erotica*, *ars theoretica*, *ars politica*, we can disrupt such hetero-normative binaries; we can learn how to imagine a more expansive possibility of politics as a collaborative public pedagogy – we become the insinuating body.

Coercion of the real: détournement and unrepresentability

How we perceive and encounter sex and sexuality in self and other underlies one of the most virulent dysfunctions of US culture. We are living in a body-phobic and difference-phobic culture-of-collusion. Ethnocentrism is rooted in an opaque authoritarianism in which, as Weber reminds me, anxiety is utilised as fear. Internalised norms ranging from fear of germs, our own bodies, nature, 'terrorists' or anyone/anything outside of our zone of familiarity and habit operate as the scaffolding of our ironically both open-ended and violently restrictive period in contemporary history. Foucault declared that simultaneously, we are living in the most sex-saturated and body-phobic period in history (Foucault, 1978, p. 78). For example, in 1994 at the United Nations on World AIDS Day, Surgeon General Elders addressed the fact that at that time, half of all HIV infections occurred in people under the age of 25. One response she offered was to encourage masturbation as part of a safe-sex curriculum. One week later, President Clinton fired Elders for promoting values counter to the administration. Although Elders did not explicitly say so, autoeroticism is a productive sexual agency that resists medical (STDs) and social diseases (body-phobia). Additionally, pornography videos became a substitute for public sex to avoid AIDS. Of course, conservatives and liberals were not pleased with this tactic. Equally, they could not rely on the myth of scarcity – the myth that porn undermines relationships (like sex toys detracting from masculinity in a heterosexual relationship). The 'sex-drenched, sex-obsessed West' (Hall, 1995, p. 11) proliferates both the ob-scene and the confession: 'Today, sex is avoided as it has probably never been avoided before, in any culture. Why? Because this avoidance occurs under the cover of a diffuse sexualization of all the consumer objects (human beings included) of our society' (Durfourmantelle, 2007, p. 82).

This hypocritical hyperbole is exacerbated as we enter the treachery of the Trump presidency. By operating strictly through the fantasy of the knowable or the real, contemporary Western sexuality inhabits the very heart of binary oppositional thinking. The regulation and enforcement of what is considered real predetermines the question of *how* and *where* in our bodies we read public forms of sexual exchange.[2] Butler reminds us, 'what pornography delivers is … a text of insistent and faulty imaginary relations that will not disappear with the abolition of the offending text, the text that remains for feminist criticism relentlessly to read' (Butler, 1997, p. 69). If we ignore pornographies' multifarious relations, we constrain our own sexual potential, our libidinal plenum. We render ourselves impervious to our own capacities. My reference is to Deleuzian capacities as relational and open-ended. When examining what constitutes the real, this 'feminist reading of pornography' too easily slips into the double bind entrained assumption that women who enjoy sex too much are sluts. Additionally, '[p]orn is too often expected to mirror the Real. As if it weren't cinema. For example, actresses are criticized for faking orgasms. That's what they are here for, and paid for, and have learned how to do' (Despuentes, 2010, p. 86). Similarly, one justification for my work being censored is the recrimination that my images constitute a reality. In response, I invoke Schirmacher's (2009) insistence on the audience's responsibility to determine the 'truth' of material. Although my images have been categorised as pornographic, the censors' understanding of how my images actually *are* pornographic missed the mark.

They are not pornographic because they depict naked bodies or fragments of bodies engaged in illicit activities, but because, like pornography, my images fail to constitute a *familiar* reality.

It is precisely the amplification of the beyond that invites the erotics of the uncanny to operate as pedagogical liberatory possibilities of pornographies. For example, Probst's black and white still analogue photographs of often humorous, often surrealist behind-the-scenes gay porn reiterate pornography's failure to constitute reality. As scholars of freedom of speech, we must ask: Who is making the porn? And for which audience?

The cross-fertilisation between art and pornography expands the creative and pedagogical boundaries of each. *The Operation*, an infrared film that focuses on the temperature changes in the skin during a het-sex doctor scenario, won the 1995 Award for Best Underground Film at the Chicago Film Festival. In his *Melancholia and Moralism*, Crimp (2002) theorises what I identify as one version of Kristeva's *Carrefour* (Kristeva, 1982) – the fluid intersection between art and sex. Crimp discusses the significance of the site, which is often more important than the act committed there; Escoffier observes that the setting is as significant as the sex itself. Examples of the import of a public staging of porn material range from 1970s male gay porn set at the NYC piers to Genet's prison scene in *Un chant d'amour* (1950) (see Genet, 1988). Congruently, my photographs are 'literary' texts in the sense of Weber's definition of the literary in contrast to the theoretical: 'A text can be considered literary to the extent that its propositional, semantic, thematic *content* is *exceeded* or undermined by its syntactic movement. *What* it says is never separable from the *way* it says it' (Weber, 2000, p. 1).

The primacy of context, the act of viewing that is always in flux and infinitely repetitive as the how rather than the what, parallels my photographs' censorship history – a history of the *extimate*. Nietzsche's theorisation of the a-substantive (see Ulfers, 2008) is an example of the *extimate*; the non-local co-relations theory in quantum physics reflects this a-substantive field. The *extimate* defies ethnocentricity – engendering the intimacy of the 'I' as profoundly collaborative, as enfoldments of collective continual non-arrival – the embodied unknown. The way we choose to experience our bodies can provide a framework of intersubjectivity that moves beyond the narrow limits of what we think we know – engaging contradiction and difference as inevitable and replete with collaborative potential. Erotic politics exert 'libidinal zones [which] are continually in the process of being produced, renewed, transformed, through experimentation, practices, invocations, the accidents or contingencies of life itself, the coming together of surfaces, incisive practices, inscriptions' (Lingis, 1983, p. 198). Although my photographs are consciously constructed, the relationships are born out of an improvised collaboration, practising this repetition of contiguities. My images offer a cathartic opening into the becoming-vulnerable of *extimité*. Intensive differences drive this ever-expanding process.

Carnal activities proliferate the possibility of political agitation and social (ex)change. These libidinal intensities reorganise our social body's scopic drive. They provoke subversion and transgression in the workplace – conditions of production that when examined can no longer slip through the cracks of normalcy. The Sex Workers Project Urban Justice / Network of Sex Workers Projects (SWOP, a New York-based sex workers' union) participation in the Construction Workers' Rally (whose focus is middle-class 'made in America' unions), illuminated how the nine-to-five labourer is engaged daily in officially sanctioned prostitution – the socially accepted and expected coercion of the worker's body in domestic servitude, agricultural or construction labour, and service industries, as well as the hetero-married female body.[3] Moral authorities decide what constitutes honest work. As a sex worker radical, El Saadawi explicitly chooses to inhabit her insinuating body – to be a 'free prostitute, rather than an enslaved wife ... An employee ... pays the price her illusory fears with her life, her health, her body, and her mind. She pays the highest price for things of the lowest value ... [M]en force women to sell their bodies at a price, and that the lowest paid body is that of a wife' (El Saadawi, 1990, p. 75).

In a 1912 study of 647 prisoner women prostitutes living in New York, most 'said they earned between $5 and $9 a week before turning to prostitution and from $46 to $72 a week after. This was at a time when high paid male workers earned under $25 per week. Prostitutes were among the highest paid members of the Jewish community and their money must have contributed substantially to the upward mobility of their families' (Schulman, 1986, p. 273). In contrast to unchallenged, institutionalised coercive labour, sex-positive activism (including sex work and public affirmations of uncanny eroticisms such as female ejaculation) shifts the focus from Bataille's (1989) warning of production as inherent repetitive destruction to Goethe and Nietzsche's consciousness of instinct:

> As with Goethe, "all is redeemed and affirmed in the whole". Here is the affirmation of life, the essence of *Amor Fati*: we must learn the joy of perishing for the life of the species, of being sacrificed, as we have no choice but to be, for the continuance of life that both is ours and is not ours: not our individual lives but the life of the whole of which we are a part. We must learn to face with joy, with the Yes of affirmation, our part in a world that "lives on itself: its excrements are its food, and we are among what is consumed". (Nietzsche, 1886, p. 548)

Echoing both Baudrillard's challenge to consumer society and Glissant's poetics of relation (Baudrillard, 1983; Glissant, 1997), I examine the potentially expansive/elastic dialectical nature of sex work in the context of *Amor Fati*. To cannibalise, to swallow the other, becomes a simultaneous self and other sacrifice and expansion (affirmation), a discursive negotiation among differences: 'women – and whores – do not exist to be sexually used by men ... any sexual interaction, including a paid one, benefits from *negotiation*' (Queen, 1997, p. 129).

When we take into consideration the unintended consequences of negotiation, we can begin to play with the generative capacities/ tendencies of co-implications. Negotiation as a multilogue (an expansion of dialogue) of promiscuous crossings reposition Grosz's concern. Grosz (1995) is wary of sex workers who describe themselves as 'health workers': 'they justify their roles in terms of maintaining the "health" of their clients ... It is a model of sexuality based upon the equation of sexual desire with orgasmic release, with instrumental or functional relief of the body' (Grosz, 1995, p. 204) – literally buying into heteronormative sexuality. Why must Grosz dichotomise the 'purposes' of orgasmic release? Particularly, within a simultaneously sex-drenched, body-phobic culture such as ours, orgasm breeds and serves multiple 'functions'. Although Grosz exhorts the 'formlessness of sexual pleasure, the indeterminacy of the objectives of desire' (1995, p. 248), it appears as though she is denying the importance of fucking – for any given reason. Whether 'using' the oxytocin hormone that is released during orgasm to help calm an agitated nervous system or to help realign someone's psyche who has internalised too many sex-negative messages, sex with orgasm can be healthful without replicating the repressive heteropatriarchal status quo that Grosz condemns.

Given our market-driven consumer culture's stigmatisation of sexual pleasure for its own sake, Grosz's assertion is eerily reminiscent of right-wing censors. Again, we are caught in the enfoldments of the *détournement*. I am reminded of Keating Jr. During Reagan's administration, Keating served on the Commission on Obscenity and Pornography: 'Any form of sexual activity which is impersonal, which uses the body alone for pleasure, violates the integrity of the person and thereby reduces him [sic] to the level of an irrational and irresponsible animal' (*The Report of the Commission on Obscenity and Pornography*, September 1970). Clearly, Grosz is a pro-pleasure feminist. Perhaps her argument would be better served if she would distinguish amongst the sexual variations of sexual activities – examining why this kind of 'health-care' may be a crucial need within our somatically impoverished culture that continuously reproduces the sanctity of normalcy.

Feminists who fight for the right to have an abortion, but simultaneously condemn sex work as shameful are caught in a hypocritical boomerang. 'Rather than take it upon themselves to tell other women which professions to choose, feminists should defend every woman's work-place rights' (Reed, 1997, p. 184). If anti-sex-work demagogues would de-stigmatise sex-work as a profession, it would no longer be an outlet for men and women who have internalised their victim-status and seek dehumanising forms of interaction: 'Again the answer lies not in abolition or extreme regulation but in confronting the various fabrications about [sex work]' (Reed, 1997, p. 180). Bataille (1989) reminds us that historically prostitution was not initially perceived as degrading for women (or men). It began as a sacred exchange – a religious prostitution. Only with the onset of servile poverty did prostitutes become monsters. Economics and new social divisions between the public and private reconfigured the public role of women 'using' their bodies.

Hierarchical ethnocentric attitudes, differing very little from humanitarian imperialist tendencies, perceive sex-workers as devoid of agency. The image of the prostitute stripped of her rights, independence and capacity to make positive decisions about her own body functions as a political strategy to victimise all sex-workers (Reed, 1997, p. 189). Rescue-missionary tactics of sex industry abolitionists concretise homogenous concepts of equality emblazoned in the fantasy of neutrality. Both mainstream and 'alternative' media position the dirty sex worker through a lens of shame and lack. The myth that most sex workers have been sexually assaulted feeds both the invisibility of sexism and misinformed feminists: one out of four women in our culture have been sexually assaulted in some capacity. It is assumed that the sex worker is forced into her role of prostitution: 'The worry isn't that the women won't survive; quite the contrary. The worry is that they might come and say that it isn't such a dreadful job after all. And not only because all work is degrading, difficult, and demanding – but because plenty of men are never as affectionate as when they are with a whore' (Despuentes, 2010, p. 63).

Additionally, laws and the media conflate sex trafficking with sex work – criminalising any and all sex work. The gendered stigma of a 'whore' (Pheterson, 2010) extends to all sexuality becoming implicitly degrading to women; sex is essentially constructed as inherently abusive (implicit in the unchallenged assumptions of what sex is 'supposed to be'). Despuentes cites Pheterson: 'What is transgressive for women is neither providing services to men nor is it receiving money or goods for sexual service: women's transgression is in asking for and taking money for sexual services' (Pheterson in Despuentes, 2010).

Within the rhizomatic detours of internalised fascistic tendencies (habituated norms), the boundaries between collusion and agency become even more unstable and circuitous. Whether sex workers who straddle the private-public corporeal construction of desire (Preciado, 2013), or myself as photographer (mother, teacher, writer), who consciously deploys a radical perversity of subject–object interplay in order to illuminate the how of what we do not know, I believe it is possible to mobilise contradictory possibilities for creativity and vulnerability as personal and cultural healing. The conscious choice to decriminalise prostitution extends into a denaturalisation of the suburban (coerced) body. Jiddu Krishnamurti's warning, 'It is no measure of health to be well adjusted to a profoundly sick society' (Krishnamurti, 2010, p. 21) characterises *both* our global humanitarian, educational, economic, environmental crises and *our* potential to intervene in hegemonic convenience-culture – becoming the insinuating body. Such promiscuous crossings underscore the interlocking mechanisms among multiple infrastructures that enable *both* collusion (perpetuating apathy and its concomitant loss of agency) *and* emancipation (allowing creativity and connectivity to flourish).

1997–2001. San Francisco. During the years I reviewed pornographic films and erotic literature for the Good Vibrations sales team, I focused on how my affective psyche could slip into interstitial corporeal narratives. I was interested in getting lost, not knowing my way as I migrated through each labyrinth of sexual alterity. My only compass was my body. Its affective antennae located my desire as I traversed polyvalent visual, textual materials. Embodying the radical potential of vulnerability – the fertile directionlessness of quantum unfamiliarity, uncertainty – we can take on Annie Sprinkle's challenge:

> Pornography is like a mirror through which we can take a look at ourselves. And sometimes what we see doesn't look pretty, and it can make us feel *very* uncomfortable. But how beautiful to take that look, to see (truth), and to learn. The answer to bad porn is not no porn, but to make better porn! (Sprinkle, 2001, p. 81)

Straddling the private and the public, our collaborative insinuating body incites deterritorialised embodied thought. When we recognise the value of re-'discovering' our innate capacities to think and act beyond the habitual, we can expand a transformative corporeal politics; explicitly making our private public, we can generate ethical individual and collective sexual justice.

Notes

1. Images from my photographic project referred to in this chapter can be viewed at: plate 1: www.cara. zazudreams.com/fire/; plate 2: www. cara.zazudreams.com/self-portraits/; plate 3: www.cara.zazudreams. com/video-stills/; plate 4: www.cara. zazudreams.com/theater-of-space/; plate 5: www.cara.zazudreams. com/gender-adaptations/; plate 6: www.cara.zazudreams. com/creative-dream-circle/.

2. For a Deleuze-Reichian integration of politics and pornography see The Feminist Porn Awards and Madison Young's Feminists for Facials Manifesto (available on YouTube).

3. See the civic rights lawyer and previous labour lawyer, Andrea Ritchie's activism addressing workers' compensation claims in the context of the connection between conventional labour abuses and sex workers' rights.

References

Bataille, G. (1961, rpt. 1989) *Tears of Eros* (trans. P Connor), San Francisco, CA: City Lights Books.

Baudrillard, J. (1983) *Simulations* (trans. P. Foss, P. Patton and P. Beitchman), New York: Semiotext(e).

Butler, J. (1997) *Excitable Speech*, New York: Taylor and Francis.

Caws, M.A. (1990) 'Ladies Shot and Painted: Female Embodiment in Surrealist Art' in Broude, N. and Garrad, M.D. (eds) *The Expanding Discourse: Feminism and Art History*, New York: Harper Collins Icon Editions.

Cioran, E.M. (1956) *The Temptation to Exist*, Chicago, IL: University of Chicago Press.

Commission on Obscenity and Pornography (1970) *The Report of the Commission on Obscenity and Pornography, September 1970*, Washington, DC: US Government Printing Office.

Crimp, D. (2002) *Melancholia and Moralism: Essays on AIDS and Queer Politics*, Cambridge, MA: MIT Press.

Deleuze, G. (1989) *Masochism*, New York: Zone Books.

Deleuze, G. and Guattari, F. (1980, rpt. 2004) *A Thousand Plateaus, Volume 2 of Capitalism and Schizophrenia* (trans. B. Massumi), London and New York: Continuum.

Derwent, M. (1986) *Hannah Arendt*, Ann Arbor, MI: Penguin Books at the University of Michigan.

Despuentes, V. (1991, rpt. 2010) *King Kong Theory: A Manifesto for Women Who Can't or Won't Obey the Rules* (trans. S. Benson), New York: The Feminist Press at the City University of New York.

Duden, B. (1991) *The Women Beneath the Skin*, Cambridge, MA: Harvard University Press.

Dufourmantelle, A. (2007) *Blind Date: Sex and Philosophy*, Urbana and Chicago, IL: University of Illinois Press.

El Saadawi, N. (1990) *Woman at Point Zero*, New York: Zed Books.

Ellman, M. (1968) *Thinking About Women*, New York: Harcourt, Brace and World.

Foucault, M. (1978) *The History of Sexuality, Volume 1: An Introduction*, New York: Random House.

Genet, J. (1988) *Ce qui est resté d'un Rembrandt déchiré en petits carrés bien réguliers, et foutu aux chiotte*. New York: Hanuman Books.

Glissant, E. (1997) *Poetics of Relation*. Ann Arbor, MI: University of Michigan Press.

Grosz, E. (1994) 'Of Bugs and Women: Deleuze and Irigaray on the Becoming Woman' in Burke, C. and Schor, N. (eds) *Engaging with Irigaray: Feminist Philosophy and Modern European Thought*, New York: Columbia University Press.

Grosz, E. (1995) *Space, Time, Perversion*, New York: Routledge.

Hall, E. (1995) 'Sex Works', *Hungry Mind Review*, (Spring).

Krishnamurti, J. (2010) 'Freedom from the Known'. Web document serial no./id: JKO 237. Krishnamurti Foundations. J. Krishnamurti

Online, the official repository of the authentic teachings of Jiddu Krishnamurti.

Kristeva, J. (1982) *Powers of Horror: An Essay on Abjection.* New York: Columbia University Press.

Lingis, A. (1983) *Excesses: Eros and Culture*, Albany, NY: State University of New York Press.

Nietzsche, F. (1886, rpt. 1968) *The Will to Power*, ed. W. Kaufmann (trans. W. Kaufmann and R.J. Hollingdale), New York: Vintage Books.

Pheterson, G. (2010) 'The Social Consequences of Unchastity'. Available at http://biblioteca-alternativa.noblogs. org/files/2010/10/social_consequences_unchastity.pdf.

Preciado, B. (2013) *Testo Junkie: Sex, Drugs, and Biopolitics in the Pharmacopornographic Era* (trans. B. Benderson), New York: Feminist Press.

Queen, C. (1997) 'Sex Radical Politics, Sex-Positive Feminist Thought, and Whore Stigma' in Nagle, J. (ed.) *Whores and Other Feminists*, New York: Routledge.

Queen, C., Bell, S., Baja and Sundahl, D. (1992) *How to Female Ejaculate*, Santa Fe: Desaro Isis Media.

Reed, S. (1997) 'All Stripped Off' in Nagle, J. (ed.) *Whores and Other Feminists*, New York: Routledge.

Ronell, A. (1991) 'Angry Women' in Juno, A. (ed.) *Re/Search Magazine*, San Francisco, CA: Re/Search.

Schirmacher, W. (2009) 'Spinoza Seminar', New York University.

Schulman, S. (1986) 'When We Were Very Young: A Walking Tour through Radical Jewish Women's History on the Lower East Side, 1879–1919' in Kantrowitz, M. and Klepfisz, I. (eds) *The Tribe of Dina: A Jewish Women's Anthology*, Boston, MA: Beacon Press.

Sprinkle, A. (2001) *Hardcore from the Heart: The Pleasures, Profits, and Politics of Sex in Performance*, New York: Continuum.

Stewart, S. (1984) *On Longing: Narratives of the Miniature, the Gigantic, the Souvenir, the Collection*, Baltimore, MD: Johns Hopkins University Press.

Sundahl, D. (1998) *Tantric Journey to Female Orgasm: Unveiling the G-Spot and Female Ejaculation*, Santa Fe, NM: Desaro Isis Media.

Ulfers, F. (2008) *Nietzsche in Contemporary Thought Seminar*, Saas-Fee, Switzerland: European Graduate School.

Weber, S. (2000) *Legend of Freud*, Stanford, CA: Stanford University Press.

2 | MAKING SENSE OF AMBIGUITY: THEORY AND METHOD

Eva Cheuk-Yin Li

Abstract

This chapter aims to suggest ways to approach ambiguity that arises in the social research of genders and sexualities by reflecting on doctoral research on the discourse and practice of the *zhongxing* phenomenon in East Asian Chinese-speaking societies. The *zhongxing* phenomenon is a substantial mediated and gendered phenomenon referring to heterosexual and queer women doing non-normative gender by using the ambiguous term *zhongxing*, which literally means 'neutral gender/sex' in the Chinese language. I specifically focus on how to engage with inter-disciplinary knowledge and how to collect data empirically. Theoretically, I suggest a critical integration of queer theory and sociology to resist the poetic/textual reading of ambiguity and to avoid reducing complexity and contradiction for the sake of 'systematic' analyses. Methodologically, I propose the indirect 'method of ambiguity' which emphasises openness and reflexivity, in order to delineate and clarify ambiguity to capture a wider range of data and minimise the risk of imposing preconceived definitions. It is hoped that by making sense of ambiguity which is a realistic and complex realm of social experience, we can begin to consider its effects on issues of agency, subjectivity, identity politics, as well as the implications for resistance and incorporation.

> But the lived, empirical world is never that simple. "Reality" has to be more messy than this [binary]. (Plummer, 2003, p. 524)

Ambiguity is a realistic and complex realm of social experience which presents challenges to gender and sexualities researchers across cultural contexts. It includes: the discursive use of ambiguity in social interactions, uncertainty in decision-making that shapes one's behaviour and perceptions of social life, and indeterminacy that influences an agent's relations with social structure.

This chapter reflects on my journey of researching the discourse and practice of the *zhongxing* (中性) phenomenon in the post-millennial East Asian Chinese-speaking societies of Hong Kong and urban China. *Zhongxing* literally means 'neutral gender/sex' in the Chinese language.[1] The *zhongxing* phenomenon, which I will introduce in detail later, is a substantial mediated and gendered phenomenon referring to women doing non-normative gender by using the ambiguous term *zhongxing*. This reflection is also invoked by my intellectual journey. Having been trained in sociology, I moved to a humanities department for my doctoral studies. This has provided me with opportunities to rethink various issues around research practice and knowledge production.

The aim of this chapter is to open up a conversation on how to approach ambiguity in order to achieve nuanced social analysis. I specifically reflect on two questions. The first one is theoretical: How do we make sense of ambiguity? This concerns the critical integration of queer theory and sociology in particular. The second is methodological: How do we study ambiguity in the empirical world? In the following, I will first illustrate how a personal encounter with *zhongxing* unleashed my interest in researching ambiguity in relation to gender and sexualities, then I will provide a brief introduction to the *zhongxing* phenomenon.

Encountering ambiguity

My first encounter with the term *zhongxing* occurred in the mid-2000s when I was a form-four student (Year 10 in the UK) in Hong Kong. It was an ordinary day and my mother and I were returning from grocery shopping. Inside the lift of the 30-

storey apartment block in which my family and I lived, there was another neighbour, a middle-aged woman, whom I had barely met before. The silence inside the lift was first broken by her asking my mother: 'Your daughter is no longer a kid, but why does she *still* dress like a boy?'

During my teenage years, I usually went out in 'boyish' outfits – short and spiky hairstyles, loose-fitting unisex fashion and boy's trainers. Although it was reported that more than two-thirds of homosexuals in Hong Kong had experienced discrimination at that time (MVA Hong Kong Limited, 2006, p. iv), such explicit scrutiny of my gender expression (and sexual orientation) was rare. To my surprise, my mother replied calmly, 'She's just a bit *zhongxing*'. Then, the lift arrived at the floor on which we lived, and put an end to the awkward conversation.

This incident reveals several issues, which can be seen as a snapshot of the ambiguity of *zhongxing*. Firstly, the neighbour's 'question' was actually a scrutiny of my mother's parenting practice, because a daughter's masculine display in public is considered to bring shame to the parents, who will lose face (Tang, 2011, p. 32). More importantly, the conversation was silenced by an ambiguous response. Invoking *zhongxing* was my mother's act of 'saving face' to avoid public scrutiny. It also manifested her ambivalent approach of 'don't ask, don't tell' towards my gender and sexuality.

When I was characterised by my mother as *zhongxing*, I felt simultaneously relieved and nervous. I was relieved because my neighbour's scrutiny was silenced, but I was uncertain about what my mother meant, and we never discussed that conversation afterwards. This prodded me into studying how Chinese women use the ambiguity of *zhongxing* to negotiate gender, sexuality and selfhood. I am also interested in investigating the differences between Chinese-speaking societies because, although the outcome of the phenomenon looks similar, the process of struggle and negotiation may differ, given their distinctive historical and socio-political trajectories.

The *zhongxing* phenomenon

The *zhongxing* phenomenon in contemporary Chinese societies refers to the widespread representation and self-representation of women doing non-normative gender.[2] The ambiguity of *zhongxing* lies in its equivocal state of not being either a gender identity or a sexual practice (Li, 2015). It is a way of re-doing gender without taking up a specific gender or sexual identity position within the binaries of masculine/feminine and heterosexual/homosexual (Li, forthcoming, 2015; West and Zimmerman, 2009). Hence, heterosexual-identified and queer-identified women can all do *zhongxing*, albeit with different consequences.

The phenomenon has been largely popularised by a generation of androgynous female idols in transnational Chinese-language popular culture in the post-millennial era, such as Li Yuchun (aka Chris Lee) in China, Denise Ho (aka HOCC) in Hong Kong and Jing Chang in Taiwan (Li, forthcoming, 2015). Their popularity is strongly associated with the transforming entertainment industry in their respective locales, the increased transnational flow of popular culture, the rise of youth culture due to the availability of new mobile technologies, and the quest for female independence. These idols are categorised as *zhongxing* by the media and audiences because of their aesthetic presentation of self and their ambivalent sexual orientation (Li, 2015, pp. 85–86). They have attracted huge numbers of female followers by emphasising individuality and authenticity, which is used as the justification for their non-normative gender expression and enigmatic sexuality. *Zhongxing* therefore became an ambiguous and generic euphemism for women doing non-normative gender.

Elsewhere, I have argued that the *zhongxing* phenomenon is socio-culturally peculiar due to its ambiguity, mundanity and depoliticised overtones; and that there are no existing academic concepts in the English language able to sufficiently encapsulate it (Li, 2015, pp. 76–78, forthcoming). In brief, *zhongxing* is unlike androgyny because it is defined by negation, captured by the Chinese expression *bunan bunü* (neither men nor women), which expresses disapproval of 'unclassified' gender expression and sexuality. Instead of a theoretical performance of male impersonation, *zhongxing* is an everyday embodied practice.[3] Unlike queer (*ku'er* in Chinese translation), an originally derogatory term that was taken up by non-heterosexuals to destabilise categories and resist normalisation politics, *zhongxing* carries depoliticised overtones due to its surface meaning of 'neutral'.[4]

My key research question is: What does *zhongxing* mean to different women and how does it shape the process of doing gender? I am less interested in the positivist question of determining 'who is *zhongxing*?' My concern is how Chinese women, both heterosexual-identified and queer-identified, use the ambiguity of *zhongxing* to negotiate gender and sexuality in their specific sociocultural milieu. Sociological studies of gender have suggested that ambiguity is the mechanism of hegemony and structurally created contradictions (Connell and Messerschmidt, 2005, p. 838; Connidis and McMullin, 2002). Thus, the ambiguity of *zhongxing* can be seen as a contested and contradictory site of meanings, repertoires of gender expression, embodiment, sexualities and selfhood in contemporary Chinese societies.

Queer theory and sociology

When conducting the literature review for my research, I went through the work of several disciplines: textual analysis of ambiguous gender performances in humanities writings, ethnographic accounts of the everyday lives of women and lesbians in sociological research and audience reception studies from the interdisciplinary field of media research. These have provided insights from diverse perspectives; yet, I still need new conceptual tools to approach the ambiguity of *zhongxing*. Thinking about ambiguity and the instability of identities, it was inevitable that I would turn to queer theory. As Valocchi (2005, p. 768) reminds us, sociologically informed queer concepts 'can result in gender and sexuality research that represents individuals' lived experience in ways that honour the complexity of human agency, the instability of identity, and the importance of institutional and discursive power'.

My question is: How can we engage with theories and concepts of both queer theory and sociology for empirical analysis? This question has been thoroughly discussed by others (Green, 2007; Plummer, 2003; Plummer and Stein, 1994; Seidman, 1996b). With my specific focus on researching ambiguity, I would like to raise three issues that require particular attention.

The first concerns queer theory's impulse to deconstruct. The primary strategy of queer theory is to denaturalise and destabilise categories such as man/woman, heterosexual/homosexual and masculine/feminine. What concerns me is the tendency to romanticise and force potentiality upon the fluidity and ambiguity found in some of the writings in 'queer textualism' (Seidman, 1997, p. 153). Sociologist Steven Seidman provides two relevant suggestions to tackle this concern. Firstly, he calls for rethinking the ethical and political standpoint of deconstructive critiques of queer theory (Seidman, 1995, p. 132). He also draws attention to the different understanding of 'empirical' in queer textualism and sociology – the former locates it in literary texts while the latter finds it in agents' interactions with social structures (Seidman, 1997, p. 75). And it is researchers' responsibility to consider which theorisation of the 'empirical' and 'social' better suits the objectives of a specific research project.[5]

Secondly, queer theory and sociology seldom acknowledge each other's work (Seidman, 1996a, p. 13; 1997, p. 94). Queer theory often claims innovation for concepts that have already been developed within sociology (Brickell, 2006; Green, 2007). Indeed, as Seidman (1996a) argued more than two decades ago, it is necessary to create dialogues between the two in order to advance an analysis that remains attuned to the contingency, contradictions and complexity of social life. An obvious example of the 'mutual indifference' that I came across is the 'performance' of gender – Judith Butler's widely cited theory of performativity and the notion of 'undoing gender' (Butler, 1990, 1993, 2004) and 'doing, re-doing, un-doing gender' in sociological writings (Deutsch, 2007; Risman, 2009; West and Zimmerman, 1987, 2009). Good research practice needs to critically evaluate its epistemological difference and theorisation of the 'social', since gender is not only citational repetition but also a more deep-rooted social structure (Risman, 2004). Examples include the works of Jackson and Scott (2001) and Brickell (2003, 2005).

Thirdly, when bringing both into dialogue, we need to work on conceptual clarity. When I was asked whether the *zhongxing* phenomenon is female masculinity (Halberstam, 1998) or 'tomboy femininity' (Yue and Yu, 2008, p. 130), I hesitated because they only capture part of the phenomenon, since my findings show that heterosexual and/or normatively feminine women also do *zhongxing*. More importantly, sociologists have critiqued the concept of female masculinity for lacking clarity and overlooking the constraints of embodiment when applied to empirical analysis (Francis, 2010; Paechter, 2006). The heavy reliance on highly dualistic definitions of gender risks reifying a dichotomy that we aim to challenge (Francis and Paechter, 2015). To address this dilemma, researcher reflexivity and sensitivity to local discursive and material conditions are the most important attributes (Francis, 2012; Francis and Paechter, 2015, pp. 785–786).

Method of ambiguity

Besides theoretical issues, ambiguity has also posed a major methodological challenge: What types of selection criteria should I use to recruit interview participants? The ambiguous and generic use of *zhongxing* as a euphemism for doing non-normative gender is too broad, but searching for 'self-identified' *zhongxing* individuals inevitably imposes my preconceived understanding and risks forcing interview data.

When studying the less well-defined empirical phenomenon of heterosexual casual sex, Farvid (2010) put forward the idea of 'benefits of ambiguity'. She suggests that starting from a more general idea of sex would give her access to the complex and multi-faceted aspects of the phenomenon. Similarly, I adopt an indirect approach when interviewing the fans of *zhongxing* stars by considering the constructivist approach of grounded theory (Charmaz, 2006, 2008).[6] I call this approach 'the method of ambiguity'. Instead of starting from the ambiguity of *zhongxing*, I use 'doing gender' as the sensitising concept to structure my interview questions, which can simultaneously avoid reifying existing binaries and imposing a predefined understanding of *zhongxing*.[7]

Concern about the selection criteria for research participants can be addressed by the strategy of theoretical sampling – a strategy rather than an explicit procedure, which can be useful in specific studies (Charmaz, 2006, p. 107). It aims to gather pertinent data instead of achieving representativeness and allows the development of conceptual categories with a specific analytical focus and research puzzles (Charmaz, 2006, pp. 96, 108).

There are three advantages. Firstly, it sidesteps the paradox of recruiting self-identified *zhongxing* informants. Secondly, because doing gender is a deeply internalised everyday accomplishment, it may not be easy to verbally articulate their experience without a nodal point. The *zhongxing* stars can serve as the point of departure. By staying attuned to the mediated nature of *zhongxing*, it is easier to elicit a discussion of gender and sexuality by starting from one's consumption and affective engagement with popular culture. Through this, I can understand how fans, as gendered and sexual subjects, appropriate these meanings and practices into their everyday lives and what additional resources and knowledge they drew from.

Thirdly, without assuming that fans of *zhongxing* stars necessarily take up the position of *zhongxing* themselves, this method reaches out to research participants of diverse gender, sexual orientation, age and educational level, as suggested by fandom studies of *zhongxing* stars, which challenged the stereotypical assumption that associates *zhongxing* stars with lesbians only (Li, 2012; Yang, 2012). Since *zhongxing* is an integral part of their stardom, fans, whatever their own stance on *zhongxing*, unavoidably have to negotiate and re-appropriate the discourse and practice of *zhongxing*.

The interview schedule

When recruiting fans for my semi-structured interviews, I made it clear that I was also interested in their lives beyond fandom – as a 'gendered and/or sexual subject'. The interview guide was structured according to the sensitising concept and divided into several parts that progressed according to several themes: the experience of being a fan, interpretation of their idol's stardom, discussion about *zhongxing* as media discourse and personal experience, and fans' gender-related experiences in everyday life.

The interview schedule is also divided into softer and harder questions. Softer questions ask about fans' practice and experience with the purpose of understanding their background and establishing rapport before discussing more personal experiences related to gender and sexuality. The harder questions began with asking fans to comment on the various discourses of *zhongxing* in relation to their idol. Since *zhongxing* is ambivalently related to homosexuality, which is considered a social taboo, questions regarding the sexuality of *zhongxing* stars were asked indirectly, in order not to offend the fans. Instead, I asked them to comment on relevant news reports. Based on their responses, I proceeded to ask about their understanding of *zhongxing* beyond fandom, such as their relation with their family, peers and significant others, and whether they are attracted to *zhongxing* individuals or identify with being *zhongxing*.

There are both advantages and drawbacks to this approach. In most of the interviews, the softer questions got fans engaged; yet, sometimes they were extremely talkative, which made it difficult for me to proceed to the harder questions about their own experience of doing gender and negotiating *zhongxing*. For example, a lesbian-identified fan eloquently recounted how she overcame hardship and how the fandom experience transformed her life. I was grateful for her sharing for more than an hour before I could politely interrupt and lead the way to the harder questions. And the interview resulted in a more solid rapport. Later, I was given the chance to re-interview her about more personal issues regarding her negotiation of gender and sexuality and the ways in which the discourse and practice of *zhongxing* had enabled and/or limited such a process.

Moreover, the ambiguity of gendered pronouns in *Putonghua* spoken in China and Cantonese in Hong Kong helped me to ask about informants' sexual orientation in a less intrusive manner. I did not explicitly ask for their sexual orientation at the beginning of the interview for fear of intimidating informants, because some of them might not see the relevance of their own sexual orientation to the interview. Therefore, only when the interview had progressed to a point that touched upon their everyday lives and personal aspirations, did I ask whether they were 'dating someone' or what their ideal partners would be like. In spoken *Putonghua*, the gender-specific pronouns 'he' and 'she' share the same sound, *ta*, while, in colloquial Cantonese, the third-person pronoun *keoi* is not gender specific. The ambiguity of these pronouns can reduce the embarrassment of posing a potentially intrusive question but, at the same time, informants could use the same tactics of ambiguity to avoid providing any hints about their sexual orientation.

Since qualitative interviewing is a process of co-constructing knowledge, at the end of each interview I encouraged informants to reflect on the experience and asked if they had any questions for me. Some informants were curious about my research motivation because they usually found talking about popular culture and gender trivial. In these situations, I reaffirmed them by acknowledging their contribution to my research. I also asked them to describe the aura of their idol with a colour and explain why they had chosen that colour. The question was originally formulated as a reflection of my interest in the affective dimension of doing gender. Most of the informants found this question interesting. Although their answers might not be directly relevant to my theorisation of the discourse and practice of *zhongxing*, it helped to end the interviews with a lighter mood and imaginative answers.

'Failed' interviews and veiled silence

Researching *zhongxing* ambiguously touched upon both gender and sexuality, and the interview process has not been as straightforward as I had anticipated. Due to the method of ambiguity, I also encountered several interviews which I initially considered 'failures' because informants seemed not to be engaged and gave short responses. A few fans whom I interviewed kept playing with their mobile phones during the interview. On some occasions, I successfully asked what was keeping them distracted, and they showed me photos of other *zhongxing* celebrities and fashion models in the West, such as Freja Beha and Andreja Pejić, which enhanced my understanding of my research question. However, with some of the others, I seemed to fail.

Nairn and colleagues (2005) argue that an apparently 'failed' interview should be revisited for a reflexive analysis since it teaches us about our research practice. When I listened to the recordings after the interviews, I found that some informants considered gender to be a 'non-topic', which they had taken for granted because it was deeply embedded in everyday life. Hence, they had little to say and did not find much vocabulary or narrative to articulate their thoughts. This motivated me to improve my probing skills and develop more diverse ways to ask for their views – for example, by citing more examples from popular culture.

As well as actual silence, I also encountered 'veiled silence' during interviews. 'Veiled silence' is silence in a metaphorical sense. It is a situation in which informants spoke, but what they said responded to a different question than the one I had posed (Morison and Macleod, 2014, p. 695). During interviews, there were signs of avoidance of some issues on *zhongxing* that informants 'spoke without speaking' (Mazzei, 2007, p. 633). An example is the group discussion with four Chris Lee fans in Shanghai, China. It was initially scheduled with Tung, a migrant worker in her mid-twenties from central China. On the day of our interview, she brought three other fans, despite my preference for conducting individual interviews. I did not seek a group discussion since it was likely to quickly become a fan talk session, which hindered the progression to harder questions. At last, I met Tung and the three other fans, Hong, Han and Chi, who were also migrant workers in Shanghai. Two of them, Han and Chi, looked very alike with a similar short hairstyle and unisex outfits. They were exceptionally quiet during the interview. Tung also occasionally interrupted my conversation with Han and Chi on their experience of being classified *zhongxing* and misrecognised in public:

Li: You've mentioned that some people stare at you in public because of your appearance. Has your appearance got you into ... unexpected situations?

Han: Sometimes I was expelled from the female toilet. Those old ladies [toilet attendants] thought I was a boy.

Chi: When we hang out [with Han], some people think we're a gay couple.

Tung: People always classify others according to their hairstyle. But wearing a short hairstyle is great.

Li: Why?

Tung: It saves on the water bill [*chuckle*].

Li: So, do you all consider a short hairstyle an element of *zhongxing*?

Hong: Can a person wear a long hairstyle and be *zhongxing* at the same time?

Tung: Many people think that *zhongxing* girls lack *nürenwei* [lit. scent of femininity]. It's hard to understand. For example, Chris Lee is just full of *nürenwei*, isn't she?

> She's so adorable and everyone falls for her ... Sexiness
> is delivered through the tiny details of a person. At the
> end of the day, girls are girls. At least 80 per cent of us
> want men to take care of us.

To interpret veiled silence, research reflexivity is needed
in order to re-examine the power relations and language used
during interviews (Morison and Macleod, 2014). Pillow (2003,
p. 193) argues that 'messy' examples in qualitative research in fact
demonstrate complex and uncomfortable realities. Reviewing the
above interview, it is clear that there was an unspoken avoidance
of certain topics, such as the gender expression of Chi and Han,
and also the sexuality of Chris Lee. To them, *zhongxing* star
Chris Lee was by default (normatively) feminine and therefore
'normal'. In hindsight, this interview illustrates an important
concept regarding the *zhongxing* phenomenon – avoidance
and denial, which also occurred in other interviews. It also
highlights the situatedness of the discourse of *zhongxing*, since
such responses were less observed among interviews conducted
in Hong Kong. While literal silence in the discussion of non-
normative gender and sexuality is considered a 'violent form of
symbolic erasure' (Kam, 2012, p. 92), *zhongxing*, on the other
hand, is an example of veiled silence, which is more ambiguous
and contested; it is usually spoken without actually speaking. It is
acknowledged ambivalently through avoidance, which manifests
its entanglement with the complex web of domination through
gender, sexuality and class.

Reflexivity of discomfort

Moreover, uncomfortable moments during interviews helped
to refine my understanding of *zhongxing* and informed subsequent
interviews and data analysis. To better engage with the complexity
of the empirical world, the 'reflexivity of discomfort' repositions
reflexivity 'not as clarity, honesty, or humility, but as practices of
confounding disruptions – at times even a failure of our language

and practices' (Pillow, 2003, p. 192). Uncomfortable reflexivity continuously challenges 'the representations we come to while at the same time acknowledging the political need to represent and find meaning' (Pillow, 2003, p. 192).

During the interviews, I never made judgmental comments on informants' gender expression. When asking whether they desire *zhongxing* – being attracted to *zhongxing* individuals or identify with being *zhongxing*, I asked indirectly and progressed carefully, in order to avoid any potential discomfort or embarrassment. However, when informants made comments about my appearance, I felt uncomfortable. There was one occasion when an informant said to me during the interview: 'You look quite *zhongxing* too. You've a light skin tone, cute face, and short hairstyle'. I was slightly nervous and stammered a bit before returning to the questions that I was asking. In hindsight, it was the ambiguity of *zhongxing* that caused my discomfort. Recalling my experience of being described by my mother as *zhongxing* when I was younger, I felt anxious because being described as *zhongxing* is different from being described as fat or 'gay', for instance. 'Being fat' is a definite statement referring to my physical shape, while 'being gay' implies that I do not look feminine *enough*; and I could easily know what to 'improve' in order to 'fit in' if necessary. Being characterised by an informant whom I had only known for 30 minutes as *zhongxing*, I felt as though I was 'being caught' for doing something wrong without a concrete reason. I could not read exactly what she meant. Was she saying that I was not feminine enough? Was she implying that I was *bunan bunü*? Was she hinting that she 'smelled' that I might be a lesbian?

Again, *zhongxing* would not need to be named if it were normalised in society, if there were space for everyone to do their gender and express their sexuality comfortably without the need to account for it. When *zhongxing* is named, it means that something ambivalent is being acknowledged, but without being addressed directly. While one may happily embrace the ambiguity, most subjects, including my informants, live in a binary gender/sex system. Not everyone desires, or can afford, to embrace the ambiguity or to challenge the binary. In this sense, normativity was one of the key themes running through most of the interviews. By taking this uncomfortable experience into account, I was more reflexive in understanding why some informants embraced or avoided *zhongxing* as a discursive and embodied practice. Moreover, in subsequent interviews, I felt more comfortable when informants used my appearance as the point of reference to discuss *zhongxing* and gender, which, in turn, facilitated the interview process. Therefore, I argue that the method of ambiguity is indeed better to sketch and delineate the ambiguity of *zhongxing* by capturing a broad range of discourses and practices.

Conclusion: making sense of ambiguity

When talking about gender-ambiguous performances in Hong Kong popular culture, Hong Kong sociologist and cultural critic Dr Chun-Hung Ng (2017) observed: 'you could choose to see it, or not see it, because it was "ambiguous"'. In a similar vein, we can choose to address and delineate the complexity of ambiguity, or ignore it by reducing it to classifiable patterns for 'systematic' analysis. What I want to reiterate in this chapter is that, in order to achieve a better understanding of the lived experience of gender and sexuality, ambiguity as a realistic realm of social experience can and should be acknowledged by the critical and theoretical integration of queer theory and sociology and the method of ambiguity that reflects on uncomfortable and ambivalent experiences.

To recap, this chapter reflects on the theoretical and methodo-logical issues that arose when I researched the discourse and practice of the ambiguous *zhongxing* phenomenon in Chinese-speaking societies. Making sense of ambiguity requires the critical integration of queer theory and sociology by resisting the temptation to merely engage in a poetic/textual reading of ambiguity. Instead, we need to locate ambiguity and fluidity firmly within everyday interactions situated in the web of domination, such as that of gender, heterosexual marriage, class structures, the media industry and so on. Methodologically, it requires an indirect method, the method of ambiguity, to help in *delineating* and *clarifying* ambiguity in order to capture a wider range of data and minimise the risk of forcing interview data and imposing preconceived definitions. By employing the method of ambiguity, it is hoped that we can begin to consider the effects of gender and sexual ambiguity on individual agency and their implications for resistance and incorporation.

Author's note

Many thanks to Dr Charlotte Morris for inviting me to write this chapter. Thank you to Miss Chloe Chow at M+ for providing information on the exhibition 'Ambiguously Yours'. I also thank Professor Ken Plummer and the participants of the *Researching Sex and Sexualities* conference at the University of Sussex in 2015 for their feedback.

Notes

1. Although the same written characters are used in East Asian Chinese-speaking societies, the transliteration differs – *zungsing* in Hong Kong (Cantonese) and *chung hsing* in Taiwan (Mandarin).

2. Men who are not performing the 'correct' gender tend to be labelled with derogatory adjectives instead of *zhongxing* (Li, 2015, p. 76).

3. For historical traces of gender ambiguity in Chinese history, see Huang (2013) and Li (forthcoming, 2015).

4. Moreover, the Chinese translation of queer, *ku'er*, literal meaning 'being cool', is seldom used in everyday life.

5. It should be noted that there is also an impulse to deconstruct in sociology. See Plummer (2003) and Green (2007).

6. I interviewed the fans of Chris Lee in China and Denise Ho in Hong Kong due to their popularity in the respective locales. For details of their stardom, see Au (2012) and Li (2015).

7. Sensitising concepts are the concepts that give a researcher initial ideas and a general sense of orientation in approaching the empirical world (Blumer, 1969, pp. 147–148).

References

Au, W.V. (2012) *The Queer Female Stardom: Emerging from Transnational Chinese Singing Contests*. MPhil, Hong Kong: The University of Hong Kong. Available at http://hub.hku.hk/handle/10722/183061 (accessed 1 June 2014).

Blumer, H. (1969) *Symbolic Interactionism: Perspective and Method*, Berkeley and Los Angeles, CA and London: University of California Press.

Brickell, C. (2003) 'Performativity or Performance? Clarification in the Sociology of Gender', *New Zealand Sociology*, 18(2), pp. 158–178.

Brickell, C. (2005) 'Masculinities, Performativity, and Subversion: A Sociological Reappraisal', *Men and Masculinities*, 8(1), pp. 24–43.

Brickell, C. (2006) 'The sociological construction of gender and sexuality', *The Sociological Review*, 54(1), pp. 87–113.

Butler, J. (1990) *Gender Trouble: Feminism and the Subversion of Identity*, New York and London: Routledge.

Butler, J. (1993) 'Imitation and Gender Insubordination' in Abelove, H., Barale, M.A. and Halperin, D.M. (eds) *The Lesbian and Gay Studies Reader*, London and New York: Routledge, pp. 307–320.

Butler, J. (2004) *Undoing Gender*, New York and London: Routledge.

Charmaz, K. (2006) *Constructing Grounded Theory: A Practical Guide through Qualitative Analysis*, London: Sage.

Charmaz, K. (2008) 'Grounded Theory as an Emergent Method' in Hesse-Biber, S.N. and Leavy, P. (eds) *Handbook of Emergent Methods*, New York and London: Guildford Press, pp. 155–170.

Connell, R. and Messerschmidt, J. (2005) 'Hegemonic Masculinity: Rethinking the Concept', *Gender and Society*, 19(6), pp. 829–859.

Connidis, I.A. and McMullin, J.A. (2002) 'Sociological Ambivalence and Family Ties: A Critical Perspective', *Journal of Marriage and Family*, 64(3), pp. 558–567.

Deutsch, F.M. (2007) 'Undoing Gender', *Gender and Society*, 21(1), pp. 106–127.

Farvid, P. (2010) 'The Benefits of Ambiguity: Methodological Insights from Researching "Heterosexual Casual Sex"', *Feminism and Psychology*, 20(2), pp. 232–237.

Francis, B. (2010) 'Re/theorising Gender: Female Masculinity and Male Femininity in the Classroom?', *Gender and Education*, 22(5), pp. 477–490.

Francis, B. (2012) 'Gender Monoglossia, Gender Heteroglossia: The Potential of Bakhtin's Work for Re-conceptualising Gender', *Journal of Gender Studies*, 21(1), pp. 1–15.

Francis, B. and Paechter, C. (2015) 'The Problem of Gender Categorisation: Addressing Dilemmas Past and Present in Gender and Education Research', *Gender and Education*, 27(7), pp. 776–790.

Green, A.I. (2007) 'Queer Theory and Sociology: Locating the Subject and the Self in Sexuality Studies',

Sociological Theory, 25(1), pp. 26–45.

Halberstam, J. (1998) *Female Masculinity*, Durham, NC: Duke University Press.

Huang, X. (2013) 'From "Hyper-feminine" to Androgyny: Changing Notions of Femininity in Contemporary China' in Fitzsimmons, L. and Lent, J.A. (eds) *Asian Popular Culture in Transition*, London and New York: Routledge, pp. 133–155.

Jackson, S. and Scott, S. (2001) 'Putting the Body's Feet on the Ground: Towards a Sociological Reconceptualization of Gendered and Sexual Embodiment' in Backett-Milburn, K. and McKie, L. (eds) *Constructing Gendered Bodies*, Houndmills: Palgrave, pp. 9–24.

Kam, L.Y.L. (2012) *Shanghai Lalas: Female Tongzhi Communities and Politics in Urban China*, Hong Kong: Hong Kong University Press.

Li, C.Y. (2012) 'The Absence of Fan Activism in the Queer Fandom of Ho Denise Wan See (HOCC) in Hong Kong', *Transformative Works and Cultures*, 10. Available at http://journal.transformativeworks.org/index.php/twc/article/view/325/286.

Li, E.C.Y. (2015) 'Approaching Transnational Chinese Queer Stardom as Zhongxing ("Neutral Sex/Gender") Sensibility', *East Asian Journal of Popular Culture*, 1(1), pp. 75–95.

Li, E.C.Y. (Forthcoming) 'Zhongxing Phenomenon' in Chiang, H (ed.) *Global Encyclopedia of Lesbian, Gay, Bisexual, Transgender, and Queer History*, Farmington Hills, MI: Gale, Cengage Learning.

Mazzei, L.A. (2007) 'Toward a Problematic of Silence in Action Research', *Educational Action Research*, 15(4), pp. 631–642.

Morison, T. and Macleod, C. (2014) 'When Veiled Silences Speak: Reflexivity, Trouble and Repair as Methodological Tools for Interpreting the Unspoken in Discourse-based Data', *Qualitative Research*, 14(6), pp. 694–711.

MVA Hong Kong Limited (2006) *Survey on Public Attitudes towards Homosexuals*, Hong Kong: Home Affairs Bureau, The Government of Hong Kong Special Administrative Region. Available at www.legco.gov.hk/yr05-06/english/panels/ha/papers/ha0310cb2-public-homosexuals-e.pdf.

Nairn, K., Munro, J. and Smith, A.B. (2005) 'A Counter-narrative of a "Failed" Interview', *Qualitative Research*, 5(2), pp. 221–244.

Ng, C.-H. (2017) Curatorial Advisor Dr Ng Chun Hung on Anita Mui. Exhibition entitled 'Ambiguously Yours: Gender in Hong Kong Popular Culture', M+, West Kowloon Cultural District. Available at www.facebook.com/mplushongkong/videos/905260919634800/?pnref=story.

Paechter, C. (2006) 'Masculine Femininities/Feminine Masculinities: Power, Identities and Gender', *Gender and Education*, 18(3), pp. 253–263.

Pillow, W. (2003) 'Confession, Catharsis, or Cure? Rethinking the Uses of Reflexivity as Methodological Power in Qualitative Research', *International Journal of Qualitative Studies in Education*, 16(2), pp. 175–196.

Plummer, K. (2003) 'Queers, Bodies and Postmodern Sexualities: A Note on Revisiting the "Sexual" in Symbolic Interactionism', *Qualitative Sociology*, 26(4), pp. 515–530.

Plummer, K. and Stein, A. (1994) 'I Can't Even Think Straight: Queer Theory and the Missing Sexual Revolution in Sociology' in Seidman, S. (ed.) *Queer Theory/Sociology*, Oxford: Blackwell.

Risman, B.J. (2004) 'Gender as a Social Structure: Theory Wrestling with Activism', *Gender and Society*, 18(4), pp. 429–450.

Risman, B.J. (2009) 'From Doing to Undoing: Gender as We Know It', *Gender and Society*, 23(1), pp. 81–84.

Seidman, S. (1995) 'Deconstructing Queer Theory or the Under-theorization of the Social and the Ethical' in Nicholson, L. and Seidman, S. (eds) *Social Postmodernism: Beyond Identity Politics*, Cambridge: Cambridge University Press, pp. 116–141.

Seidman, S. (1996a) 'Introduction', in Seidman, S. (ed.) *Queer Theory/Sociology*, Oxford: Blackwell, pp. 1–29.

Seidman, S. (ed.) (1996b) *Queer Theory/Sociology*, Oxford: Blackwell.

Seidman, S. (1997) *Difference Troubles: Queering Social Theory and Sexual Politics*, Cambridge and New York: Cambridge University Press.

Tang, D.T.-S. (2011) *Conditional Spaces: Hong Kong Lesbian Desires and Everyday Life*, Hong Kong: Hong Kong University Press.

Valocchi, S. (2005) 'Not Yet Queer Enough: The Lessons of Queer Theory for the Sociology of Gender and Sexuality', *Gender and Society*, 19(6), pp. 750–770.

West, C. and Zimmerman, D.H. (1987) 'Doing Gender', *Gender and Society*, 1(2), pp. 125–151.

West, C. and Zimmerman, D.H. (2009) 'Accounting for Doing Gender', *Gender and Society*, 23(1), pp. 112–122.

Yang, L. (2012) *Zhuansing shidai de yule kuanghuan: Chaonü fensi yu dazhong wenhua xiaofei* [*Entertaining the Transitional Era: Super Girl Fandom and the Consumption of Popular Culture*], Beijing: China Social Sciences Press.

Yue, A. and Yu, H. (2008) 'China's Super Girl: Mobile Youth Cultures and New Sexualities' in Smaill, B. and Rodrigues, U. (eds) *Youth, Media and Culture in the Asia Pacific Region*, Newcastle upon Tyne: Cambridge Scholar Press, pp. 117–134.

3 | CAN QUANTITATIVE APPLIED SEXUAL HEALTH RESEARCH BE CRITICAL AND FEMINIST? TOWARDS A CRITICAL SOCIAL EPIDEMIOLOGY TO SUPPORT TARGETED STI TESTING AND CONTRACEPTION IN PRIMARY CARE

Natalie Edelman

Abstract

In this chapter I discuss issues of methodology and research practice in the context of applied sexual health research. I explore the notion of a critical epidemiology for applied sexual health research, and how we might conceive of and practise it in a way that draws on critical traditions in the humanities. Applied sexual health research tends to employ a bio-medical approach that focuses on sexual 'risk behaviours', on adverse sexual health outcomes (particularly sexually transmitted infections and unintended pregnancy) and on the design and uptake of sexual health interventions designed to address these behaviours and outcomes.

Describing my experiences and concerns as a mixed methods researcher in this field for 15 years, I discuss how an interest in research as a feminist political activity has led me to attempt to bring criticality to social epidemiology in the context of sexual health research. Specifically, I critique current social epidemiological practice concerning the socio-political agendas of public health regarding: pregnancy ambiguity; the 'depersonalised' researcher; the notion of 'risky individuals'; a reliance on health psychology constructs assumed to be causal; and descriptive treatment of socio-demographic variables. I suggest how these concerns might be addressed in a way which is methodologically sound, enriching in knowledge and emancipatory in intent.

Introducing myself as an applied sexual health researcher

The experiences and ideas presented in this chapter are born of my own trajectory working as a researcher in the field of applied sexual health research, in which I have moved from a non-reflective approach uninformed by my feminist politics, to the development of a critical epidemiology which directly speaks to them.

Applied sexual health research is a particular field within sex research, which focuses on studying the causes of ill-health, the distribution of ill-health in populations, and best means for preventing, identifying and treating ill-health. Much applied sexual health research is therefore characterised by a biomedical focus on sexually transmitted infections (STIs) and unplanned pregnancies as 'adverse outcomes'; on the sexual 'risk behaviours' which may precede these outcomes; and on the development and evaluation of sexual health interventions designed to ameliorate these outcomes (e.g. STI screening programmes, and contraception advice and supply (CAS) services).

In the context of applied sexual health research, sexuality is commonly investigated as either a potential 'risk factor' for ill-health or in behavioural terms as a defining quality in populations experiencing disproportionate sexual morbidity – particularly Men who have Sex with Men (MSM) ill-health. In particular, Men who have Sex with Men (MSM) are a behaviourally defined population who are known to experience higher rates of Sexually Transmitted Infections (STIs), as are 'swingers' who regularly engage in group sex. Sex is a topic of interest precisely because of its impact on sexual health so that there is a concomitant focus on particular 'sexual behaviours' such as use of condoms and contraception, number of sexual partners and concurrency of sexual partners.

Applied sexual health research tends to address pragmatic and narrowly defined research questions that are then able to inform public health and clinical practice. This focus lends itself particularly to quantitative research designs – often combining clinical data with patient self-report via closed-response questionnaires. These quantitative designs fit most readily within positivist or critical realist epistemologies (Crotty, 1998). However, there is little tradition of learning about – or considering epistemological positions in this field where quantitative research predominates and 'objective' clinical data are a mainstay. Similarly, qualitative applied sexual health research often fails to do so, particularly where mixed methods are used to address narrowly defined research questions.

Personal influences on research

I have become increasingly aware of how research is underpinned not only by our epistemological positions but also by our own life experiences, values and ways of seeing and understanding the world (in the informal sense). This underlies the scope and focus of our enquiries, and our approach to analysis as well as our interpretation of the data then generated. Some of these positions will be explicitly recognisable as 'theoretical perspectives' which are also political in nature – e.g. feminism (Inhorn, 2001). To notice, query and work with epistemological, theoretical and personal influences is important in order to acknowledge research as a practice, and to employ reflexivity with regard to that research practice. Reflexivity is then a key component of criticality, as it invites us to critique, re-dress and improve our research practice.

However, just as applied quantitative health research has little tradition of epistemological enquiry, so it has little tradition of reflexivity either. As a primarily quantitative researcher without a social sciences background, I have been introduced to criticality, reflexivity (Crotty, 1998) – and even epistemology informally through colleagues and recommended reading. I have found my way to texts addressing feminist epidemiology and critical epidemiology (Breilh, 2008; Krieger, 2000a). Feminists particularly have written about the role of personal values and experience in the research process – particularly the notion that personal values cannot be left behind in intellectual work, nor should they be acknowledged purely to prevent their influence, but instead should be interrogated as part of that work. Oakley (1993) suggests that even 'Quantitative data are mediated by the perception and position of the observer just as much as, though less obviously than, accounts of experience or feeling' (Oakley, 1993, p. 214).

These issues often lie un-noticed in quantitative research, likely compounded by their nebulous and fractured nature. For example, I bring to my research a variety of experiences, values and positions including: myself as a woman, my feminist beliefs, my interest in research as a political activity and my epistemological position as a critical realist (discussed later). Much harder to explicate is how each of the experiences and positions I bring to my research informs the other, and how together and separately they impact my research.

Reflexivity around research practice can lead one to challenge the boundaries between the researcher and the researched, an idea taken up in feminist research (Allen et al., 2007; Reinharz and Davidman, 1992). This false distinction is very salient to Patient and Public Involvement (PPI) in applied health research. PPI involves consultation or collaboration with lay people about research design, management and dissemination. Where the distinction between the lay person and the researcher has been disrupted so that patients have themselves conducted research, this has led to wonderfully enriched data (Gillard et al., 2010). Although contested, myself and others (Edelman and Barron, 2015) have argued that lay people can hold the position of researcher without losing lay perspective.

The corollary of this idea is that professional researchers can carry lay perspectives, and may in fact be 'depersonalised' where relevant personal experiences are denied or diminished. I find it problematic to refer to the population I am currently researching (sexually active women who use GP services) as other than myself, because I fit this description. Key to my research practice is that I seek to acknowledge, interrogate and embrace how being a woman informs my research.

Feminism and research as a political activity

Forays into feminist research reveal a range of research methods and approaches, which are primarily qualitative but not inherently so (Oakley, 1993; Reinhartz and Davidman, 1992). I consider myself a feminist researcher in so far as (1) I identify as a feminist and (2) I have moved into researching women's sexual health with the precise intention of empowering women to maintain and improve our sexual health. This represents a political rather than theoretical understanding of feminism – unschooled in feminist theory I nonetheless identify as feminist because I consider gender to be the primary form of inequality which humanity must address.

For me, being a critical realist (Parr, 2015) is a feminist decision. Critical realism holds that 'the social world is both socially constructed and real', with 'real' referring not to material existence but rather to possession of 'causal powers' (Parr, 2015, p. 195). To recognise a knowable and real world (albeit imperfectly captured) is to recognise gender inequality as a real and potent phenomenon. The privileging of certain types of knowledge in critical realist approaches may clash with egalitarian feminist principles (Parr, 2015), but I believe quantitative research founded in critical realism is a potent way of seeking concrete change through research (Reinharz and Davidman, 1992).

My subscription to critical realism and to feminism also fits an interest in health research as a political activity. Firstly, the motivations for certain topics to receive research funding can be political. Margaret Thatcher's government withdrew funding for the 1990 National Survey of Sexual Attitudes and Lifestyles (Overy et al., 2011) as it was deemed politically inexpedient to fund research responding to the AIDS epidemic and associated changes in sexual mores and lifestyles.

More generally what actually gets researched is political and can have huge implications for the nature and extent of health care provision for different populations of people. This is particularly true in the context of Evidence-Based Medicine (EBM) (Mayer, 2010), which privileges interventions that have a positive evidence base, but may result in under-provision for under-researched populations and conditions. For example, the lack of evidence-base for the sexual health needs of substance-misusing women can be understood as a lack of political and societal investment in this population, which then leads to a lack of services.

As I have increasingly sought to embrace reflexivity, criticality and feminism in my research, I have grown aware that how something is defined and researched is also politically charged. For example, Rothman (1990) discusses how 'reproductive technologies' (e.g. contraception) are in fact procreative technologies. In biological terms reproduction is a singular activity – the use of the term 'reproductive' then reflects and perpetuates how the onus of fertility regulation is placed on women, in both research and the social world. The fine tuning of research questions, the choice of methods, approaches to analysis and interpretation of findings are all steps in the research process which can disrupt or reinforce received wisdom in research disciplines and subject areas, in popular consciousness and in government policy and plans.

Early research career: being inspired by MSM research to focus my research on women

My research with women has incorporated and rejected aspects of earlier studies around Men who have Sex with Men (MSM) that I was involved with. In particular I worked on the Brighton Syphilis Outbreak Project (BSOP) screening and mixed methods research study (Imrie et al., 2006; Lambert et al., 2005; Lambert et al., 2006).

This study introduced me to the sensitive nature of applied sexual health research in which certain sexual practices, STI acquisition and transmission and unplanned pregnancies each entail stigmatised experiences. The studies I encountered commonly incorporated constructs from social cognition models (such as risk perception and self-efficacy) which have been adopted by mainstream quantitative health psychology.

Recruiting and collecting data within sexual health clinics, I noticed how much mental health and social determinants of health seemed manifest amongst those experiencing sexual morbidity – both men and women, heterosexual and otherwise. This interest in the mental and social determinants of health inspired me to research them in the context of STI acquisition, unplanned pregnancy and contraception among women. As a female researcher this was a response to both a paucity of research looking across these issues and to the fact that these issues are not discrete. For example, if I want to get pregnant without contracting an STI, modern science affords me few options for enabling that.

Researching women with problematic drug use: becoming politicised as a researcher

Following the BSOP I led a National Institute for Health Research (NIHR) funded study to model sexual health interventions for substance-misusing women (Edelman et al., 2013; Edelman et al., 2015). I undertook this study when I became aware of the poor quality of existing evidence on this population and the lack of service recommendations that therefore existed. For me, this study was a feminist endeavour, as there was little existing research and therefore no evidence-based service provision.

This study further politicised me and informed my thinking. Examining the evidence, I was struck by how the existing studies did not examine individual service use in the context of individuals' actual sexual risk, nor did they compare those levels of risk to the 'general population'. Equally the social contexts in which women experience – and which contribute to – sexual risk, are often absent from these studies despite known social factors such as high prevalence of child sexual abuse among those experiencing problematic drug use (Jarvis and Copeland, 1997). Neglect of social factors can be viewed as part of a wider sexist interpretation of women's mental health and behaviour, in which 'even if many individual women have the same problem, the explanation of a defective psychology rather than that of a defective social structure is usually preferred' (Oakley, 1993, pp. 7–8).

As a feminist and critical researcher working within the 'restrictions' of applied quantitative health research I believe I have a moral duty to adapt my research methods to avoid excluding the more vulnerable from research and to gain a picture of women's sexual experiences and health that enables us to develop meaningful solutions. For example, I chose to use convenience sampling for the quantitative survey, to maximise participation as well as to avoid the bias that can arise with random sampling of disenfranchised populations (Faugier and Sargeant, 1997). This meant that population estimates could not reliably be obtained, and so the study was considered 'methodologically flawed' by some peer reviewers and publication required perseverance.

It was also in this study that I first explicitly drew on my own experiences as a woman – in particular the qualitative component of the research required that women talk about historical uptake of cervical screening (smear testing), STI testing, contraceptive advice and supply, abortion services and pregnancy care. In order to help women recall and reflect on their experiences I began by thinking of my own, attempting to notice what techniques I was using in order to recall them. This led me to an approach that began by mapping out menarche, sexual debut, sexual relationships and encounters, as a prompt to recollections of service use.

My experience of carrying out this research both consolidated the importance of pursuing the links between mental, social and sexual health and also made concrete to me an inadequacy in my research methods. However, this was not only born of the limitations of quantitative methods, but rather the reductive and non-critical nature of both my qualitative and quantitative findings.

Applying criticality

Wishing to bring a critical and feminist approach to future qualitative and quantitative studies, I encountered very little precedent for the latter. Although the notion that quantitative research cannot be feminist has also been proposed and challenged, I have found that more general discussion of criticality almost inevitably veers into a methodological impasse, in which the relative merits of qualitative and quantitative approaches are posited against each other.

The notion of a 'critical epidemiology' occurred to me one evening and I discovered a small body of literature – largely within South America where the term has been used to describe research examining the socio-political causes of disease (Arreaza, 2012; Breilh, 2008; Waitzkin et al., 2001) and leading to the persecution of many of its academics. Outside of this context the term has been used occasionally on disparate studies of suicide (Hopper and Guttmacher, 1979), environmental genomics (Robert and Smith, 2004), and by Krieger in her critiques of epidemiology (Krieger, 1994; Krieger, 2000b; Krieger, 2014). In particular Krieger has challenged the degree to which the discipline adheres to a bio-medical model characterised by individualism and the construction of populations as simple aggregates of the individual. Alongside this, a more specific critique has emerged of epidemiology's focus on 'individual risk factors' (Wemrell et al., 2016). This literature chimed with my concern over the predominance of health psychology constructs within applied sexual health research – in particular concepts such as 'self-efficacy' and 'risk perception' which provide a reductive understanding of sexual risk in which the individual is the primary agent of change (Krieger, 2014).

In order to envisage how I might enact a critical epidemiology for sexual health research I therefore began by attempting to distil the core features of criticality. Murray (2014) and Siedman (2012) identify key features of critical theory as applied to specific disciplines:

1. critical attention to structural concerns, power and norms, particularly as explanatory of both behaviour and health outcomes;
2. an intention to bring about positive change in response to these critiques.

In addition, the term 'critical' has been used to refer to:

3. critical attention to the practices of research/bringing reflexivity to the practice of one's discipline;
4. critical attention to the production of knowledge.

Murray (2014) also notes how a morality is always present in the actions of any discipline, with the task of the critical professional being to notice, reflect upon and challenge that morality where necessary. Similarly, Oakley (1993) argues that 'knowledge itself must serve social ends' (Oakley, 1993, p. 208) and goes further to suggest that health itself 'is impossible without a moral basis of good social relations' (Oakley, 1993, p. 4).

Notably, these criteria are all congruent with feminist approaches, in particular the notion of bringing about social change (Reinharz and Davidman, 1992). Thus criticality can be identified as a core feature of feminism.

Importantly, these four core features of criticality represent a particular focus of interest, intent and approach (Siedman, 2012) but not of methodology. That is to say, criticality is not inherently qualitative. In principle then, criticality should not be incompatible with social epidemiology – which is defined by both its topic area (the social determinants, spread and distribution of disease in populations) and by its methodologies (usually case-control, cross-sectional survey and longitudinal observational studies). Notably however, although social epidemiology is concerned with the social world, it is widely critiqued for paying scant attention to the experience of structural issues, of agency and power (Jayasinghe, 2011).

Different topics within social epidemiology may have different conventions of method and interpretation, may privilege different models and ideas, and will probably differ in the assumptions which underlie these. The practice of social epidemiology as applied to sexual health research is likely different from its practice in other fields of health research. Therefore, it might be more helpful and realistic to consider the idea of critical epidemiologies.

Core components of a critical social epidemiology for applied sexual health research

Addressing the four core components of criticality set out above, I propose that a critical social epidemiology specifically for applied sexual health research would seek to do the following:

1. notice and address the socio-political agendas of public health in the context of sexual health;
2. challenge the notion of the 'depersonalised' researcher;
3. challenge the notion of 'risky individuals', a reliance on health psychology constructs which are assumed to be causal;
4. address descriptive treatment of socio-demographic variable.

By adhering to these objectives, I hope to begin to address within sexual health research some of the broader issues which Oakley (1993) explicates when she asks 'How do we recognise the subjective validity of the problem without enclosing it in a terminology that inhibits political insight? How do we name it in such a way that we remain interested not only in what the problem is but also on how it might be caused and in what might be done to prevent it on a social and not purely individual level?' (Oakley, 1993, p. 15). In the final paragraphs of this chapter I give examples of how these concerns might be addressed using the critical epidemiological objectives set out above.

1. Noticing and addressing the socio-political agendas of public health in the context of sexual health

Examining critically the existing epidemiological literature on pregnancy and public health, it is noticeable that 'unplanned pregnancy' is privileged over 'unintended', 'unwanted' or 'mistimed' pregnancy, though there is considerable literature on all these differing concepts. This reflects firstly that epidemiology's key purpose is to answer public health questions, and unplanned pregnancy is a behavioural notion. More poignant and less obvious is that this reflects how public health has itself become increasingly interested in changing population behaviour rather than the circumstances in which populations live. A focus instead on 'unintended' pregnancy incorporates more of women's experiences as 'unplanned' pregnancies will form only a sub-set of those which are 'unintended'.

This latter point also speaks to a second critique, which is of the way in which within epidemiological studies, women categorised as 'ambivalent' about pregnancy are aggregated (combined) with those who express they don't plan or intend pregnancy unintended/unplanned pregnancies. This operationalises a particular public health agenda – which is to describe and therefore target contraception to all women who are not actively seeking to get pregnant. Instead ambivalence could be treated as its own category (or aggregated with intended if the sample size is too low for certain analyses to then be performed). This approach to analysis explicitly recognises that choosing not to use contraception when one is ambivalent about pregnancy is a valid choice, and not a neglect of one's sexual health, which requires correction.

2. Challenging the notion of the 'depersonalised' researcher

In reality most of the sexual health researchers I know draw on their own experiences as individuals experiencing particular illnesses or social circumstances, as parents, as users of services. In order to interrogate and work with that process and to recognise its power in critiquing convention and underlying socio-political agendas, it needs to be treated as an explicit and meaningful activity that sits alongside more 'traditional' Patient and Public Involvement (PPI).

3. Challenging the notion of 'risky individuals', and a reliance on health psychology constructs which are assumed to be causal

Quantitative health psychology has fully embraced the constructs developed in social cognition models. 'Self-efficacy', 'risk perception' and similar constructs have been adopted by social epidemiological studies. Not only are they quantitatively measured (and so methodologically compatible) but they were developed as a way of explaining the behaviour of individuals, and so meet the contemporary interests of public health in changing behaviour. It is ironic that social epidemiology of sexual health has roundly adopted this area of enquiry, yet it barely incorporates the 'social' at all – instead focusing largely on how the internal psychological world impacts on one's behaviour. This approach then sites risk within the individual, reinforcing the notion of the individual as the primary agent of change by positing that our cognitions are the primary key to unlocking that change. Particularly worrying is that, although most epidemiological studies are unable to infer causality due to design constraints, this inference is often made in applied sexual health research literature.

Moving our focus away from the notion of the 'risky individual' and towards the notion of the 'risky encounter' would allow us to disrupt this locus of responsibility on individual cognition and invite us to consider the dynamic and shifting nature of 'sexual risk'. This in turn invites us to consider the subjective experience of sexual encounters – and the social contexts which frame those encounters.

4. Addressing descriptive treatment of socio-demographic variable

Not only are observed associations between cognition and behaviour frequently interpreted as causal (even when the study design allows no such inference) but socio-demographic variables are frequently interpreted as descriptive (non-causal). This convention has arisen partly because a key use of epidemiological studies is to socio-demographically describe populations that carry a greater burden of ill health (so that resources can rightly be allocated based on that distribution). But it may also reflect the lack of theorising on how socio-demographic factors might lead to differing burdens of disease. Some models – such as Krieger's eco-social model (2001) – posit socio-demographic factors as 'distal' predictors of morbidity – but they do not draw out the nature of those associations. These issues, combined with their positioning as 'distal' rather than 'proximal' risks, can lead to the neglect of socio-demographic variables in analysis.

In contrast, I advocate for more detailed and broad use of 'socio-demographics', perhaps informed by preliminary qualitative enquiry. I also challenge the idea that variables such as ethnicity, sex, class or age are merely descriptive or 'weakly' causal. Rather I view them as representative of key components of our lived experience as humans. Being a middle-aged white woman is an essential part of my lived experience. In practice, this means that I am treating socio-demographic factors 'symmetrically' in the analysis of my data (rather than merely controlling for them, or using them to describe the women who report risk). This is not an uncommon practice, but again is something I am doing explicitly in order to enact a critical epidemiology. Equally, where I use stratification of factors such as ethnicity and class and gender I do this in order to explore the prevalence of sexual risk and morbidity within the intersection of these factors – this investigation of intersectionality differs from the 'control' of socio-demographic factors, for which cross-tabulation is more commonly used. Finally, when interpreting my analyses, I am taking care to afford the same degree of causal or non-causal interpretation to all the exposures that I am modelling – rather than assuming some to be causal and others as non-causal.

The steps I propose in these last paragraphs represent only the beginning of the development of a feminist, critical epidemiology for applied sexual health research. Many of these and other steps will probably be novel in their explicit intention and interpretation rather than implementation (e.g. symmetrical treatment is well-established but for other explicit purposes). Equally, other disciplines such as critical and medical anthropology have sought to investigate how human experience, behaviour and health are shaped by structural factors (Lambert, 1998). Despite the paradigmatic differences which exist between biomedical and social sciences, fields such as anthropology and sociology may have much to offer in developing critical epidemiology further.

Nonetheless I hope I have demonstrated that feminism and criticality can be enacted in quantitative research and more specifically in social epidemiological studies, and that they have the potential to be of great value in advancing both scientific knowledge and inequalities in health. For me, the possibility of bringing criticality to bear in quantitative studies is a tremendously exciting possibility, particularly in the field of applied sexual health research in which power relations, disenfranchisement and social inequality not only affect but direct both individual and population health. I believe that the ways in which we research sexual behaviour, experience and identity can only be improved by greater criticality in our work.

References

Allen, E., Bonell, C., Strange, V., Copas, A., Stephenson, J., Johnson, A.M. and Oakley, A. (2007) 'Does the UK Government's Teenage Pregnancy Strategy Deal with the Correct Risk Factors? Findings from a Secondary Analysis of Data from a Randomised Trial of Sex Education and Their Implications for Policy', *Journal of Epidemiology and Community Health*, 61(1), pp. 20–27.

Arreaza, Antonio Luis Vicente (2012) 'Critical Epidemiology: For a Theoretical Praxis of Knowing How and When to Act', *Ciência & Saúde Coletiva*, 17(4), pp. 1001–1013.

Breilh, J. (2008) 'Latin American Critical ("Social") Epidemiology: New Settings for an Old Dream', *International Journal of Epidemiology*, 37(4), pp. 745–750.

Crotty, M. (1998) *The Foundations of Social Research: Meaning and Perspective in the Research Process*, London: Sage.

Edelman, N.L. and Barron, D. (2015) 'Evaluation of Public Involvement in Research: Time for a Major Re-think?', *Journal of Health Services Research and Policy*, 21(3), pp. 209–211.

Edelman, N.L., Patel, H., Glasper, A. and Bogen-Johnston, L. (2013) 'Understanding Barriers to Sexual Health Service Access among Substance-Misusing Women on the South East Coast of England', *Journal of Family Planning and Reproductive Health Care*, 39(4), pp. 258–263.

Edelman, N.L., de Visser, R.O., Mercer, C.H., McCabe, L. and Cassell, J.A. (2015) 'Targeting Sexual Health Services in Primary Care: A Systematic Review of the Psychosocial Correlates of Adverse Sexual Health Outcomes Reported in Probability Surveys of Women of Reproductive Age', *Preventative Medicine*, 81, pp. 345–356.

Faugier, J. and Sargeant, M. (1997) 'Sampling Hard to Reach Populations', *Journal of Advanced Nursing*, 26(4), pp. 790–797.

Gillard, S., Borschmann, R., Turner, K., Goodrich-Purnell, N., Lovell, K. and Chambers, M. (2010) '"What Difference Does It Make?" Finding Evidence of the Impact of Mental Health Service User Researchers on Research into the Experiences of Detained Psychiatric Patients', *Health Expectations*, 13(2), pp. 185–194.

Hopper, K. and Guttmacher, S. (1979) 'Rethinking Suicide: Notes toward a Critical Epidemiology', *International Journal of Health Services: Planning, Administration, Evaluation*, 9(3), p. 417–438.

Imrie, J., Edelman, N., Mercer, C.H., Copas, A.J., Phillips, A., Dean, G., Watson, R. and Fisher, M. (2006) 'Refocusing Health Promotion for syphilis prevention: results of a Case-Control Study of Men Who Have Sex with Men on England's South Coast', *Sexually Transmitted Infections*, 82(1), pp. 80–83.

Inhorn, M.C. and Whittle, K.L. (2001) 'Feminism Meets the "New" Epidemiologies: Toward an Appraisal of Antifeminist Biases in Epidemiological Research on Women's Health', *Social Science and Medicine*, 53(5), pp. 553–567.

Jarvis, T.J. and Copeland, J. (1997) 'Child Sexual Abuse as a Predictor of Psychiatric Co-morbidity and Its Implications for Drug and Alcohol Treatment', *Drug and Alcohol Dependence*, 49(1), pp. 61–69.

Jayasinghe, S. (2011) 'Conceptualising Population Health: From Mechanistic Thinking to Complexity Science', *Emerging*

Themes in Epidemiology, 8(1),
pp. 2–8.

Krieger, N. (1994) 'Epidemiology
and the Web of Causation: Has
Anyone Seen the Spider', *Social
Science and Medicine*, 39(7),
pp. 887–903.

Krieger, N. (2000a) 'Epidemiology
and Social Sciences: Towards a
Critical Reengagement in the 21st
Century', *Epidemiologic Reviews*,
22(1), pp. 155–163.

Krieger, N. (2000b) 'Refiguring "Race":
Epidemiology, Racialized Biology,
and Biological Expressions of Race
Relations', *International Journal of
Health Services*, 30(1), pp. 211–216.

Krieger, N. (2001) 'Theories for
Social Epidemiology in the
21st Century: An Ecosocial
Perspective', *International Journal
of Epidemiology*, 30, pp. 668–677.

Krieger, N. (2014) *Epidemiology and
the People's Health: Theory and
Context*, New York, NY: Oxford
University Press.

Lambert, H. (1998) 'Methods and
Meanings in anthropological,
epidemiological and Clinical
Encounters: The Case of Sexually
Transmitted Disease and Human
Immunodeficiency Virus Control
and Prevention in India', *Tropical
Medicine and International Health*,
3(12), pp. 1002–1010.

Lambert, N.L., Imrie, J., Fisher, M.J.,
Phillips, A., Watson, R. and Dean,
G. (2006) 'Making Sense of
Syphilis: Gay Men's Experiences
of Syphilis Diagnosis and the
Implications for HIV Prevention
and Sexual Health Promotion',
Sexually Transmitted Infections,
3(3), pp. 155–161.

Lambert, N.L., Fisher, M., Imrie,
J., Watson, R., Mercer, C.H.,
Parry, J.V., Phillips, A., Iversen,
A., Perry, N. and Dean, G.L.
(2005) 'Community Based
Syphilis Screening: Feasibility,
Acceptability, and Effectiveness
in Case Finding', *Sexually
Transmitted Infections*, 81(3),
pp. 213–216.

Mayer, D. (2010) *Essential Evidence-
based Medicine*, 2nd edition,
Cambridge: Cambridge University
Press.

Murray, M. (2014) *Critical Health
Psychology*, 2nd edition, New
York: Palgrave Macmillan.

Oakley, A. (1993) *Essays on Women,
Medicine and Health*, Edinburgh:
Edinburgh University Press.

Overy, C., Reynolds, L.A. and
Tansey, E.M. (2011) 'History of
the National Survey of Sexual
Attitudes and Lifestyles' in
*Wellcome Witnesses to Twentieth
Century Medicine*, Volume 41,
London: School of History,
Queen Mary, University of
London.

Parr, S. (2015) 'Integrating
Critical Realist and Feminist
Methodologies: Ethical
and Analytical Dilemmas',
*International Journal of Social
Research Methodology*, 18(2),
pp. 193–207.

Reinharz, S. and Davidman, L.
(1992) *Feminist Methods in
Social Research*, Oxford: Oxford
University Press.

Robert, J.S. and Smith, A. (2004) 'Toxic
Ethics: Environmental Genomics
and the Health of Populations',
Bioethics, 18(6), pp. 493–514.

Rothman, B.K. (1990) 'Recreating
  Motherhood: Ideology and
  Technology in a Patriarchal
  Society', *Journal of Midwifery and
  Women's Health*, 35(2), p. 116.
Siedman, S. (2012) *Contested
  Knowledge: Social Theory
  Today*, 5th edition, Chichester:
  Wiley-Blackwell.
Waitzkin, H., Iriart, C., Estrada, A.
  and Lamadrid, S. (2001) 'Social
  Medicine in Latin America:
Productivity and Dangers
  Facing the Major National
  Groups', *The Lancet*, 358(9278),
  pp. 315–323.
Wemrell, M., Merlo, J., Mulinari,
  S. and Hornborg, A.C. (2016)
  'Contemporary Epidemiology: A
  Review of Critical Discussions
  within the Discipline and a Call
  for Further Dialogue with Social
  Theory', *Sociology Compass*, 10(2),
  pp. 153–171.

4 | SEX SHOP STORIES: SHIFTING DISCIPLINES IN DESIGN RESEARCH

Fran Carter

Abstract

Both popular and academic writing about upmarket sex toys and the shops they are sold in has focused on the ways in which the market has repositioned itself to appeal to the female consumer. While existing research has tended towards a disembodied decoding of objects, my work prioritises the voices of female consumers. By using sociological research methods, I have uncovered women's understanding of the various discourses embedded in the materiality of sexualised things and spaces, asking how women's sex shops speak to women about their sexuality.

This paper introduces a framework for exploration of the intersections between sexuality, consumption and designed objects, acknowledging the struggle to honour precepts and adapt methods foreign to one discipline or prized by another. Primarily it focuses on those dilemmas of the research process which have resonated most markedly in the life of this project, highlighting the need to adapt an analysis method steeped in one ontological framework to encompass selves in relationship to objects rather than people. Furthermore, it explores the challenges of exploring a sensitive subject and documents the search for a fluid methodology, leaving space for research trajectories to be shaped by participant readings of the spaces of sexual consumption.

Introduction

The disciplines of design history and design studies have not been fertile ground for exploration of sexualised objects, spaces or the practices of sexual consumption. The lack of design and material culture studies focusing on the sexual object or space is perhaps due to female sexuality still being seen as a 'difficult' subject, as evidenced by the reaction of various colleagues to my earliest research proposals. However, in recent years innovatory sex toy designs have featured repeatedly in mainstream design publications such as *Dezeen*[1] and *Design Week*,[2] sex 'toys' are retailed in both Selfridges and Superdrug, Ann Summers is visible on every suburban high street and the newer, women friendly, sex shops sell high-end sex products to a female consumer who sees herself as both sexually enlightened and design literate. Nonetheless, an assumption remains that actually visiting (any sort of) sex shop is an act of consumption best conducted in private and sex shopping is a practice and transaction seen by some academic colleagues as difficult to admit to, let alone discuss with a researcher.

In broader disciplinary terms, design history has tended towards a focus on design in production and representation rather than by engaging empirical evidence for the experience of the consumer in the act of consuming designed objects. Hence the aim of my research has been to bring together sexualised design and its consumers, to move away from a disembodied decoding of objects or spaces to focus on how the spaces and objects of sexual consumption speak to women shoppers about sexual matters. Overarchingly, my research has aimed to uncover the multiple meanings women attach to the processes of sexual consumption by listening to the voices and paying attention to the understandings of women who shop in sex shops designed to appeal to the female consumer – to talk to women about their experiences of sex shopping and the meanings they make of the visual presence of both shops and goods. However, for colleagues in the field of design studies my initial research proposal seemed not only alien to the discipline but fraught with difficulty on two counts – it proposed a focus on consumption which prioritised talking to consumers and it intended talking to those consumers about sexuality! A raft of questions 'hung in the air': What is the place of interview research in a study which prioritises the design of objects? Into what interpretative framework will such data fit? And how would one find these interview 'subjects' prepared to talk openly about their sex shopping habits and experiences? These reservations and concerns were summed up by one of my colleagues, a design historian, who asked me, 'why do interviews, why don't you just look at the shops?'

This paper reflects on just two of the issues and challenges arising from conducting empirical research into consumer engagement with and interpretation of, the women-orientated sex shop – its spaces and its objects. Firstly, it offers a background to the research, proposing that things are active in materialising and producing discourse around female heterosexuality. Secondly, it describes an epistemological and methodological journey somewhat outside the traditional remit of the design historian; asking how can we address the challenges of using interviews with women consumers to unlock the ways in which objects function ideologically?

Background to research

The heterosexual male sex shop has traditionally been seen as a masculine environment, 'uncomfortable' for and even hostile to the female consumer. Invoked as a visual materialisation of a hegemonic masculine sexuality, it has also been popularly characterised as a nucleus for ongoing debate around pornography. Whether my research participants had visited a 'traditional' sex shop in actuality or whether for them it existed only in the hinterlands of their imaginations, women uniformly began their narratives of sex shopping by describing what they saw as the 'traditional' masculine-defined sex shop. These shops were vividly described by participants in visual terms, as dark, forbidding spaces, with blacked out windows and stuttering neon signs. Words such as seedy, sordid and sleazy emerged repeatedly in testimony:

I imagine it as being dark, my imagining is that they're not
particularly clean, tidy and neat because the outsides often
look so grubby ... Erm, my imagining is lots and lots of
magazines with covers with pornographic pictures of women
that would make me very uncomfortable ... I can't imagine
what they sell, I really can't, I can't imagine that, I don't want
to imagine what they sell. (Louise)

In order that it may open up a new space in the market,
female sexual consumption has been subject to a project of re-
appropriation, a branding of women's sexual consumer culture
as liberating, stylish and overwhelmingly 'empowering'. Feona
Attwood acknowledges the centrality of aesthetics to this process
of re-making:

The sleazy style of sexually explicit practices is rearticulated
as tasteful and sometimes ironic. Aestheticizing and
domesticating the sexual is crucial to the marketing of
sex to women enabling its re-articulation as a new set of
things – art, dance sport, thing of beauty. (Attwood, 2009,
p. 179)

In 1992 Sh! opened, situated in London's Hoxton, designed
as both an antidote to the 'sleazy' male sex shop and a site for
agentic female sexual expression. Sh! and subsequent female-
orientated shops (Myla, selling sex toys alongside luxury lingerie,
came to London's Notting Hill in 1999 and Sam Roddick's
luxury erotic boutique Coco de Mer arrived in London's Covent
Garden in 2001) all utilise a range of design strategies, for both
the interior and the façade of shops, employed to re-gender and
re-code the 'traditional' sex shop as a feminine environment and
eradicate all traces of a masculine sexual culture. The exterior of
Sh! for example is decorated in a ferocious sugar pink, Coco de
Mer has windows featuring a tasteful assemblage of lingerie and
ambiguously suggestive 'objet d'art' and the interior of She Said

(an 'erotic boutique' in Brighton) re-imagines the turn-of-the-century boudoir. Variously the shops seek to normalise the act of sex shopping by positioning it within the apparently oppositional frameworks of domesticity and luxury and style. Thus on the one hand the design of shop interiors may reference a supermarket and on the other a turn-of-the-century bordello. All offer a range of sexualised goods which prioritise a blend of aesthetics and cutting-edge technology, aesthetics being key to the appeal the re-imagined sex shop makes to the female consumer.

Unfailingly, my research participants defined and described the female-orientated shops in terms of resistance to the paradigmatic male shop, this challenge for them was articulated in the design of windows, lighting, layout and the goods for sale. However, constructions of female sexuality were also found to constrain the design of sexualised goods and spaces. For some participants, the version of sexuality on offer in the women's sex shop was still reliant on the dominant masculinist model. 'Harder' or less 'acceptable' products were described as hidden downstairs, 'round the back' or along darkened passageways. The functionality of products was sometimes concealed and even, for some women, de-sexualised by luxury materials and high cost as well as by their mode of display, which for some participants hinted at the sex toy's new status as art object.

> I think I felt a look but don't touch kind of thing, it did very much seem to be, even designer, which is a little bit crazy at the end of the day – most of the things are just going in one hole or another ... I think it made the sexual experience very detached ... that it's something that you wouldn't ... that you would put on your table rather than actually use ... I did feel it was much less sexual, that you wouldn't use these things. (Veronica)

Straightforward correlations in which 'hardcore' equals private and 'vanilla', public were obfuscated for women in the design of the women's sex shop, the embedded challenge of items designed for women's self-pleasure obscured by their high design specifications. In these and other ways design was seen as supporting a dominant sexual culture to which women have limited or prescribed access. In describing the layout of shops she had visited, Heidi queried a spatial design which located some goods near the entrance to the store and others downstairs: 'For me it's almost like this is the bit that's OK and that other bit, you know' (Heidi).

In the entwined and often contradictory narratives embedded in the objects and spaces of the women's sex shop, stories of both liberation and constraint emerged from the in-depth interviews I conducted with women sex shoppers. Testimony showed clearly that the women's sex shop holds out sexual empowerment, materialised in designed goods and spaces as an appealing new model for feminine sexual identity and sexual display. My task then was to find a method of data analysis which would allow me to account for the ways in which things are active in materialising and producing discourse around female heterosexuality.

Disciplinary dilemmas

An interest in the methodological issues arising from interview research meant that from the start of the project, I was inevitably drawn to concerns somewhat outside the traditional remit of the design historian. While sex research has a long history of studying sexuality through field research, it was acknowledged early on that research into sexuality would always push at the margins of qualitative research, that in 'extreme' qualitative research, reflexivity and transparency is central and an appropriate methodology must be found to deal with a subject which is potentially 'difficult'. Sanders (2006, p. 450) proposes that early sex researchers railed against the expectations of a 'scientific and objective approach to inquiry'. She suggests, 'This tradition has influenced those who have studied the sex industry; exploring the

depths of sex work through small scale, intimate methodology'
(2006, p. 450).

My own small-scale study uses empirical methods to explore
how sexuality is done by and on behalf of women consumers.
Most particularly it has a sustained focus on the shop's claims
to offer autonomous sexual empowerment to women, a claim
materialised in marketing and representation but also explicitly
located in the design of shops and their goods. Where existing
work has investigated the women's sex shop (Malina and Schmidt,
1997; Kent, 2006; Feona Attwood, 2005), it has tended to focus
on the ways in which the women's sex shop has been moved
representationally from sleazy to stylish and has repositioned
itself as a feminine rather than wholly masculine space. Malina
and Schmidt (1997), writing specifically on Sh!, suggest:

> Sex shops targeted exclusively at women can be seen as a new
> and ground breaking phenomenon. As such it may signify the
> end of the dichotomies of the modernist perspective and the
> advent and celebration of the leisurely exploration of female
> sexual diversity and creativity – the consumption of "sex
> toys" on the one hand and the shopping experience on the
> other.

However, the interests of sociologically based and media-
focused projects do not pivot principally on discourse as
materialised in things or space. A significant aim of my research
design then, was to move the disciplines of design studies and
design history in territorial terms. Its intention was to provide a
framework which might account for the lived experience of sex
shoppers, drawing on the processes, the places and objects of
sexual consumption in order to arrive at an exegetical understanding of the ways in which contemporary female sexuality is
visually represented and understood.

I knew early on that, loosely in line with a grounded theory[3]
approach, I was committed to letting theory emerge in a fluid way

from participant testimony, as well as to maintaining transparency about my own place in the research. The women I met and interviewed had formulated their own interpretation around the significance and place of the women-focused sex shop in their lives and to their sexuality and I felt it was essential not to make the assumption that this was (necessarily) an unconscious process on their part, or that, in many cases, they did not participate in the research without a cogent and significant agenda of their own. Several of the women, both consumers and retailers, were actively enthusiastic about participating in interviews and appeared genuinely pleased to have their voices heard on the topic. Anne Oakley in her article of 1981 on the values implicit in feminist research herself argues that this type of research can be: 'A tool for making possible the articulated and recorded commentary of women on the very personal business of being female in a patriarchal capitalist society' (Oakley, 1981, p. 48).

Oakley's words resonated considerably for me over the life of the project, in that research extended beyond the process of interviewing women in order to allow them a voice in 'a patriarchal capitalist society' to a discussion of whether a visit to a sex shop may be an act, or site, of real articulation for women, in what may be seen as the most personal business of being female.

Having completed a number of in-depth, semi-structured interviews with women consumers, sex shop workers and shop owners, I was left with substantial and rich material in the form of interview tapes and transcriptions. However, I lacked an analysis framework through which to begin unpacking the relationship between consumer and designed commodity. Daniel Miller (1998) characterises the aims of his work on the shopping habits of north London residents in the following terms:

> Our main interest is in how they (the subjects) narrate
> their identities drawing on a relatively limited repertoire of
> available images and representations. Thus we do not seek to
> describe the purchasing habits of different social family, class,

ethnic or gender groups. Rather, we are interested in the way that narrative identities are constructed by these different groups and in the different discourses on which people draw as they relate to particular types of goods in particular kinds of places. (Miller, 1998, p. 24)

This notion of 'narrative identities' became central to my analytic approach and served to encompass a sense of the personal nature of these accounts. My hope was that interviews should be an opportunity for participants to ruminate on the part that sex shopping played as an outlet for sexual self-expression, exposing their relationship to and opinion of, a commodified feminine sexuality embodied in the frontage of shops, design of internal space and objects for sale. Thus the process of telling was, for some, an opportunity to reflect on the ways in which the design of the sex shop works to open up or close down individual sexual self-expression. Like Miller's, my own research does not aim to be representative of a particular female experience but to map both the narrative identities employed by the women who describe shopping for sex items and the visual narratives employed by these shops in order to advocate themselves effectively to the consumer as a site via which a woman might explore her sexuality.

We increasingly recognise that all narratives, whether oral or written, personal or collective, official or subaltern, are "narratives of identity" (Anderson, 1991); that is, they are representations of reality in which narrators also communicate how they see themselves and wish others to see them (Stein, 1987; Volkan, 1988). (Errante, 2000, p. 16)

After several false starts I was drawn to the work of Mauthner and Doucet in their 'Reflections on a Voice-centred Relational Method of Data Analysis' (1998). Mauthner and Doucet's account of their use of the method positions the interviewees as active participants in the research process, asking the researcher to look for the story or narrative in the data, an approach that chimed with my interest in exploring consumption as a means of identity creation. The authors relate their experience of using the method in their respective doctoral research projects exploring motherhood and postnatal depression and the attempts of heterosexual couples to share house work and child care.[4] The method revolves around three or more readings of the texts generated from interviews, beginning with 'Reading 1: Reading for the plot and for our responses to the narrative'. While clearly this is a method drawn from disciplines far removed from the traditional concerns of design studies, the method appealed to me on a number of counts. Not least because their account of data analysis recognises the role of the researcher in shaping the data:

> The particular issue which strikes us as central, yet
> overlooked, in qualitative data analysis processes and
> accounts is that of how to keep respondents' voices and
> perspectives alive, while at the same time recognising the
> researcher's role in shaping the research process and product.
> (Mauthner and Doucet, 1998, p. 119)

Their account of the analysis process acknowledges not only the impossibility of taking an 'objective' position in relation to data but the ways in which a potentiality for bias pervades the whole process. For example, in the control the researcher has over the trajectory of the interview, following up some leads and ignoring others. My analysis of the data showed me where I had done this myself, sometimes to the detriment of the data. I had a particular experience of this when I interviewed one participant who called herself 'Sexy Kitten' and I regretted it bitterly. I was conducting an interview that didn't start until 8.45pm, it had been a difficult week, I was tired and not really 'on the ball'. When I listened to the interview subsequently and read the transcript there was a point at the end of the session at which my participant talked about how far she had come from her mother's experience of sexuality as an Irish woman growing up in the 1950s. This was not only an emotional point for Sexy Kitten but may have been a rich seam of material in terms of how she viewed the development of her own sexual attitudes in the context of her consumption practices and experiences. Unfortunately, having listened to her point I did not follow this up but brought her back to my list of questions, ignoring this personal disclosure.

This issue of transparency regarding my own place in the research was key to the ethos of my research project. The voice-centred relational method works to unearth the ways in which the researcher impacts on the data by taking account, not only of dimensions such as race, class, gender and so on, but explicitly by 'tracking' the 'feelings' of the researcher in response to the material: 'particularly those feelings that do not resonate with the speaker's experience' (Brown, 1994, cited in Mauthner and Doucet, 1998, p. 127). I found my intuitively felt difficulties articulated in a useful article by Molly Andrews who characterises this as 'The problem of the omniscient feminist'. She suggests:

> Feminist researcher[s] ... feel that we know better than those who participate in our research about the underlying structures that give or deny meaning their lives. It is argued that sexism, like other forms of oppression can be deeply internalized and hidden from the conscious. (Andrews, 2002, p. 57)

Thus while one of the most attractive tenets of feminist research is its quest to acknowledge and validate a diversity of feminine experience, conversely, it may struggle to deal with women research participants whose experience or views do not fit with those of the feminist researcher. I was to encounter this myself in the first 'reading' suggested by the method: reading for the plot and for our responses to the narrative. At this point I will quote from my own research notes:

I was very ambivalent about doing this reading to start with,
particularly when I tried to locate myself in the transcript.
I couldn't really do it from the transcript of the interview
and felt that there was very little evidence of any bias – a few
rather leading questions and points at which I changed the
subject. However, when I decided to listen again to the taped
interview it was quite different. I could feel and hear my
lack of sympathy for the participant. I was aware that I was
irritated by her rather insistent, bombastic manner and her
assumption that she was speaking about sexuality on behalf of
all women, particularly when my own sexual identity felt so
different to hers. I realised that for this reason – that what she
was expressing was at odds with my own feelings but also that
[it] didn't chime with much of the other interview material
– I could very easily ignore or slant her testimony. (Author's
research notes, 2010)

This was an epiphany in the life of the research process, a point
at which the methodological concerns that had interested me in
an abstract sense, were made concrete and challenging in my own
work!

Another instance of researcher bias became clear when it took
me a long time to acknowledge one particular discourse in the
testimony of my participants. This narrative became unavoidable
when I interviewed Emily, a psychologist who inevitably utilised
psychological language and terminology. However, the reason that
this woman had been suggested to me (as a potential interviewee)
was that she had once considered opening a women's sex shop
of her own. When she described how her ideas had crystallised
into a sex shop come therapy rooms, café, nail bar and so on, it
became clear that her therapeutic perspective on female sexual
consumption chimed, very explicitly in some respects, with that
of some of my other interviewees. I wondered why this discourse
had not emerged previously. At this point the notion of sexual
consumerism as therapeutic did not even exist in my coding

structure and yet it was clearly a significant and repeated discourse amongst my participants. I have concluded that this is because I was resistant to such a notion and for that reason – although in some vague inarticulate way I knew it was there – I refused to recognise it in these terms. It was Emily's testimony that required me to acknowledge the presence of this discourse and forced me to address it. Thus, in its insistence on reflexivity, the method had enabled me to unearth a source of potential bias and resistance of which I had not previously been aware and I was able to mine a seam of data that had been at risk of being side lined.

Shifting disciplines

The voice-centred relational method was used by Mauthner and Doucet (1998) in a project that had a sociological focus, therefore they stress that central to this method is its: 'Relational ontology, [which] posits the notion of "selves in relation"' (Ruddick, 1989, cited in Mauthner and Doucet, 1998, p. 125) – a view that prioritises the notion of human beings as part of a network of social relations. While I recognise the centrality of sociological approaches and research methods to my own work, my challenge was to extend this ontological framework to a study framed by the interests of material culture and design studies – to include, therefore, selves in relation to the consumption of sexualised things. Thus clearly, from the start of my project I was aware that I needed to find a method of analysing the rich interview material I had gathered, which would facilitate me in revealing the way participants accounted for the meanings embedded (for them) in objects and spaces. Mauthner and Doucet (1998) stress the flexibility and intuitive nature of the process. While the first two readings of interview transcripts are fundamental, they suggest that the third and fourth readings can be adapted to the particular interests of the research in question. However, my initial attempts to transform the third reading – Reading for relationships into Reading for relationships with things – was not fruitful; somehow this seemed to presuppose or encompass only a static relationship between participants and objects. It did not sit well with material which told of an active process – participants were skilled in reading objects, uncovering a raft of meanings inscribed for them in the design of the women's sex shop. I moved to the fourth suggested reading: Placing people within cultural contexts and social structures; a ruminatory excerpt from my research notes illustrates the flavour of the struggle at this point and hints at its resolution:

> This reading seemed more difficult although I am convinced of its appropriateness to my work. I scrutinised Mauthner and Doucet's (1998) account [of their own research] to find a clue as to how I could relate it to my own participants' shopping accounts. One of the problems with applying this methodology is that Mauthner and Doucet's accounts, if not life histories, are about significant life events or aspects of participants' lives. On the surface my accounts are simply about a few shopping expeditions. However, I do strongly maintain that embedded in these seemingly superficial and flimsy experiences of sex shopping, are accounts of the way in which my participants experience, not simply their own personal sexual identity but how feminine sexuality encounters a wider social context. These sex shops are sites of exchange in that they are places in which women are invited to consume a notion of female sexuality on offer, they are also one of the very few environments in which feminine sexuality is contextualised beyond the personal. In a female-orientated sex shop feminine sexuality is social, political, liberatory, therapeutic and recreational – empowering, subjugatory and status-conferring. So what are the cultural contexts and social structures, the prisms or frameworks through which participants experience the sex shop? It seems in Heidi's testimony that her encounters with these shops are framed by her in terms of gender difference. The narrative thrust of her story is one of how these shops do not cater to the

more "holistic", sensual and aesthetic, needs of women …
Thus my understanding of "reading 4" looks at frameworks
through which the participant "reads" the shop. (Author's
research notes, 2010)

By focusing on shopping (or navigating the sex shop) as an
active process, I was able to re-interpret the analysis method and
unpack accounts participants gave of their shopping experiences.
This reading seeks to: 'place … respondents' accounts and
experiences within broader social, political, cultural and structural
contexts' (Mauthner and Doucet, 1998, p. 132). Reading the
material in this way meant that I was able to identify a number
of shared discourses emerging from testimony, discourses which
began to define the ways in which participants viewed the spaces
of sexual consumption alongside or counter to their identity as
sexual consumers.

This research has introduced a fresh perspective for the
examination of current constructions of heterosexual female
sexuality by prioritising the study of designed spaces and
recognising the ways in which things are active in materialising
and producing discourse around female heterosexuality. It has
done so by harnessing a multi-disciplinary approach, using
empirical methods borrowed from the social sciences. Research
has uncovered the ways in which design is utilised in an attempt
at relocating the paradigm of sex shop – to utilise a formulation
used repeatedly in testimony: to transform sex shopping from
an uncomfortable experience to a comfortable one for female
shoppers – but concludes that the route between these states is
circuitous. Participant testimony reveals an understanding of both
the act and the products and spaces of sexual consumption, which
is complex and sometimes contradictory. Sexual consumption is
framed as being an individualised and therapeutic activity but also
at times a social one. Competing conceptions of resistance and
appropriation, public and private space, the domestic, luxurious
and humorous are all harnessed in the project of commoditising

female sexuality. The stories told by women about sex shopping dictated the organisation and trajectory of research and in exposing and tracking these discourses I uncovered implications for our understanding of the ways in which female sexuality is visually mediated. While empirical research findings show that for some of the women I interviewed, sexual consumption in the women's sex shop had been a liberatory, therapeutic or self-actualising experience, research has also revealed the ways in which the shops' offer of sexual empowerment was inhibited for others by design strategies drawing on a still dominant masculinist sexual paradigm.

Notes

1. *Dezeen* is a popular online architecture and design magazine which has featured sex toys many times over recent years from the perspective of innovatory design. For example, in an article of 29 March 2016: www.dezeen.com/2016/03/29/erotic-sex-toys-opportunity-for-new-designers-objects-of-desire-book-rita-catinella-orrell/.

2. *Design Week* is a UK-based website magazine for the design industry which has also featured new design innovation in sexualised products.

3. Grounded theory is closely associated with the American sociologists Glaser and Strauss. It was first outlined in their hugely influential work of 1967 and later further developed by them (Glaser, 1978 and Strauss and Corbin, 1997, 1998). Grounded theory, which suggests that theory may be generated directly out of work done in the field rather than field work being used to substantiate a pre-existing theory, has proved very attractive to researchers. However, their strategy is not 'soft' but highly developed and specific in its methods of application and while it seems many studies, like this one, find the fundamental concept appealing and useful, not many adhere to its methodology with rigidity.

4. See Mauthner and Doucet (1998, pp. 8–9) for more information about the disciplinary origins of the method as well as further reading on the processes and applications of this analysis method.

References

Anderson, B. (1991) *Imagined Communities*, London: Verso.
Andrews, M. (2002) 'Feminist Research with Non-feminist and Anti-feminist Women: Meeting the Challenge', *Feminism and Psychology*, 12(1), pp. 55–77.

Attwood, F. (2005) 'Fashion and Passion: Marketing Sex to Women', *Sexualities*, 8(4), pp. 392–406.

Attwood, F. (ed.) (2009) *Mainstreaming Sex: The Sexualization of Western Culture*, London: IB Tauris.

Errante, A. (2000) 'But Sometimes You're Not Part of the Story: Oral Histories and Ways of Remembering and Telling', *Educational Researcher*, 29(2), pp. 16–27.

Glaser, B.G. (1978) *Theoretical Sensitivity: Advances in the Methodology of Grounded Theory*, Mill Valley, CA: Sociology Press.

Kent, T. and Berman Brown, R. (2006) 'Erotic Retailing in the UK (1963–2003): The View from the Marketing Mix', *Journal of Management History*, 12(2), pp. 199–211.

Malina, D. and Schmidt, R.A. (1997) 'It's Business Doing Pleasure with You: Sh! A Women's Sex Shop Case', *Marketing Intelligence and Planning*, 15(7), pp. 352–360.

Mauthner, N. and Doucet, A. (1998) 'Reflections on a Voice-centred Relational Method' in Ribbens, J. and Edwards, R. (eds) *Feminist Dilemmas in Qualitative Research*, London: Sage, pp. 119–146.

Miller, D. (1998) *Shopping, Place, and Identity*, London: Routledge.

Oakley, A. (1981) 'Interviewing Women: A Contradiction in Terms' in Roberts, H. (ed.) *Doing Feminist Research*, London: Routledge, pp. 30–61.

Sanders, T. (2006) 'Sexing up the Subject: Methodological Nuances in Researching the Female Sex Industry', *Sexualities*, 9(4), pp. 449–468.

Stein, H.F. (1987) *Developmental Time, Cultural Space: Studies in Psycho-geography*, Norman, OK and London: University of Oklahoma Press.

Strauss, A. and Corbin, J. (1997) *Grounded Theory in Practice*, Thousand Oaks, CA: Sage.

Strauss, A. and Corbin, J. (1998) *Basics of Qualitative Research Techniques*, Thousand Oaks, CA: Sage.

Volkan, V.D. (1988) *The Need to Have Enemies and Allies: From Clinical Practice to International Relationship*, New York: James Aronson.

PART TWO
CREATIVE METHODOLOGIES

INTRODUCTION

Laura Harvey

Creative methods are increasingly used for data collection, analysis and dissemination in qualitative research. The four chapters that follow explore the use of different forms of creative methodology in sexualities research. On the surface, the chapters draw on data from very different research projects. Catherine Barrett explores the use of body mapping in research about the sexual rights of older people. Catherine Vulliamy uses cultural patchworking to look at feelings, ideas and experiences of sexuality and love. P.J. Macleod examines the use of poetry in a project about the consumption of pornography. Ester McGeeney, Lucy Robinson, Rachel Thomson and Pam Thurschwell explore the use of cover versions and re-animation of data in two research projects about youth sexualities. While each of these projects used a wide variety of creative methodologies and addressed different questions, there are some striking threads that connect their analysis and reflection on creativity in sexualities research. In this introduction I have pulled out four strands that weave across the chapters: the potential for creative methods to capture the ephemeral nature of sex and sexualities; issues of voice and authorship in the use of creative methods; the ability for creative methods to create engaging and provocative ways to disseminate research; and the accessibility of methods that emphasise 'creativity'.

Collecting data

The chapters in this section all suggest that creative methodologies can offer a way to explore sexual experiences and feelings that are intangible or difficult to articulate. In Catherine

Barrett's research older women were asked to produce body maps – drawing, painting and using collage to represent their bodies and sexual experiences. Barrett argues that body maps can be a useful tool to open up space for reflection, including about painful experiences like sexual assault. Catherine Vulliamy similarly points to the reflective potential of creative methods – exploring the use of 'cultural patchworks' which included the creation of collages, a 'mix tape', private journals and interview discussions about objects chosen by participants on the subject of sex and love. Both Vulliamy and Barrett point to the temporal nature of such creative methods – in which creating something with the hands, or taking time to choose a song or object, enables time for research participants to reflect before talking about their feelings or experiences.

P.J. Macleod notes that researching sex and sexualities often requires us to look at intangible experiences, feelings, memories and ideas and suggests that poetry can be one way to capture some of the elusive aspects of sexual experience. The research presented in each of the chapters highlights the rich data that can be generated using creative methods – particularly in projects that seek to understand the embodied and affective dimensions of sex and sexuality that can sometimes be hard to put into words. The objects, lyrics, sounds and drawings resonate – sometimes creating space for verbal reflection, and at other times expressing what is hard to say by using other voices or other kinds of expression.

The creative methodologies that the authors discuss foreground the messy and fragmented nature of sexualities. McGeeney and colleagues draw attention to this in their discussion of 'ventriloquism' in research on sexualities with young people. Exploring the re-animation of data from research transcripts and the use of 'cover versions' of songs in participatory research, their chapter highlights the layers of meaning and interpretation in performances and stories about sexualities. Similarly, Vulliamy's cultural patchworks draw attention to the untidiness of desire –

allowing for multiple stories and meanings to exist alongside and in conversation with each other. Macleod, too, argues that poetry can create a space in which fragmented and complex experiences can be spoken.

Authorship/voice

Taking a creative methodological approach can open up different possibilities for the voices of research participants and researchers to be expressed. Barrett argues that body maps can be used to address the absence of older people's voices in sexualities research – privileging their narratives about their sexual experiences.

A concern to make visible personal stories has long been at the heart of sexualities research concerned with power and inequality, as McGeeney and colleagues note in their chapter. They argue, along with Macleod and Vulliamy, that creative methods acknowledge that sexual cultures and practices are 'always already thoroughly mediated'. Sexual stories are social creations – complicating ideas of personal voice and authorship. Speaking through the voices of others can create what McGeeney et al. call 'scaffolding' to articulate ourselves – creating new voices, new representations and conversations in the process. Methods that draw on, re-use and craft creative representations of sexualities shed light on these practices of mediation, as well as highlighting the role of research and researchers in constructing sexualities.

Creative methods can also enable different kinds of collective voices to emerge – whether in borrowing lyrics from a song, or working as a group to create and discuss body maps. This can create safer (or less safe, depending on the context) ways to talk about personal life and sensitive or controversial topics, perhaps offering some protection against the vulnerability that these might bring. The ability of some creative methodologies to capture and analyse non-verbal or textual data brings other kinds of 'voices' into the research too. Vulliamy reflects on the 'voice' of objects chosen and presented by participants – data that has texture beyond the verbal or written accounts given of them.

Creative projects like those discussed in the following pages pose a challenge to ideas of authorship that dominate contemporary academia. Acknowledging and inviting a messiness of voices, borrowing, re-using and collective voice sit in contrast with much of the discourse of individualism that characterises neoliberal capitalism. Projects that use or create 'covers' of existing creative materials also face challenges in terms of institutional regulations around copyright and ownership. This poses difficulties for researchers seeking to present work in both academic and non-academic contexts.

Dissemination/representation

Nonetheless, creative methodologies can bring the otherwise potentially elusive sphere of sex and sexualities into view, enabling audiences to experience, empathise and understand. Barrett argues that personal narratives enabled by creating body maps do just this. Macleod discusses using spoken word to present research on the consumption of pornography at an academic symposium – immersing the audience in poetry that explored participant experiences and researcher reflexivity. Vulliamy exhibited interactive and experiential collages at conferences, inviting attendees to contribute their own responses, blurring the boundaries between researchers, data, audiences, analysis and dissemination. McGeeney and colleagues explore the possibilities opened up by re-animating transcripts using both audio and video, creating new collaborative mediations that can help us to understand contemporary sexualities. Creative methods can also offer different kinds of visibility to research participants – whether enabling anonymity or providing space for their own authorship to be recognised.

Accessibility

One of the challenges of creative methods is their accessibility. In some senses, creative methods like music, collaging and drawing allow space for participants to express themselves in ways that can be more accessible than conventional interviews, surveys and focus groups. However, assumptions or fears about what counts as 'creativity' or participant perceptions of their own 'skill' can have an impact on how people feel about using creative methods. Two of the older participants in Barrett's body mapping project decided not to create maps as they did not feel they had the right skills. Similarly, McGeeney and colleagues describe a young participant who feared that their singing voice wouldn't be as good as another participant's. In both cases, the authors discuss the possibilities opened up and closed down by collective, creative methods. It is possible to hold onto greater anonymity – by being a quieter member of a bigger group, or by using other materials or words instead of our own. But creative methods with groups also create the potential for visibility, and the risks that can emerge from that. Both Barrett and McGeeney et al. discuss the use of existing materials – a template for body maps, song lyrics and backing tracks from YouTube – as creative expressions that don't require the potentially intimidating sight of a blank page.

Conclusion

The rich interdisciplinarity of sexualities research is animated in the work discussed in this section. Insights from literature, social science, music, history and art connect in conversations between practice, theory and research. Each chapter shows these connections taking place in research projects that have borrowed ideas from different academic disciplines and practices. The section as a whole also enables these conversations to continue beyond the boundaries of the chapters, creating a collage of reflections and insights that speak to the challenges sexualities researchers face in exploring and articulating diverse experiences. The chapters also grapple with questions of power in intimacy – both the potential that creative methods have to illuminate and challenge inequalities, but also the place that such methods might have in relations of power in research. The ideas in these chapters are part of a conversation in which you, the reader, is also involved – in reading, taking up and reworking the collection of ideas that follow.

5 | BODY MAPPING, STORIES AND THE SEXUAL RIGHTS OF OLDER PEOPLE

Catherine Barrett

Abstract

This chapter begins by outlining the need for an innovative approach to promoting the sexual rights of older people. It presents ageism as a significant barrier to retaining our sexual rights as we age and proposes that current approaches to researching older people's sexuality often limit their focus to sex. Such a reductionist, biomedical focus fails to promote recognition of older people sexual rights. Furthermore, the lack of older people's narratives in the research reinforces the belief that older people's sexuality is not important to them.

There is a compelling need for innovations in researching older people's sexuality in order to achieve social, policy and legislative reforms recognising their sexual rights. To achieve such reforms this chapter draws on the emerging field of critical sexuality studies methodologies and presents a body mapping method. Body mapping is a process in which a storyteller traces an outline of their body and utilises this as a canvas for telling a story about their life. The chapter describes piloting this approach with older women to document their sexual narratives. Despite the limitations of the pilot the body maps generated sexual narratives that were rich and compelling and could be a useful catalyst for the recognition of sexual rights.

We are ceaselessly creating stories and dwelling in story telling societies. As we humans tell our stories, listen to the stories of others, and story our lives, our tales come to haunt, shape and

transform our social worlds. We really need our stories in order
to live. (Plummer, 2013a)

This chapter outlines an innovative research methodology and
method for promoting the sexual rights of older people. It draws
on the emerging field of critical sexuality studies as a methodology
to frame a body mapping method – utilising an arts and story-
based approach to qualitative research. It describes a small body
mapping pilot and makes recommendations for future research.

The centrality of sexuality to the lives of older people is
recognised by the World Health Organization. They note that
sexuality is a fundamental aspect of being human 'throughout life'
and add that the sexual rights of all people must be 'respected,
protected and fulfilled' (2006, p. 5). The World Association of
Sexual Health (WAS) reinforces this position in their Declaration
of Sexual Rights, with explicit reference to equality and non-
discrimination without distinction relating to age (WAS, 2014).
This acknowledgement of rights is important. Rights are pivotal
to recognition of human potential – including sexual potential
(Plummer, 2013a) and encompass the human and sexual
potential of older people.

However, the human rights of older people are not recognised
explicitly under the international human rights laws, and their
human rights continue to fall short across the globe. The violations
of older people's human rights include their sexual rights. Very
little has been done to explore or address the sexual rights of older
people (Aboderin, 2014). This is largely due to ageism and the
longstanding myth that older people are asexual.

The myth of asexuality is commonly held by service providers
and community members. It is embedded in ageist beliefs of
beauty as the prerogative of youth, and ageing as a series of declines
and losses. Few older people encounter affirming or celebratory
discourses relating to their sexuality and as a result many believe
that sexual wellbeing is not something they can reasonably expect.
The myth of asexuality also contributes to a lack of education and

awareness of older people's sexual rights; and older people who have diminished capacity for self-determination may find their sexual expression is restricted by family members and service providers who disapprove (Barrett, 2011a).

The repression of older people's sexuality is a violation of what WAS (2014) refers to as the right to positive approaches to sexuality. It also leads to other sexual rights violations, including violation of the right to be free from sexual violence and coercion (WAS, 2014). A significant barrier to primary prevention of the sexual assault of older women is the misguided belief that older women do not experience sexual assault because they are asexual (Mann et al., 2014). Old age is mistakenly believed to be a protective factor against sexual assault by those who think sexual assault is about sexual attraction.

Myths about asexuality and older people also result in a failure to address the changes to sexuality that occur with disease and disability. For example, many clinicians fail to address sexuality after stroke (Green and King, 2010) because most stroke victims are older people (Barrett and Whyte, 2014). Consequently, sexuality has been described as one of the most neglected parameters determining quality of life after a stroke (Chadwick et al., 1998). There is also a lack of attention to the sexual wellbeing of people living with dementia. People with dementia may find their sexual expression labelled 'challenging behaviour' by service providers who don't understand the sexual need being expressed (Barrett et al., 2009).

Perceptions of asexuality have also contributed to a failure to recognise the rights of older gay and lesbian people (Barrett et al., 2015b; Crameri et al., 2015). Attention to gay and lesbian rights has focused predominately on youth because older people are expected to be asexual and therefore not sexually diverse (Barrett et al., 2015a).

The list of adverse consequences of ignoring older people's sexuality is significant. We do not provide older people with information about the growing rates of sexually transmissible infections (Kirby Institute, 2012) or information about how to safely use online dating sites and social media to negotiate new relationships (Barrett, 2015). There are few discourses that celebrate sexuality and ageing or that give older people the space to assert their sexual rights.

But perceptions of older people's sexuality are changing. Still embedded in ageism, there is an emerging discourse on 'active' or 'successful ageing' which encourages older people to 'fight' the signs of ageing and 'sexual decline' in order to be 'sexy' in their old age. While this represents a significant shift in perceptions of older people's sexuality, it is still embedded in ageist beliefs. Bodily ageing is viewed as a pathology to be cured (Lamb, 2014, 2015). This biomedical approach represents a push towards maintaining youthful standards of sexual function and attractiveness as indicators of 'successful' ageing (Gott, 2006; Marshall, 2011). This is particularly apparent in what Tiefer (1994) calls the 'viagracization' of older men's sexuality – vascular discourses that reframe age related erectile decline as erectile 'dysfunction' and encourage what Marshall (2010, 2012) calls 'virility surveillance'. This discourse has been driven by the profit motives of pharmaceutical companies (Conrad and Leiter, 2004) who manufacture sexopharmaceuticals that enable older men to regain the levels of erectile function they experienced in their youth. Missing from these discourses is discussion about how older people's sexual lives can be fulfilling despite declining erectile function.

Rethinking methodologies

There is a need to recognise older people's sexuality beyond a reductionist, biomedical focus on sex. A broader approach is needed to ensure older people's rights to affirmative responses to their sexuality and comprehensive information about sexuality are enacted (WAS, 2014). To achieve this we need to recognise the sexual contexts and the meaning of sexuality in the lives of older people. The limited focus on heterosexual, penetrative sex challenges myths of asexuality – but does so in ways that are reductionist. This new approach fails to create momentum for change to address sexual rights, particularly the right to comprehensive sexuality education that is age appropriate and grounded in a positive approach to ageing and sexuality (WHO, 2006). Older people's sexuality encompasses sex, but it is not limited to sex. Sexuality needs to be understood or made operational within a broad understanding of sexuality (WAS, 2014).

One strategy to achieve this shift is to provide space for older people to narrate their own sexual stories. At present older people's voices are largely absent from the thousands of research papers describing their sexuality. Their sexual stories are overpowered by the voices of researchers and are often limited to a focus on sex. This may explain why even very large data sets like the Global Study of Sexual Attitudes and Behaviours (Laumann et al., 2005) has achieved little in terms of recognition of older people's sexual rights. When reading research papers, it is difficult to hear, see or feel the importance of sexuality in the lives of older people. The absence of narratives fails to compel us to create a world where older people's sexual rights are recognised. It also enables reductionist biomedical discourses to prevail. Providing opportunities for older people to narrate their own sexual stories could also ensure that the focus is not limited to sex, but includes sexuality more broadly.

Hearing older people's sexual stories could create momentum for recognition of their sexual rights. Plummer (2013b) suggests that humans cannot bear too much abstraction or generalisation. Abstraction of older people's sexuality may contribute to a failure to engage with the capacity to implement reforms. We need to reconsider researcher monologues and provide space for older people to speak for themselves. Plummer (2013a) suggests we cannot live with monologue, but rather we need dialogue to help us understand how people make sense of others. Such a dialogue necessitates hearing older people's sexual stories.

Stories are powerful tools for social change. Plummer (2013a) notes that we are 'story telling animals' and that hearing the stories of others is required for democratic functioning and social change. Stories generate empathy and help us to connect with others (Plummer, 2013b). Our empathetic responses to the stories of others have been attributed to mirror neurones, or brain cells that are activated in response to hearing about the experiences of others (Manney, 2008). When stories are told, the listeners' and the storytellers' brains exhibit similar physiological responses (Stephens et al., 2010). Harnessing this power by sharing older people's sexual narratives could help to generate understandings about the importance of sexuality in the lives of older people and provide a catalyst for social reforms.

We need to rethink what we want to achieve by researching older people's sexuality. If the outcome is recognition of sexual rights then our research methods need to be reconsidered. Are we engaged in what Plummer (2011) refers to as 'zombie research' – an approach that has now passed its use-by date? Is our focus limited to research that increases our understanding of older people's sexual lives – but does not seek to directly influence recognition of their sexual rights? This paper suggests that there is a need for innovative approaches to researching older people's sexuality that create momentum for social and political change. The following section outlines critical sexuality studies as a methodology to frame a body mapping method to documenting older people's sexual stories and promoting change.

Methodology: critical sexuality studies

Research can be a powerful tool for social and political reform and this needs to be acknowledged when selecting a research methodology. The emerging field of critical sexuality studies has been developed to recognise the potential for reform. Critical sexuality studies is concerned with shifting relationships of power, knowledge, context and culture (Fletcher et al., 2013). It focuses on the social and sexual feeling worlds and connections between sexuality and key divisions of social life such as age, ethnicity, disability, nation and class (Plummer, 2012). It asks questions about inequality (Fletcher et al., 2013).

Critical approaches also concern themselves with action. They have an emancipatory interest (Carr and Kemmis, 1986) concerning themselves with injustice (Kemmis and McTaggart, 2000) and the liberation of people from habit (Kemmis and McTaggart, 1982), custom, illusion and coercion (Kemmis, 2001). Critical research involves developing knowledge of how communication and social action occur (Carr and Kemmis, 1986) in order to enable them to be reconstructed differently (Kemmis and McTaggart, 2000). It focuses on freeing people from the actions or beliefs which restrict their practice (Grundy, 1982; Kemmis, 2001).

Given this methodology generates knowledge about sexuality and power, it could be utilised to help transform the sexual rights of older people. It could explore the barriers and enablers to sexual rights and invite older people to narrate stories beyond sex and inclusive of their sexuality. Research reports could privilege the voices of older people in order to shift relationships of power. Such research could create momentum for change and build a sense of urgency about addressing the sexual rights of older people. We need to convince people that business as usual is not enough (Kotter, 1995) – that recognising older people's sexuality is not an optional extra, but a question of fundamental human rights. This is an essential step towards enlightenment and creating momentum for change (Beer et al., 1990; Kotter, 1995).

In the following section, body mapping is presented as a critical sexuality studies method to documenting older people's sexual stories in a way that privileges their voices and creates momentum for recognition of their sexual rights. We need to hear narratives in order to progress the development of sexual rights (Plummer, 2010b). The process of body mapping can empower older people to be creators of their own sexual stories.

Body mapping

Body mapping is an approach to story-telling that was first developed in South Africa in 2002 as an art-therapy method for women living with HIV/AIDS (Devine, 2008; MacGregor, 2009; Weinand, 2006) and later adapted using narrative processes (Solomon, 2007). A body map is usually a life-size body image created by storytellers who trace the outline of their body and then use drawing, painting or other art-based techniques within the outline to visually represent their lives, their bodies and their world (Gastaldo et al., 2012). It is a useful approach to visually representing older people's sexual lives, bodies and worlds.

While initially developed as a therapeutic tool, body mapping has been adapted as a qualitative research method. Gastaldo and others (2012) describe augmenting body maps with brief first-person accounts as a key to assist in narrating the body map and to enable interpretation by others (Gastaldo et al., 2012). The shape and meaning of the story is determined by the storyteller and in this way the integrity of the story is enhanced. The role of the researcher is to facilitate the story-telling.

The centrality of the storyteller's body to this research method provides the opportunity to document the sexual stories written on their bodies. It could facilitate stories of sexuality lived and the meanings made by older people. Storytellers may be more reflective because they are making something with their hands (Gauntlett and Holzwarth, 2006) and may be supported to express emotions and make connections that are often missed in more linear approaches to research (Gastaldo et al., 2012).

Body mapping also provides the opportunity to explore embodied sexualities. The focus on the body enables embodied experiences and meanings to be shared (Gastaldo et al., 2012) and encourages integration of mind and body (Meyburgh, 2006). Storytellers who trace the outline of their bodies are guided to reflect on the stories held in their bodies and then use this outline as a starting point for decoding and representing their sexual stories.

The centrality of the body in this approach provides an opportunity to recognise older people's sexual bodies and stories. In ageist societies young bodies are often prized and older bodies ridiculed. Ageing bodies are associated with a series of losses (elasticity, power, sexual attractiveness) and considerable money and energy is often invested in fighting the physical and visible signs of ageing. Older people's bodies are not seen and their voices are not heard. In this context, body mapping provides an opportunity to celebrate older people's bodies and challenge ageism. It offers the opportunity to explore the rich stories held in older people's bodies. Plummer (2010a) describes how human sexualities accumulate across a life and leave stains or traces of the lives left behind. These stains and traces provide important contexts for understanding older people's sexual lives. They help us to understand power relationships and how sexual rights can be addressed. The end product, an image and narrative, retains its completeness and meanings attributed by the storyteller. The image provides a focal point that is compelling and can only be understood in relation to the storyteller's overall story and experience (Gastaldo et al., 2012).

The body mapping technique lends itself to the context of an in-depth interview to assist interviewees' focus on embodied sexuality. Art and story-telling have previously been utilised to raise awareness of older people's sexual rights (Barrett, 2011b). Despite the potential value in body mapping older people's sexual stories, this does not appear to have been previously utilised with older people or sexuality more broadly. Ludlow (2012) used body mapping with a small number of older patients on haemodialysis and found it helped to give voice to their experiences and the needs of their bodies. There remains an opportunity to explore the potential of this approach for documenting older people's sexual narratives and the power of these in providing impetus for recognition of sexual rights.

Body mapping pilot

Body mapping older people's sexuality was explored in a small pilot conducted by the Australian Research Centre in Sex, Health and Society at La Trobe University in partnership with the Australian Women's Health Network and Women's Health in the South East. The pilot was undertaken in response to earlier research on the sexual assault of older women, which failed to recruit any older women willing to talk about their experiences of sexual assault (Mann et al., 2014). There was an identified need to explore new ways of opening up conversations with older women about their experiences of sexual assault – to understand inequalities of power and strategies for primary prevention.

The aim of the pilot was to explore ways in which research could create safe spaces for older women to talk about their experiences of sexual assault. Analysis of factors contributing to the failure to recruit older women in previous research identified an opportunity to broaden the research focus from 'sexual assault' to 'sexual wellbeing and safety'. It was felt that broad conversations might be more likely to capture the interest of older women.

The project was conducted in 2015 once ethics approval was obtained from the La Trobe University's Human Research Ethics Committee. Prior to commencing the study the body mapping method was tested with an older woman who was an artist. The usual approach to body mapping, tracing an outline of the storyteller's body, was unachievable as the woman was physically unable to straighten her body. As an alternative, she drew her body freehand onto an A3 sized piece of paper. As she drew we talked about her sexual wellbeing and safety. Feedback on the method was positive and the image she drew was a compelling representation of her sexuality. There was agreement the method needed to be modified to enable older women to work on A3 sized paper to ensure accessibility to older women with limited movement.

Following the testing, a recruitment flyer was distributed through the project partner's networks with the aim of developing body maps and conducting interviews with around six women. The recruitment period was brief and the only response to the flyer was from a social support group for older women. The group invited the researcher to attend one of their group meetings to outline the project. They expressed interest in participating but were concerned they didn't have the artistic ability to produce a body map. In response, a template or tracing of a human figure, was developed for the women to use as a starting point for their individualised body maps. The women also reported they wanted to be interviewed as a group because they did not want to be 'picked off' and felt more powerful together.

Six women participated in the pilot, ranging in age from 60 to 82 years, with an average age of 67.4 years. All were provided with information sheets and signed consent forms. Four women made body maps and two elected to participate in the group interview but felt they did not have the skills to produce a body map, even using the templates provided.

Two body mapping sessions were facilitated, lasting around two hours each and held a month apart. Art materials were provided in each session and included paints, pencils, collage materials and body templates for the women to trace. During the first session the women worked on their body maps as they talked about their sexuality and the body maps they were making. The conversation was spontaneous and at times the women were guided with questions about what sexuality meant to them, whether it changed over time, how their bodies had changed, what sex was like for them and what sexual wellbeing and sexual safety meant to them.

The sessions were taped and transcribed. The transcription process was difficult as the group sessions were animated and the women frequently talked over each other. Individual narratives were identified from the first session – ranging from a few paragraphs to several thousand words in length. Where possible transcribed comments were linked to body maps and returned to women in the second session for verification, de-identification and further comment. The group reviewed a draft report that included their body maps and individual narratives as well as an edited transcription of interactions within the group.

Reflections on the pilot

The research did not progress as anticipated. The women's requirement that they participate as a group meant it was difficult to explore their body maps and individual narratives in depth. However, the body mapping process opened up new conversations that the group had not previously had. One woman shared a story about an earlier experience of rape and the impacts this had on her subsequent relationships and life. She reflected on issues of gender equity and provided significant insights into why some older women may not talk about sexual assault. The sense of safety and cohesiveness in the group appeared to have created a space where she felt safe to disclose. This should be explored further given body mappers may be more reflective because they are making something with their hands (Gauntlett and Holzwarth, 2006).

The resultant report (Barrett, 2015) includes powerful narratives about sexual wellbeing and safety, in older women's own words. The stories make for compelling reading and have been utilised by project partners in the education of service providers and to lobby elder abuse prevention services for strategies to address the sexual safety of older women.

A further challenge experienced was that the women were uncertain of their artistic abilities and chose to work on the tracing templates provided, rather than creating their own unique maps. It would have been easier to work with the women individually to explore their capabilities, but the group work and the animated conversation prohibited this. There is a need to explore strategies to make body mapping accessible to older people who have limited physical capabilities and those who are not confident with their artistic abilities. As a novice body mapper, I also recognise the opportunity to build skills to be able to support participants regardless of their skill levels and confidence. Despite this limitation the powerful images and stories produced by such a small pilot are encouraging.

Discussion

The body mapping method provided a useful focus for working with older women to document their sexual wellbeing and safety narratives. While the pilot was complicated by the group approach and the novice researcher, it showed significant promise. One narrative in particular is broad and encompasses an understanding of gender and power as barriers to reporting and preventing sexual assault. It alludes to the suitability of body mapping as a critical sexuality studies approach.

The research report privileges the voices of the participants and these first person narratives are rich and compelling. They demonstrate the potential of body mapping to generate narratives that build empathy and momentum for recognition of older people's sexual rights. Further research is currently being undertaken to explore body mapping older people's sexual stories. The research will explore sexuality broadly and will identify strategies such as computer assisted drawing to assist older people who are not confident making art.

The pilot demonstrated the potential for body mapping to position older people as narrators of their own sexual stories and it draws attention to the importance of respecting their rights as storytellers and sexual citizens. The privileging of older people's voices in this way does not suggest that the researcher has no influence. Narratives are shaped by the questions asked, the ways in which they are asked and when they are asked. Story facilitation is not an impartial process – but body mapping may take us a step closer to positioning older people as narrators of their own sexual stories. As Plummer (2013b) notes we need to listen to the stories of others to transform our worlds.

References

Aboderin, I. (2014) 'Sexual and Reproductive Health and Rights of Older Men and Women: Addressing a Policy Blind Spot', *Reproductive Health Matters*, 22(44), pp. 185–190.

Barrett, C. (2011a) 'Auditing Organisational Capacity to Promote the Sexual Health of Older People', *Electronic Journal of Applied Psychology*, 7(1), pp. 31–36.

Barrett, C. (2011b) 'Storyboarding: Using the Arts to Promote the Sexual Health and Emotional Wellbeing of Older Australians', *Culture, Health and Sexuality*, supplemental volume, 13(1).

Barrett, C. (2015) 'It's Gone Wild Out There: Women's Stories about Sexuality and Ageing', Australian Research Centre in Sex, Health and Society, La Trobe University, Melbourne Australia. Available at: www.opalinstitute. org/uploads/1/5/3/9/15399992/ wildoutthere.pdf.

Barrett, C. and Whyte, C. (2014) *Sexuality after Stroke: A Report on the 2013 SOX Program*, ARCSHS Monograph Series no. 100, Australian Research Centre in Sex, Health and Society, La Trobe University, Melbourne.

Barrett, C., Harrison, J. and Kent, J. (2009) *Permission to Speak: Towards the Development of Gay, Lesbian, Bisexual, Transgender and Intersex Friendly Aged Care Services*, Melbourne: Matrix Guild Victoria and Vintage Men.

Barrett, C., Crameri, P., Lambourne, S., Latham, J.R. and Whyte, C. (2015a) 'Understanding the Experiences and Needs of Lesbian, Gay, Bisexual and Trans Australians Living with Dementia and Their Partners', *Australasian Journal on Ageing*, LGBTI Special Edition, 34(2), pp. 34–38.

Barrett, C., Whyte, C., Comfort, J., Lyons, A. and Crameri, P. (2015b) 'Social Connection, Relationships and Older Lesbian and Gay People', *Sexual and Relationship Therapy*, 30(1) (Special Issue), pp. 131–142. doi: 10.1080/14681994.2014.963983.

Beer, M., Eisenstar, R. and Spector, B. (1990) 'Why Change Programs Don't Produce Change', *Harvard Business Review*, November–December, pp. 158–166.

Carr, W. and Kemmis, S. (1986) *Becoming Critical: Education, Knowledge and Action Research*, Burwood, Vic.: Deakin University Press.

Chadwick, L., Saver, J., Biller, J. and Carr, J. (1998) 'Stroke and Quality of Life', *Loss, Grief and Care*, 8(1), pp. 63–69.

Conrad, P. and Leiter, V. (2004) 'Medicalization, Markets and Consumers', *Journal of Health and Social Behavior*, 45, pp. 158–176.

Crameri, P., Barrett, C., Latham, J.R. and Whyte, C. (2015) 'It's More Than Sex and Clothes: Culturally Safe Services for Older Lesbian, Gay, Bisexual, Transgender and Intersex People', *Australasian Journal on Ageing*, LGBTI Special Edition, 34(2), pp. 21–25.

Devine, C. (2008) 'The Moon, the Stars, and a Scar: Body Mapping Stories of Women Living with

HIV/AIDS', *Border Crossings*, 27(1), pp. 58–65. Available at www.catie.ca/pdf/bodymaps/BC_105_BodyMapping.pdf.

Fletcher, G., Dowsett, G., Duncan, D., Slavin, S. and Corboz, J. (2013) 'Advancing Sexuality Studies: A Short Course on Sexuality Theory and Research Methodologies', *Sex Education*, 13(3), pp. 319–335.

Gastaldo, D., Magalhaes, L., Carrasco, C. and Davy, C. (2012) *Body-Map Storytelling as Research: Methodological Considerations for Telling the Stories of Undocumented Workers through Body Mapping*. Available at www.migrationhealth.ca/undocumented-workers-ontario/body-mapping.

Gauntlett, D. and Holzwarth, P. (2006) 'Creative and Visual Methods for Exploring Identities', *Visual Studies*, 21(1), pp. 82–91.

Gott, M. (2006) 'Sexual Health and the New Ageing', *Age and Ageing*, 35(2), pp. 106–107.

Green, T. and King, K. (2010) 'Functional and Psychosocial Outcomes 1 Year after Mild Stroke', *Journal of Stroke and Cerebrovascular Diseases*, 19(1), pp. 10–16.

Grundy, S. (1982) 'Three Modes of Action Research', *Curriculum Perspectives*, 2(3), pp. 23–34.

Kemmis, S. (2001) 'Exploring the Relevance of Critical Theory for Action Research: Emancipatory Action Research in the Footsteps of Jurgen Habermas', in Reason, P. and Bradbury, H. (eds) *Handbook of Action Research*, London: Sage, pp. 91–102.

Kemmis, S. and McTaggart, R. (eds) (1982) *The Action Research Planner*. Geelong, Vic.: Deakin University.

Kemmis, S. and McTaggart, R. (2000) 'Participatory Action Research', in Denzin, N. and Lincoln, Y. (eds) *Handbook of Qualitative Research*, London: Sage, pp. 567–605.

Kirby Institute (2012) *HIV, Viral Hepatitis and Sexually Transmissible Infections in Australia*, Annual Surveillance Report 2012, Sydney: The Kirby Institute, the University of New South Wales.

Kotter, J. (1995) 'Leading Change: Why Transformation Efforts Fail', *Harvard Business Review*, March–April, pp. 59–67.

Lamb, S. (2014) 'Permanent Personhood or Meaningful Decline? Toward a Critical Anthropology of Successful Aging', *Journal of Aging Studies*, 29, pp. 41–52.

Lamb, S. (2015) 'Beyond the View of the West: Ageing and Anthropology', in Twigg, J. and Martin, W. (eds) *Handbook of Cultural Gerontology*, London: Routledge, pp. 37–44.

Laumann, E., Nicolosi, A., Glasser, D., Paik, A., Gingell, C., Moreira, E. and Wang, T. (2005) 'Sexual Problems among Women and Men Aged 40–80 Years: Prevalence and Correlates Identified in the Global Study of Sexual Attitudes and Behaviors', *International Journal of Impotence Research*, 17, pp. 39–57.

Ludlow, B. (2012) *Body Mapping with Geriatric Inpatients Receiving*

Daily Haemodialysis Therapy for End-stage Renal Disease at Toronto Rehabilitation Institute: A Qualitative Study. Open access dissertations and theses. Paper 7542.

MacGregor, N. (2009) 'Mapping the Body: Tracing the Personal and the Political Dimensions of HIV/AIDS in Khayelitsha, South Africa', *Anthropology and Medicine*, 16(1), pp. 85–95.

Mann, R., Horsley, P., Barrett, C. and Tinney, J. (2014) *Norma's Project: A Research Study into the Sexual Assault of Older Women in Australia*, ARCSHS Monograph Series no. 98, Australian Research Centre in Sex, Health and Society, La Trobe University, Melbourne.

Manney, P. (2008) 'Empathy in the Time of Technology: How Story Telling Is the Key to Empathy', *Journal of Evolution and Technology*, 19(1), pp. 51–61.

Marshall, B.L. (2010) 'Science, Medicine and Virility Surveillance: "Sexy Seniors" in the Pharmaceutical Imagination', *Sociology of Health and Illness*, 32(2), pp. 211–224.

Marshall, B.L. (2011) 'The Graying of "Sexual Health": A Critical Research Agenda', *Canadian Review of Sociology/Revue canadienne de sociologie*, 48(4), pp. 390–413.

Marshall, B.L. (2012) 'Medicalization and the Refashioning of Age-related Limits on Sexuality', *Journal of Sex Research*, 49(4), pp. 337–343.

Meyburgh, T. (2006) *The Body Remembers: Body Mapping and Narratives of Physical Trauma*. MA thesis, Pretoria: Dept. of Psychology, University of Pretoria.

Plummer, K. (2010a) 'Generational Sexualities, Subterranean Traditions and the Hauntings of the Sexual World: Some Preliminary Remarks', *Symbolic Interaction*, 33(2), Spring, pp. 163–190. Available at http://kenplummer.com/publications/selected-writings-2/generational-sexualities/.

Plummer, K. (2010b) 'The Social Reality of Sexual Rights: A Critical Humanist View' in Aggleton, P. and Parker, R. (eds) *The Routledge Handbook of Sexuality, Health and Rights*, Abingdon, Oxon.: Routledge, pp. 45–55. Available at http://kenplummer.com/publications/selected-writings-2/the-social-reality-of-sexual-rights/.

Plummer, K. (2011) 'Critical Humanism and Queer Theory: Living with the Tensions' in Lincoln, Y.S and Denzin, N. (eds) *The Sage Handbook of Qualitative Research*, 4th edition, Thousand Oaks, CA: Sage, pp. 195–212.

Plummer, K. (2012) 'Critical Sexuality Studies' in Ritzer, G. (ed.) *The Wiley-Blackwell Companion to Sociology*, Chichester: Wiley-Blackwell, pp. 243–269.

Plummer, K. (2013a) 'A Manifesto for a Critical Humanism in Sociology on Questioning the Human Social World' in Nehring, D. (ed.) *Sociology: An Introductory Textbook and Reader*, Harlow: Pearson, pp. 498–517. Available at http://kenplummer.com/

manifestos/a-manifesto-for-a-critical-humanism-in-sociology/.

Plummer, K. (2013b) 'A Manifesto for Stories: Critical Humanist Notes for a Narrative Wisdom' in Stanley, L. (ed.) *Documents of Life Revisited: Narrative and Biographical Methodology for a 21st Century Critical Humanism*, London: Routledge, pp. 209–220. Available at http://kenplummer.com/manifestos/a-manifesto-for-stories/.

Solomon, J. (2007) *Living with X: A Body Mapping Journey in the Time of HIV and AIDS, Facilitator's Guide*, Johannesburg: REPSSI.

Stephens, G., Silbert, L. and Hasson, U. (2010) 'Speaker-Listener Neural Coupling Underlies Successful Communication', *Proceedings of the National Academy of Sciences of the United States of America*, 107(32), pp. 14425–14430.

Tiefer, L. (1994) 'The Medicalization of Impotence: Normalizing Phallocentrism', *Gender and Society*, 8(3), pp. 363–377.

Weinand, A. (2006) *An Evaluation of Body Mapping as a Potential HIV/AIDS Educational Tool*, Centre for Social Science Research, working paper no. 169, Cape Town: CSSR, University of Cape Town, pp. 1–32. Available at www.cssr.uct.ac.za/sites/cssr.uct.ac.za/files/pubs/wp169.pdf.

World Association for Sexual Health (2014) *Declaration of Sexual Rights*. Available at www.worldsexology.org/wp-content/uploads/2013/08/declaration_of_sexual_rights_sep03_2014.pdf.

World Health Organization (2006) *Defining Sexual Health: Report of a Technical Consultation on Sexual Health*, Geneva: WHO. Available at www.who.int/reproductivehealth/publications/sexual_health/defining_sexual_health.pdf.

6 | PATCHWORKING: USING CREATIVE METHODOLOGIES IN SEX AND SEXUALITIES RESEARCH

Catherine Vulliamy

Abstract

This chapter discusses the use of creative visual, textual and aural methodologies in my doctoral research on the relationship between sexuality and love. Alongside the more traditional interview and group discussion approaches to data collection, my fieldwork also makes use of participatory visual and audio collages, creative reflexive journals and the sharing of 'objects' (including visual, textual and audio 'objects' as well as physical objects) to explore individuals' experiences of love, desire and sexuality, and the relationships between them. I argue that the use of these creative approaches to studying desire, love and sexuality allows for new entry points into conversations about potentially difficult, intimate and abstract issues. Simultaneously, these approaches can make space for an additional dimension to our understanding of issues around sex, sexuality and emotion in their production of a dynamic account of personal and interpersonal experiences of and relationships to the topics in question. Drawing from some of the data generated with my participants, I aim to demonstrate the ways in which these kinds of methodologies can generate a richly textured and multi-dimensional picture of the lived experience of sexuality and desire.

Introduction

This chapter will outline and explore the use of a range of methodological tools employed in my PhD research on love and sexuality. My work has used a combination of methods, including more traditional one-to-one interviews and small group discussions, alongside a number of more 'creative' methods which I conceive of as producing a series of 'cultural patchworks' relating to individuals' thoughts, feelings, ideas and experiences of sexuality and love, as well as beginning to map a cultural context for these. I will describe these creative methods, explaining how they functioned and the kinds of data they generated, and will suggest that creative qualitative methodological approaches like these can produce new vitality in the research relationship in terms of opening up communication beyond the verbal, which simultaneously expands the potential to generate multi-dimensional and vibrant accounts of experiences of love and sexuality. I want to argue that the use of creative methods allows for a complex mapping of personal, interpersonal and cultural experience, practice and understanding that takes account of the 'untidiness' and ambiguity of both relational experience and the 'inner worlds' of desire and affect. I will explore the value of using creative approaches in research on sexuality, sex and love in relation to a number of issues: the impact of creative approaches on the research relationship; the potentials offered for new entry points to conversations about abstract and intimate issues; the production of dynamic accounts of personal and interpersonal experience; and the ability to situate individual experience within wider cultural contexts.

Cultural patchworking: creative methods in researching desire, sexuality and love

There is wide-ranging work from many perspectives on love and sexuality (see for example, Barthes, 1977/1979; de Beauvoir, 1949/1997; Berlant, 2011, 2012; Firestone, 1971; Fisher, 2004; Giddens, 1992; Gunnarsson, 2014; hooks, 2000; Ilouz, 2012; Jackson, 1993; Rich, 1980; Swidler, 2001, amongst many others), but research that explores the particular nature of the relationship between love and sexuality as experienced by subjects appears to be thin on the ground. My own work was concerned with the ways in which my participants do sexuality and love, rather than with defining them, and as such, draws on both feminist and queer theory to look at the ways in which participants might be understood as engaging in projects of 'queering love'. Participation was invited from people of all genders and sexualities, with the majority describing a level of 'fluidity' to their sexuality. Although recruitment was not restricted, in practice all participants were British and white, with the majority living in the north of England. My research began, without making the assumption that love necessarily ought to have a relationship with sexuality, or vice versa, but from the supposition that it seems reasonable to imagine that individuals might understand some kind of association or influence between these aspects of their experience. In dealing with the abstract realm of emotion, feeling, desire, relational intimacy and identity, I wanted to use methodological approaches that could maximise the available space for participants to express these deeply personal, often sensitive and opaque aspects of their lives. Recognising that both sexuality and affective emotion are communicated and generated culturally as well as within and between individuals, I also wanted to be able to try to understand these intensely personal accounts within their wider cultural context. As such, I used a combination of creative qualitative methods alongside or in addition to interviews and discussion groups: visual and textual collages, a collectively produced 'mix tape', personal journals and participant-chosen 'objects'.

Participants in the project fell broadly into three categories; those who participated in one-to-one interviews, those who participated in small group discussions, and a small 'Core Group' who met regularly with me throughout the fieldwork year to contribute to and reflect on the issues arising, participate in specific research tasks and to offer an alternative perspective to balance my own observations and understandings of the emerging themes. Beyond these modes of participation, the project's Facebook page also generated contributions from individuals who were unwilling or unable to participate in interviews or discussion groups, but who still wished to engage with the project in other ways.

The visual and textual collages and the mix tape all generated contributions from both those who formally participated in the project, and others who engaged less formally. People were invited to suggest visual images, poetry, literary quotes (and other textual submissions) as well as music and song that was meaningful to them in relation to sexuality, desire and love. I then assembled the visual data into eight large (A1) collages, which offer a striking visual representation of collective cultural expression and understanding of desire and love. I also created a CD and online playlist of musical submissions, alongside a track listing and a copy of the song lyrics which were bound into a book. I did not impose a specific curation or ordering of these data, but simply pulled them together as the submissions arrived, though I was conscious of wanting the collages to be attractive to the viewer; to look 'beautiful', and so mounted some of the text contributions on brightly coloured tissue paper, rather than simply reproducing lines of typed text in black on white.

The personal journals were kept by myself and the Core Group participants over the course of the fieldwork year. I had requested that they include visual, as well as text entries, and invited us all to use the journals to reflect on the issues and experiences we were discussing as part of our work, as well as to reflect on our experiences of being involved in the project.

Finally, I invited all interview participants to bring to interview three objects which they felt were meaningful in some way to their experience of love and/or sexuality. Some participants, particularly those who conducted their interview via Skype, sent me photographs of their chosen objects; others had physical objects available during the interview.

Collages

Some of the contributions were intensely personal; images, text or song that had deep personal meaning that might be

unlikely to be shared with others in the same ways. Some contributions, particularly the images, were chosen specifically because
of the possibility of collective cultural meaning; following discussion with the Core Group, internet searches were conducted for
images according to both broad and specific search terms, relating to love, desire and sexuality. For example, we made a point of
seeking out images of 'iconic' lovers, book covers of relationship
manuals and self-help books, albums of love songs, film posters
etc. Beyond these, some images were offered with short explanations – one man messaged me a selection of images followed by
a short note explaining that he realised with hindsight that they
were mostly images of people he desired either to 'have' or to be,
or both. Some images were abstract and offered without explanation, leaving their meanings unclear. While some of the textual
contributions were incorporated into the visual collages, several
collages were created just with textual data, based largely upon
extracts of poetry and prose, and some quotes about desire and/
or love. Once again, these sometimes were offered as very personal offerings about an individual's experience, but more often
as a cultural reference that articulated an aspect of an individual's feeling or experience in a way that had resonance for them.
The textual contributions were less likely to be accompanied by
explanations – participants were perhaps more comfortable with
the idea that words could communicate meaning clearly in ways
that images might not.

Between them, these visual, textual and musical collages
encourage interaction with the viewer in a way that I hope
illustrates experientially how we draw from these cultural references as we find meaning, understanding and articulation of
our feelings and experiences of sexuality and love in a dynamic,
responsive and evolving communicative process. This process
operates within and between our individual life stories and a
constantly shifting collective outpouring of cultural expression
and production.

Personal journals

As well as this collective creation of visual, textual and audio 'cultural patchworks', the Core Group and myself kept reflexive journals throughout the fieldwork year. The content of these was not particularly intended to be shared between us on an ongoing basis, though sometimes we did share particular journal entries by way of introducing or illustrating particular topics we were discussing during our meetings, or in shared communications in between meetings. However, the journals were designed as a record of the year, with the intention that they be returned to me as a complete record at the end of the year in order that they could be included as part of my data. The journals contain a combination of broad musings upon and responses to the issues we were dealing with; descriptions of our personal narratives, feelings and experiences in relation to desire and love; and reflections on our experiences of participating in this work.

The personal nature of journaling, and the assurance that though the contents of the journals would form part of my analysis, they would not be reproduced in the final thesis, meant that some of the journal entries, visual and textual, were powerfully personal, intimate and sometimes explicit. The entries chart intense explorations of personal history and experience, and intellectual and emotional engagement with the issues and themes of the research. Although the journals are too few to offer meaningful opportunity for stand-alone analysis, they are a compelling part of the broader dataset. The timescale over which they were compiled (12 months) also offers a fascinating overview of the reflexive processing that happened over the course of our work together, the developing relationships between us as individuals, and the expansion and shift of ideas and responses to the material over time.

Interview objects

Finally, participants in one-to-one interviews were invited to bring to their interviews three 'objects' that were meaningful to them in relation to sexuality and love. The objects could take any form – physical objects or references to music, poetry, websites etc.

Physical objects were photographed and stored alongside interview transcripts; references were noted and stored similarly. Some objects were also recorded in other ways, for example, one participant shared a large antique Tibetan singing bowl with me, explaining that the sound and physicality of the bowl were significant for her, so as well as photographing it, I also made a sound recording of the bowl being 'played', and a written record of my own physical experience of holding it while it was played. The objects functioned in a number of different ways both in the context of the interviews and in relation to my analysis. The objects are data in themselves, representing the stories, feelings and experiences that their owners attached to them or generated through them, and sometimes (as with the singing bowl) the objects 'spoke' with their own voice. They also offered a 'beginning point' for conversations about desire and love, a route into complex and abstract ideas, reflections and feelings. Both as data themselves and as methodological tools, the objects were involved in the generation of dynamic, vibrant and multi-layered accounts of sexuality, desire and love, adding a compelling richness to the verbal data generated in interviews and discussions.

The value of creative methods in sex and sexualities research

There are many and varied accounts of the advantages and challenges of using creative and visual methods in social research. In her work on family relationships, Jacqui Gabb has noted that research tackling the abstract realms of interpersonal connection, emotion and feeling can benefit from a qualitative mixed methods approach because of the ways such an approach can generate multidimensional data which 'produces a dynamic account of … sensual, emotional and embodied interactions' (2009, p. 37). David Gauntlett argues that visual and creative methodologies enable people 'to communicate in a meaningful way about their identities and experiences, and their own thoughts about their identities and experiences' (Gauntlett and Holzwarth, 2006, p. 82). Ongoing developments in understandings of pictorial data in social sciences move us beyond dealing with it as a record of 'reality', and towards a deeper recognition of the visual as 'producing or constructing particular realities, and as mediated by culture, ideology and subjectivity' (Frith et al., 2005, p. 188). It is my intention now to briefly explore four key ways in which the use of creative methods has enriched my own work, and which I suggest offer broad potential for sex and sexualities research generally.

The quality of the research relationship

There are challenges for the social researcher in working on areas of social life like sexuality, desire and love, which can be complex, abstract, intimate and sensitive, and however short-term it might be, the quality of the relationship between researcher and participant in exploring these areas of social life is profoundly important. The use of the 'objects' within the context of one-to-one interviews supported the quality and rapport of the research relationship in expansive ways. Stanczak (2007) proposes that visual methods encourage research participants to feel more comfortable within the research process, and deepen rapport in ways that unlock 'what otherwise might be closed off' (2007, p. 12), making way for deeper reflection and discussion within an interview process (2007, p. 15). In my own work, the objects brought to interview were usually selected as a result of particular personal associations or memories that were attached to them, and the sharing of these stories, memories and descriptions at the beginning of the interview ultimately supported a real depth of intimacy as the interview unfolded. People might begin hesitantly, uncertain if they had made the 'right' selection, or if they were talking about it in the 'right' ways, but as their talk about their objects unfolded, it would be peppered with thoughtful pauses, smiles, side tracks, laughter or far-off gazes as participants relaxed into both their communication and my willingness to receive it, however it was offered. Individuals' handling of their objects as they spoke often had a visibly soothing effect for them, as well as offering me another layer of insight into their responses to their objects and the stories they 'contained'. David Gauntlett (Gauntlett and Holzwarth, 2006) suggests that creative methods offer an approach that is 'optimistic and trusting about people's ability to generate interesting theories and observations about themselves' (Gauntlett and Holzwarth, 2006, p. 82). It is, in part, this optimism about and trust in people's ability that I believe enhances the quality of the research relationship; because people are able to experience their material contributions (and through them, themselves) as valued within the relationship and the wider research process.

New entry points for difficult conversations and abstract issues

There are challenges in approaching work on sexuality, desire and love, and seeking to explore relations between them. Not only are these intimate and sensitive aspects of our lives, but trying to articulate thoughts, feelings and experiences about such abstract and hard-to-grasp concepts can be daunting for people. However, the creative approaches used in my research helped to create new entry points into those conversations as well as supporting the expression of the intricate connections between emotion, experience and subjectivity. The interview objects very often paved the way for a conversation to begin; the material presence of the object demanding its story is told. As Whincup (2004) says, visual methods allow us to 'visualize' the 'intangible dimensions of human activity' (Whincup, 2004, p. 79); in my interviews, the visibility of the object served as a raft in the wide-open sea of the less tangible – emotion, experience and 'self' – offering a concrete starting point from which to launch. On the other hand, opening up the opportunity for a wider population to contribute to the collages and mix tape meant that it was possible for people to share particular 'objects' without necessarily participating in the 'deeper conversation' of an interview.

Creative methods allowed opportunities for people to communicate their thoughts and experiences both with and beyond the verbal. A person might offer an object, or share an image and accompany it with a verbal story or explanation, but the words attached to the object/image did not render the object itself obsolete; they were simply another dimension of the communication. Some of the collage and mix tape contributions came without a verbal narrative, with the implication that the contributions 'spoke for themselves'. Gauntlett (Gauntlett and Holzwarth, 2006) cautions against imposing interpretation on an artefact: 'My own guesses or speculation about someone else's meanings are just that – guesses and speculation' (Gauntlett and Holzwarth, 2006, p. 87), however in the absence of an expressed meaning, I can only take these offerings at face value. Part of the value of recording the lyrics of song contributions has been that the whole collection can be analysed textually, an addition to, but distinct from analysis of any particular meanings expressed in relation to contributions.

Dynamic, multi-faceted and 'messy' data

Creative methodologies can generate data that are rich and dynamic, but also 'untidy', demonstrating 'the emotional messiness, uncertainties and fluidity that constitute relational experience', and echoing the 'contingency of lived lives' (Gabb, 2009, p. 49). Gabb argues that the 'loose ends' themselves have salience in making sense of complicated lives and relational experiences (2009, p. 44).

Creative methods can also construct space for different levels of reflection. As Gauntlett and Holzwarth (2006) highlights, language-based research generally demands an instant response from participants, which, particularly in exploring identities and emotions, can be challenging. Crucially, creative methods allow time, making space for a reflective process, and resulting in data that is the result of that process – thoughtful, considered and often particularly insightful (Gauntlett and Holzwarh, 2006, p. 84). Participants talked about the time involved in choosing objects, images or music; their selections had been made consciously, and many had reflected deeply on the reasons and meanings behind their choices, the experience of choosing, and on the ways they wished to communicate these to me. One man who brought a scarf knitted for him by a former lover told me that he had spent several days trying to decide which of a number of scarves he would choose, as each had particular meanings and representations, and he had wanted to choose the one that was most appropriate for what he wanted to convey through it.

Noting Merleau-Ponty's work on the relationship of the body to experience and perception, Gauntlett also draws attention to the 'embodied' nature of creative methodologies, arguing that social research needs to embrace the body as a key element of experience, alongside the people's creative and reflexive responses (Gauntlett and Holzwarh, 2006, p. 85). Creative methodologies can offer new dimensions for exploring and communicating emotional and embodied experiences of sexuality, desire and love; the singing bowl example mentioned earlier illustrates how an object can convey a vibrant combination of bodily and emotional information. In describing her choice of the singing bowl, 'Sarah' explained:

> The thing that works for me is the physicality of the sound of
> it and the fact that when you hear it you can move yourself
> closer or away from it and the resonance of it in relation
> to your body is quite significant ... Now for me that says
> a lot about sensuality and love and I find it quite a darkly
> passionate thing.

Similarly, contributions to the mix tape frequently conveyed bodily as well as emotional meanings. In her exploration of queer relationships with music, Sarah Hankins (2014) stresses the relationship with music as 'embodied, aroused, and situated' (Hankins, 2014, p. 87) and argues that 'arousal opens, extends, and receives; it dissolves boundaries not only between our bodies and objects in the outside world but also between different and even contradictory parts of our selves' (2014, p. 101). Musical 'objects' were often chosen because of the ways they made the listener feel, how the music facilitated that arousal state, emotionally, physically or both.

Situating the research: linking the personal and the cultural

Finally, the creative methods I have used here have enabled me to situate my work within a cultural context. Part of my concern has been with examining the ways in which individuals 'acquire' love, as well as exploring how love and sexuality/sexual desire might interrelate. In collecting data for the collages and the mix tape, I have been able to build a visual representation of some of the ways in which our experiences, articulations and understandings of the affective realms of desire and love are situated within, and mediated by the cultural context in which they arise. Several interviews and discussions reflected on the ways in which we learn about love, desire and relationships through the media which surround us; Disney's various renditions of the rescue of the princess in order to live happily ever after in monogamous heteronormative bliss were mentioned, as was the peculiar construction of gender and sexuality in 'Ghostbusters' that implied that a man's persistent pursuit of an uninterested woman was 'cute' rather than 'creepy'. In a world in which we are receiving cultural media messages constantly and from all kinds of places, it is important to recognise that we are not simply observers or consumers of these cultural products, but that we are actively engaged with them, and processing them constantly (Gauntlett and Holzwarh, 2006, p. 85).

The creation of these tangible 'cultural patchworks' also enables me to disseminate aspects of my findings in ways that are interactive and experiential: I have exhibited the collages and mix tape in conference settings and encouraged conference participants to make their own responses to the data, allowing them to encounter first-hand how the work might contribute to understanding how we perceive and make meaning of our experiences of love and desire in culturally situated and co-constructed ways.

Conclusion

The integration of creative methodologies with more conventional interviews and group discussions in my research has offered opportunities for rich and complex understandings of individual's experiences of sexuality and love, and the dynamic and evolving relationships between these facets of their experience. While I can't assert that the methodological approach I have used has enabled me to apprehend a fixed 'reality' or 'truth', it has facilitated the capture of a 'thick' account of these experiences, complete with various contradictions and loose ends, and allowed an exploration of the assorted facets of self and experience with which individuals make meaning of their worlds.

I have tried to show some of the ways in which these kinds of methodologies might offer valuable opportunities for sex and sexualities research, and there are many other ways which might be useful, as well as other creative approaches beyond those I have outlined here. While there are challenges as well as opportunities in designing creative methodologies and analysing the data collected in this way, the diverse layers of perception and meaning that arise through these processes support the production of a richly textured and multi-dimensional portrayal of the lived experience of sexuality and desire, which take account of bodily, emotional, cultural and relational aspects of our lives.

References

Barthes, Roland (1977/1979) *A Lover's Discourse: Fragments*, London: Penguin.

Berlant, Lauren (2011) 'A Properly Political Concept of Love: Three Approaches in Ten Pages', *Cultural Anthropology*, 26(4), pp. 683–691.

Berlant, Lauren (2012) *Desire/Love*, Brooklyn, NY: Punctum Books.

De Beauvoir, Simone (1949/1997) *The Second Sex*, London: Vintage.

Firestone, Shulamith (1971) *The Dialectics of Sex*, London: Jonathan Cape.

Fisher, Helen (2004) *Why We Love: The Nature and Chemistry of Romantic Love*, New York: St. Martin's Griffin.

Frith, Hannah, Riley, Sarah, Archer, Louise and Gleeson, Kate (2005) Editorial in *Qualitative Research in Psychology*, 2(3), pp. 187–198.

Gabb, J. (2009) 'Researching Family Relationships: A Qualitative Mixed Methods Approach', *Methodological Innovations Online*, 4(2), pp. 37–52.

Gauntlett, David and Holzwarth, Peter (2006) 'Creative and Visual Methods for Exploring Identities', *Visual Studies*, 21(1), pp. 82–91.

Giddens, Anthony (1992) *The Transformation of Intimacy: Sexuality, Love and Eroticism in Modern Societies*, Cambridge: Polity Press.

Gunnarsson, Lena (2014) *The Contradictions of Love: Towards a Feminist-Realist Ontology of Sociosexuality*, Abingdon, Oxon.: Routledge.

Hankins, Sarah (2014) 'Queer Relationships with Music and Experiential Hermeneutics for Musical Meaning', *Women and Music: A Journal of Gender and Culture*, 18, pp. 83–104.

hooks, bell (2000) *All About Love: New Visions*, London: The Women's Press.

Ilouz, Eva (2012), *Why Love Hurts: A Sociological Explanation*, Cambridge: Polity Press.

Jackson, Stevi (1993) 'Even Sociologists Fall in Love: An Exploration in the Sociology of Emotions', *Sociology*, 27(2), pp. 201–220.

Rich, Adrienne (1980) 'Compulsory Heterosexuality and Lesbian Existence', *Signs* 5(4), pp. 631–691.

Stanczak, Gregory Charles (2007) *Visual Research Methods: Images, Society and Representation*, Thousand Oaks, CA: Sage.

Swidler, Ann (2001) *Talk of Love: How Culture Matters*, Chicago, IL and London: University of Chicago Press.

Whincup, T. (2004) 'Imagining the Intangible' in Knowles, C. and Sweetman, P. (eds) *Picturing the Social Landscape: Visual Methods and the Sociological Imagination*, London: Routledge, pp. 79–92.

7 | DIRTY TALK: ON USING POETRY IN PORNOGRAPHY RESEARCH

P.J. Macleod

Abstract

Researchers in the social sciences have frequently bemoaned the difficulty in accessing and expressing the nuances inherent in human experience (Offord and Cantrell, 1999; Rath, 2012; Hoskins, 2015; Hallett and Allan, 2017). For academics working within sex and sexuality studies – and on porn audience research in particular – the focus of study is often precisely which is least easily tangible: namely how sex and sexuality are experienced by the individual. The contention of this paper is that creative methods, specifically the written and spoken poetic form, can give texture to some of these more elusive experiential complexities. By drawing upon my own work in the field of porn studies, I also contend that poetry in research can speak to issues of ontology, epistemology and reflexivity experienced within the field of sex and sexuality studies, in a way that traditional academic language and research methods may otherwise struggle to achieve.

'The poetic moment': the emergence of poetry in research

Despite our tendency to separate arts and science following the dualist influences of the modernist era, in recent years we have witnessed academics 'knitting back together the strands of the sciences and humanities' (Sherry and Schouten, 2002, p. 219). Following this, whilst the use of creative writing in scholarship remains uncommon, poetry is beginning to venture outside its traditional literary home, towards the world of academic research and the sciences. The reasons for this are manifold – from the ability of non-traditional formats to increase engagement with academic audiences and enhance accessibility in research representation (Cahnmann, 2003), to the ways in which poetry can be used to gain access to, or more aptly express, aspects of human experience or emotion that are inaccessible or difficult to articulate by other means (Maslow, 1964).

With this in mind, we have seen poetry being utilised in a number of ways within diverse fields, including marketing (Zinkhan, 1994), consumer behaviour (Stern, 1998) and education (Cahnmann, 2003). It has been posited that the interest in using poetry in the research context can in part be attributed to some of the shared goals common to both poets and social science researchers, namely with regards to a mutual interest in observation, reflexivity and acknowledging one's own positionality (Faulkner, 2009). This notwithstanding, we have also seen poetry being employed for the purposes of data collection and representation in the 'hard sciences', such as mathematics and medicine, where poetry has proven useful 'to deliver with economy what normal speech, scholarship, or pedagogy can do only with greater difficulty, if at all' (Sherry and Schouten, 2002, p. 219).

This recent revival of poetry in research, and indeed, poetry as research, has been attributed to the 'crisis of representation', which has interrogated the relationship between language and experience (MacLure, 2003). Arguably, as academics have continued to expose research as a discursive practice in itself, the inclination to resist the authoritative voice of realism in favour of a more reflexive and multi-faceted conceptualisation of the research topic, has gained ever-more potency and continues to do so today. It is upon observation of this inclination, which acknowledges and addresses tensions between the emotional and the 'objective', that Gurevitch (2002, p. 403) announced 'the poetic moment' in social science research.

Gurevitch maintains that poetry constitutes an important method for addressing the instability of the relationship between the empirical world and its representation in language by researchers, claiming that the poetic form is 'a performative one, shifting the focus from the figure to the act of writing' (2002, p. 404). This illumination of the role of language in the representation of findings, and of the researcher as an invariably biased filter of those representations, is one that is often acknowledged as a regrettable inevitability in research practice. However, with some exceptions – for example, the use of 'thick description' (Geertz, 1973) to highlight subjectivity in ethnographic work – these issues are rarely taken forward in their own right within research. Accordingly, moving beyond a surface-level recognition of the discursive nature of research practice towards a more explicit challenge and overt problematisation thereof, emerges as one way in which that poetry might be usefully implemented.

The use of poetry in research remains controversial (Poindexter, 2002), however Lahman et al. (2011) contend that we have yet to fully appreciate the methodological advantages it could yield. I will discuss some of those uses, their potential contributions to research, and some of the concerns that must be navigated, specifically within my own area of research (porn audiences) and within the field of sex and sexualities more broadly.

Poetic form and function in academic research

Whether a source of data or method for data collection, an analytical tool, or a means of representation, poetry has been shown to have a place at each stage of the research process (Furman, 2006). Nonetheless, it is still the case that the modes by which to best make use of this tool are not widely recognised. Sherry and Schouten (2002) provide a comprehensive summary of the range of ways in which poetry has been employed in research practice, which include poetic transcription, auto-ethnographic poetry, investigative poetics as well as 'found' and interpretive poetry. Further to this, Faulkner (2009) provides an overview of the different goals and intended outcomes for the various configurations of poetry utilised in research. These include a desire to convey phenomenological nuance or fragmentation, a wish to elicit emotional and visceral responses in audiences, and attempts to more closely tie academic work with the personal and political.

Amongst the literature that incorporates these creative tools, we find work that makes use of, or even produces, poetry as part and parcel of the research process. For an example of this, we might look to the study by Furman et al. (2007), during which the authors use open and axial coding of participant responses to construct interpretive research poems, based around the inducted themes. We might also draw upon examples of 'poetry journals' written during the fieldwork stage, as demonstrated by Schouten (1990). In addition, the more tangential use of poetic techniques can be identified in work such as that of Cahnmann (2003), who points to the ways in which attention to meter, pitch, tone and metaphor can be usefully employed in speech and discourse analysis. She goes on to claim that this and other poetic techniques have the capacity not only to enhance the impact and accessibility of research, but also the value and substance of qualitative data, analysis and representation.

This enhancement of 'value' has been said by many to come from the way in which poetry, and indeed other creative tools are able to forge a more intimate relationship between science and art (Faulkner, 2009), with each contributing to the research process in distinct ways. Some of these contributions have included the ways in which poetry can evoke an emotional response and a sense of shared experience between researchers and audiences (Carr, 2003; Glesne, 1997); how it can stimulate cultural critique and political change in a way that more neutral academic language may struggle to achieve (Denzin, 1999); how poetry is better able to capture contextual worlds as experienced by the subject (Leggo, 2008); the ways in which it expresses the introspective and emphasises humanity (Richardson, 1998); how poetic language and performance is able to convey multiple, sometimes contradictory, creative and political meanings (Madison, 2003);

and thus how poetry can draw attention to the constructedness of knowledge and of how we understand reality itself (Witkin, 2007).

This challenge to dominant ontological and epistemological discourses within and beyond the academy forms the backbone of Leggo's (2008) argument in favour of poetry's place in research. If everything we know about the world is constructed in language, as Leggo argues, making use of language to draw attention to this very fact becomes a priority for those wishing to take seriously the question: 'How do I know what I know?' (2008, p. 166). It is for this reason that Leggo makes use of autobiographic poetry, which he claims leaves open the possibility for multiple interpretations, fragmented meaning, and the acknowledgement of that which we don't – and can't – know. In a similar vein, Richardson (1994, p. 520) emphasises that using a variety of writing styles in research can help shift the focus from simply an attempt to get it right towards getting it 'differently contoured and nuanced'. Furthermore, being able to effectively express such nuances is of increasing concern for academics in terms of maximising impact and retention, and reaching audiences in a way that is meaningful: 'Why do we, as researchers and scholars whose work needs to have more community currency than ever before, remain wedded to telling rather than showing or imagining?' (Neilson, 2008, p. 99).

Cahnmann (2003) posits that poetry provides an effective tool with which to undertake this task, by virtue of its capacity to convey information in multi-vocal, incisive and more understandable ways. Indeed he goes on to specify 'spoken word', or 'stand-up poetry' performed in poetry slams, as a particularly accessible format. Occupying an important place within African American culture and history (Fisher, 2003), we now see spoken word poetry increasing in popularity worldwide, amongst African diaspora communities and beyond. Gurevitch (2002, p. 405) states that this type of performative representation highlights the personal and the emotive, and perhaps thereby helps redress what Daniel and Peck (1996, p. 7) refer to as the 'expressive inadequacy of prose'. Such claims serve to support Faulkner's (2009) assertion that poetry best serves researchers when more traditional methods of knowledge transfer would fail to capture or represent that which they feel should be foregrounded in their work.

However, as Brady (2000) contends, it is nonetheless the case that just because poetry can add value in certain contexts and particular research endeavours, this does not necessarily render it an appropriate method or tool for every project. Specifically, concerns have been raised about the 'sample of one' that poetry tends towards. Whilst Wallendorf and Brucks (1993) rightly argue that the introspective form makes no claims to generalisability, questions of validity and reliability at the heart of much social science research remain significant obstacles. Moreover, whilst Cahnmann (2003) claims there is little to lose by adopting creative methods that promise to enhance research practice, Eisner (1997) warns against the risk of substituting the novelty that poetry might appear to bring for the substance and rigour that academic work ultimately requires.

Indeed, the same argument has been made in reverse – that research poetry must not serve simply as a scholastic novelty, but works best when literary techniques are used skilfully. As such, meaningful consideration of how to go about using poetry in research is perhaps necessary in order to ensure that neither artistic nor academic ends are diminished. Sherry and Schouten (2002, p. 229) provide an example of such points for deliberation when elaborating on the ways in which poetry-as-research 'may reasonably require a more methodical and permanent record of observations'. This, they suggest, resolving through the use of footnotes – uncommon in poetry-as-art, but necessary when presenting poetry within an academic context. Thus, it becomes important to ensure that any attempts to make use of poetry as part of our research, are also accompanied by a critical discussion of the means by which we intend to go about it, what it can offer us that other tools cannot, and the ways in which these contributions will facilitate our particular research endeavours.

The use of poetry in sex and sexualities research

Taking stock of the areas in which poetry in research has already proved valuable, and the literature around how creative methods can be usefully employed in the social science context, it seems there exists a number of ways in which poetry could make meaningful contributions to sex and sexualities research. Firstly, the multifaceted expressiveness attributed to the poetic form arguably constitutes an invaluable tool for researchers in this field, by virtue of the possibilities it offers for capturing the 'myriad intangible qualities' associated with sex:

> Sex is entwined with ideas of romance, attraction, commitment, independence, orientation, crime, identity, hygiene, waste, fantasy, confidence, despair, nature, abnormality, deviance, degradation, fulfilment, liberation, status, sin, perversion ... It would, of course, be wrong to talk of sex as a singular activity or having only singular meaning. (Attwood and Smith, 2013, p. 325)

The complexities of people's experiences and practices with regards to sexual activity are often hidden, overlooked or disavowed by simplistic definitions that associate sex purely or primarily with corporeality and conception. Across the field we have seen work that explores sex not only in terms of reproduction, but also with reference to emotion, identity, kinship, power, economy, industry, education and countless other facets of that which constitutes the complex terrain of sex and sexualities. Accordingly, the potential for poetry in this area of research may lie in its ability to represent such coexisting perspectives; to access the less concrete characteristics that nonetheless remain central to sexual experience; and to thereby work towards a more authentic representation of affect and experience that may sometimes prove difficult to communicate.

Whilst such challenges to achieving nuanced representation of human experience and identity are undoubtedly encountered across the social sciences, they seem especially pertinent in the field of sex research. Specifically, I would argue that the task of representing the 'ineffable' takes on a renewed urgency with regards to pornography audience research, by virtue of the complex interplay between cognitive processing and physical response that sexual stimuli are thought to provoke (Laan and Janssen, 2007). If we are to understand pornography as a 'body genre' (Williams, 1991) with a filmic imperative not only to produce an emotive but also a physical response on the part of the viewer, the focus of study for many porn audience researchers often becomes precisely that which is least easily tangible: the mental and corporeal responses pornographic material elicits, and how these are experienced by the consumer. Poetry may thus be able to offer sex and sexualities scholars the potential to access and express something internal or intangible that may otherwise resist description.

This is something that Rath (2012) puts to the test in her paper on poetic and participatory research with rape crisis workers, which describes the co-creation of poems by both participants and researcher, based on interview transcripts. The benefit of this approach proves to be the capacity for the poems to more effectively convey the nuances of the experiences described at interview, without losing the authenticity of participant voices. Such poems can thus go a long way towards helping the reader understand and even relate to some of the more complex emotive elements of sexual experience and identity that often remain hidden and/or unspeakable. In this way, we see how poetry in research, and indeed poetry-as-research, can add value to the knowledge transfer process in a way that other creative methods, such as 'thick description', may struggle to accomplish; the latter, for example, most commonly serving as a mode for articulating the researcher's observations of human behaviour, and the former – as demonstrated in this instance – offering a means by which to engage with the emotional and affective elements of human experience itself.

With reference to my own research into consumers' experiences of using pornography, knowledge transfer has similarly proven a productive avenue for employing poetry in research. Here I draw upon an occasion on which I presented a spoken word set at an academic symposium, in lieu of a traditional conference paper. The poems recited covered a range of themes related to my work, from the history of pornography to personal experience of sexual harassment – the latter framed as researcher subjectivity and reflexive practice. The intention was to provide a more immersive and impactful means for understanding the research context, my own positionality and emergent results based on recounted participant experiences, many audience members reporting enhanced engagement with the paper accordingly. Additionally, the decision to create a conference paper that would not only be received, but could also be experienced in some way was reflective of the centrality of experiential knowledge to the project, in light of its inductive methodological approach and firm grounding in participant narratives.

This project made use of grounded theory to explore feminists' experiences using online pornography, and thus emphasised a 'bottom-up', theory-building approach to the research process. Grounded theory's focus on inductive theory development, and its iterative approach to data collection and analysis, lent itself to a number of key aims for the research. Chief amongst these was a quest to capture the subtleties of those insights that lie between and beyond harm/empowerment discourses and apathy/ victimhood perspectives, which have been widely criticised for their somewhat simplistic understandings of pornography and its consumption (Duggan et al., 1993; Segal, 1993). Other objectives include eschewing, as far as possible, commonly held assumptions about the research topic and research subjects; resisting agenda-driven frameworks that seek to validate pro- or anti-porn stances; and allowing for the voices of porn consumers themselves to be heard and taken seriously, in a way that hasn't tended to be prioritised in pornography effects research or the public arena more widely (Mowlabocus and Wood, 2015, p. 119). However, whilst grounded theory brings many virtues, its positivist influences can simultaneously pose significant challenges, particularly when they stand in contrast to the researcher's own ontological and epistemological allegiances. Addressing such tensions is an area in which creative and poetic methods can arguably add further value to our research.

Glaser and Strauss (1967) established grounded theory during the time Denzin and Lincoln (2000, p. 3) refer to as the 'golden age of rigorous qualitative analysis', and that Birks and Mills (2011) call 'the second moment'. This era was characterised by post-positivism and an inclination to work within a philosophical frame that assumes a singular, objective reality and the possibility of a detached, impartial observer. It wasn't until later that questions about the researcher's place in the process, and the 'crisis of representation' began to gain traction. Following these critiques, a weakness of grounded theory might be said to be in its call for researchers to 'bracket' their prior knowledge and assumptions about the subject matter and initially refrain from engaging with pre-existing literature, in order to remain impartial during theory development (Glaser and Strauss, 1967; Glaser, 1992; Strauss and Corbin, 1994). Indeed, the weakness here may lie in its inference that such a task could, itself, ever truly be unproblematically accomplished. If notions of sex and sexuality are, in fact, central to humanity's 'self concept' (Pangman and Seguire, 2000) it would be unwise to assume that sex researchers, by virtue of being researchers, could easily detach themselves from their personal experiences, attitudes, knowledge and identities.

In reality, despite faithful adherence to the well-elaborated guidelines for inductive data collection, analysis and theoretical sensitivity put forward by Glaser and Strauss, it inevitably remains the case that I, the researcher, continue to be influenced by existing debates around pornography, and so am in some ways informed by exactly those harm/empowerment agendas that I seek to eschew in my work. As such, another place for poetry in sex and sexualities research reveals itself, in the context of grounded theory as well as with other social science methodologies. Namely, it presents an opportunity for moving beyond a simple disavowal of existing emotive, political and intellectual inclinations during the research process, towards a more meaningful engagement with and reflection upon subjectivity's place within it. This follows Richardson's (1994) suggestion that poetry act as a tool for foregrounding – rather than renouncing – issues of legitimacy, transparency and truth:

> When we read or hear poetry, we are continually nudged into recognizing that the text has been constructed. But all texts are constructed – prose ones, too; therefore, poetry helps problematize reliability, validity, and "truth". (Richardson, 1994, p. 522)

Accordingly, poetry holds the potential to become a means not only for acknowledging the impossibility of complete impartiality in research, but also for rejecting ontological and epistemological dualism, and actively resisting the supposition that the research we undertake could or should ever be detached from us as the researchers.

With this in mind, poetry can be said to constitute an overlooked and underused reflexive tool for researchers seeking to undertake what Stoller (1997) might call 'sensuous scholarship' or academic work that seeks to speak to the meaning-making process itself. Moreover, we have identified ways in which poetry can be usefully employed to help address potential epistemological and ontological conflicts in our research efforts, as well as its capacity for enhancing our ability to access and express human sexual experience. That the benefits of poetic interventions in research have not yet been widely exploited within the field of sex and sexualities, nor in the social sciences at large (Lahman et al., 2011) perhaps provides a timely opportunity to embark upon such an undertaking in our own research endeavours.

References

Attwood, F. and Smith, C. (2013) 'More Sex! Better Sex! Sex Is Fucking Brilliant! Sex, Sex, Sex, SEX' in Blackshaw, T. (ed.) *Handbook of Leisure Studies*, Oxford: Routledge.

Birks, M. and Mills, J. (2011) *Grounded Theory*, London: Sage.

Brady, I. (2000) 'Anthropological Poetics' in Denzin, N. and Lincoln, Y. (eds) *Handbook of Qualitative Research*, 2nd edition, London: Sage.

Cahnmann, M. (2003) 'The Craft, Practice, and Possibility of Poetry in Educational Research', *Educational Researcher*, 32(3), pp. 29–36.

Carr, J.M. (2003) 'Poetic Expressions of Vigilance', *Qualitative Health Research*, 13(9), pp. 1324–1331.

Daniel, E.V. and Peck, J.M. (1996) *Culture/Contexture: Explorations in Anthropology and Literary Studies*, Berkeley, CA: University of California Press.

Denzin, N.K. (1999) 'Two-stepping in the '90s', *Qualitative Inquiry*, 5(4), pp. 568–572.

Denzin, N.K. and Lincoln, Y.S. (2000) *Handbook of Qualitative Research*, 2nd edition, London: Sage.

Duggan, L., Hunter, N.D. and Vance, C.S. (1993) 'False Promises: Feminist Anti-Pornography Legislation', *New York Law School Law Review*, 38, p. 133.

Eisner, E.W. (1997) 'The Promise and Perils of Alternative Forms of Data Representation', *Educational Researcher*, 26(6), pp. 4–10.

Faulkner, S.L. (2009) 'Research/Poetry: Exploring Poet's Conceptualizations of Craft, Practice, and Good and Effective Poetry', *Educational Insights*, 13(3), pp. 1–23.

Fisher, M. (2003) 'Open Mics and Open Minds: Spoken Word Poetry in African Diaspora Participatory Literacy Communities', *Harvard Educational Review*, 73(3), pp. 362–389.

Furman, R. (2006) 'Poetry as Research: Advancing Scholarship and the Development of Poetry Therapy as a Profession', *Journal of Poetry Therapy*, 19(3), pp. 133–145.

Furman, R., Shears, J. and Badinelli, M. (2007) 'Mexican Men and Their Fathers: Analyzing and Representing Data through the Research Poem', *Journal of Poetry Therapy*, 20(3), pp. 141–151.

Geertz, C. (1973) 'Thick Description: Toward an Interpretive Theory of Culture' in *The Interpretation of Cultures: Selected Essays*, New York: Basic Books.

Glaser, B.G. (1992) *Basics of Grounded Theory Analysis: Emergence vs Forcing*. Mill Valley, CA: Sociology Press.

Glaser, B.G. and Strauss, A. (1967) *The Discovery of Grounded Theory*. London: Weidenfeld & Nicolson.

Glesne, C. (1997) 'That Rare Feeling: Re-presenting Research through Poetic Transcription', *Qualitative Inquiry*, 3(2), pp. 202–221.

Gurevitch, Z. (2002) 'Writing Through: The Poetics of Transfiguration', *Cultural Studies ↔ Critical Methodologies*, 2(3), pp. 403–413.

Hallett, F. and Allan, D. (2017) 'Architectures of Oppression: Perceptions of Individuals with Asperger's Syndrome in the Republic of Armenia', *Journal of Research in Special Educational Needs*, 17(2), pp. 123–131.

Hoskins, K. (2015) 'Researching Female Professors: The Difficulties of Representation, Positionality and Power in Feminist Research', *Gender and Education*, 27(4), pp. 393–411.

Laan, E. and Janssen, E. (2007) 'How Do Men and Women Feel? Determinants of Subjective Experience of Sexual Arousal' in Janssen, E. (ed.) *The Psychophysiology of Sex*, Bloomington, IN: Indiana University Press.

Lahman, M.K., Rodriguez, K.L., Richard, V.M., Geist, M.R., Schendel, R.K. and Graglia, P.E. (2011) '(Re) Forming Research Poetry', *Qualitative Inquiry*, 17(9), pp. 887–896.

Leggo, C. (2008) 'Astonishing silence', in Knowles, J. and Cole, A.L. (eds) *Handbook of the Arts in Qualitative Research: Perspectives, Methodologies, Examples, and Issues*, London: Sage.

MacLure, M. (2003) *Discourse in Educational and Social Research*, Maidenhead: Open University.

Madison, D.S. (2003) 'Performance, Personal Narratives, and the Politics of Possibility', in Lincoln, Yvonna and Denzin, Norman, K. (eds) *Turning Points in Qualitative Research. Tying Knots in a Handkerchief*, Walnut Creek, CA: Sage, pp. 469–486.

Maslow, A.H. (1964) *Religions, Values, and Peak-Experiences*. Columbus, OH: Ohio State University Press.

Mowlabocus, S. and Wood, R. (2015) 'Introduction: Audiences and Consumers of Porn', *Porn Studies*, 2(2), pp. 118–122.

Neilsen, L. (2008) 'Lyric Enquiry' in Knowles, J. and Cole, A.L. (eds) *Handbook of the Arts in Qualitative Research: Perspectives, Methodologies, Examples, and Issues*, London: Sage.

Offord, B. and Cantrell, L. (1999) 'Unfixed in a Fixated World: Identity, Sexuality, Race and Culture', *Journal of Homosexuality*, 36(3–4), pp. 207–220.

Pangman, V.C. and Seguire, M. (2000) Sexuality and the Chronically Ill Older Adult: A Social Justice Issue', *Sexuality and Disability*, 18(1), pp. 49–59.

Poindexter, C.C. (2002) 'Research as Poetry: A Couple Experiences HIV', *Qualitative Inquiry*, 8(6), pp. 707–714.

Rath, J. (2012) 'Poetry and Participation: Scripting a Meaningful Research Text with Rape Crisis Workers', *Forum: Qualitative Social Research*, 13(1), art. 22.

Richardson, L. (1994) 'Writing: A Method of Inquiry', in Denzin, N. and Lincoln, Y. (eds) *Handbook of Qualitative Research*, Thousand Oaks, CA: Sage.

Richardson, M. (1998) 'The Poetics of a Resurrection: Re-seeing 30 Years of Change in a Colombian Community and in the Anthropological Enterprise', *American Anthropologist*, 100(1), pp. 11–22.

Schouten, J.W. (1990) 'Drum Song', *Korea Journal*, 30(11), p. 95.

Segal, L. (1993) 'False Promises: Anti-Pornography Feminism', *Socialist Register*, 29, pp. 92–105.

Sherry, J.F. and Schouten, J.W. (2002) 'A Role for Poetry in Consumer Research', *Journal of Consumer Research*, 29(2), pp. 218–234.

Stern, B.B. (1998) 'Poetry and Representation in Consumer Research: The Art of Science' in Stern, B. (ed.) *Representing Consumers: Voices, Views, and Visions*, London: Routledge.

Stoller, P. (1997) *Sensuous Scholarship*, Philadelphia, PA: University of Pennsylvania Press.

Strauss, A. and Corbin, J. (1994) 'Grounded Theory Methodology' in Denzin, N. and Lincoln, Y. (eds) *Handbook of Qualitative Research*, Thousand Oaks, CA: Sage.

Wallendorf, M. and Brucks, M. (1993) 'Introspection in Consumer Research: Implementation and Implications', *Journal of Consumer Research*, 20(3), pp. 339–359.

Williams, L. (1991) 'Film Bodies: Gender, Genre, and Excess', *Film Quarterly*, 44(4), pp. 2–13.

Witkin, S.L. (2007) 'Relational Poetry Expressing Interweaving Realities', *Qualitative Social Work*, 6(4), pp. 477–481.

Zinkhan, G.M. (1994) 'From the Editor: Poetry in Advertising', *Journal of Advertising*, 23(4), pp. 3–7.

8 | THE COVER VERSION: RESEARCHING SEXUALITY THROUGH VENTRILOQUISM

E. McGeeney, L. Robinson, R. Thomson and P. Thurschwell

Abstract

In this chapter we propose 'ventriloquism' as a practice with potential to create new knowledge, and in this sense as a mode of research. Our definition of ventriloquism is broad and encompasses the practice of re-voicing of verbatim interview material and singing cover versions of songs. What is common to both practices is that they combine a sense of comfort and safety (working with a script) while also offering the potential for something new to happen, both on the part of the performer who may gain new insights by occupying another's words and subject position but also on the part of the audiences who witness these performances. Our experiments in ventriloquism arise from two projects explicitly concerned with knowledge exchange in the area of sexuality research, and our insights are contextualised by the theoretical and methodological landscape of sexualities studies. Our collaborative research draws on interdisciplinary understanding from sociology and history conducted along the boundaries of research and youth work practice. We conclude with reflections on how ventriloquism might be explored as a productive practice for both.

> Covers do a lot of different things: they imitate, they critique, they ironize, they render homage, they acknowledge debts, they revel in the power or beauty of a prior song. Every single instance of a cover is mobile and crosses boundaries of some

sort: genders, genres, races, decades, eras, cultures, continents. Covers are particularly good for summoning up not just the original songs on which they are modeled but moments associated with it: a summer of love, a winter of discontent, a time when there was a riot was going on. Covers make and re-make history. (Ian Balfour, 2014)

In this chapter we propose 'ventriloquism' as a practice with potential to create new knowledge, and in this sense as a mode of research. Our definition of ventriloquism is broad and encompasses the practice of re-voicing of verbatim interview material, singing cover versions of songs and engaging in different forms of 'karaoke'. What is common to these practices is that they combine a sense of comfort and safety (working with a script) while also offering the potential for something new to happen, both on the part of the performer who may gain new insights by occupying another's words and subject position but also on the part of the audiences who witness these performances. Our experiments in ventriloquism arise from two projects explicitly concerned with knowledge exchange in the area of sexuality research, and our insights are contextualised by the theoretical and methodological landscape of sexualities studies. Our collaborative research draws on interdisciplinary understandings from sociology, performance studies and history conducted along the boundaries of research and youth work practice. We conclude with reflections on how ventriloquism might be explored as a productive practice for both.

Two projects one solution

The two projects that we draw on here were both conceptualised in terms of knowledge exchange between academic and practice communities. The first, the Good Sex project,[1] was a collaboration with the UK young people's sexual health organisation Brook which sought to find ways to turn the findings of a doctoral research project into sexual health learning materials.

The doctoral research project (McGeeney, 2013) had involved in-depth interviews with young people exploring sexual experiences including the meanings of 'good' and 'bad' sex. These recorded testimonies proved to be powerful and ethically challenging documents – portraying sex that might be non-consensual and underage as well as joyful, experimental or plain mundane. 'Showing' and 'sharing' these stories was complicated both by promises to participants concerning confidentiality and limits to the use of audio recordings and by organisational anxieties on the part of Brook about showcasing examples of underage sex. However, experiments with peer educators and young actors revealed the value of using drama techniques to re-animate the testimonies and to document these performances (McGeeney, 2017).

The second project was called Sounds of Sexology[2] and involved working alongside a group of young women and music practitioners over a ten-week period, with the aim of producing a public performance and engaging young women in sexuality research as part of a public engagement project. The original plan for this collaboration was that the young women would be introduced to academic research methods and encouraged to undertake original sexuality research, which in turn would feed back into a song-writing initiative. In practice the young women wanted simply to sing, and the researchers settled into a more ethnographic practice of 'being there', reflecting on how their singing might be understood as a research practice in its own right. The young women's interest in singing cover versions marked a decisive analytic moment for the research team. In this chapter we take examples from each of these projects as starting points for thinking about how and why ventriloquism and its associated practices might give rise to new insights and critical reflective space. Before going on to share these examples we consider the conceptual resources that are informing our discussion, drawing on scholarship from a range of disciplines.

Conceptual resources: performance, mimesis, ventriloquism and karaoke

The starting point for thinking about sexuality and performance must be Judith Butler's work on gender and performativity (Butler, 1990), which, by employing a dramatic metaphor, undermines claims to nature and normality for practices that are simply repeated and sedimented. If sex/gender is an act then it is an act that can be parodied, and Butler's interest in drag points to the ways in which performances of sex/gender are not only recognised but regularly undermined in queer subcultures. The performance of gender in the mainstream has also long been the focus of feminist intervention, informed by ideas of front and backstage in symbolic interactionism (Goffman, 1959) and by insights into the artifice and compensations of femininity captured by Simone de Beauvoir's assertion that one becomes a woman rather than being born that way. In 1929 British psychoanalyst Joan Riviere introduced the idea of womanliness as 'masquerade' – a cover that deflects attention from what she terms 'female masculinity' and what we might think of as forms of power that do not fit with a feminine identity. This is an idea developed in 1980s British feminism by Valerie Walkerdine (1989) who writes about femininity as a performance that results in the uncanny experience where women experience their power 'as if' belonging to someone else.

Queer studies have expanded notions of performativity as a critical practice. For example Elizabeth Freeman coins the phrase 'temporal drag' to expose the importance of the passage of time between performances as well as the productive incongruities that make space between the embodied actor and speaking subject – 'suturing two times but leaving both times visible as such' (Freeman, 2010, p. 69). For Freeman, re-enactment, re-voicing and 'covering' feminist texts from the past provides a site for conversation between generations of feminists as well as creating critical spaces that unsettle notions of what was, what is and what should be. There are resonances here with ideas of mimesis, which emerge from the discipline of anthropology and which have been used to understand ritualised actions and performances as sites for the contestation and reworking of meaning. So for example in *Mimesis and Alterity* Michael Taussig (1993) suggests that through ritualised practices we try both to adopt and to assimilate another's nature or culture while also distancing ourselves from it. These ideas all point toward the centrality of repetition and performance to the construction of gender and sexuality, as well as to the ways in which such sedimented practices might be contested.

Engaging with ventriloquism and the cover version, through critical and feminist practice, indicates the uses to which 'throwing voices' can be put. The idea of ventriloquism has been a cornerstone of media studies, explored through the flexible relationship between sound and image associated with film, and the potential of electronic devices to amplify, distort and transmit the human voice.[3] Certainly each new wave of media technology presents new possibilities for the production of dissonances between voices, bodies and objects.[4] The 'throwing of the voice' involved in different forms of ventriloquism raises questions about identity, ownership and accountability. We are not sure whose word this is. This opacity can be thought of a kind of 'cover', as something that allows us to show ourselves in a way that does not make us overly vulnerable to rejection or being 'known' in too direct a way.

British artist Gillian Wearing has operationalised these ideas exhaustively in her video work using *Signs that say what you want to say and not Signs that say what someone else wants you to say* (1992), transposing the words of children into the mouths of adults and vice versa (*2 in 1* and *10–16*, 1997); and using masks to facilitate confession through the occupation of other times and identities (*Confess all on video: don't worry you will be in disguise*, 1994; *Family series*, 2003). These kinds of artistic techniques have been taken up in advertising and popular production practices including the use of animation to mask the voices of vulnerable people in an ethical way by charities and researchers.[5] Popular television programmes such as *The X Factor* and *The Voice* showcase this opacity as contestants are tasked with singing a new 'cover' each week and 'making it their own'. Contestants and their mentors are taken to task if their song choices are unfamiliar to the programme audience, whilst also being criticised if the contestant fails to use the 'cover' to express their individuality and unique sound.

Sound studies scholars Sarah Kessler and Karen Tongson (2014) have explored the relationship between the terms ventriloquism and karaoke as 'sound technologies and technologies of power' with the potential to be 'transformed into critical, intellectual, and affective methodologies' (2014). While the term 'karaoke' is used to denote a lack of originality, notions of ventriloquism are imbued with a sense of the 'sinister', suggesting that 'one individual acts as the communications medium ... which originate with someone else' (Kessler and Tongson, 2014). This wariness is echoed by sociologist Nirmal Purwar who warns against a 'violating ventriloquism', which consists of speaking for others and leaving them lost for words (Purwar, 2006, cited in Back, 2009). Technologies can be used to colonise and assimilate the words and value of research participants and a cut and paste media affords both opportunities and dangers for academics. In the advent of 'live sociology' (Purwar and Back, 2012) and 'digital history' (Hitchcock and Shoemaker, 2015) we find digital methods transcending the temporal and spatial gaps that once shaped research projects – turning the past into the present, voices into data and data into reports and papers. Archives and voices may just be a click away (Eichhorn, 2013) allowing a new and iterative relationship between 'collecting', 'sharing' and 're-using' material. Importantly, the researcher needs to be understood as part of the culture that she researches, intra-acting (Barad, 1997; Davies, 2014) with the phenomena in which they are interested; inciting, catalysing, perhaps interrupting or distracting processes of meaning making. Sarah Kessler encourages us to think about ventriloquism as inciting *bifurca-*

tion, the notion of being inside and beside ourselves, a condition that makes us all researchers:

> A ventriloquist has to exist in both the future and the past to make her practice work. She has to anticipate what's going to be said next while remembering what's just been said, and she has to keep her lips still while moving her tongue – acts that circumvent linearity and synchronization. In saying this I'm not arguing for ventriloquism as a "resistant cultural practice"; rather, I'm simply pointing out the temporal perversion to which the art lends itself. (Kessler and Tongson, 2014)

Different and complex histories of value accrue to ventriloquism, karaoke and the cover version; all three are cultural forms implicated in relations of power but also to hopes for the future. The expansive definition of ventriloquism used in this chapter encompasses the practices of voicing others' words, and singing others' songs. It is brought to life by the participants in the two projects profiled below, revealing the ways in which theories of performance are never just theories. The differences in the valences of these practices – ventriloquism, the cover, karaoke – might help us think through what happens when teenage girls, and adult researchers, find themselves speaking or singing in different tongues, using words that are not their own, but which they make their own.

In drawing this section to a close we suggest that these ideas have the potential to push us into new ways of thinking and talking about sexual cultures. Traditionally feminist and sexuality researchers have conceptualised their task as making the personal visible (or audible) as a strategy for making it political, gaining glimpses into hidden private worlds through the 'stories' that we invite people to tell us in research projects. But what if we think of sexual cultures and practices as always already thoroughly mediated? By researching sexuality we are *making* sexualities in a particular and very public way. Ventriloquism is both a tool for doing this, and also an idea that gives insight into digitalised, mediatised sexualities. Similarly the cover can simultaneously keep things private (be, in fact, a cover story), and make things visible or audible (sing it loud!). These are ideas and possibilities that we return to through the examples explored below.

Revealing moments within a process

During the period when we were working on these two projects we collaborated on a number of blogs through which we documented and reflected on our practice. The following three examples are taken from blog posts written by us over a nine-month period between July 2014 and April 2015. The blog posts were an active form of 'documentation' (Prior, 2008), forging a space between field notes and publication that allowed us to share emergent lines of interpretation with our community of interpretation, which includes participants (Davies and Gannon, 2006). They are presented here in edited form with links to the original documents from which they are taken. They capture an embedded 'then', a register that is more personal, closer to the field and distinct from our collective, analytic and abstract 'now' voice that top and tail the chapter.

Experiments in re-animating data, by Ester McGeeney, July 2014[6] At the first session we looked at an extract from an interview with a 19-year-old young women called 'Kat'. In the extract Kat describes her first sexual experiences with her first boyfriend and reflects on how their relationship developed over time. She describes her boyfriend as 'controlling' and states that she enjoyed the 'rough' sex that they had together. Later in the extract Kat goes on to talk about her subsequent sexual partners – her second boyfriend who just 'popped it in' one day when she was lying in bed with him and her current boyfriend – a 'good boyfriend' who is 'not that good' in bed …

As homework, we asked the group to go away from the first session and collect photos that they thought visualised the extract I had read out. The following week two young women [Megan and Elesha] brought along a series of images both of which captured the unsettling interplay between pleasure and pain that is inherent in Kat's narrative.

Running in parallel to this participatory film-making group I had been in contact with an East London young acting company [and] asked if any of the volunteer actors would be able to come into the office, stick their heads in our makeshift sound booth and record a few takes of 'Kat's story' ...

My plan was to take the audio recordings from my two volunteers ... back to the group and play around with using them alongside the images that the group were collecting and visualising. I could imagine their voice telling Kat's story as the images of twisted hands and bedsheets, captured as part of the groups homework, appeared on the screen. Or I hoped that the audio recordings might generate new ideas about new photos to take or footage to collect. The group, however, had different ideas. They wanted a young person speaking to camera. Less fussy. More powerful. [Film-maker and collaborator] Susi Arnott encouraged us to focus on what exactly would appear in the frame – did we want the whole body? Just the face? Any close ups?

Here was our list: Head and shoulders. Head. Mouth. Eyes. Hands. Struggling hands. A response to the extract.

The following week we met at Susi's studio. Megan agreed to be our camerawoman and Carlos our actor. Tirelessly he performed extracts from Kat's story to camera as Megan experimented with different frames; Carlos's head and shoulders, his face, mouth, eyes and hands. We also played with the ideas that Megan and Elesha had captured in their photos and filmed two sets of hands untwined to convey moments of pleasure, tenderness, force and pain.

From the outset we had also been interested in finding a way of capturing on camera not just the young person's story, but different responses to the story. Opening up a critical space that suggests there is more than one interpretation of this story. This had been Megan's idea and on our first week of filming she had brought along her response to Kat. Not wanting to appear on camera Megan read out her response as Carlos pointed the camera at her hands, holding the piece of paper.

When we watched the footage back the following week the group were critical. They felt Carlos's performance was too depressing – conveying a level of trauma and distress that they had not experienced when they first heard, or re-read the extracts. I was secretly pleased. I remembered the original interview with the 19-year-old young woman and she had not seemed sad or traumatised. She told her story with energy, anger and vigour as if it was in the telling that she realised the injustice of her experience and the way in which she had been compromised in her previous relationships with her partner. This was not a young woman who saw herself as a victim however, or one that lacked burning sexual desire.

That was my interpretation anyway. My memory of the young women I had met four years previously and my ongoing analysis of her interview transcript, which I had now read – selectively – endless times.

The group were excited about the way that the shots looked: they loved the black backdrop, the close ups on the eyes, the hands and the full body shots. They wanted to do more but they were tired of Kat's story – unhappy about the way it had been voiced and wanting to have a go at filming other young people's stories.

Full and empty handed by Rachel Thomson, 8 December 2014[7]   In the second half of the workshop we got down to work. One group were developing the original 'Wild and Tamed' song that had emerged from working with Ester's 'Good Sex' data. The other group wanted to concentrate on singing. The issue of covering other people's songs vs creating a song came up as a discussion point. Some members of the group were only interested in singing covers, while others were engaged with the task of making music and lyrics from scratch. The Wellcome Trust, who are funding this project, only want new songs and this is a sticking point for some of the girls. Moving between the language of the musician and the researcher we talked a bit about places in-between the 'raw' of song-writing and the 'cooked' of covers. We could think about 'sampling' as a strategy for taking from the past or present and making the material our own by putting it together in new ways. We also talked about writing new words to old songs and got excited by the idea of rewriting 'Jolene' from the perspective of an old woman after Ester's account of Dolly Parton's Glastonbury performance where she joked with the audience how in retrospect maybe Jolene should have taken her man after all.

After the break the 'Wild and Tamed' group worked to build a melody for their embryonic song. A combination of improvisation and experiment enabled different members of the group to make their mark on the song and to build a richer sound. After a while I went downstairs to check out the 'singing group' finding R and C with musician Zoe in a cavernous dance studio with great acoustics and plenty of background noise from what sounded like an indoors football match next door. The group were sitting with a laptop, guitar, sheets of lyrics and mobile phones. It took me a while to understand the method, which involves calling up backing tracks and lyrics on YouTube, working out the chords and strumming along. We started together with 'Jolene' – once on our own with Zoe's guitar and once with Dolly and her band, which made us all feel like amateurs. The girls remarked how great the room was because the background sound made it easier to sing without being too self-conscious. After lots of fussing and texting we got onto solos and C began with a rendition of 'Keep Your Head Up' by Ben Howard. The girl has an awesome voice! Even the five-a-side football went quiet as we all listened. I realised that singing covers is an entirely different game to songwriting. Then we listened to Ben Howard doing the original on YouTube and I recognised how distinctive C's cover was. One of his lyrics described looking for happiness between 'the sheets', and I thought how this captures the place of sexuality as part of a wider canvas of longing, desire and emotion. The song describes the physical pleasure of experiencing nature's force (the wind, the sun, the tides' pull) and comparing it to erotic pleasure. Howard has a moment of realisation; physical pleasure, regardless of whether it is erotic or elemental, is a form of self-actualisation. In the end the search for pleasure is a search for self-recognition.

We agreed that it was a beautiful lyric. It is, however, not a lyric that we can reproduce here. The irony of the project being that whilst the girls we worked with were able to make complex negotiations of identification and ownership, we are not. We were unable to gain appropriate permissions to reproduce the lyrical content for this publication, hence the only lyrics we can actually include will be those of the girls themselves, the rest are paraphrased.

R is nervous about singing a solo, saying how she will sound crap in contrast to C, who then has another go, this time giving her rendition of 'Electric Feel' a much more sexy and upbeat number. It is much less lyrical, a series of sexual invitations to an unnamed girl in praise of her 'electric feel'. Just when it seems too late R gets brave and sings Ella Henderson's 'Yours'. It is exquisite and heart-felt. She knows the words without the lyric sheet. We listen with reverence as her voice and feeling fills the room. It is only later that I discover this is the first time she has sung solo. A big moment for her and the group.

Again the lyrics seemed to fit perfectly in our exploration of what it means to talk or sing about sex or desire. The power of waking up with someone you love next to you gives you power to speak. Whereas the song's narrator used to find it difficult to speak, love/sex 'untame[d]' her mouth. The group reworked her song to make it their own. They took the connection between Henderson finding her voice and the group finding theirs and ran with it. They wrote a song about what it feels like to be made to write a song.

> I'll wear my winter coat, the one I love to wear
> So I keep feeling safe to what's beyond compare
> The moments waking up, feel tense, my stomach churns
> Let's shout and scream and shout
> Just wanna let it out

So what have I learned this week about sex and social change? Well, I am aware that some things don't change. That young people are fragile and that our hopes and dreams are made in private and built in interaction. Sometimes the only power young people have is the power to say no. Audiences are important and can be very small and ephemeral. Other people's music gives us a scaffolding to express ourselves in more or less safe ways. We make ourselves vulnerable in performance yet this itself is a route to recognition and community. Starting from scratch is a big ask, and there are lots of ways in which creativity can emerge from the re-use and re-animation of existing material. This is true of the research process as well as the process of being in a media saturated culture characterised by proximity to a vast digital archive. And sexuality – it's always there, sometimes in the foreground, more often in the background – all mixed up with love, hope, loneliness and desire. I hope that I was able to bring something to the party, even as an audience of one: eager to hear, witness, document and share the ephemeral work of the project. Making the private a bit more public in a safe and honest way. That for me is the essence of research.

How many historians does it take to start a cover band? By Lucy Robinson, April 2015[8] We came to realise that our assumptions about what constituted research, and what constituted song-writing both privileged a certain sort of production. The young people we worked with were very clear that they didn't want to be either sexologists or songwriters. But they wanted a space to go to and this was a way of getting it funded. Girls are really good at getting what they wanted out of an agenda that isn't really set up for them. After all, if they didn't they'd never get anything at all. What they wanted was to not write songs about sexology. What they wanted was to sing and arrange cover songs of the songs that they already loved. Although we had been tasked with writing 'original' music, it didn't seem appropriate to make the young women become songwriters when they didn't want to be. And it was not clear how enforcing our agenda would fit with our wider responsibility to facilitate a sense of ownership of the project and enable the young women's self-expression. When two slightly different points came together the problem shifted out of the way. Firstly, we could read cover versions as a creative active engagement rather than a lack of creativity; secondly, we could read historical research as much closer to a cover version than it is to singer songwriting. We weren't training the young women to be researchers – rather they were training us in their modes of re-enactment; an active and creative intervention in a cultural circuit – one that brought together the legitimacy of publically celebrated singer-songwriters, with their own experiences and voices ...

In the media-literate group of young women in the songwriting project, it wasn't surprising therefore that the act of choosing what song they would cover was in itself an active process. It was also a process that ended up fulfilling both sets of practitioners' expectations: it helped cohere the group and allow the project members to situate themselves within that group as individuals. The discussions around finding a song that spoke to everyone, or that everyone knew, involved developing a shared musical language. Being the person who had their song chosen, or insisted that they would only sing their own song choice, positioned individuals in the group. Having your choice of cover chosen by the rest of the group had a status of its own. Just as fans are not passive consumers – they are a collective of emotional producers

– cover versions are not poor facsimiles: they are a collective production.

In other words, the participation in this project was less focused on the participation in the production of a song, and at least as much focused on participation in, and negotiation of, a collective experience ... The choice to cover rather than write songs makes sense of the cultural world that they inhabit. They demonstrated agency in the covers that they chose and how they sung themselves into the established songs. Their imagined communities were far bigger than those of us in the room. They were working *with*, not *on*, Beyoncé, Adele, Lily Allen, Ella Henderson and Amy Winehouse. One of the songs that they performed at the Roundhouse shows just how they did it. They took the song 'Yours' by Ella Henderson, tweaked it a bit and used it to map their journey through the project itself. They called it 'I'm Adored' and described it as a 'love song to themselves'.[9]

These young people were not worried about the inauthenticity of the cover version. The cover band is bigger business than ever. The karaoke machine and the dance mat provide regular opportunities to put yourself in the original artist's place. Computer games like Sing Star combine karaoke with role play of the journey from starlet to stardom. Singers get their break at audition by singing someone else's songs, chosen from a list of pre-agreed choices. The line between the competitor, the original artist and the star-maker behind them blurs all the time. It gets pretty hard to work out who has won, or failed.

So what is the difference between historical analysis and a 'cover'? The lesson of the Sounds of Sexology songwriting project for me was to put my historical methods into practice. Just because something isn't unique, or new doesn't mean it doesn't matter. Authenticity, originality, is a value judgement. Historical meaning isn't produced in the genesis moment of production alone, but in the dissemination, consumption and memory of a cultural artefact. Singing someone else's songs, like re-using someone else's interviews, is therefore a way of having a conversation with the past that keeps track of how it has been valued and maintained over time. I have no problem re-analysing someone else's sources, so why shouldn't they want to sing someone else's song? In fact, let's go one step further, and take up their lead, exploring re-enactment, collectively but in our own voices.

Getting under the covers: lessons for sexuality research and activism

The impact agenda[10] and focus on knowledge exchange within the academic community could go two ways: making us anxious and instrumental about the communities that have a role and investment in academic work (and the ways that they may represent value in a new way), or intrigued by the invitation to think critically about the boundaries of research in contemporary culture and the role of the university and the academic in inciting research practices. Both projects documented in this chapter are responses to the invitation to think critically about the synergistic relationship between research and practice as critical and creative modes of enquiry. Here we 'cover' our own research documents, re-using our voices and records to reveal the knowledge creation practices that are part and parcel of our research practice and of the everyday.

The projects are *interdisciplinary* – involving conversations between sociologists, historians and literary scholars – and *inter-professional*, involving collaboration between researchers and practitioners of different kinds (youth workers, musicians, educators). Working across the social sciences / humanities divide has enriched our vocabularies and methodologies, providing us with new places to stand and think from. Working across the academic/practice divide multiplies the audiences and agendas with whom we communicate, again in productive ways.

We can think of these projects as examples of action-research in that the action of the project constitutes a mode of enquiry and as practised researchers we were able and interested to experiment and reflect on our practice with and through others. Interestingly both projects lead us into practices of mediation as a mode of critical enquiry. In the Good Sex project this involved engaging with the experiences of others through the re-animation of audio recordings and the representation of meaning through visual means. In the Sounds of Sexology songwriting project this involved the researchers tuning into the different ways in which meaning was being made and the particular affordances offered by working with existing cultural artefacts and making them our own. Neither project ended up creating new material from scratch; even the 'original' song created and performed by the Sounds of Sexology group was written by re-using and reanimating quotes from research materials about 'good sex'.

The examples that we have shared in this paper suggest that ideas of performance, ventriloquism, mimesis, karaoke are not simply good ways of thinking about sex/gender but that they provide us with a route into the phenomenology of a range of creative practices that includes informal education, academic research and arts practice. It may no longer be such a breath-taking revelation that identities might be 'performed', yet there is still value in thinking about how the space and the opacity offered by the tools of artifice that are available to the performer may be utilised to enable the emergence of new thoughts, feelings and connections between us. Becoming 'other' and incorporating parts of others within us through referencing, homage and imitation are accessible and pleasurable practices. Our use of such practices places us firmly within a wider popular culture and Zeitgeist characterised by an expanded intimacy that is simultaneously digitalised, democratised and extrovert yet enduringly self-effacing. It may be that an ideal of individual ownership, whether of our sexual identities, or our popular culture and research practices, is in the process of changing in ways we as researchers both respond to and enact.

It is possible that these participatory methodologies are the ideal method for researching teenage sexualities in a culture that is media saturated and where sexuality is highly mediated. Every era has its own 'methods' be that the psychoanalysts' couch of the nineteenth century, feminist testimonies of the 1970s and 1980s or the graphs, checklists and films of Masters and Johnson in the 1950s and 1960s. The young people we worked with gave us the cover version as a method for getting up close and personal – a way of having intimacy without too much vulnerability or visibility. A great lesson for sexuality research and activism.

In conclusion, this chapter offers an account of how the university and its scholars might play a meaningful role within a wider culture and polity in an age of digital saturation and shrinking public spaces. When we work with outside communities, partners and publics, we can move beyond the metrics. We can work reflexively with the processes and negotiations our collaborators have to make to get what they need out of us. We have provided an exemplar of interdisciplinary academic collaboration – bringing together scholars of the humanities and social sciences – as well as inter-professional knowledge exchange – working across the boundaries of research, youth work and the creative arts. It demonstrates that impact and knowledge exchange projects, if done well, demand critical and creative thinking and have the potential for conceptual and methodological discovery while also creating vital spaces for collective and personal development.

Notes

1. The Good Sex project was a knowledge exchange initiative undertaken at the University of Sussex between June 2013 and 2014 funded by the ESRC to identify and share the learning from Ester McGeeney's PhD project co-funded by the Open University and Brook. A report on the project can be found at www.researchcatalogue. esrc.ac.uk/grants/ES.K005421.1/ read.

2. This public engagement project was funded by the Wellcome Trust during 2015 as part of its Sexology season which focused on the history of sex research. Our public engagement project was one of a number of regional collaborations. The Brighton team involved the University of Sussex (Rachel Thomson, Lucy Robinson, Pam Thurschwell and Ester McGeeney), the Brighton Youth Centre and a community

music organisation called Rythmix. See https://wellcomecollection. org/whats/sounds-sexology.

3. https://lucian.uchicago. edu/blogs/mediatheory/keywords/ ventriloquism/.

4. See for example Real-time face capture and re-enactment that can transpose facial expressions from a source actor to a target face using video. www.graphics.stanford.edu/ ~niessner/thies2016face.html.

5. For example the use of animation by RELATE to showcase the value and nature of their sensitive work in couples counselling. www.bbc. co.uk/news/health-13317604.

6. https://goodsexproject.

wordpress.com/2014/07/11/kats-story-experiments-in-reanimating-data/.

7. https://goodsexproject. wordpress.com/2014/12/08/full-and-empty-handed/.

8. https://goodsexproject. wordpress.com/2015/04/01/how-many-historians-does-it-take-to-start-a-cover-band/.

9. Listen and watch at www. youtube.com/watch?v=3JzLKlhDG_s.

10. UK academic research is subject to periodic audit by the Higher Education Funding Council and since 2014 this has included a focus on the non-academic impact of the research. See www.hefce. ac.uk/rsrch/REFimpact/.

References

Back, L. (2009) 'Global Attentiveness and the Sociological Ear', *Sociological Research Online* 14(4), 14.

Balfour, I. (2014) 'Critical Karaoke: We Drop the Mic Right', *Journal of Popular Music Studies*. Available at http://popmusicstudies.org/ck/?p=7 (accessed 2 January 2017).

Barad, Karen (1997) 'Meeting the Universe Halfway: Realism and Social Constructivism without Contradiction', in Nelson, L.H. and Nelson, J. (eds) *Feminism, Science, and the Philosophy of Science*, Dordrecht and Boston, MA: Kluwer, pp. 161–194.

Butler, Judith (1990) *Gender Trouble: Feminism and the Subversion of Identity*, London: Routledge.

Davies, B. (2014) *Listening to Children: Being and Becoming*, London: Routledge.

Davies, B. and Gannon, S. (2006) *Doing Collective Biography*, Maidenhead: Open University Press.

Eichhorn, K. (2013) *The Archival Turn in Feminism: Outrage in Order*, Philadelphia, PA: Temple University Press, 2013.

Freeman, E. (2010) *Time Binds: Queer Temporalities, Queer Histories*, Durham, NC: Duke University Press.

Goffman, E. (1959) *Presentation of Self in Everyday Life*, London: Penguin.

Hitchcock, Tim and Shoemaker, Robert (2015) 'Making History Online', *Transactions of the Royal Historical Society*, 25, pp. 75–93.

Kessler, S. and Tongson, K. (2014) 'Karaoke and Ventriloquism: Echoes and Divergences', *Sounding Out!*, May 2014. Available at

https://soundstudiesblog.
com/2014/05/12/karaoke-and-
ventriloquism-echoes-and-
divergences/.

McGeeney, E. (2013) *What Is 'Good
Sex'?: Young People, Sexual
Pleasure and Sexual Health
Services*. DPhil, The Open
University. Available at https://
goodsexproject.files.wordpress.
com/2014/03/ester-mcgeeney-
theses-with-ammendments.pdf.

McGeeney, E. (2017) 'Possibilities for
Pleasure: A Creative Approach to
Including Pleasure in Sexuality
Education' in Allen, L. and
Rasmussen, M.L. (eds) *The
Palgrave Handbook for Sexuality
Education*, New York: Palgrave
Macmillan, pp. 571–589.

Prior, L. (2008) 'Repositioning
Documents in Social Research',
Sociology, 42(5), pp. 821–836.

Purwar, N. and Back, L. (2012) 'A
Manifesto for Live Methods:
Provocations and Capacities',
Sociological Review, 60(1),
pp. 6–17.

Riviere, J. (1929) 'Womanliness as a
Masquerade', *International Journal
of Psychoanalysis*, 10, pp. 303–313.
Reprinted in *Hurly-Burly*, 3 (2010),
pp. 75–84.

Taussig, M. (1993) *Mimesis and Alterity:
A Particular History of the Sense*,
London: Routledge.

Walkerdine, V. (1989) 'Femininity as
Performance', *Oxford Review of
Education*, 15(3), pp. 267–279.

PART THREE

NEGOTIATING RESEARCH CONTEXTS

INTRODUCTION

Yingying Huang

A review of sex and sexuality research indicates its methodological shifts from psychoanalysis, invented by Freud and his followers since the early 1900s, to laboratory observations on human beings' sexual responses such as Masters and Johnson's research in the 1960s and large-scale survey investigations on sexual behaviours and relationships pioneered by Kinsey in the 1940s–1950s, moving towards more diverse and comprehensive methods on people's sexual practices, identities and meanings, with the emergence of the social constructivism paradigm since the late 1970s (Gagnon and Parker, 1995; Vance, 1991). Along this journey from 'sexology' to 'sexuality', methodological foci have moved from psychiatry and biologically centred to relational and contextual, and more importantly, toward a lived desiring body in everydayness that goes beyond the constraints of a dualistic ideological framework (Lock and Farquhar, 2009).

Dating back to the 1920s, anthropologists such as Malinowski and Margaret Mead have contributed their work to enriching knowledge about sexualities in terms of documenting diverse sexual behaviours and practices in cross-cultural settings, acknowledged in the history of sexuality research (Gagnon and Parker, 1995). Ethnography since the 1980s has further brought in the researcher's subjective body to the field, and critically examined the myth of 'scientific' observation claimed in the earlier phase. It thus reached a new wave of unpacking the research process, examining and reflecting on the researcher's social position, bodily and emotional presence in the field and the politics involved in data collection and cultural writing, especially in cross-cultural contexts (Clifford and Marcus, 1986).

Although in comparison with other topics, less literature has cast an eye on sexualities, sexuality researchers are sensitive to methodological thinking with respect to our own gender, sexual body, desire and emotion while we are trying to explore those of others (e.g. Cesara, 1982; Newton, 1993). The embodied thinking and reflections on the position of our own sexuality and gender are even more urgently and profoundly experienced because of the topic we are trying to explore. Moreover, as our subjects are often sexually marginalised groups or social groups somehow marginalised because of complex intersections of sexuality, gender, age, class, ethnicity and poverty, we tend to be more easily aware of ethical confusions and ambiguities in everyday life and sometimes frustrations when we try to enter the field and situate ourselves within the local context, physically, psychologically and culturally.

Although cross-cultural ethnography has been questioned and challenged for its tendency to be 'ideal' or poetic in uncovering its political agenda (Clifford and Marcus, 1986), the work of Shostak (1982) about Nisa in *The Life and Words of a !Kung Woman* – on her personal stories from giving birth, childhood sexual games to multiple husbands and lover, and her return to Nisa many years later while suffering from breast cancer – revealed that doing research in another culture, about another woman's body, sexuality and everydayness is a way of knowing about our own society and ourselves. 'Who am I?' is equally important as, if not even more important than 'who are they?' We are not only trying to be insiders, experience being close to our participants who are living in different cultural and political contexts in order to learn and better understand their erotic body (Gagnon and Parker, 1995), but also being aware of the existence and (re)production of our own sexualities in fields which are strange to us, and the dynamic inter-subjectivity between us and our subjects in the process of sexual knowledge production.

With the progress of reflective anthropology and social-historical constructivism approaches, a politics of sexuality is emerging within research. Sexuality researchers are increasingly aware that the power relationships and politics of doing research among people from different cultures, especially those labelled as subalterns or less developed, and positioned in a different layer of sexual hierarchy (Rubin, 1984), has engendered obstacles in sharing languages and experiences, interpreting sexual meanings and the practising logic of one's lived sexual body in everydayness. Through critical reflections on dominant Western (the centralism of Europe and America) discourses (Said, 1978) and the heterosexual hegemony in knowledge production, methodological attention has been specifically paid to local knowledge and situated bodies and gender and sexualities in a global context (Haraway, 1988; Parker and Easton, 1998; Rofel, 1999; Sang, 2014).

As with the history of research methodology in general, I myself as a female sociologist – a discipline which still largely relies on Western theories – who is doing research on female sex work (illegal and immoral) and sexualities among women living with HIV/AIDS (who are expected to be asexual) in the Chinese context, have also gone through my own methodological shifts and gradually made local knowledge and situated thinking, as well as researcher's subjective bodily presence in the fieldwork some of my key words (Pan et al., 2011). As with the authors who contribute to this section and the whole book, questions such as 'Is my research work ethical?' and the relationship between ethical thinking and the quality of research often emerge from my fieldwork. While doing sexuality research in various contexts, especially those contexts and experiences which are far from ours, it is urgent to call for more constructive and detailed discussions on the importance and different layers of cultural translations, including but far beyond language (Parker, 1999; Clifford and Marcus, 1986). And there is nowhere to hide my own desire, body and sexualities, and also those social and sexual values which have been embedded deep within and sometimes constrained my mindful body in fieldwork (Huang, 2017).

As sexuality researchers, when we enter into a field located far from our own, learning about a language that is strange to ours, observing bodily performances with which we are not familiar, interpreting meanings of the behaviours and identities of different sexual subjects, questions as such arise: How can we understand people's sexual bodies located in a different culture, experiencing different lives and expressed in different words? What kinds of cultural translation should we do while doing sexuality research in a different setting and among different groups? And How? Where are our sexual bodies located or produced while dialoguing with our subjects, and negotiating with people from different disciplines and with different social and sexual positions – our potential readers, publishers, who we believe share the same culture with us? What is that nuanced and embodied thinking in one's fieldwork that is full of thrill, struggle and embarrassment? These are also the questions raised and addressed by the four chapters collected in this section, from different angles and through different sexual story-telling, situated in various cultural and sexual contexts.

Among these four pieces, Johnson focuses on contexts negotiated in interdisciplinary research, occasioned through a 'youth-led' sexual and reproductive programme carried out for the International Planned Parenthood Federation (IPPF) in Benin, Kenya, Nepal and Nicaragua. Johnson firstly highlights the importance of and strategies involved in linking young people to their context in order to be youth centred and youth led. She then further explores three key issues discussed as ownership and the extent of participation of young peer educators in the research, ethics and how globally agreed protocols were rolled out in the youth-led research, and flexibility and creativity in methods versus comparability across cultural contexts. As a global programme, the negotiations of social and sexuality contexts at various levels are in evidence, including collaboration across academia and practitioner worlds, communicating to decision-makers and practitioners at all levels throughout the research, and how youth centredness is being applied across international organisations such as IPPF.

In the following chapter, Day brings us to her fieldwork in Lençóis, a small town in the northeast interior of Brazil, while she was working on her PhD research about the sexual learning processes and practices of heterosexual young women there. Using concrete examples, Day describes in detail several methodological and ethical challenges faced by a first-time female fieldworker from a Western country. Being aware that some important aspects of her research were 'lost in translation', Day specifically examines and reflects on 'wrinkles in the messy process of conducting research'. She attempts to capture three methodological challenges. The first one is the linguistic – specifically the variety and creativity of sexual slang shared by local young women. The nuances of sexual slang in the lençoense context influenced her strategy of interview, and also impacted on how she worked with the resulting audio recordings of interviews in order to better capture the meanings while doing translations. The second was about the translation of cultural grammar, which goes beyond language and refers to multiple meanings and social values of sex and certain sexual practices and relationships. This not only fed into interpretations, but influenced the recruitment process and methods. Her third methodological thinking is on 'me-as-researcher', that is how the young women 'translated' her as a sexuality researcher and ways in which her motivations and intentions impacted on the likelihood of their participation in the research. Reflections on the ethical dilemmas and emotions involved and produced in the research process – joys, frustrations, anxieties, isolation – also contribute to her naming sexuality research as one type of 'emotion work'.

In the third chapter, Barbé i Serra situates us in a Barcelona swinger club, where erotic and sensorial experiences act as mediators in the construction of particular images and meanings around cross-dressing. Based on her ethnography conducted on cross-dressing practices, Barbé i Serra reflectively discusses the erotic subjectivity of the anthropologist, more precisely the dynamic contingency of bodily contact, and how that could be epistemologically productive in sexuality research. Her being young, a lesbian and a woman has defined the internal key monitors of this research, and forced her to consider certain variables that have implied risks for analysis. She therefore places the researcher's erotic desire at the forefront, making it visible as an aspect of sexuality research, breaking silences around the dynamics of reciprocity and the circulation of power and desire that occur within the field. Two cutting-edge methodological questions are specifically raised and explored in her research: is a non-transphobic writing possible by a 'cisgender' researcher being immersed in a socio-cultural context in which transphobia operates? And how can the erotic subjectivity of the anthropologist be epistemologically productive (Kulick and Willson, 1995) within this dynamic? Her discussions and reflections are balanced between a positioning and repositioning as activist-subject and erotic-subject. In this paper, Barbé i Serra insightfully borrows from and dialogues with important anthropological and feminist concepts, such as Wacquant's concept of 'carnal knowledge' (2009) and Esteban's 'emotional ethnography' (2011) among others, and regards body as an epistemological device, not as a device for access to knowledge but part of its coproduction.

In the last chapter, Cornwall brings us to the context of Sangli in India, the location of one of the most famous sex workers' self-organisations in the world. While sex workers have often been the objects of other people's (including researchers') curiosities and preoccupations and while the ethics has been widely debated in academic research, Cornwall describes in detail the process of her personal encounters with the participants, including her original concerns and doubts as an outsider feminist anthropologist from a Western country, and how a research project on sex workers' intimate lives was finally initiated and developed. As she points out, so often the focus of writing on sex work is on the business of sex, less on sex workers' daily lives involving a diversity of other people, including those they love as well as those who make their lives difficult. In this research project, biographical narrative story-telling is used as the methodological approach to allow sex workers to tell their own intimate stories and lived experience. Cornwall clearly explains how this kind of approach, which creates the possibility of open-ended dialogue and exchange, can serve to acknowledge and give recognition to the stories told by those who are all too often objectified in popular media and social science research.

Thus, the four articles address the negotiation of research contexts concerning geopolitics, language and more broadly cultures with different sexual meanings, and the various social and sexual positions that we need to dialogue with our subjects and other interdisciplinary cooperators, and to reflect on ourselves. Based on their own research experience and embodied and emotional thinking on what happens in the research process (where we see 'I' as a researcher and the personal interactions between 'us' and 'our participants' throughout the narratives), the authors demonstrate well that researchers and research encompass subjective desiring bodies; they enrich nuanced methodological and ethical discussions on different layers of cultural translation in different layers occurring in various contexts, and in so doing provide insights related to cosmopolitan sexualities (proposed and framed by Plummer in his book on this theme, 2015).

References

Cesara, M. (1982) *Reflections of a Woman Anthropologist: No Hiding Place*, London and New York: Academic Press.

Clifford, J. and Marcus, G.E. (eds) (1986) *Writing Culture: The Poetics and Politics of Ethnography*, Berkeley, CA: University of California Press.

Esteban, M.L. (2011) *Crítica del Pensamiento Amoroso. Temas contemporáneos*, Barcelona: Bellaterra.

Gagnon, J.H. and Parker, G. (1995) 'Introduction: Conceiving Sexuality' in Parker, G. and Gagnon, J.H. (eds) *Conceiving Sexuality: Approaches to Sex Research in a Postmodern World*, New York and London: Routledge.

Haraway, D. (1988) 'Situated Knowledges: The Science Question in Feminism and the Privilege of Partial Perspective', *Feminist Studies*, 14(3), pp. 575–599.

Huang, Y.Y. (2017) 'Women's Body and Desire: Research Methods and Ethical Thinking', *Journal of Exploration and Free Views*, 1, pp. 97–103.

Kulick, D. and Willson, M. (1995) *Taboo: Sex, Identity and Erotic Subjectivity in Anthropological Fieldwork*, London and New York: Routledge.

Lock, M. and Farquhar, J. (2009) *Beyond the Body Proper: Reading the Anthropology of Material Life*, Durham, NC: Duke University Press.

Newton, Esther (1993) 'My Best Informant's Dress: The Erotic Equation in Fieldwork', *Cultural Anthropology*, 8(1), pp. 3–23.

Pan, S.M, Huang, Y.Y. and Wang, D. (2011) *Social Research on Methods: Quantitative and Qualitative Sociological Studies in Chinese Contexts*, Beijing: Renmin University Press.

Parker, R.G. (1999) '"Within Four Walls": Brazilian Sexual Culture and HIV/AIDS' in Parker, R.G. and Aggleton, P. (eds) *Culture, Society and Sexuality: A Reader*, London and Philadelphia, PA: UCL Press, pp. 253–266.

Parker, R.G. and Easton, D. (1998) 'Sexuality, Culture, and Political Economy: Recent Developments in Anthropological and Cross-Cultural Sex Research', *Annual Review of Sex Research*, 9(1), pp. 1–19.

Plummer, K. (2015) *Cosmopolitan Sexualities: Hope and the Humanist Imagination*, Cambridge: Polity Press.

Rofel, L. (1999) 'Qualities of Desire: Imagining Gay Identities in China', *GLQ: A Journal of Lesbian and Gay Studies*, 5(4), pp. 451–474.

Rubin, G. (1984) 'Thinking Sex: Notes for a Radical Theory of the Politics of Sexuality' in Vance, C. (ed.) *Pleasure and Danger: Exploring Female Sexuality*, Boston, MA: Routledge, pp. 267–319

Said, E. (1978) *Orientalism: Western Conceptions of the Orient*, London: Routledge & Kegan Paul.

Sang, Z.L. (2014) *The Emerging Lesbian: Female Same-Sex Desire in Modern China* (trans. Q.F. Wang), Taibei: Taiwan University Publication Centre.

Shostack, J. (1982) *Nisa: The Life and Words of a !Kung Woman*, New York: Vintage.

Vance, C.S. (1991) 'Anthropology Rediscovers Sexuality: A Theoretical Comment', *Social Science and Medicine*, 33(8), pp. 875–884.

Wacquant, Loïc (2009) 'The Body, the Ghetto and the Penal State', *Qualitative Sociology*, 32, pp. 101–129.

9 | HESITATING AT THE DOOR: YOUTH-LED RESEARCH ON REALISING SEXUAL RIGHTS INFORMING ORGANISATIONAL APPROACHES

Vicky Johnson

Abstract

This chapter will consider methodological issues confronting youth-led participatory research that was carried out for International Planned Parenthood Federation (IPPF) in Benin, Kenya, Nepal and Nicaragua. Photo narratives were used by young peer educators to tell stories about being young in different cultural contexts, and what helped and hindered them to realise their sexual rights. Young people were supported to analyse their evidence and present recommendations to local decision-makers. Presentations by young researchers in the four country cases were analysed alongside the interviews conducted by a team from Panos London and the University of Brighton. The chapter addresses questions around interdisciplinary collaboration and conversation and the relational and negotiated nature of youth agency. The findings from the youth-led research, taken to national, regional and global levels have informed a process of reconceptualising youth programming in sexual rights in IPPF. Building on Johnson's Change-scape framework, the research informed a youth centred approach to sexual and reproductive health and rights across IPPF and Member Associations. This socio-ecological framework places young people's identities, inclusion and interests at the heart of developing youth-centred services and programming. It includes young people's priorities to: find safe spaces in which to interact with each other and access services; work with adults, religious leaders and service providers in communities; and to influence policies and laws that affect their health and rights. It builds on IPPF's strategies of youth-friendly services, advocacy and comprehensive sexuality education.

Introduction

This chapter has three main sections. In the first, I provide a short introduction to the youth-led research on youth sexual rights and reproductive health carried for the International Planned Parenthood Federation (IPPF) by Panos London and the University of Brighton. This includes a snapshot of some key findings from the youth-led aspect of the Nepal case study. I then present findings from the cross-case analysis highlighting issues that confronted young peer educators in their research on sex and sexuality across the four countries in West and East Africa, South Asia and Central America. Lastly, I consider the interdisciplinary collaboration and conversations that led to this research informing youth programming across IPPF in their global strategy. Champions for youth within IPPF have worked to move towards youth-centred approaches to realising sexual rights by providing practical advice on implementation to the Member Associations in the 152 countries where they work. IPPF's global strategy (IPPF, 2016–2022, p. 8) discusses the intention to empower youth by moving from being a youth-friendly organisation to becoming a youth-centred organisation. To conclude, the chapter discusses possible ways forward in taking youth seriously more systematically in rights-based research so that young people can move towards being agents of change in realising their sexual rights.

The importance of linking young people to their context

Introduction to the research   The research on youth sexual rights was commissioned by the International Planned Parenthood Federation (IPPF). It was carried out during 2012 within a broader assessment, managed by Panos London, of a Dutch government-funded programme of youth-friendly service delivery implemented in 2010–2013 to realise sexual youth rights across 16 countries. Mixed methods were used in the assessment with case study research in four countries led by the University of Brighton. Creative visual methods formed the basis of the youth-led aspect of the case studies in Benin, Kenya, Nepal and Nicaragua. The assessment research asked the questions: What it is like to be young in that particular place and how this has changed? How have local and national cultural and political/policy changes affected young people's feelings about sex and sexuality? And how have strategies, including making services youth friendly, sexuality education and advocacy, helped youth in realising their sexual rights? (see Johnson et al., 2013a).

The case study research (following for example Stake, 2003) was comparative across the particular locations chosen by 'youth focal points' who are tasked in Member Associations in the IPPF to share learning on youth sexual rights and programming. The methodology for this aspect of the research included an element of youth-led research but was also rights-based (following Beazley and Ennew, 2006) in that it: included youth perspectives as well as research with other key stakeholders, followed ethical protocols and employed a mix of methods so that research took into account the complexities of young people's lives as well as being convincing as rigorous to decision-makers within the Federation. The youth-led research in each of the country case studies examined what it is like to be young in the different cultural and political contexts in the chosen locations in Benin, Kenya, Nepal and Nicaragua and established youth perspectives on what helped or hindered them in realising youth sexual and reproductive health and rights (SRHRs). In the case studies young peer educators were both informants and researchers. For example, in Nepal after a team of 12 young peer educators received training, they went back to their villages in the Himalayan region of Kaski to carry out their own research using photo narratives with their peers and other community members (Johnson, 2013).

The research was youth-centred in that it followed a 'Change-scape' approach that links young people to their contexts through mechanisms that address intergenerational and institutional power dynamics (for example, Johnson, 2011, 2017). The 'Change-scape' provides a socio/cultural-ecological framework to systematically analyse cultural and political contexts and link the identities, inclusion and ideas of young people to decision-makers in communities and service providers locally and nationally. Mechanisms that help to ground findings in youth perspectives include: building the capacity of young people as researchers who then present their own evidence and findings to local key stakeholders; and supporting them to make recommendations to policy makers at local and national levels (Johnson, 2017). Evidence from youth-led research lay alongside research carried out by adult team members in the same locations and was analysed across the four country case studies to provide recommendations at national, regional and global levels to IPPF and their federation of Member Associations (see Johnson et al., 2013a).

During a two-week period in each location, young peer educators identified key issues that they wanted to investigate further and, after research training, conducted qualitative participatory research. Sexual and reproductive health and rights touches all aspects of our lives including our psychological wellbeing and can lead to distress as well as happiness (Cornwall and Welbourn, 2000). It was therefore important to find creative methods that would help young people to express stories of power and change in their complex lives. The use of visuals with metaphors can help young people to express sensitive issues and feelings in their complex lives. Photo narratives were therefore used in the youth-led research so young peer educators could carry out research with peers and community members to develop their stories of change. Once they shared their photos and stories they prioritised how to present their analysis and get their message across. They selected key photos, stories, quotes and recommendations and then presented their evidence to groups to local decision-makers.

Their presentations were then taken to national, regional and global levels. Further details can be found in IPPFs process document *Learning from Our Peer Educators* (Johnson et al., 2013b).

In this chapter, I focus on the youth-led research from Nepal. Young peer educators identified barriers to progress in realising young people's SRHRs that included the attitudes of adults within local communities, especially those uneducated and living remotely in deprived rural areas. They chose to further investigate cultural and religious beliefs that they felt countered progress in making services more youth friendly and comprehensive sexuality education. One of the young male peer educators from Nepal said: 'We may not be able to change cultural beliefs but at least we can edit them'.

As young researchers, the young men and women from the Kaski hills wanted to highlight specific aspects of local culture and intergenerational and gender power dynamics that they felt were important to their peers in local communities. Talking openly about sex is often taboo, especially for young people in many cultural contexts (Cornwall and Welbourn, 2000), as are issues surrounding menstruation (Roose et al., 2015). Peer research therefore employed creative photo narrative using metaphors and role-playing that allowed young people and adults to express their feelings. The young peer researchers identified the key themes they felt needed to be addressed in order to gain a greater understanding of how to realise sexual rights in the Himalayan region of Kaski. They then interviewed peers and adults in their communities but worked in pairs or threes so that there were researchers from different communities on each team. A snapshot of key findings from the youth-led photo narrative research is presented in the next section.

Young people suggested that as well as making services more youth friendly and delivering comprehensive sexuality education in schools, they would need to address the way in which traditional belief systems and power worked in their communities. They prioritised working with adults to change their attitudes towards young people, love, sex and sexuality. They made very specific recommendations to changing programmes and services locally. For example advocating for spaces where young men and women can talk to each other and form relationships, working on comprehensive sexuality education with adults, as well as children in and out of school, and providing stronger condoms that don't split. In Nepal, peer educators also suggested that services of the Member Association need to reach out to more marginalised young people who were working in hard labour and unable to attend school or any form of peer group discussions about sexual health services, those involved in selling sex and drugs to tourists, and young people of the third gender.

Snapshot of findings from youth-led research Here I provide a brief snapshot of findings from the youth-led research in the case studies and focus on the Nepal case study (see Johnson et al., 2013a, and Johnson, 2013, for further details). In the mountainous region of Kaski, in the foothills of the Himalayas, youth researchers carried out photo narrative research in their remote hill communities. In these areas mobile health services provide much needed access to basic contraception and advice. In many communities it may take most of the day to walk to the nearest government health post.

Two of the young researcher groups decided to address cultural and traditional beliefs and power dynamics and decision-making in households. The young peer researchers presented what it was like to be young in Kaski and described how traditions meant that they are not able to meet with members of the opposite sex until they are married. They also discussed how they wanted to change the safe spaces where young men and women could meet and talk to each other and form relationships. They named their groups after the great peaks of the Anapurna range of the Himalayas.

The 'Genesh Group' researched early marriage and the effect of cultural and religious beliefs on young people's sexual rights.

The young researchers had found cases of young people marrying early despite national campaigns against this practice, so that they could have a sexual relationship. Their photos showed role plays of the traditional practices still prevalent in the area: when menstruating girls do not wash their hair, eat or sleep with the family and sometimes sleep with animals, they are also not meant to touch plants in case they cause leaves to die. Girls and women felt they had no power in household decision-making and had to put up with situations of bad behaviour and abuse in their families.

The 'Annapurna Group' prioritised issues of violence and gender discrimination. They presented a picture of a tree bare of leaves and said that this is how it feels to be a young woman in the local communities. Young women felt lacking in any power in household decision-making and had to put up with situations of bad behaviour and abuse in their families. They also told other stories of the damage to the bodies of older women who had married early and how in marriage women could not choose when they had sex.

The 'Dhaulagiri Group' presented the issue of reaching out to the most marginalised. Their role plays showed young people smoking and selling drugs and carrying bricks and rocks in hard labour. The marginalised groups could not talk openly about sex or relationships and did not have information or access to family planning services. The young researchers also presented a rose coming into bloom and talked about how, despite national policies to reduce discrimination towards young people of the third gender, these young people could not talk openly about their sexuality.

Young researchers from the 'Machhapuchhare Group' supported IPPF reaching more remote areas with mobile clinics and suggested that the information and peer education for young people about relationships, sexual rights and how to access services should be continued. They also suggested this extend outside schools and utilise engaging approaches such as street theatre so that adults would be engaged.

Challenging aspects of methodology for this youth-led research are discussed in the next section of this chapter giving specific examples from Nepal as this was the case study that I facilitated. After gathering youth perspectives in the four countries, I analysed the youth-led research alongside interviews carried out by the adult research lead and local facilitators across the case studies. A model that was developed has been shared and acted on by the youth programme and subsequently informed the new global strategy of IPPF. This is further discussed in the third section of this chapter.

Issues confronting sex researchers in their methodologies

This section further explores some of the key issues discussed under the following areas of reflection:

- Ownership and extent of participation of young peer educators in the research;
- Ethics and how globally agreed protocols were rolled out in the youth-led research;
- Flexibility and creativity in methods versus comparability across cultural contexts.

Ownership and extent of participation of young peer educators in the research In order to carry out research that was meaningful for young peer educators, time was planned in the overall assessment for research training. This included facilitating young people working with IPPF Member Associations to identify local issues that they felt affected their perspectives on sex and sexuality. It also involved learning about the overall ethical protocols and further developing how they would implement ethical procedures in their research (following, for example, Alderson and Morrow, 2004). Also piloting methods with the young people as participants first so that they could then become facilitators, including, for example, focus group discussions and photo narratives. The research training took place over two weeks and included the young peer educators going into villages or urban areas where they lived and worked in order to gather evidence from their peers and adults in communities about the topics that they had chosen to explore further.

The participation of young people in the research was, however, limited as the research had been initiated at the global office level by the youth team. The research team that I worked with designed the overall approach to be comparative so as to have some consistency in methods, although there was some limited flexibility in the way that these methods were applied across the four country case studies. Had there been more time in planning then young peer educators could have been involved in design at the global level, but instead were involved to some extent in choice of topic, choice from a range of methods, piloting and design in the application of methods and what they presented at local level. They identified key topics that they felt were priorities for the realisation of youth sexual rights, carried out the research in their local communities, and analysed and presented their evidence and key conclusions to local decision-makers. All of the recommendations at national, regional and global levels were informed by the youth-led research that was carried out as the starting point of the international analysis.

Ethics and how globally agreed protocols were rolled out in the youth-led research   Ethical protocols were developed and agreed at an international level for the assessment as a whole, including the research carried out for the four country case studies. These ethical protocols included obtaining informed consent from young people and adults in communities, maintaining confidentiality on sensitive issues discussed in the research, ensuring meaningful participation of young people as discussed above, including their identification of research topics and questions, and taking the lead in analysis and presentation of findings.

As creative methods such as photo narratives were used to discuss sex and sexuality, part of the research training was to practice taking photos of symbols that would represent feelings, and using role play to ensure that individuals photographed were not directly associated with the stories that were told. For example, in Kaski in Nepal young people took photos of trees that were bare of leaves to represent how it feels to be a young woman in the area and a photo of a rose coming into bloom was taken to show how young people of the third gender (including transsexuals, transgendered and intersex) should be able to feel about expressing their sexuality. Role play was used by the young people in Nepal, for example, to show issues facing girls who had to eat separately from their families and sleep with the animals during menstruation, and to highlight the importance of including marginalised young people involved in hard labour, sex tourism, drug and substance abuse and drug dealing (see Johnson, 2013).

A particularly challenging ethical procedure was that, as well as signing the informed consent for participating in the research, young peer educators had to gain informed consent from young people and adults in communities, many of whom were not literate. Clear concise information sheets were developed so the young researchers felt happy to explain their intentions and simple signing sheets developed so that community participants including young people could sign or make an indication that they were giving their informed consent to the research and to photos being used in local, national and global presentations.

Flexibility and creativity in methods versus comparability across cultural and political contexts As mentioned in the section above on the limited extent of participation, there was a trade-off between flexibility/creativity and comparability across the four country case studies. The methods that were developed and used were piloted in Kenya and modified for the training in the other three youth research training sessions in Nepal, Benin and Nicaragua (see Johnson et al., 2013b). Although after the pilot, methods used were the same across the country case studies, they were creative and young peer educators in Kenya had enjoyed the process and felt they had worked to help to co-construct the research.

As young peer educators were encouraged to explore issues of relevance to their cultural and political context, they were still able to lead research that they were interested in and construct powerful presentations to present their findings. In Nepal and Benin, the young people presented to local decision-makers with help from the team adult facilitator, then taking it to national and regional levels. In Nicaragua the young people prepared the PowerPoint presentation with the facilitator who then presented it locally as well as to Member Associations and IPPF at the different levels of decision-making.

The young people in Nepal that had participated in the research felt that they had gained skills that they would like to continue to develop more widely in their peer educator roles. This was included in their recommendations. The creative methods have also proved applicable with other marginalised young people, for example in UNGEI-funded research with street-connected girls in Nairobi.

Interdisciplinary collaboration and conversations

Globally, the research is informing a new youth-centred model of programming. This model was formulated through new conceptual thinking that arose from the youth-led research across four countries described above. It also builds on IPPF's 'triangle approach', including youth-friendly services, advocacy and comprehensive sexuality education, with youth participation, gender and partnership as cross cutting. Inductive theorising during this research on realising sexual rights suggested a socio-ecological model that places young people at the centre and considers their interest, identities and inclusion. The model gives attention to identifying and developing safe participatory spaces for peer discussion, building relationships, identifying the support they need and how to access services. It also highlights the importance of analysing intergenerational and gender power dynamics and considering changing adult attitudes to youth sexual rights. It provides a framework to increase understanding of cultural and political contexts. This model is fully explained in the output from the research, *Love, Sexual Rights and Young People: Learning from Our Peer Educators* (Johnson et al., 2013a).

The adoption of this model across programming is discussed under the following headings:

• Collaboration across academia and practitioner worlds;
• Communicating to decision-makers and practitioners at all levels throughout the research;
• Youth centredness and how this is being applied across IPPF.

Collaboration across academia and practitioner worlds   How this research has contributed to reconceptualising youth programming has largely been down to the commitment of IPPF management and staff to be critical of their existing approaches, and to learn from and build on their experience of youth programming. In order to move forward they supported the research to engage with young people and conducted consultations with youth focal points and networks globally to inform the journey forwards. Issues of power were addressed through building into the research mechanism spaces for youth to express their perspectives but also to enter into dialogue with adults in communities and decision-makers in positions of power in order to seek more transformational change for youth in realising their sexual rights (as suggested by Johnson, 2017). The combination of academics and practitioners in the research was also key to bridging theory with practice. This helped to build a new conceptual model, based on Johnson's (2011, 2017) 'Change-scape' socio-ecological model of child and young people's participation, that is understandable to practitioners at different positions across the federation.

Key issues that were highlighted in the youth-led research, such as the importance of safe and participatory spaces for peer interaction and youth-friendly ways of accessing services, were incorporated into an iterative process in which the 'Change-scape' model continued to develop. Members of the South Asia Regional Office of IPPF worked with me to fine-tune the model and this was further developed through discussion with global youth advisors. The language that builds bridges between academia and practice, and between disciplines, was important in developing a model that IPPF felt ownership of and that was relevant to their vision of working with youth as partners and agents of change. How this is being implemented years after the youth-led research and incorporation of youth centredness needs to be assessed.

Communicating to decision-makers and practitioners at all levels throughout the research The youth-led research and complementary research carried out by adult facilitators, was communicated with decision-makers and practitioners at different levels, from local to national to regional to global. The importance of creating spaces for dialogue and communication with the purpose of negotiating social relationships with adults and improving decision-maker understanding of children's perspectives is starting to be recognised across childhood and youth research (for example Percy-Smith and Thomas, 2010). The research process included research participants as active agents of change who could also translate their own findings of research into practice in their lives and work as peer educators, members of communities or service providers. It was important that during the youth-led research, where possible, young people interacted with decision-makers and practitioners to express their views and explain the recommendations that they were making at local level. In the 'Change-scape' model that informed youth programming in IPPF, these mechanisms of communication and collaboration were seen as key to translating research into change and resulting in positive impact in the lives of young people.

The co-construction of presentations with young people was a powerful way to help young peer educators to get their key issues heard at different levels of decision-making, and to encourage further commitment to take their research evidence seriously. To treat them as agents of change rather than as recipients of programmes (Johnson, 2017) and to understand agency of children as negotiated, mediated and relational (Oswell, 2013).

Youth centredness and how this is being applied across IPPF   In order to turn new conceptual thinking in the research into a youth-centred model that was accepted by the youth team as a new theory of change for IPPF globally, it needed to be presented and discussed at a global strategic level by the board of IPPF. In order to do this the youth programme produced a strategic document, *Young at Heart,* that described the journey of IPPF from being an organisation that would not turn young people away from services, to one that made services youth friendly, to one that regarded young people as partners and agents in social change. The development of the new socio-ecological model that arose from the research was discussed alongside the experiences of IPPF and its Member Associations in youth programming globally.

A user-friendly guide was written by an academic (Vicky Johnson, myself) and an experienced manager and practitioner in youth programming (Doortje Braeken from IPPF). This was intended to give practitioners globally, in Member Associations of IPPF in 152 countries, the background to the new model of youth centredness and a way to understand the transitional steps to implementation. Markers of success were offered to organisations so that they could embark on journeys to put youth-centred programming and strategic thinking into practice across the Federation in different cultural and political global contexts. Markers needed to be flexible enough to allow for differing contexts and institutional settings, but to indicate what kind of capacity building and changes in thinking would be needed, locally and nationally, to reach a vision where young people are treated as agents at the centre of change. The approach to youth centredness acknowledges the heterogeneity of young people and how important it is to include those that feel most marginalised in their societies, rather than just counting those young people who access contraceptive services. Principles of treating young people as sexual beings and embracing the values of youth centredness also underpin implementation of the model.

Conclusions

Treating young people as agents of change and taking their perspectives seriously is key to realising youth sexual rights. Progress has been made in moving from turning young people away from sexual and reproductive health services, to programmes of youth friendly services, and comprehensive sex education in schools (IPPF, 2016–2022). There is, however, distance to travel to address some of the entrenched beliefs and traditional practices in communities where changing gender norms can be precarious, and there are deep-rooted feelings of powerlessness in decision-making around love, relationships and sex. Children and young people's agency needs to be understood as relational and as contested, negotiated and bound within the constraints of the societies in which they live (Oswell, 2013). In order to address issues of importance to young people in realising their sexual rights, research also needs to seek deeper understandings of the multiple ways in which young people construct their sexual identities and position themselves within their experiences of marginalisation (K. Johnson, 2015). Hemmingway (2006, p. 313) and colleagues, in a special issue on reframing sex education, recognise sexuality as an integral part of young people's lifeworlds and suggest that we illuminate how culture works in society and how value systems and circuits shape sexual learning. In different global cultural contexts we need to gain a better understanding of how young people interact with traditional beliefs and practices about transitions to adulthood that maintain heteronormativity and gender discrimination, and how they can be supported to express themselves more freely about love, sex and relationships in their complex lives and communities. Understanding both how young people develop ideas and meanings about sexual relationships and practices, and what they view as supportive enabling environments, is central to recognising young people as sexual beings and in providing support and services that can reduce their vulnerability (Keys et al., 2006).

Youth-centred approaches to realising youth sexual rights has young people as agents of change and suggests analysis of the contexts and power dynamics in which they live (following Johnson, 2011; Johnson et al., 2013a; and Johnson, 2017). Research that engages young people can apply creative methods that support them in safe spaces to engage in dialogue with peers and adults in communities and organisations and start to negotiate their gendered and intergenerational relationships. As young people in this youth-led research reminded us, the intergenerational power dynamics that govern their lives need to be understood and comprehensive sexuality education extended to adults in communities for traditional practices to change. In a similar way, *Stepping Stones with Children* (Gordon, 2016) recognises that realising sexual rights is about social justice and building up skills amongst young people and carers to negotiate relationships between genders and generations. With support and capacity building young people can help to change contexts by communicating important issues that affect their lives and the solutions that they suggest to realise their rights. In this IPPF youth-led research, young people showed sensitivity to how entrenched power dynamics could be changed. They suggested negotiating complex relationships in different cultural contexts and highlighted safe spaces where they could talk with their peers about relationships. They didn't just want to discuss their problems and ideas with supportive adults and youth-friendly service providers, but felt that if they could gain support to work with community and religious leaders to start to change adult attitudes towards youth sexual rights, they would have the space to become agents of change in order to try to influence practices, policies and laws that affect their lives.

References

Alderson, P. and Morrow, V. (2004) *Ethics, Social Research and Consulting with Children and Young People*, Essex: Barnardos.

Beazley, H. and Ennew, J. (2006) 'Participatory Methods and Approaches: Tackling the Two Tyrannies' in Desai, V. and Potter, R.B. (2006) *Doing Development Research*, London: Sage.

Cornwall, A. and Welbourn, A. (2000) 'From Reproduction to Rights: Approaches to Sexual and Reproductive Health', *PLA Notes*, 37, pp. 14–21.

Gordon, G. (2016) *Stepping Stones with Children*, Rugby: Practical Action Publishing.

Hemmingway, J. (2006) 'Reframing Sex Education', *Sex Education: Sexuality Society and Learning*, 6(4), pp. 313–316.

International Planned Parenthood Federation (2016–2022) *Locally Owned Globally Connected: A Movement for Change, Strategic Framework*, London: International Planned Parenthood Federation.

Johnson, K. (2015) *Sexuality: A Psychosocial Manifesto*, Cambridge: Polity Press.

Johnson, V. (2011) 'Conditions for Change for Children and Young People's Participation in Evaluation: "Change-scape"', *Child Indicators Research*, 4(4), pp. 577–596.

Johnson, V. (2013) *Hesitating at the Door: Differences in Perceptions between Genders and Generations on Sexual and Reproductive Health Rights in Kaski, Nepal*, London: International Planned Parenthood Federation.

Johnson, V. (2017) 'Moving Beyond Voice in Children and Young People's Participation', *Action Research*, Special Issue: *Development, Aid and Social Transformation*, 15(1), pp. 104–124.

Johnson, V., Leach, B., Beardon, H., Covey, M. and Miskelly, C. (2013a) *Love, Sexual Rights and Young People: Learning from Our Peer Educators in How to Be a Youth Centred Organisation*, London: International Planned Parenthood Federation. Available at www.ippf.org/sites/default/files/ippf_lsr-yp_full_020813.pdf.

Johnson, V., Leach, B., Beardon, H., Miskelly, C. and Warrington, S. (2013b) *Learning from Our Peer Educators: A Guide for Integrating and Reflecting Participatory Youth Research in the A+ Assessment Country Case Studies*, London: International Planned Parenthood Federation.

Keys, D., Rosenthal, D. and Pitts, M. (2006) 'Young People, Sexual Practices and Meanings' in Aggleton, P., Ball, A. and Mane, P. (eds) *Sex, Drugs and Young People: International Perspectives*, Oxford: Routledge.

Oswell, D. (2013) *The Agency of Children: From Family to Global Human Rights*, Cambridge: Cambridge University Press.

Percy-Smith, B. and Thomas, N. (eds) (2010) 'Conclusion' in *A Handbook of Children and Young People's Participation: Perspectives from Theory and Practice*, Oxford: Routledge.

Roose, S., Rankin, T. and Canvill, S. (2015) 'Breaking the Next Taboo: Menstrual Hygiene within CLTS', *Frontiers of CLTS: Innovations and Insights*, 6 (July), Sussex: Community Led Total Sanitation Hub, IDS.

Stake, R.E. (2003) 'Case Studies' in Denzin, N.K. and Lincoln, Y.S. (eds) *Strategies for Qualitative Inquiry*, 2nd edition, London: Sage, pp. 134–165.

10 | SEXUALITY RESEARCH 'IN TRANSLATION': FIRST-TIME FIELDWORK IN BRAZIL

Natalie Day

Abstract

In the summer of 2013, I embarked on nine months of fieldwork in Lençóis, a small town in the northeast interior of Brazil. It soon became clear to me that certain aspects of my research were getting somewhat 'lost in translation' – and that these aspects merited further reflection. This seemed particularly important, given that '[r]eaders are seldom provided an in-depth view of the inevitable wrinkles in the messy process of conducting research' (Rubenstein-Ávila, 2009, p. 1). In this chapter, I examine some of the methodological and ethical challenges I faced as a first-time fieldworker, attempting to capture the literal, cultural and social 'meanings' of sex and sexuality in a small-town, semi-rural fieldsite.

My PhD explores the sexual learning processes and practices of heterosexual young women in northeast Brazil, examining cultural and social influences alongside formal state interventions targeting the transformation of certain sexual practices. Over the fieldwork period, I carried out 27 semi-structured interviews with young women aged 18–29, encouraging them to reflect on their sexual learning processes. I also held more informal conversations with health care professionals and sex educators to increase my understanding of the local context, and observed and collected materials from sex education sessions. Finally, I kept fieldwork diaries in which I noted down events, issues, conversations, song lyrics, slang, rumours and observations which seemed pertinent to the discussion of sexuality in the lençoense[1] context. Though in no way an ethnography, these field notes contributed to my wider understanding of the place and culture in which my research is situated. The key research questions were:

1. What are the dominant cultural understandings of sex and sexuality held by young women in Lençóis?
2. Where do they get their information about sex, both formally and informally, and how does this information interact with pervasive cultural norms and beliefs about sex and sexuality?
3. What do young women perceive to be the consequences of the exercise of youth sexuality for their bodies (e.g. teenage pregnancy), identities (e.g. reputation) and futures (e.g. economic support)?

Sexual slang

Clearly, challenges of 'meaning' around sex and sexuality permeate my project, and the first of these challenges was linguistic. I have a degree in Spanish and Portuguese, and had previously worked for a charity for children and young people in my fieldsite. As a result, I was reasonably confident with my Portuguese fluency, and had a fair understanding of everyday Brazilian slang. I was, however, unprepared for the variety and creativity of sexual slang, and how important my use and understanding of such terms would be. Sexual slang is an extremely important lens through which to view sexual culture – the terms used reflect the (un)popularity and (un)acceptability of certain sexual practices and behaviours, and slang changes and adapts as these do: 'New terms are created, old terms are reinterpreted' (de Jesus, 2005, p. 67, my translation). To illustrate this point, I will explore the example of the term *ficar*.

Despite its literal meaning, 'to stay', suggesting permanence, *ficar* is '[a] relationship code marked by a lack of commitment and by a plurality of desires, rules and uses' (Chaves, 1994, p. 12). I heard it innumerable times 'fiquei com ele', 'a gente ficou', 'estamos ficando', but the actual relationship practices encompassed by the term remained unclear. The literature on the topic was similarly ambivalent – understood as anything from kissing up to, but not including, penetrative sex (de Jesus, 2005); a possible starting point for a relationship (de Oliveira et al., 2007); 'a night of partying and fun' (Justo, 2005, p. 71, my translation) – the only points of agreement were the fleeting nature of the relationship and its lack of commitment.

What was clear from my interviews was that *ficar* was vastly different from *namorar*, which suggested a more lasting relationship with deeper commitment and involvement:

> *Ficando*. It's for pleasure. *Namorando* – it might be that it's not love, but you've got some sort of strong feeling there, because you're with that person all the time. It's when you go, you *fica* with someone, like, you like a guy, he likes you, it might be that there are only a few kisses, but it might also be that you have sex. (Joana, 23)

Knowing and understanding this difference brought with it the opportunity to examine contraceptive practices more closely. Many participants felt that young women were more likely to use condoms with a *ficante* than with a *namorado*, with whom they went on the pill:

> they say "Oh, he's my boyfriend", but guys, he's a man! He's a man! ... She thinks that she's never going to – it's not that she's afraid, but she thinks "Oh, my boyfriend, he's not going to give me anything". (Maria, 24)

Understanding the slang use of *ficar* was necessary to clarify the cultural differences between *ficar* and *namorar*, and thus expose the different associated sexual practices. This is just one example of how Brazilian youth sexual slang was a vital methodological tool for better understanding the experiences of the young women in the study. As Groes-Green states in his 2009 study with Mozambican youth: 'Only by gradually learning the language in which young people talk about sex ... was I let into their erotic universe' (2009, p. 665). This does not mean to say that my 'translations' of the young women's sexual stories were always correct, or that this was an unproblematic process. However, my naïveté of the local sexual language was often useful within the interview process. Many of the young women assumed I was ignorant about 'the way things worked' in the town, so happily explained terminology and slang in a way they might not have done for a local researcher. My genuine ignorance on some issues also endeared me to some participants: for example, Betina was reserved at the start of her interview, but warmed to me when she discovered my ignorance of the term *pós*-love (post-love) as a euphemism for the morning-after-pill, which she found extremely amusing.

The nuances of sexual slang in the lençoense context impacted on how I worked with the resulting audio recordings of my interviews, in order to render English-language quotes to use within my thesis. I decided to engage in this process in two separate stages – to fully transcribe all my recordings in Portuguese, and then translate each in full into English – because I felt the translation itself was a distinct phase of analysis. Given my experience in the interviews, my observations and my local contextual knowledge, I was interpreting the Brazilian Portuguese words of my participants and finding the best fit in English, as 'it may be necessary to try to convey meaning using words other than literally translated equivalents' (Temple, 1997, p. 610). This was particularly true when participants used slang terms about sex and sexual practice: it was only through context that one could determine the nuances of such accounts. I did feel, however, that I was the best-placed person to undertake this translation work because, as Temple (1997) argues, '[w]hen the translator and the researcher are different people the process of knowledge construction involves another layer' (1997, p. 614). Regarding transcription and translation as separate and meaningful phases of data analysis process prompted me to take responsibility for my interpretations of the language used by my participants, and the process of representation I undertook in turning their words into 'useful' English-language quotations (Temple and Young, 2004).

Translating 'cultural grammar'

Researchers have struggled when faced with the reality that familiar concepts do not apply in the same way in new contexts (Brislin, 1986; Nsamenang, 1993; Groes-Green, 2009; Rubenstein-Ávila, 2009). During my own research, I soon realised that issues of meaning went far beyond the specific words I employed, to what were essentially different understandings of sex and sexuality altogether. Different cultures have different understandings of the multiple meanings of sex and sexuality – indeed this idea is key to theories of social constructionism (Parker and Easton, 1998). This brings me to my second methodological challenge – truly understanding the cultural positioning of 'sex' in the town, a positioning which seemed, at times, downright paradoxical.

Accordingly, to Parker and Easton (1998), '[w]ith whom one is permitted to have sex, in what ways, under what circumstances, and with what specific outcomes are never simply random questions. Such possibilities are defined through the implicit and explicit rules and regulations imposed by the sexual cultures of specific communities' (1998, p. 9). In the process of 'translating' sex and sexualities research to my northeast Brazilian research context, it was not just lençoense sexual slang I needed to understand, but also these sexual rules, which medical anthropologist and Brazilianist Richard Parker (1999) terms the 'cultural grammar' of a place. A more complete understanding of my fieldsite's cultural grammar would impact on my entire study, making it a key methodological element.

Many people might feel familiar with the cultural grammar of Brazilian sexuality. Certainly the country holds a strong position in the popular imaginary – beaches, sunshine, minute bikinis, samba and Carnival abound in media and tourism depictions of the country. These images come with ideological baggage about sexuality in Brazil: 'Brazilians are generally considered to be very uninhibited, "hot", sultry, and always up for anything in the bedroom. It's as though the country were some kind of sexual paradise' (Heilborn, 2006, p. 49, my translation). This image is very commonly gendered – it is the Brazilian woman (and specifically the mulata[2]) who most usually embodies the country's hypersexuality (Piscitelli, 2001; Adelman and Ruggi, 2008; Pravaz, 2012; Selister Gomes, 2013). However, this common-sense understanding of Brazilian sexual culture is not only racist, sexist and colonialist, it also masks the true complexity of the country's cultural grammar of sexuality. Certainly in my fieldsite it was far from easy to determine the limits of acceptability and desirability, perhaps because 'northeastern Brazilian society is a combination of tolerance for sexual and sensual expression and a traditional patriarchy in which the double standard remains strong' (Willson, 1997, pp. 29–30). This means that young women must walk a tightrope between sensuality and sexuality and traditionally accepted modes of femininity, a tightrope you might not necessarily see if you persist in viewing Brazil as 'an exotic Other ... populated by beautiful, available women' (Adelman and Ruggi, 2008, p. 561).

This tightrope was difficult for the women in my fieldsite to negotiate. The cultural prominence of *ficar* as a preferred relationship type (de Jesus, 2005), socially valued by young people (Justo, 2005), meant pressure on young women to engage in varying degrees of sexual behaviours from dancing, flirting, kissing and 'preliminares'[3] to 'o ato em si',[4] whilst at the same time monitoring and managing their reputations to avoid being seen as 'easy':

Like "*ficar*" to me (coughs) "*ficar*" is, for me it's kisses, cuddles, talking to that person, and the next day you don't see each other again … But there are people who, no, *ficar* means sexual relations … With people they've never seen before in their lives … You just met them and you're doing it. So what's the first impression that gives? You're that thing that he's going to think "My god, she's so easy!" (Janaina, 21)

Women, therefore, have to walk a very fine line between being happy to '*ficar*' and becoming a girl who is seen as good to 'shag' but not to marry:

if a man pulls more women, he's great. If a girl pulls more, she's going to be slagged off, that's she's been around, right? It'll go round "Oh, that one's been around, everybody's already been with her. That one's not marriage material". Because they always diff, differentiate, which I think is horrible, "That one's for marrying, that one's just for shagging". (Michele, 19)

This fine line had strong implications for my recruitment. Such a balancing act is precarious, and might easily be affected, for example, if it became public knowledge that that a young woman was participating in research about sex. No matter how much I reassured potential participants that the research was about sexual learning and not sexual partners or activity, the very word 'sex' placed them on the defensive. Proactive recruitment tactics such as a Facebook group advertising the research or publicising it during adult-only classes at the local high school[5] yielded almost no participation.

The issue, it seemed, was trust – especially as Lençóis is a small town and a very close-knit community. Elsewhere in the interviews, several women told me that teachers and health care workers could not be trusted to maintain confidentiality – so possibly similar concerns extended to me. The only answer was to rely on snowballing, and allow the young women in this community to vouch for me through word-of-mouth. In this way, they could relay to one another that I had been honest about the content of the interview, and that I was respecting confidentiality. It is in this sort of methodological challenge that the nuances of carrying out sexualities research, as opposed to other forms of sensitive qualitative research are most clearly reflected. Those areas of life culturally deemed most private are interrogated and discussed, in a manner which runs contrary to the acceptable standards of a given community – a factor certainly at play in my research, and which impacted on my recruitment of participants.

This element also intersects with the third and final challenge to be discussed here – how potential and eventual participants decoded and understood the meaning of me-as-researcher. How the young women in my fieldsite 'translated' me and my motivations and intentions impacted on the likelihood of them trusting me with their participation in my research.

Me-as-researcher

As mentioned earlier, I had lived and worked in the fieldsite previously and, to some extent, this helped me – I was aware of the organisations and institutions I would need to access, I had some contacts who would help me and introduce me to others, and, most importantly, I had a network of friends to support me during the stresses of fieldwork. However, my previous experience of the fieldsite was also problematic – because my fieldsite had previous experience of me. In my previous life in the town, I was a 21-year-old student, there to work with local children but also to learn Portuguese, get a great tan and have an amazing time – nothing out of the ordinary, but not the same things now on my agenda as a researcher. I needed to break with the idea that I was there 'só pra curtir',[6] in order to be taken seriously – leaving friends bemused when I told them I couldn't come to the river to swim, chat and hang out, as I had to work!

Whilst this understanding of me-as-volunteer over me-as-researcher was frustrating, it was far easier to deal with than the most common 'translation' of me – as a white, middle-class,

Anglophone woman, I was frequently understood first and foremost as a *gringa*.[7] If the only connotations of the word *gringa* were foreignness, I would not have struggled with the term as I did – after all, as a white woman speaking fluent but not native Portuguese in a predominantly Afro-Brazilian town, it was no secret that I was foreign. Unfortunately, the word has become increasingly loaded, and its use increasingly pejorative – giving me what I call here the *'gringa* problem'.

Gringas, on the whole, do not have good reputations in Latin America: 'the term "gringa" generally refers to a foreign white woman who is considered not to take enough care over her appearance, who will have sex with anyone, who is easy to deceive and who is easily parted from her money' (Willson, 1997, p. 31). The most damaging impact of the *'gringa* problem' was the suspicion it aroused amongst local women. It was common knowledge in the town that many men preferred, or would only date, foreign women.

> There's battling over *gringas* ... Lots of it. Because here, for
> example, the guides, when they see the *gringas* getting off the
> bus, it's all "Oh wow", right, all that, right? I think that it's
> because they've seen lots of people here in town, who have
> changed their lives, improved their lives, through doing that
> ... They, they get blinded by it "Oh, I want a *gringa*".
> (Luiza, 28)

This 'preference' put foreign women in direct competition with local women, producing hostility[8] – I was insulted in the street and suffered (completely fictitious) gossip. Because they saw me as a *gringa* – 'a cultural stereotype of foreign women being sexually promiscuous or "loose"' (Willson, 1997, p. 30) – many local women positioned me as seeking sexual relations with local men, and so as a potential threat. Several of my participants were keen to discover if it was my intention to find myself a local man, and seemed pleased when I told them it wasn't:

I don't know about you, right, if you like big black men? (both laugh)

N – I've got a boyfriend in England

Ah, that's good! (laughing) But here, lots are like that. My, my, my cousin, he's married to a Spanish woman. (Carolina, 29)

Having experienced the '*gringa* problem' during previous visits, I had anticipated that it might lead to difficulties recruiting participants and building rapport. I pre-empted this by talking a lot about my boyfriend back home – about how much I missed him, how hard it was to be away from him for nine months, how we planned to get married and how excited I was for his visit – and when he arrived, I showed him around the town, introducing him to many members of the community. Whilst this did not entirely eliminate the '*gringa* problem', I believe it certainly went some way to reducing its impact. In addition, I was extremely conscious of how I dressed and behaved. Whilst in her work with Caribbean men, Joseph (2013) joined in with popular styles of dance and wore short shorts to encourage flirtation and therefore make contact with possible research participants; I was very careful not to dress in a way which could be deemed provocative, and did not dance with men, other than close friends, at local *festas*[9] or nights out *na rua*.[10] Groes-Green describes a similar struggle over his reputation during fieldwork in Mozambique: 'I managed to keep a balance between "being part of the game" by dancing and having fun like the rest of the crowd and yet persistently rejecting sexual offers' (2009, p. 657). I also went out of my way to show organisations I worked with that I was not just another *gringa*, passing through the town and contributing nothing to the community. I mostly did this through reciprocity – I offered English lessons and translation work at one organisation, helped a community radio station at a second and covered some youth-work sessions at a third. In combination with my efforts to reassure women, my public 'good' behaviour, and my extended stay in the town, this work helped me to build a reputation for myself which benefitted my research, rather than threatening it.

It is important to recognise that my social positioning was not always, and never wholly, negative. More than one participant told me that it was easier to open up to me because I was a stranger, so not involved in the internal politics of the community. Another possible positive was the fact that all my participants knew I was not staying, so they perhaps understood me as a 'safe' person to open up to. I also found common ground easily with many of the women – from our age, to our shared experiences of coming from a big family, to the pains of getting your heart broken! – allowing us to develop rapport, despite our clear differences.

It is, of course, important to acknowledge that there were many other dynamics at play in the research interactions between my participants and me, and that we were each marked by our race, class, gender, education and sexuality, amongst other factors. However, discussion of the '*gringa* problem' demonstrates, rather usefully, how the issue of meaning in sex and sexualities research works both ways: it is not solely about what I understood of, from and about my participants, but equally – and at times more importantly – how they read me.

Ethical implications

Having explored some of the methodological struggles I faced in 'translating' my sexualities research to my semi-rural, northeast Brazilian context, and in understanding the different meanings I encountered, I now turn to the ethical debate I had with myself as a result. Given the blurring and inconsistencies of meaning, was my research ethical? Was it ethical to encourage young women to participate in research which might interfere with the delicate process of reputation management? Was it ethical for me to attempt to interpret their accounts when still less than fluent in their cultural grammar? What might I do to mitigate the impact of these ethical dilemmas?

In a study on violence in London and South Africa, Parkes (2010) talks about the indirect harm which can come of research – as researchers, we often focus on the direct harm to participants of talking about a distressing subject or self-implicating in illegal activity, however 'research can also harm indirectly through, for example, violating group rights or reputation' (Parkes, 2010, p. 350). I was very aware of the latter risk, and the implication my research might have had on my participants' ability to walk the tightrope of reputation in the fieldsite. To mitigate this, all I could really do was keep my promises to anonymise transcripts and maintain the confidentiality of the study, and adhere to the other ethical practices outlined in my institution's ethical approval procedures.

Another indirect harm identified by Parkes was that 'research might further disempower marginalised groups, through the imposition of the (adult, western) researcher's knowledge and values over the deficit "other"' (2010, p. 350). My fear was that I might, unwillingly, distort my participants' experiences and narratives by imposing my own cultural grammar over theirs in my analysis. One way to avoid this was to engage in reflexive practice, as I have attempted to do both in this text and in my research as a whole, and question my own positionality as a researcher and the assumptions I carry with me as baggage. Another was to adhere to feminist principles of giving voice, and ensure that my participants' own stories and voices are privileged and included extensively, as recommended by Tolman et al. (2005), rather than subjugated to my own.

Finally, I reminded myself that the research was done for a purpose – to add to existing knowledge about sex education and sexual learning in northeast Brazil, and possibly contribute to helping make state interventions more appropriate to the needs of the young women at whom they are aimed. This means that any risk of harm, direct or indirect, was not risk for risk's own sake, but for a possible future benefit.

A further ethical consideration came from the fact that the final product of this research – my PhD thesis – is in English, whilst the data was co-produced and created in Portuguese. This means that none of my participants could read the outputs, even if they wanted to. Therefore, it has been extremely important to me to write in a way which is accessible and easy to understand, in order to make my work readable for the widest Anglophone audience possible. This preference for an accessible, readable style seemed logical to me, given the hope of future applicability of my work to policy development: 'Presumably we would like not only academics, but also professionals ... to read and comment on our work. Paradoxically, in conforming to our implicit assumptions regarding a scientific style of writing, our writing may well discourage other audiences from engaging it' (Golden-Biddle and Locke, 2007, pp. 11–12). It is also my intention to publish from my thesis in Portuguese, as well as English, in order that my interpretation of the sexual stories shared with me during fieldwork might be accessible to a Lusophone[11] audience.

Emotion work

As the purpose of this chapter is to share and reflect on the methodological and ethical challenges of 'translating' sex and sexualities research to a northeast Brazilian cultural context, and shed some light on the inevitable 'wrinkles' in such a process, it would be remiss of me to pretend that I did not find this experience incredibly emotional. Although there were times of great joy and feelings of triumph throughout, I also suffered intense feelings of self-doubt, frustration and isolation, as I attempted to negotiate the differences in meaning I have discussed in this chapter. Given these struggles in the field, I felt it important to explore the emotional aspects of sexualities research, using the concept of 'emotion work'.

It has been increasingly acknowledged that sensitive research, particularly qualitative interviewing, carries 'a potentially high cost for the health and well-being of researchers' (Sampson et al., 2008, p. 920). One such cost is that researchers are required to carry out extensive 'emotion work': monitoring participants' emotions and intervening if harm is perceived; building rapport and trust with participants, whilst simultaneously maintaining the boundaries of the research relationship; gaining access in the first place; managing their own emotions and feelings of anxiety, isolation and inferiority; and leaving the field in a way which is respectful and non-damaging (Dickson-Swift et al., 2007). It could be argued that this 'emotion work' is still more important in sexualities research, where stories of abuse or illegal activity are potentially close, and where information which could damage reputations or identities is so frequently shared.

My concerns and fears over how I was 'translating' the words and socio-cultural contexts and experiences of my participants and how they were 'translating' me led to intense feelings of anxiety, isolation and inferiority (Dickson-Swift et al., 2007), as demonstrated in the fieldwork diary extract below:

12th November 2013
I feel like a failure, I'm here to do one job – get 30 interviews – and can't even do that. I feel like I shouldn't be doing a PhD at all, I'm not up to it. I've been trying so hard and just not getting anywhere, I feel like I'm doing everything I can.

Several characteristics of my fieldsite contributed to such feelings, for example the site's unpredictable internet connection made contacting friends, family and supervisors challenging and, at times, impossible. Similarly, the alteration in my relationship to my fieldsite and participants, from friend and volunteer to 'serious' researcher, at times left me feeling isolated from my existing friendship networks. The research itself also contributed to these feelings: whenever a participant failed to show up for a scheduled interview I felt increasingly desperate, frustrated and alone. Several scholars have discussed the emotional, mental and physical consequences of 'emotion work' (e.g. McCosker et al., 2001; Seear and McLean, 2008): for me these included stress, anxiety, sadness, increased homesickness and insomnia – especially early on in the research as I felt the research 'clock' ticking. To combat these issues, Dickson-Swift et al. (2007) advocate 'self care': maintaining a peer network, developing a protocol for emotional safety, scheduling rest breaks during fieldwork and conducting a debriefing on return (2007, p. 345).

This brief focus on 'emotion work' could be interpreted as overly personal, even self-indulgent. However, I feel that such a focus not only fits with my commitment to explore my research process honestly and transparently, it is also consistent with the feminist desire to 'acknowledge the "messiness" of the research process' (Letherby, 2003, p. 6) and how this messiness impacts on research outcomes. Not only this, but taking the time to consider how the research affected me personally has made me more aware of the impact it may have had on my participants, prompting me to engage more fully in the ethical process: 'exploring the emotional experiences of doing research on such sensitive topics is a productive and meaningful project ... It can help to foster intellectual clarity and a deeper understanding of the issue(s) being studied, the research participants, and the researchers themselves' (Blakely, 2007, p. 59).

In this chapter, I have attempted, in a very personal and reflexive way, to analyse the methodological and ethical obstacles I faced when 'translating' my research project to a small-town northeast Brazilian context. It was an immensely challenging process, and one which did not end when I flew home. Transcribing, translating and analysing gave way to write-up and the new challenges of accurately presenting the cultural grammar of sexuality in my fieldsite within my thesis. In this regard, this piece has been extremely useful in helping me think through some of the 'wrinkles in the messy process' (Rubenstein-Ávila, 2009, p. 1) of my own research.

Notes

1. Term meaning of or from Lençóis.

2. Portuguese-language term for a mixed-race Brazilian woman, with specific racial characteristics such as light brown skin and smooth, dark (but not afro) hair.

3. Foreplay.

4. The 'act' itself.

5. Classes were run in the evenings for adults who wanted to finish their secondary education.

6. Just to have a good time.

7. The term *gringa* literally refers to a foreign, Anglophone woman and was originally used for US women, before expanding to encompass British, Australian and South African women. In my fieldsite, the term was indiscriminately used to refer to any white foreign woman, and its masculine equivalent, *gringo*, to any white foreign man – though without the sexualised connotations.

8. This dynamic also meant it would have been almost impossible to include men within my research, although the richness their contributions would have added to understandings of the topic.

9. Parties/festivities.

10. Literally meaning in the street, going out, *na rua* refers to going on a night out, or partying.

11. Portuguese-speaking.

References

Adelman, M. and Ruggi, L. (2008) 'The Beautiful and the Abject: Gender, Identity and Constructions of the Body in Contemporary Brazilian Culture', *Current Sociology*, 56(4), pp. 555–586.

Blakely, K. (2007) 'Reflections on the Role of Emotion in Feminist Research', *International Journal of Qualitative Methods*, 6(2), pp. 59–68.

Brislin, R.W. (1986) 'The Wording and Translation of Research Instruments' in Lonner, W.J. and Barry, J.W. (eds) *Field Methods in Cross-cultural Research*, Newbury Park, CA: Sage, pp. 137–164.

Chaves, J. (1994) *Ficar com: um novo código entre os jovens*, Rio de Janeiro: Revan.

de Jesus, J.S.O. (2005) 'Ficar ou namorar: um dilema juvenil', *Revista de Psicologia da Vetor Editora*, 6(1), pp. 67–73.

de Oliveira, D.C., Tosoli Gomes, A.M., Corrêa Marques, S. and Thiengo, M.A. (2007) '"Pegar", "ficar" e "namorar": representações sociais de relacionamentos entre adolescentes', *Revista Brasileira de Enfermagem*, 60(5), pp. 497–502.

Dickson-Swift, V., James, E.L., Kippen, S. and Liamputtong, P. (2007) 'Doing Sensitive Research: What Challenges Do Qualitative Researchers Face?' *Qualitative Research*, 7(3), pp. 327–353.

Golden-Biddle, K. and Locke, K. (2007) *Composing Qualitative Research*, Thousand Oaks, CA, London and New Delhi: Sage.

Groes-Green, C. (2009) 'Health Discourse, Sexual Slang and Ideological Contradictions among

Mozambican Youth: Implications for Method', *Culture, Health and Sexuality*, 11(6), pp. 655–668.

Heilborn, M.L. (2006) 'Entre as tramas da sexualidade brasileira', *Revista Estudos Feministas*, 14(1), pp. 43–59.

Joseph, J. (2013) 'What Should I Reveal?: Expanding Researcher Reflexivity in Ethnographic Research', *Sport History Review*, 44, pp. 6–24.

Justo, J.S. (2005) 'O "ficar" na adolescência e paradigmas de relacionamento amoroso da contemporaneidade', *Revista do Departamento de Psicologia*, 17, pp. 61–77.

Letherby, G. (2003) *Feminist Research in Theory and Practice*, Buckingham and Philadelphia, PA: Open University Press.

McCosker, H., Barnard, A. and Gerber, R. (2001) 'Undertaking Sensitive Research: Issues and Strategies for Meeting the Safety Needs of All Participants', *Forum Qualitative Sozialforschung/ Forum: Qualitative Social Research*, 2(1), pp. 1–14.

Nsamenang, A.B. (1993) 'Psychology in Sub-Saharan Africa', *Psychology and Developing Societies*, 5(2), pp. 171–184.

Parker, R.G. (1999) '"Within Four Walls": Brazilian Sexual Culture and HIV/AIDS' in Parker, R.G. and Aggleton, P. (eds) *Culture, Society and Sexuality: A Reader*, London and Philadelphia, PA: UCL Press, pp. 253–266.

Parker, R.G. and Easton, D. (1998) 'Sexuality, Culture, and Political Economy: Recent Developments in Anthropological and Cross-

Cultural Sex Research', *Annual Review of Sex Research*, 9(1), pp. 1–19.

Parkes, J. (2010) 'Research on/as Violence: Reflections on Injurious Moments in Research with Friendship Groups', *International Journal of Qualitative Studies in Education*, 23, pp. 347–361.

Piscitelli, A. (2001) 'On "Gringos" and "Natives": Gender and Sexuality in the Context of International Sex Tourism in Fortaleza, Brazil'. Paper at Meeting of the Latin American Studies Association, 5–8 August 2001, Washington D.C., pp. 1–28.

Pravaz, N. (2012) 'Performing Mulata-ness: The Politics of Cultural Authenticity and Sexuality among Carioca Samba Dancers', *Latin American Perspectives*, 39(2), pp. 113–133.

Rubinstein-Ávila, E. (2009) 'Reflecting on the Challenges of Conducting Research across National and Linguistic Borders: Lessons from the Field', *Journal of Language and Literacy Education*, 5(1), pp. 1–8.

Sampson, H., Bloor, M. and Fincham, B. (2008) 'A Price Worth Paying? Considering the "Cost" of Reflexive Research Methods and the Influence of Feminist Ways of "Doing"', *Sociology*, 42(5), pp. 919–933.

Seear, K. and McLean, K. (2008) 'Breaking the Silence: The Role of Emotional Labour in Qualitative Research', *The Australian Sociological Association Refereed Proceedings*.

Selister Gomes, M. (2013) 'O Imaginário Social "Mulher Brasileira" em Portugal: Uma

Análise da Construção de Saberes, das Relações de Poder e dos Modos de Subjetivação', *DADOS: Revista de Ciências Sociais*, 56(4), pp. 867–900.

Temple, B. (1997) 'Watch Your Tongue: Issues in Translation and Cross-cultural Research', *Sociology*, 31(3), pp. 607–618.

Temple, B. and Young, A. (2004) 'Qualitative Research and Translation Dilemmas', *Qualitative Research*, 4(2), pp. 161–178.

Tolman, D.L., Hirschman, C. and Impett, E.A. (2005) 'There Is More to the Story: The Place of Qualitative Research on Female Adolescent Sexuality in Policy Making', *Sexuality Research and Social Policy*, 2(4), pp. 4–17.

Willson, M. (1997) 'Playing the Dance, Dancing the Game: Race, Sex and Stereotype in Anthropological Fieldwork', *Ethnos*, 62(3–4), pp. 24–48.

11 | THE CONTINGENCY OF THE CONTACT: AN INTERPRETIVE RE-POSITIONING THROUGH THE EROTIC DYNAMICS IN THE FIELD

Alba Barbé i Serra

Abstract

Through an investigation based on the practice of cross-dressing in Barcelona I reflect on the 'contingency of the contact'. I aim to move into public and academic space a 'privacy' that reveals itself in the socio-political field. Following Ahmed, I do not propose a radical subjectivism mode, but 'I am suggesting that "no thing" or "no body" has positive characteristics, which exist before contact with others ... Rather, subjects as well as objects are shaped by contact' (Ahmed, 2014, p. 40). I consider the complexity that characterises the definitions of socio-symbolic and sexual value of the people involved in the research. These values are locally and temporarily redefined in the interactions through erotic dynamics and through the bodily contact.

> I am convinced that there are ways of thinking that we don't yet know about. (Adrienne Cécile Rich, 1977)

The question underlying my research is as follows: Is a non-transphobic writing by a 'cisgender' researcher possible, when immersed in a socio-cultural context in which transphobia operates? Thence, how could we open research practices from a radical depathologisation paradigm? The second question is to understand ways in which the erotic subjectivity of the anthropologist can be epistemologically productive (Kulick and Willson, 1995) in thinking about these last questions.

Managing boundaries: touch, loss and shock in fieldwork

Kulick and Willson posited in *Taboo* (1995) how the 'erotic sub-jectivity' of the ethnographer can be epistemologically productive. Such an insight would entail a new contribution to the strength of partial perspectives and situated knowledges bequeathed by authors such as Haraway (1988, 1991) or Strathern (1991), as well as by many other non-academic feminists preceding them. Other anthropologists had pointed to its 'usefulness' for fieldwork in remote societies: its access, its deep understanding of 'culture' and ease of an unfelt presence as intrusive.

Contemporaneously, Stacey (1988) wrote that as the ethno-graphic method 'adapts' to feminist research: 'this method draws on those resources of empathy, connection, and concern that many feminists consider to be women's special strength' (Stacey, 1988, p. 22). Then, she warned: '[it] masks a deeper, more dan-gerous form of exploitation' (1988, p. 22). This concern forced me to reinforce a careful and critical look at the ethnographic process and writing. This ethnographic process went beyond what the postmodern turn called 'the reflective stance anthropol-ogist' (largely worked by Bourdieu and Wacquant, 2005). It was a necessary epistemological and methodological vigilance that feminisms were enabling, and this entailed pointing to contra-dictions and refinements of possible power relations in a context where the intertwinings of affection and complicity are strong. Taking into account what Spivak (2008) says in relation to the deconstructionist approach, the virtue of such care was to ques-tion myself as a researcher, yet without invoking paralysis in terms of creativity and analysis. I have attempted this vigilance through what Wheatley (1994) has called in her critique of Stacey, 'femi-nist imagination'.

To this purpose, I attend to the procedures of interpretation following from phenomenology studies (Merleau-Ponty, 2002 [1945]; Csordas, 1994; Ahmed, 2004, among others). The alliance between conceptions and practices from the worlds of what scientific work has named the 'subject' and 'object' is unavoidable. Both are generated through the interpretive process itself, and the interpretative process of all the subjects involved within. Therefore, it is a process of mutual and reciprocal bases. These conceptions and practices are impossible to separate from the 'habitus' (Bourdieu, 2006) and therefore, these require addressing the 'body-reflexive practices' (Connell, 2010) of both people with whom we research and ourselves as researchers. This starting point becomes my orientation[1] for the production of ethnographic knowledge.

This chapter is developed through an ethnography carried out in a swinger club – a club of erotic-sexual exchange in Barcelona – which has allowed me to reflect on a 'contingency' that is directly linked to the temporariness of cross-dressing. To summarise, cross-dressing is characterised for a contemplation and gender expression not persistent in time and space. It refers to a presentation and social representation of the 'own body', and therefore gender, depending on the social spheres in which this is expressed; in particular, among people socially interpreted and assigned as men, and many who identify as heterosexual.

In this club, erotic and sensorial experiences act as mediators in the construction of a particular image and meaning of cross-dressing. 'Flirtation' (including inviting for a drink or a dance, leading her into a corner, touching her thighs under her skirt, whispering in her ear that 'she's the most beautiful woman in the club'), appears as an erotic encounter that, beyond referring to corporal pleasure, is related to a production process and the dynamics of recognition and negotiation of a 'femininity' (and consequently a 'masculinity') that is being constructed through the interaction itself. Through erotic tensions, gazes, affects and the way that the people touch another's body, people 'see' and 'feel' the structures of distinct borders.

The dynamics of negotiation and recognition (or non-recognition) that appear in the bodily contact or erotic interactions become mediators of social knowledge. However, sometimes they also generate power relationships intrinsic to research. These erotic experiences, understood as a 'bodily process' (Spronk, 2014, p. 6), that comprise a view of my own erotic subjectivity, have placed me not only in a confrontation with my own questions but in a network of tensions and lack of recognition, and in a particular position within the dynamic of power circulation, attractions, conflicts and mutual reflections. They all relate to emotions that operate at the same time shaping the surface of individual and collective bodies (Ahmed, 2014).

My reflections are 'swinging' between positioning and re-positioning as activist-subject and erotic-subject, so that I should challenge myself to a completely unexpected process of selective perception. This links me to the approaches towards 'participant perception' and the bodily commitment of the researcher.[2] I intend with this to 'undress' some analytical limitations that have eventually become key elements for understanding cross-dressing. They are related to a necessary critique of the asymmetries that the researcher role may bring with it but it highlights one of the problem areas that is yet to be addressed: we are placed within a framework in which thinking self-critically about our own position of power as researchers means that we continue to conceive of ourselves within a hegemony. It is, within an opposite and static relation to the people with whom researchers investigate. What happens when the researcher is not situated as hegemonic subject? Until now, these methodological innovations result in a 'politically correct' posture, seeking to understand 'hierarchies of oppression' (Brah, 1992). This position blurs the analysis by not allowing for analytic strategies based on the way in which the vectors of oppression and privilege (gender, erotic-sexual orientation, social class, age, etc.) are temporarily interconnected through their dialectical relations within the field.[3]

Internal key-monitors in fieldwork The revelations of Malinowski's field notes (1989 [1967]) placed on the 'game board' anthropologist sexuality and the role of 'imagination' or 'fantasy'.

Of the latter, less has been written. Cardín (1989, p. 11) speaks of the 'I-witness', naming Geertz, referring to one who realises the facts as an inner witness.[4] Up until then, sexuality not only seemed invisible or non-existent, but its effects remained silenced in marginalised communities and removed from data collection, interpretation and writing of research; therefore, in the construction of ethnographic knowledge. Although scientific developments that followed were timid, in the 1980s, under the pseudonym of Manda Cesara (1982), an anthropologist published a book about her sexual experiences and emotions involved in the field; also of love. In the years that followed, others directly addressed the role of desire and eroticism in the field (Newton, 1993; Caplan, 1993; Plummer, 2008).

Two aspects have been most significant for me in the work of Kulick and Willson (1995). The former is the notion of 'risked involvement' introduced by Cesara (1982, p. 217). Authors emphasise that the involvement with others carries a 'risk'. In my case, the bodily co-entanglements through touch or distance has involved the 'sensitive zones'. According to Cohen-Emerique's (2011) definition: these are areas where we encounter another's touch, and this relates directly to our identity, what we know about ourselves. When this part of one self comes into play (concretely, to be cisgender and lesbian),[5] it can generate feelings of loss, shock and above all, a transformation of one's own position and also of the analytical positions that one assumes. The latter the authors highlight as the 'risk' warns anthropology '[to] makes its own vulnerability central' (Dwyer to Kulick and Willson, 1995, p. 15). Such a warning has revealed to me that the 'vulnerability' of all people involved in a process of interpretation, can model the same frames of understanding.

I cannot separate the notion of 'risked involvement' from the following discussion. Whitehead and Conaway (1986) warned about something that resonates today and ignites discussions with my colleagues (men) talking about the possible vulnerability of doing fieldwork in spaces explicitly eroticised and/or sexualised.

In a discussion related to an awkward flirtation in the swinger club, I received an answer, 'you know where you were, right?' This fact astonished all of my colleagues (women) who were in the debate. Whitehead and Conaway (1986) wrote down as specifically addressing 'sexual' and 'gender' issues, men – both gay and heterosexual – have been commissioned, managed in the field and write about issues related to desire or sex practices rather than issues of 'gender' per se; and in particular, how they are touched. This concern lies inherently with many anthropologists (women), being by action or omission positioned (I do not exclude positioning oneself) as erotic subjects.

Such discussions are one of the many effects of what Butler (1994), inspired by Rubin (1989), warned in her article 'Against Proper Objects': the institutional separation (and political-activist) of queer studies or radical sexual theories, and feminisms. The former would correspond to 'sexuality' and the latter to 'gender'. This is an illusory distinction that not only compresses the research, obviating the necessary problematising of the boundaries between these two categories, but reproduces a (hetero)normative view of the ethnographic process. This generates specific analysis or circumvention of material and bodily impacts on those who investigate and of the people with whom we investigate.

Made aware of the impacts of research that may involve fielding not only a question or research questions but the body of the anthropologist, is one aspect of the learning process that I consider more complex. I approached the body and I used the body, not as a device enabling access to knowledge but involved in its coproduction.[6] What follows are some of the issues that arise when that unpredictable element plays a decisive role during the investigation.

To be touched: between complicity and the impact of desire

26 November 2012. Swinger club Fidelité: Maribel lies in the bed with delicacy, taking care that her skirt does not lift more than halfway above her thigh. She begins to touch and caress different

men who are encircling the big bed. A man in his later forties gets close to her, undressing the towel and he offers himself up to be masturbated, and she does. A moment later, the man tries to get into the big bed. Maribel turns around while she removes her hair to see the orgiastic scene that is taking place behind her. After this, she looks for my gaze, she smiles and disappears. I respond to her with an uncomfortable smile.

The contact is, par excellence, characterised by contingency. The proposition, the scene could be diverse, or not even occur, if there were different possibilities for existence, hers and mine. And if these possibilities really were different, I wonder how this would affect the evocation of gesture, or the evocation of gaze, and my attribution of value to it.

The atmosphere of intimacy that I feel between Maribel and myself becomes a shared intimacy in the context of the swinger club, revealing the relational norms within the same. Probably, only she and I are witnesses to the fleeting glance (although a glance is never a private experience). I would rather suggest that there is complicity between us. And I would say that through this gaze, I become witness and at the same time guarantor of a Secret, or the 'Public Secret' to which Taussig (2010) refers. I am a secret accomplice to her cross-dressing practice, the desecration of which could put the most 'sacred' at risk: heteronormativity. It would expose its intrinsic fragility. Through our gaze, I find myself aware of 'knowing what could not be known'. For the Secret to be effective, and to ensure its survival as a secret, its administration must be contained in a seemingly private sphere. Indeed, its 'fetishisation' must be maintained in a floating yet controlled field of intimacy inside the spatial and temporal frame of the club.[7]

Our visual encounter reveals to me that the moral, social and sexual value of the self is established in a performative way, but above all, it is produced between us: the recognition of 'femininity' sought in cross-dressing, and what I feel to be a re-updating of my 'femininity', which surprisingly moves me and stirs me intensely.

It moves me while she is looking at me. It moves me because she looks at me. It awakens in my skin, an emotional memory that for me immediately changes the meaning of the complicity I have perceived until that moment. It forces me to breathe and appreciate my own resources in being able to remain in the field. It also leads me to reflect about how value is sometimes maintained only through the cost of vulnerability (hers and mine); since value needs expressions and solid materialisations to keep its intrinsic fragility. These expressions and materialisations are revealed in our use of clothing, rather than the nudity in which others move within the swinger's club. Our zone of contact is distance itself. Ahmed elucidates this:

> If we feel another hurts us, then that feeling may convert quickly into a reading of the other, such that it becomes hurtful, or is read as the impression of the negative ... The affective responses are readings that not only create the borders between selves and others, but also "give" others meaning and value in the very act of apparent separation, a giving that temporarily fixes another, through the movement engendered by the affective response itself. (Ahmed, 2014, p. 28)

The surface of pain masks itself / masks me with a feeling of rejection. This is the first effect. I realise later on – reflecting on what León (2011) and Sabido (2012) called the 'reappraisal' – that my reassessment of the situation has a direct bearing on the management and direction of my emotional reactions. They are outside the focus of consciousness. These appear later on when I am with Maribel in a tantric massage session to which she invites me. We are both naked. Before starting the session, she is wearing underwear and high heels. When the masseuse takes off Maribel's panties and shoes, Maribel also asks her to take off her brassiere: 'It no longer makes sense', she says. My reaction surfaces after a few long minutes, when she grabs my hand on ejaculating. And I quickly move my hand away. My reaction creates meaning and value – in the action itself of separating. It allows an accumulation of value: in my reading of her, in my reading of my own body's feelings towards her, and in my reading about myself.

In the swinger club, Maribel whispers to me that many days she goes home with 'mal d'ous' because she could not ejaculate. She tells me her desire to get home and have sex with her wife. The feeling of complicity and rejection are simultaneous for me. Both force me to attend to her emotional experience, but beyond the significance of pleasure and its intrinsic connection with the construction of gender and gender identity. My interpretation was infused with symbolic networks that have been bequeathed me through anthropology. I correlated the 'knot-ejaculation-body experience of masculinity' with the 'dress-no ejaculation body-experience of femininity'. A shift of masculinity to femininity and vice versa occurred within a continuum of heterosexuality that I could not ignore since she reinforced it (repeating 'I am not gay' or understanding masturbation and fellatio as expressions of her own femininity unlike anal sex practices). She said that, in the case of going 'dressed', it would be frustrating and difficult ejaculating, or that it could confuse her. Ejaculation would become a 'physiological' and 'mental' limitation that allowed her (unknowingly allowed me) to shield the vulnerability of the heteronormative interpretation frame.

Once more, in the refusal of the hand, the zone of contact is distance. Sustained by Ahmed (2014), I observed how materialisation of gender occurs through the 'mediation' of effects/affects (both by she grabbing my hand and by me refusing it), and how it works in the way we read the bodies of others or 'the Other'. This refusal, this reading of the impression of the negative about which Ahmed speaks, leads me to see how variables of oppression and privilege (femininity/masculinity, homosexuality/heterosexuality) are at play between us. These do not always appear within a fixed hierarchy. All variables, hers and mine, are configured in a fragile manner. Some of them more than others. Some of them at different times than others.

Displacing the border

> It is not a question of blurring boundaries or of rendering them invisible. It is a question of shifting them as soon as they tend to become ending lines. (Minh-ha, 2015)

The research entails stories (history/story[8]) of contact, connected to feminisms or activisms; if each of them can be named, separated. The research gaze here is not so much about the subjectivity of the anthropologist, but the dynamic of bodily contact. It is also present in the research because of its acting as well as of its blurring. Naming this epistemological shift is useful in positioning me in a specific field of research.

What effects/affects generate availability for bodily contact? Reflecting on this question as a starting point has allowed me to signify the intersection of values that may be in the erotic contact between the anthropologist and the people with whom we are engaged in the field. Indeed, the contact – either physical or immaterial touch (gaze or hand) – generates a corporeal emotion. Contact creates an echo of meanings that spread and shape the entangled bodies.

This scene focuses on a dynamic characterised by the circularity of the process: body contact; recognition of emotions; recognition of the other person. This recognition simultaneously generates a corporeal availability for contact. The body contact as such becomes an academic field through our negotiation of gender within it, through the feelings and emotions that regulate our availability for it, and from the recognition mediated through it.

The fundamental question is to do what Alga and I called the unthought-of and the unthinkable in our emotions, beyond something personal and political – rather, epistemological and methodological reflection (Alga and Barbé i Serra, 2015). This aspect forces collection of the direct impact on the skin itself and the 'sensitive areas' of identity (Cohen-Emerique, 2011). Deciding not to remain silent gives us the opportunity to transform the unthought-of and the unthinkable in our emotions into scientific knowledge production and creative energy. The inevitable relationship of this point with the Inappropriate/d Other of Trinh T. Minh-ha (1986–1987), allowed me to me think about how emotions imply that double reading: something that you cannot appropriate and something that is inappropriate under certain circumstances. Minh-ha (2015) has given me the key to place this dynamic analysis: 'inappropriate(d)ness does not refer to a fixed location, but is constantly changing with the specific circumstances of each person, event or struggle, it works differently according to the moment and the forces at work'.

Beyond leading to a reflection on asymmetries and estrangements, a re-reading of some episodes from the field with the 'bodily contact' lens is sustained by breaking the silence in the dynamics of reciprocity and in the circulation of power and desire that occurs within the field. If this goes un-named it would conserve the deeply exoticising and colonialist conditions that tend to permeate a unidirectional discourse about the sexuality and gender of the people with whom we study, as well as about sex and the erotic of the Other/others; a 'Sex' and an 'Erotic' which have both been widely enjoyed as an anthropological attraction.

Acknowledgements

This chapter was made possible through a lot of people from EnFemme and Fidelité that have openly shared their time, experiences and lives with me. My thanks also go to Maria Livia Alga with whom I have developed part of these reflections and Verena Stolcke for our constant methodological reflections. To Hellen Dixon and Giuseppe Aricó for having patience and putting much effort into the English revision of this work.

228 | BARBÉ I SERRA

Notes

1. Ahmed (2006) works the phenomenological notion of 'orientation' through sexual orientation, East and Orientalism. She draws upon authors like Csordas, who works on the notion of perception and 'proprioception': 'our sense of being in a body and oriented in space' (1994, p. 5).

2. I accessed the information from a presentation by Esteban (2015) quoting her colleague Carlos García of the University of the Basque Country.

3. I take the idea of vectors from Mohanty (1985), Brah (1992) and Hill Collins (1990) with a shift towards the notion of 'assemblages' from De Landa (2006) or Puar (2007). Such an approach allows me to work from how the vectors are inextricably linked to social, historical and political processes that constitute them but also to specific 'fields' of social action, or symbolic spaces in which these relations (gender, class, etc.) converge and are co-produced dynamically.

4. Geertz (1995) attributed this to Malinowski.

5. I recognise the facilities which involved me being a young and white 'bio-woman' in the swinger club: the presence in different spaces, the chance for me not to pay the entrance fee, the invitation to speak in the bed area and view orgiastic scenes, sharing stories of everyday life outside the club (connections not often made between 'unknowns').

'Bio-woman'/'Bio-man' is reflected in the Spanish context by Preciado in an attempt to underline the 'naturalised' character of cultural femininity/masculinity. The dimension of 'bio' is used to describe people who identify with the 'gender' assigned at birth, as opposed to 'techno', which is a re-conceptualisation of gender, recognising its dependence on technology (Preciado, 2008, p. 85). I do not use the concept for my analysis because of the theoretical and strategic doubts raised in me. However, the emic term 'bio-woman' appears in the field as a category of differentiation; also, but not often, 'bio-man', as many of the people who practise cross-dressing are identified. Both terms are used in the EnFemme club – from where Maribel comes – but not in the swinger club. This seems to be due to its proximity to the pro-depathologisation trans movements. Many people are influenced by queer theory, regarding which Preciado is debtor and interpreter in the Spanish state context.

6. Beyond the phenomenological tradition and legacy of Csordas's (1994) concept of 'embodiment' or the 'body memory' to which Stoller (1997) refers and 'non-discursive memory' from Del Valle (1999, p. 8), the integration of the researcher's sensory perceptions as part of the research record has been studied, taking as the starting point Bourdieu's (2006) concept of 'habitus' or Esteban's (2004) 'in-corporation'. I considered the body as an epistemological device through carnal ethnography (Wacquant's [2009, p. 1] 'carnal knowledge' or 'carnal sociology' [Wacquant, 2004]), and Esteban's (2011) related 'emotional ethnography'.

7. Taussig focused on the development of Hegel's 'labour of the negative' (1972). He wondered what if the truth was not only a secret but a Public Secret, shared. That is, the fact of 'knowing what not to know' forms the basis of social institutions (work, family, the heteronormativity regime and the state). He wondered if intrinsic to the discovery of the Secret was its destruction or its strength.

8. In Catalan or Spanish the word 'history' is written in the same way. Playing with the Anglo-Saxon words allows me to locate 'bodily contact histories' in a certain time and space, in relation to the political, social, economic, cultural and exoticising lens, etc.; also, in the multiple stories of erotic-sexual contact, intimacy, friendship and enmity, kinship, etc.

References

Ahmed, Sara (2004) 'Affective Economies', *Social Text*, 22(2), pp. 117–139.

Ahmed, Sara (2006) *Queer Phenomenology: Orientations, Objects, Others*, Durham, NC: Duke University Press.

Ahmed, Sara (2014) [2004] *The Cultural Politics of Emotion*, Edinburgh: Edinburgh University Press.

Alga, Maria Livia and Barbé i Serra, Alba (2015) 'Dosis de tensión: dinámicas eróticas, negociación y reconocimiento en la investigación entre la academia y el activismo', *Communication, International Congress Affect Embodiment and Politics*, 12–14 February, UAB Barcelona.

Bourdieu, Pierre (2006) [1980] *El sentido práctico*, Madrid: Taurus.

Bourdieu, Pierre and Wacquant, Loïc (2005) [1992] *Una invitación a la sociología reflexiva*, Buenos Aires: Siglo XXI.

Brah, Avtar (2004) [1992] 'Diferencia, diversidad, diferenciación', in hooks, b., Brah, A., Sandobal, Ch., Anzaldúa, G. et al. (eds) *Otras inapropiables. Feminismos desde las fronteras*, Madrid: Traficantes de Sueños, pp. 107–136.

Butler, Judith (1994) 'Against Proper Objects', *Differences: A Journal of Feminist Cultural Studies*, 6(2–3), pp. 1–26. Available at www.sfu.ca/~decaste/OISE/page2/files/ButlerAgainstProper.pdf.

Caplan, Pat (1993) 'Introduction 2: The Volume', in Bell, D., Caplan, P. and Karim, W. (eds) *Gendered Fields: Women, Men and Ethnography*, London and New York: Routledge, pp. 19–27.

Cardín, Alberto (1989) [1984] *Guerreros, chamanes y travestís. Indicios de homosexualidad entre los exóticos*, Barcelona: Tusquets.

Cesara, Manda (1982) *Reflections of a Woman Anthropologist: No Hiding Place*, London and New York: Academic Press.

Cohen-Emerique, Margalit (2011) *Pour une approche interculturelle en travail social: Théories et pratiques*, Rennes: Presses de L'EHESP.

Connell, Raewyn W. (2010) [2006] *Masculinities*, Cambridge: Polity Press.

Csordas, Thomas J. (1994) 'Introduction: The Body as

Representation and Being-in-the-World' in Csordas, T.J. (ed.) *Embodiment and Experience: The Existential Ground of Culture and Self*, Cambridge: Cambridge University Press, pp. 1–24.

De Landa, Manuel (2006) *A New Philosophy of Society: Assemblage Theory and Social Complexity*, New York: Continuum.

Del Valle, Teresa (1999) [1997]. 'Procesos de la memoria: Cronotopos genéricos', *La Ventana*, 9, pp. 7–42.

Esteban, Mari Luz (2004) *Antropología del cuerpo. Género, itinerarios corporales, identidad y cambio*. Barcelona: Bellaterra.

Esteban, Mari Luz (2011) *Crítica del Pensamiento Amoroso. Temas contemporáneos*, Barcelona: Bellaterra.

Esteban, Mari Luz (2015) 'La reinvención de la política y la reivindicación de la vulnerabilidad. De somatizaciones teóricas, políticas y etnográficas', Key Conference, *International Congress Affect Embodiment and Politics*, 12–14 February, UAB Barcelona.

Geertz, Clifford (1995) [1974] *La interpretación de las culturas*, Barcelona: Gedisa.

Haraway, Donna (1988) 'Situated Knowledges: The Science Question in Feminism and the Privilege of Partial Perspective', *Feminist Studies*, 14(3), pp. 575–599. Accessed May 2015. doi: 10.2307/3178066.

Haraway, Donna (1991) 'A Cyborg Manifesto: Science, Technology, and Socialist Feminism in the Late Twentieth Century' in Haraway, D. (ed.) *Simians, Cyborgs, and Women: The Reinvention of Nature*, New York: Routledge, pp. 149–181.

Hegel, Georg W.F. (1972) [1807] *Phenomenology of Spirit*, Oxford: Oxford University Press.

Hill Collins, Patricia (1990) *Black Feminist Thought: Knowledge, Consciousness and the Politics of Empowerment*, Boston, MA: Unwin Hyman.

Kulick, Don and Willson, Margaret (1995) *Taboo: Sex, Identity and Erotic Subjectivity in Anthropological Fieldwork*, London and New York: Routledge.

León, Emma (2011) *El Monstruo en el Otro. Sensibilidad y Coexistencia Humana*, Madrid: Sequitur.

Malinowski, Bronislaw (1989) [1967] *Diario de campo en Melanesia*, Barcelona: Júcar.

Merleau-Ponty, Maurice (2002) [1945] *Phenomenology of Perception*, London: Routledge and Kegan Paul.

Minh-ha, Trinh T. (1986–1987) '"She, the Inappropriate/d Other", Focusing on Postcolonial Women as Writing and Written Subjects', *Discourse*, 8 (Fall–Winter).

Minh-ha, Trinh T. (2015) 'Inappropriate/d Artificiality' [Interview of Marina Grzinic].

Mohanty, Chandra Talpade (2008) [1985] 'Bajo los ojos de Occidente. Saber académico y discursos coloniales' in Mezzadra, S. (ed.) *Estudios Postcoloniales. Ensayos fundamentales*, Madrid: Traficantes de Sueños, pp. 69–102.

Newton, Esther (1993) 'My Best

Informant's Dress: The Erotic Equation in Fieldwork', *Cultural Anthropology*, 8(1), pp. 3–23. Accessed February 2015. doi: 10.1525/can.1993.8.1.02a00010.

Plummer K. (2008) 'Studying Sexualities for a Better World? Ten Years of *Sexualities*', *Sexualities*, 11(1/2), pp. 7–22.

Preciado, Paul (Beatriz) (2008) *Testo Yonki*, Madrid: Espasa.

Puar, Jasbir K. (2007) *Terrorist Assemblages: Homonationalism in Queer Times*, Durham, NC: Duke University Press.

Rich, Adrienne Cécile (1977) *Of Woman Born: Motherhood as Experience and Institution*, New York: Bantam Books.

Rubin, Gayle (1989) [1984] 'Reflexionando sobre el sexo: Notas para una teoría radical de la sexualidad' in Vance, C.S. (ed.) *Placer y peligro. Explorado la sexualidad femenina*, Madrid: Talasa, pp. 113–190.

Sabido, Olga (2012) *El cuerpo como recurso de sentido en la construcción del extraño. Una perspectiva sociológica*, Madrid: Sequitur.

Spivak, Gayatri Chakravorty (2008) [1985] 'Estudios de la Subalternidad. Deconstruyendo la Historiografía' in Mezzadra, S. (ed.) *Estudios Postcoloniales. Ensayos fundamentales*, Madrid: Traficantes de Sueños, pp. 33–67.

Spronk, Rachel (2014) 'Sexuality and Subjectivity: Erotic Practices and the Question of Bodily Sensations', *Social Anthropology*, 22(1), pp. 3–21.

Stacey, Judith (1988) 'Can There Be a Feminist Ethnography?', *Women's Studies International Forum*, 11(1), pp. 21–27.

Stoller, Paul (1997) *Sensuous Scholarship*, Philadelphia, PA: University of Pennsylvania Press.

Strathern, Marilyn (1991) *Partial Connections*, Savage, MD: Rowman and Littlefield.

Taussig, Michael (2010) *Desfiguraciones. El secreto público y la labor de lo negativo*, Madrid: Fineo.

Wacquant, Loïc (2004) [2001] *Cos i ànima. Quaderns etnogràfics d'un aprenent de boxejador*, Barcelona: Edicions de 1984.

Wacquant, Loïc (2009) 'The Body, the Ghetto and the Penal State', *Qualitative Sociology*, 32, pp. 101–129.

Wheatley, Elizabeth E. (1994) 'How Can We Engender Ethnography with a Feminist Imagination? A Rejoinder to Judith Stacey', *Women's Studies International Forum*, 17(4), pp. 403–416.

Whitehead, Tony Larry and Conaway, Mary Ellen (1986) 'Introduction' in Whitehead, T.L. and Conaway, M.E. (eds) *Self, Sex and Gender in Cross-Cultural Fieldwork*, Urbana and Chicago, IL: University of Illinois Press, pp. 1–14.

12 | SANGLI STORIES: RESEARCHING INDIAN SEX WORKERS' INTIMATE LIVES

Andrea Cornwall

Abstract

This chapter is about using narrative biographical method with Maharashtrian sex workers and their clients-turned-lovers to hear their stories of life and love. It describes an accidental research project that emerged out of a politically-driven desire to do what sex workers charged 'western feminists' like myself with failing to do: to listen to their accounts of themselves, and their own lives, not to judge, or prejudge, but to show up, shut up and listen, and pay attention to what they were saying. They were rightly tired of stories of abjection that represented them as objects of pity, as they were of tales that disregarded the realities of abuse at the hands of the police and those who take it upon themselves to rescue sex workers. I give an account here of the unfolding process of designing the research project with the sex workers and the organisations that represent and work with them, VAMP (Veysha Anyay Mukhti Parishad, which can be translated as 'sex workers freedom from injustice') and SANGRAM. I describe how Sutapa Majumdar and I worked together to conduct the narrative biographical interviews, and the approach I took to analysing and making sense of what we learnt. And I reflect on how the method of narrative biography offered me the opportunity as a researcher to listen and learn without being overly directive in making the enquiry all about answers to my questions rather than about their reflections, memories and experiences.

Sex workers have often been the objects of other people's curiosities and preoccupations. Robust critique of research on sex workers that serves simply to reinforce politicised prejudices has highlighted the exploitative nature of this kind of social science (O'Neill, 1996; O'Neill and Campbell, 2006; Van der Meulen, 2011; Pyett, 1998). This has led to calls for, as Teela Sanders (2006) puts it, 'collaborative research partnerships that work alongside informants, offering directorship and control to those who are normally subjected to the research process' (Sanders, 2006, p. 463). Sex workers and sex worker rights activists have played an active part in defining the terms under which such research is carried out.[1] Sex worker-led initiatives such as the Network of Sex Work Projects and the Paulo Longo Research Initiative have led debates about the ethics of sex work research, as well as producing innovations in methodology and a diversity of research materials, from large-scale surveys such as the All-India Sex Work Survey (Sahni and Shankar, 2011), to case studies of project interventions (Overs, 2014) and ethnographies of international policy processes (Doezema, 2009).

Having been part of these conversations for a number of years, as an academic supervisor, commissioner of research, editor and colleague, I had no intention of engaging directly in sex work research for precisely the reasons highlighted by sex worker critics of academic researchers. And yet, as I narrate in this chapter, it was through my deliberate, politically-inspired, *non-*engagement as a researcher that I came to find myself immersed in an accidental research project on sex workers' intimate lives. In this chapter, I tell the story of developing this project. I describe the use of biographical narrative story-telling as a methodological approach that can create the possibility of open-ended dialogue and exchange (Andrews, 2014; Andrews et al., 2013; Clandinin and Connolly, 2004). I explore the ways in which this kind of approach can serve to acknowledge and give recognition to the stories told by subjects who are all too often objectified in popular media and social science research.

Beginnings

My first encounter with the sex worker collective called VAMP (Veysha Anyay Mukti Parishad, 'Sex Workers Fight Injustice'), a 5,000-plus member strong organisation based in the city of Sangli in the central Indian state of Maharashtra, was through an account of their struggles for rights and recognition given by Meena Seshu at a workshop on organising in the informal economy in Delhi in 2008 (Seshu, 2013). I had heard about VAMP many years ago, and had come to regard them as an inspiring example of community-based organising. Meena's account brought into view other dimensions of VAMP's work, chiming with two of my preoccupations at the time. The first was with instances of what Cecilia Sardenberg (2008) describes as 'liberating empowerment', which she juxtaposes with 'liberal empowerment' – the contrast invoking the distinction between transformative social action and individual self-actualisation. And the second was the use of film to convey these effects, and confront the kinds of prejudices about the 'Third World Woman' identified so powerfully by Chandra Talpade Mohanty (1988) and still so present in representations of women from the global South in the media and the marketing materials of charities in the global North.

'Come to Sangli', Meena said, enlisting me as she had many others from outside the country in seeing what VAMP were doing at first hand. With a couple of days on my hands, I took her up. Two days later, I was sitting in her car being driven from Pune to Sangli. With a translator in tow, I made my way over the next couple of days to visits to a string of households in the red-light districts of Sangli and Miraj, meeting members of VAMP. Some were female, members of the Dalit caste dedicated to the Hindu goddess Yellema as young girls, taking the identity of the never-to-be-married-to-a-man *devadasi*, many of whom work in sex work (Orchard, 2007). Others were Hindu or Muslim women who for various reasons – disastrous and abusive marriages being one, poverty being another – had gone into sex work. Others still were *hijras* (transgender), or men who identified in various ways and might be described as 'men who have sex with men' (MSM).

What intrigued me from the outset about the members of VAMP I met in that initial encounter was how confident and assertive they were. The image of the Indian sex worker conjured up by the media, and relayed in the work of NGOs specialising in rescue and rehabilitation (see for example www.freedom.firm.in), is so often one of abjection. We are led to believe that sex workers are in this business out of coercion, not out of choice. We are encouraged to think of them as victims of the brutalities of male desire, raped dozens of times a day by relentless victimisers. The reality I encountered in those rural Maharashtrian cities of Sangli and Miraj could not have been more different. In the narrow lanes that made up the red-light area, sex workers worked out of their rooms or booths made out of thin boards of wood with a sliding door in the small two-storey houses that were set up as brothels. The brothel owners (*gharwallis*) took part of their earnings as rent and protection money; some were also members of VAMP, retired sex workers or sex workers who had made enough to leave the business of sex to others. It was evident that sex workers were not spending the bulk of their time with their clients, but with their children, lovers, friends and families. Getting ready for work, domestic work and voluntary community work for VAMP like visiting people who were unwell or distributing condoms took up more of their everyday lives than having sex: I was told that the average time the sex workers spent with a client was about five minutes and that they did not generally remove their saris for a sexual encounter that was so short-lived.

As I chatted to sex workers about their lives, they sketched a contrast between those whom they called 'domestic women' and women like them. 'Domestic women' were those who were married, generally by arrangement. They were objects of pity for the sex workers; their lot was that of domestic drudgery and they were regarded as suffering with a lack of freedom, for all the respectability marriage brought them. These women, in their accounts, were often subject to being treated with disregard by their husbands and their kin, especially by mothers-in-law who could be cruel and exacting; such men could be abusive and violent with impunity. 'Domestic women' were described as trapped in their marriages, the indignity and insecurity of exit leaving them little alternative but to endure. In a vivid juxtaposition of their relative agency, sex workers told me of the conditions they set for their lovers; including, some said, telling them that if they were to lay so much as a finger on them, that would be it. After all, if a man misbehaves, they said, they could swiftly replace him with another. That's the difference between us and 'domestic women', one remarked: 'domestic women' have no such power, and if they have bad luck in the choice of husband that is made for them by their families, that is their lot in life and they just need to bear it.

The women clearly relished telling their stories. And I found them fascinating. There were so many dimensions to these tales that defied conventional perspectives on sex work. So often the focus of writing on sex work is just on the business of sex. Less often do we see sex workers represented as people with complex lives involving a diversity of other people, including those they love as well as those who make their lives difficult[2] – notably the police and those who collude with the police in the name of 'rescue'. I could see that finding a way to communicate these stories with an audience from the UK and US would be a powerful way to seek to counter some of the negative effects of abolitionist narratives on prostitution that so badly miss the mark in terms of what is actually going on in these women's lives.[3]

Here began a collaboration with Meena and VAMP that continues almost ten years later. We started with the idea of co-producing a film, which we could use to contest some of the myths about sex workers in the global South, creating a vehicle for sex workers to represent themselves and their own perspectives and experiences (Cornwall, 2016). We decided to hire a UK film company who could work with an aesthetic and narrative frame that would appeal to a Western audience. VAMP would have editorial control. The film took as its name one of their slogans: *Save Us from Saviours.* I returned in early 2009 with the film crew. In the process of making the film, I became intrigued with the teasing that was going on amongst members of VAMP when they referred to their *malaks* – a Marathi word for 'master' that was used in a tongue-in-cheek way to refer to sex workers' lovers, some of them kept husbands and others the husbands of other women who maintained love affairs with sex workers.

Out of this came an invitation to return, this time as a researcher, to document something that matters a lot in sex workers' lives, but is very rarely the topic of research: their love lives. But the idea of doing this raised for me a number of dilemmas, personal as well as political. The politics of doing research with sex workers in India as a white feminist without direct experience of doing sex work, from the country that introduced the laws, frames of reference and practices that have made such a powerfully negative contribution to the situation of sex workers added a further dimension to this. After doing anthropological fieldwork in Nigeria for my PhD, I'd been determined to never again be the quasi-colonial anthropologist; while my Yoruba 'respondents' were perfectly happy to indulge me, indulging my curiosity about their lives left me with a deeply uncomfortable feeling. Critical of the coloniality both of my own discipline and of international development, I'd got to a point where I felt the best way I could engage was in finding and channelling resources to support research initiatives led and run by people from the global South.

For almost two decades, I had not done conventional anthropological research. I had never stopped being an anthropologist; I think of my training as having cultivated a disposition that remains deeply part of me. It taught me how to listen, as well as how to remain slightly at the margins of what is going on and look on with curiosity, a life skill in itself. But I had stopped being a researcher in any formal sense. There were also practical concerns. I didn't speak Marathi, Hindi or Kannada. I had never done any research before in India, although I had lived there and gained everyday familiarity with some elements of its cultures. Plus, and importantly, I was not a sex worker.

I shared these doubts with Meena, who laughed. She reminded me that it was precisely because I was not from Sangli, not a sex worker and most importantly, because I was someone who could identify with and be identified as a 'Western feminist' that my version of the realities of sex workers' lives would be useful in challenging the myths and stereotypes that led to such abuse of sex workers' rights by foreign organisations claiming to act in their interests. Why not put my researcher's skills to work, rather than feel sheepish about accepting their invitation? And why not do the research in such a way as to ensure what I came up with was as rigorous as possible – not as an advocate, nor as a journalist, but as the academic I was trained to be. She was, of course, quite right. I was in danger of being precious. A year or so later, I was back in Sangli, this time as a researcher.

Constructing a methodology

If my research could do what the sex workers wanted me to do as a white feminist anthropologist – to provide a lens through which to look into their intimate relationships, as they themselves experienced them – then my choice of methodology was going to be critical. It needed to be sufficiently robust to be trustworthy. Lincoln and Guba (1985) usefully identify four criteria under which qualitative and interpretive research should be judged as trustworthy, highlighting key differences from the way quantitative and positivist research is assessed. The first is 'credibility': confidence in the veracity of the findings. The second is 'transferability': showing that there is applicability of the findings in other contexts. The third criterion, 'dependability', shows the findings are consistent and can be repeated. Lastly, 'confirmability' speaks to the extent to which the findings of the study are shaped by the respondents, not by the biases, motivations of interest of the researchers.

Ethnographic research wasn't going to work in this context. I lacked the time for intensive immersion. Participant observation would have been challenging, and the informal interactions that are often used by ethnographers to elucidate their object of study were going to be tricky. I didn't speak any of the languages spoken in Sangli. My presence in the sex work area would have garnered suspicions, especially since white foreigners were more often associated with collusion with the police in rights-violating raids. People had recently had their fill of a particularly aggressive American evangelist who had set up shop nearby with a mission to cause as much disruption as possible to people's lives; the stories of what had happened when young women who were visiting relatives were picked up by the police as suspected sex workers were heartbreaking. It would, in short, have been hard to produce *credible* research using the methods that I was most practised in using.

I considered the possibility of organising a series of focus groups, a method that became popular as a social research method in the 1980s (Morgan and Spanish, 1984; Kreuger, 1994). Focus groups gained popularity because they were perceived to permit researchers to be able to record interactions between participants (Kitzinger, 1994); they were seen to be a way to get people talking about sensitive issues in an environment in which they were amongst their peers, less likely to make up things to please the interviewer and more likely to offer a more authentic version of their views. Focus group discussions came to be used widely in research on sex and sexuality in the 1990s for this reason (see, for example, Munodawafa et al., 1995; White and Thomson, 1995). But I've never held much confidence in the belief that people speak more freely amongst peers on intimate matters. I found in Nigeria that women may be *least* likely to speak truthfully amidst women with whom they might share everyday encounters but not intimacies, and may be even more reluctant than in an interview setting with a total stranger from another culture. Men, in my experience, may also be less open in such settings than they would be in a one-to-one interview, for other reasons.

Survey methods are perhaps the most widely used tool in sex research. Self-completed questionnaires offer privacy and a measure of anonymity, sufficient to create the possibility of openness. Much depends, of course, on how questions are put – and just as often survey researchers receive the answers to the questions they ask, but a very partial picture of what people actually do and believe (Bleek, 1987). After all, as Laura Agustín (2004) asks in relation to sex work research, 'Why, after all, should people who are being treated as objects of curiosity tell the truth?' (2004, p. 6). In this context, survey methods were not going to work. Many of the women were not well educated enough to fill in a survey return themselves, and sending in enumerators was unlikely to yield the kind of information I was looking for. In any case, I've always felt uncomfortable with having others administer interview checklists and questionnaires on my behalf. I prefer to feel my way into a conversation, and see where it leads me.

Some of the richest insights I've gained in anthropological fieldwork have come from listening attentively as people narrate stories about their lives. I've tended to dispense with checklists and a more semi-structured approach to interviewing, and gone for a very open-ended style that begins with a simple question, and takes it from there. Ken Plummer's (1995) *Telling Sexual Stories* had been a source of immense inspiration to me as a student. The idea of working with stories of love lives seemed to promise what I was looking for in a method. Instinctively, when I carried out that very first round of exploratory interviews, I'd simply asked people to tell me their stories. I'd started wherever they wanted and gone wherever they wished, moved into doubling-back to probe and analyse, and then worked towards a closure that would leave the teller feeling as affirmed as possible. I was later to discover that this methodology had a name and a set of practices that were not far off what I'd been making up as I went along: narrative biographical interpretive method (Breckner and Rupp, 2002; Wengraf, 2009; Roseneil, 2012), narrative biographical interviewing (Clandinin and Connolly, 2004) and narrative biography (Andrews et al., 2013; Andrews, 2014).

Even with relatively little time on my hands, using a narrative biographical approach would permit me to apply sufficient methodological rigour to meet Lincoln and Guba's four criteria in *gathering* the data. And combining the conventions of interpretive analysis – coding, extracting themes, working inductively from interview transcripts – with the focus in narrative biography on stories as expressions of cultural assumptions as well as conscious concerns told would add a further layer of richness. The method would lend itself well to an intensive engagement with someone who was unfamiliar and different, as well as potentially providing a means of opening a space for dialogue with people who might be hesitant about being interviewed by enabling them to focus on their lives as lived rather than find answers to questions. As Sasha Roseneil reflects, one of its advantages is that:

> The method ... seeks narratives of past experience, rather than self-conscious statements of current belief and discourse about present and past experience, allowing the interviewee to 'wander in and out of recovered memories, in particular those that are seemingly trivial' (Bollas, 1995, p. 138 quoted in Wengraf, 2009, p. 37). (Roseneil, 2012, p. 130)

Asking people to tell their own stories, in their own words, chimes with an approach to research that I'd been involved in advocating for many years as a trainer and practitioner in participatory research (Cornwall and Jewkes, 1995; Cornwall, 2008). I recognised that in this context, other elements of a participatory approach could not only help defuse some of the suspicion with which I might be regarded as a white outsider, even with the introduction to the community that knowing Meena and VAMP could lend. It could also substantially improve the quality of the research. In conventional research, the researcher sets the frame, asks the questions, carries out or commissions others to carry out data collection, and draws together the findings into analysis. In participatory research, the relationship between researcher and participants changes: the participatory researcher becomes a facilitator as participants come to direct the action, asking the questions that are most germane to them, reflecting on the data that they themselves produce about themselves, coming up with their own analyses and ideas for action.

I'd had an experience about ten years before with one of the most effective participatory research projects I'd ever been involved in, called *Olhar Crítico* (Cornwall et al., 2008). *Olhar Crítico* consisted of a series of studies of social action in which a social movement leader directed a pair of external researchers to the people, the questions and the secondary data that would provide as rich as possible a picture of what they knew of their own context. Together, we framed what we'd ask; and together, we digested what we learnt, using participatory workshop techniques as well as the methods of the conventional qualitative researcher, interviews, coding and thematic and textual analysis. Our role as researchers was to be critical, and to investigate. But what made it different from a conventional research project was that the process of co-creation disrupted relations of knowledge and power in such a way as to put us, the researchers, in the position of deferring to the expertise of the social movement leader. And with the social movement leader directing the research process, with her knowledge of the context, the politics and the people, she was able to open doors, facilitate engagement and give us the kind of access that as researchers it would have taken us months to gain.

I could see a way of working with Meena and members of VAMP that would allow us to develop a hybrid approach to co-creating an understanding of sex workers' intimate lives. This would bring together narrative biographical method and the kind of participatory research approach we'd developed in *Olhar Crítico*. For this to work, though, I needed the right interpreter: someone who would be able to be sufficiently familiar with the women not to present a barrier to communication through body language, assumptions and the other possible obstacles to engaging women of low caste from a stigmatising profession. Meena found me exactly the right person in Sutapa Majumdar, a PhD student at the University of Pune. Sutapa had travelled the length and breadth of India supervising the pan-India survey of sex workers. She was – I quickly came to find out – warm, curious and engaging, someone who had the capacity to put people at ease very quickly.

Sharing intimate stories

Sutapa and I met for the first time at Pune airport and spent the five-hour journey to Sangli in intense conversation that ranged across our academic interests and intimate lives, touching on questions of theory and methodology along the way. Getting to know each other in this way was a vital part of the process. It permitted us to develop the dynamic between us that was to prove so invaluable in creating a relaxed, intimate ambiance for the interviews. The following day, we held a meeting with Meena and the core members of the VAMP collective to plan the research. Reflecting on the nature and purpose of the research, we began by establishing suitable criteria for selecting a sample of sex workers.

In a very useful article on the methodological challenges of doing research with sex workers, Frances Shaver (2005) reflects on the dilemmas of sampling such a difficult to reach population. Rather than using random or snowball sampling, the merits and detractions of which I explained, the group decided that purposive sampling would be the most appropriate approach. This, they argued, would allow Sutapa and I to interview a broad cross-section of female sex workers: *devadasi* and non-*devadasi*, women who had migrated from Karnataka to Sangli and Sangli-born sex workers, and women of different ages and religious faiths. Where possible, we would also speak with the *malaks* of the women who we'd interviewed. VAMP members were keen that we consider the full range of women's experiences, and, after some discussion about what that might constitute, they arrived at an initial list of women that they felt covered such a range. They included some of the 'best' and 'worst' experiences that they had come across. The rigour and care of the sampling process reflected their concern that they were persistently misrepresented with a single story. The way to contest this, they felt, was not to put a positive gloss and provide a similarly monolithic narrative; these were not to be 'happy hooker' stories, but to reflect as closely as possible the complexity and diversity of their lives and relationships as lived.

Creating a comfortable, private, space in which we could conduct the interviews uninterrupted was the next step. This was going to be essential if we were to be able to conduct long narrative biographical interviews. Sex workers' homes offered little of this privacy. Many women lived in a single room in the small houses that opened directly onto crowded alleyways, with neighbours and children milling around outside. A hotel room or office would be too impersonal. We decided to use a large, quiet, upstairs room in Meena's house. An unexpected advantage of this was that intimate conversations often spilled over into more public discussions once the interview was officially 'over' and we came down the stairs to join Meena and also sometimes other members of VAMP in her office on the ground floor. The privacy of the upstairs space permitted a sharing of confidences that included closely-guarded secrets that we were asked not to disclose to anyone. The outputs from our research respect those commitments.

Defining questions

Defining the scope of the research brought further discussion with VAMP. So often, sex workers are the subject of research about health – especially HIV – hazard and safety. Outsiders are often also curious to know why and how sex workers first began this line of work, and the details of it. But we were not looking for this, and wanted to begin in a place that made our intentions clear. If we were to run narrative interviews in such a way as to enable our participants to feel that our real interest was in them and their experiences, not as vectors of disease or victims, then we needed a way to open the interviews that could convey this intention. We began by asking them to tell us the story of their love relationships, starting with their very first love. This ran the risk, of course, that women had experienced something that we could all understand as love, and that by asking something so intimate so directly, we did not alienate them or make them feel like objects of our curiosity. But there was also something honest about it: we were there to find out about their love lives, and to represent those lives as part of the rounded fullness of life's experiences. Starting from here seemed a way we could signal that from the start.

It worked. The question often elicited laughter, and wry smiles, sometimes poignant moments of sadness, and sometimes wistful pauses as memories poured into the space we'd created for reflection on the past. But it always provoked a response and provided us with a jumping off point for an interview that generally took the shape of a narrative punctuated only by our gentle facilitative prompts and in which the speaker took the direction that they wished to take, as we'd hoped and intended. The open-ended format meant that the interviews continued for as long as the respondent wished, two to three hours on average, and on one occasion more than six. Laughter, tears, moments of intensity and stillness filled these hours. As is often the case with oral narratives of this kind, accounts circled back on themselves, returning to salient moments, reflecting on events and their consequences, and on memories that were at turns delicious, bitter sweet and painful.

Sasha Roseneil (2012) describes how narrative biographical method 'requires the interviewer to abstain from interrupting, and to offer the interviewee a sense of open-ended space within which to speak' (Roseneil, 2012, p. 130). We sought to create this space, asking very few direct questions and mostly just listening.

We probed very gently, sometimes taking the interviewee back to part of the story to explore some of what they had told us more deeply, sometimes encouraging them to step back from the detail to reflect on some of the overarching themes emerging from their narratives. We interviewed twelve women and six men. Only one of the interviewees took up my offer to reciprocate in telling my own story; that exchange, in which I was questioned in detail about my intimate relationships, led to hours of further exploration of commonalities and differences in our experiences. Out of this emerged a deeper analysis of the dynamics of power that punctuated her narrative and mine.

As our visit to Sangli drew to an end, we convened a group discussion to which we invited women of ages ranging from their early twenties to their late sixties. About 15 women came, and the lively discussion that ensued covered a range of topics from marriage normativity to social security in old age. It was definitely *not* a focus group, although we started with a simple line of questioning that might be used in one. Rather, we sought to use it to verify some of the observations we had on what the women and their lovers had told us, and explore some of the themes that emerged from the individual interviews. We also used it to reflect on ideals and realities, on representations of sex work and of how these women would like to be represented in stories about their lives.

Producing representations

Producing a representation of the lives of the women who had given so much of their time was a responsibility that I struggled to honour. The first task was to process the material we had generated. In a thoughtful analysis of the life stories of young Australian men, Connell (1991) describes a methodology for working with the transcripts of life stories that involves first working them up as case studies, and then tracing transversal themes and threads that run through them. I followed a similar approach, writing up the translated narratives in as close to verbatim as translation permitted, and then applying a meta-level analysis to explore emerging themes. I was particularly interested in variations on a theme that first sparked my interest in this project: the contrasts between the relationships sex workers had with men, and marriage. Sutapa was also intrigued by this question, and we came back to this many times in our interviews. In analysis, I came to trace this theme through the cases to explore some of the differences in discursive framing as well as reported experience.

My aim was to produce three artefacts from the interviews. The first was to be a short newspaper article, ideally for an online newspaper that is read in the US as well as the UK. I wrote a piece for *The Guardian* that captured almost half a million hits. This could have been because of the unusual juxtaposition of a self-declared feminist with the statement that the sex workers I'd worked with were amongst the most empowered women I had ever met. It could, of course, also have been because it coincided with other, more commercial, searches and drew curious or even salacious clicks. Whatever the case, it provided me with a vehicle to posit some of their realities, and speak some of their truths. The second was an anthropological article, aimed at one of the mainstream anthropology journals. I've recently finished this piece, drawing on historical and sociological as well as anthropological literature. I chose as a vehicle a device of an extended case study featuring the story of one of the older women, who recounted a string of relationships that spanned the range through from abusive (the thug, the forced sex inflicted by a policeman) to the passion of lovers and the everyday care of the man she called her 'helper', and thematic analysis that focused in on some of the surprises and contradictions emerging from the interviews. The last output is a graphic novel, and we're beginning work on this now.

Conclusion

What lessons might be drawn from this experience? For one thing, it affirmed one of the most important values of participatory research. This is not only that people know more about their own lives than researchers often given them credit for, but that in representing those lives they can be just as insistent on rigour, trustworthiness, authenticity and all those values for judging the quality of research that the academy most prizes. It was also a powerful reminder of the value of simply listening. There is nothing so revealing as a good conversation, aided by the right questions. There's something about narrating a life through the theme of love that is extraordinarily poignant. Moments of intimacy in which we shared stories of our own lives made it possible to have a different quality of conversation, one that was less the parade of questions of the semi-structured or structured interview, but more the exploratory, confidence-exchange of an unhurried, long chat.

Creating a space for this away from the bustle of everyday life gave the conversations a stolen, secret quality that added to the sense of intimacy. We'd close the heavy wooden doors in Meena's upstairs room, settle on cushions on the floor and focus our undivided attention on each other. There was something about the rhythm and pace of these exchanges that made them feel more open, more honest; and more useful, for everyone. Interviewing shades into other forms of talking therapy; there are clearly hazards here, from being triggered by painful and abusive memories to lacking the skills to safely contain what might be aroused and emerge from the conversations. And yet there is a reciprocity in this kind of exchange that is lacking in more utilitarian research methods, as well as dignity around self-disclosure that a survey questionnaire or semi-structured interview's questions might unsettle. How often do we experience people listening to us with their full attention, focused in on our memories and our feelings? I've often come away from narrative biographical interviews being thanked, in all genuineness, by the interviewee for the time, and the care, that it takes to really listen; this experience was no different.

Perhaps more than anything, what I took away from these encounters was some of the commonalities between experiences that might otherwise have appeared so entirely distant in their difference. And it was this very bridging of our worlds that took me back to the purpose of hearing these stories: to paint the lives of women living thousands of miles away in an utterly different reality not as themselves 'backward' nor as victims of 'backward' ways, with all the coloniality that word implies, but as human beings whose lives are as rich a tapestry of pleasure, pain, longing, desire, misery, laughter and joy as any of our own. Narrative biographical story-telling offered us a way of doing this that respected the integrity of the women whose stories we heard. It also lent us a sense of proximity, of empathy, that would have been difficult to access using any other method. And ultimately, what the experience of doing this research gave us was something of that sense of what it is to be fully human that is so sorely lacking in the monolithic, violating representation of sex work popularised by radical feminists whose politicised agendas so often make them so entirely unwilling to engage in that simple act of listening.

Notes

1. See, for example, the Network of Sex Work Projects' own journal, *Research for Sex Work*, at www.nswp.org/research-sex-work/.

2. For an exception to this, see anthropologists Sophie Day's (2007) *On the Game* and Angie Hart's (1997) *Buying and Selling Power*.

3. For some examples of these narratives, see Farley (2003) and Jeffreys (2008).

References

Agustín, Laura (2004) 'Alternative Ethics, or: Telling Lies to Researchers', *Research for Sex Work*, 7, pp. 6–7.

Andrews, Molly (2014) *Narrative Imagination and Everyday Life*, Oxford: Oxford University Press.

Andrews, Molly, Squire, Corrine and Tamboukou, Maria (2013) *Doing Narrative Research*, London: Sage.

Bleek, Wolf (1987) 'Lying informants: A fieldwork experience from Ghana', *Population and Development Review*, 13(2), pp. 314–322.

Breckner, Roswitha and Susanne Rupp (2002) 'Discovering Biographies in Changing Social Worlds: The Biographic-Interpretive Method' in Chamberlayne, P., Rustin, M. and Wengraf, T. (eds) *Biography* and Social Exclusion in Europe: Experiences and Life Journeys, Bristol: Policy Press.

Clandinin, Jean and Connelly, Michael (2004) *Narrative Inquiry: Experience and Story in Qualitative Research*, San Francisco, CA: Jossey-Bass.

Connell, R.W. (1991) 'Live Fast and Die Young: The Construction of Masculinity among Young Working Class Men on the Margins of the Labour Market', *Journal of Sociology*, 27, pp. 141–171.

Cornwall, Andrea (2008) 'Unpacking "Participation": models, meanings and practices', *Community Development Journal*, 43(3), pp. 269–283.

Cornwall, Andrea (2016) 'Save Us from Saviours: Disrupting Development Narratives of the Rescue and Uplift of the "Third World Woman"' in Hemer, Oscar and Tufte, Thomas (eds) *Voice and Matter: Communication, Development and the Cultural Return*, Copenhagen: Nordicom.

Cornwall, Andrea and Jewkes, R. (1995) 'What is participatory research?' *Social Science and Medicine*, 41(12), pp. 1667–1676.

Cornwall Andrea, Romano J. and Shankland A. (2008) 'Brazilian Experiences of Participation and Citizenship: A Critical Look', IDS Working Paper 389, Institute of Development Studies, Brighton.

Day, Sophie (2007) *On the Game: Women and Sex Work*, London: Pluto Press.

Doezema, Jo (2009) *Sex Slaves and Discourse Masters: The Construction of Trafficking*, London: Zed Books.

Farley, Melissa (ed.) (2003) *Prostitution, Trafficking and Traumatic Stress*, Binghamton, NY: Haworth Press.

Hart, Angie (1997) *Buying and Selling Power: Anthropological Reflections on Prostitution in Spain*, Boulder, CO: Westview Press.

Jeffreys, Sheila (2008) *The Industrial Vagina: The Political Economy of the Global Sex Trade*, London: Routledge.

Kitzinger, J. (1994) 'The Methodology of Focus Groups: The Importance of Interaction between Research Participants', *Sociology of Health*, 16(1), pp. 103–21.

Kreuger, R.A. (1994) *Focus Groups: A Practical Guide for Applied Research*, London: SAGE.

Lincoln, Yvonne and Guba, Egon (1985) *Naturalistic Inquiry*, London: SAGE.

Mohanty, Chandra Talpade (1988) 'Under Western Eyes: Feminist Scholarship and Colonial Discourses', *Feminist Review*, 30, pp. 61–88.

Morgan, D.L. and Spanish, M.T. (1984) 'Focus Groups: A New Tool for Qualitative Research', *Qualitative Sociology*, 7, pp. 253–270.

Munodawafa, D., Gwede, C. and Mubayira, C. (1995) 'Using Focus Groups to Develop HIV Education among Adolescent Females in Zimbabwe', *Health Promotion*, 10(2), pp. 85–92.

O'Connell Davidson, J. and Layder, D. (1994) *Methods, Sex and Madness*, London: Routledge.

O'Neill, M. (1996) 'Researching Prostitution and Violence:

Towards a Feminist Praxis' in Hester, M., Kelly, L. and Radford, J. (eds) *Women, Violence and Male Power*, London: Open University Press, pp. 130–147.

O'Neill, M. and Campbell, R. (2006) 'Street Sex Work and Local Communities: Creating Discursive Space for Genuine Consultation and Inclusion' in Campbell, R. and O'Neill, M. (eds) *Sex Work Now*, Cullompton: Willan Publishing.

Orchard, Treena (2007) 'In This Life: The Impact of Gender and Tradition on Sexuality and Relationships for Devadasi Sex Workers in Rural India', *Sexuality and Culture*, 11(1), pp. 3–27.

Overs, Cheryl (2014) 'Sex Workers, Empowerment and Poverty Alleviation in Ethiopia', *IDS Evidence Report*, 80, Brighton: IDS.

Plummer, Ken (1995) *Telling Sexual Stories: Power, Change and Social Worlds*, London: Routledge.

Pyett, P. (1998) 'Doing It Together: Sex Workers and Researchers', *Research for Sex Work*, 1. Available at http://hcc.med.vu.nl/artikelen/pyett.htm (accessed June 2006).

Roseneil, Sasha (2012) 'Using Biographical Narrative and Life Story Methods to Research Women's Movements: FEMCIT', *Women's Studies International Forum*, 35, pp. 129–131.

Sahni, Rohini and Shankar, V. Kalyan (2011) *The First Pan-India Survey of Female Sex Workers*, IDS Working Paper.

Sanders, Teela (2006) 'Sexing up the Subject: Methodological Nuances in Researching the Female Sex Industry', *Sexualities*, 9(4), pp. 449–468.

Sardenberg, Cecilia (2008) 'Liberal vs. Liberating Empowerment: A Latin American Feminist Perspective on Conceptualising Women's Empowerment', *IDS Bulletin*, 39(6), pp. 18–27.

Seshu, Meena (2013) 'Sex, Work and Citizenship: The VAMP Sex Workers' Collective in Maharashtra' in Kabeer, N., Sudarshan, R. and Milward, K. (eds) *Organising Women Workers in the Informal Economy: Beyond the Weapons of the Weak*, London: Zed Books.

Shaver, Frances (2005) 'Sex Work Research Methodological and Ethical Challenges', *Journal of Interpersonal Violence*, 20(3), pp. 296–319.

Van der Meulen, Emily (2011) 'Action Research with Sex Workers: Dismantling Barriers and Building Bridges', *Action Research*, 9(4), pp. 370–384.

Wahab, S. (2003) 'Creating Knowledge Collaboratively with Female Sex Workers: Insights from a Qualitative, Feminist, and Participatory Study', *Qualitative Inquiry*, 9(4), pp. 625–642.

Wengraf, Tom (2009) *Qualitative Research Interviewing: Biographic Narrative and Semi-structured Methods*, London: Sage.

White, G.E. and Thomson, A.N. (1995) 'Anonymized Focus Groups as a Research Tool for Health Professionals', *Qualitative Health Research*, 5(2), pp. 256–261.

PART FOUR

RESEARCHER BODIES, IDENTITIES, EXPERIENCES

INTRODUCTION

Hannah Frith

The sexual bodies, identities and experiences of those who research sexuality have, until recently, received very little critical reflection. Opening up such conversations often requires courage since sex research is seen as 'dirty work' (Irvine, 2014), the motivations of researchers cast as prurient or inappropriately voyeuristic, while their sexual desires and practices are subject to suspicion (Attwood, 2010; Hammond and Kingston, 2014). One approach has been to adopt an objective detachment or refusal to discuss one's own interests with the idea that this may sensationalise the research, detract from the experiences of participants themselves, expose the researcher to sexual harassment or speculation, or call their academic credibility into question. Despite these risks, there has been increasing encouragement among sexuality scholars to engage in critical reflexivity about their own sexual desires, practices, bodies, identities and experiences in order to explore how these interact with the social dynamics of the research; see Elliston (2005) for a discussion of the theoretical conditions – the 'reflexive' turn, the theorisation of subjectivity prompted by black feminism and the rise of queer theory – which enabled such a focus. The chapters by Radoslovich, Madill, Landi and Morris in the following section speak to this challenge.

Being a 'good researcher'

Discussions of reflexivity are typically bound up in two interrelated issues – the rejection of a positivist position of objectivity, neutrality and distance in favour of more intimate, engaged research which acknowledges the 'erotics of knowledge

production' (Rooke, 2009), the lusty, desiring researcher's body
(Plummer, 2008) and debates about the relative advantages and
complexities of insider/outsider research. In trying to make sense
of their confusion and uncertainty in the face of unwanted sexual
attention, for example, Diprose et al. (2013) describe worrying
about whether they had 'done something wrong' and whether
this compromised their status as 'good researchers'. Upon
reflection, they realised that they had unwittingly adopted the
historically privileged positivist (or masculine) understanding of
a 'good' researcher as someone who is disembodied, distanced
(to ensure an objective perspective), reliable (not clouded by
emotion) and importantly, non-sexual. These issues are echoed
in the following chapters. The tension between being a good,
'professional researcher' and trying to develop equitable and
ethical relationships with participants is explored and it emerges
that this largely rests on how one conceptualises what being a
good researcher means. Indeed, as Plummer in his interview
(this volume) reminds us, in a previous era there was simply no
framework for reflexivity or discussions of 'the personal' or sexual
as part of the research process – even to acknowledge the desiring
body of the researcher would have been considered taboo. Yet
conceptions of the researcher as detached and non-sexual still
predominate. Concerns about being a 'good' researcher may be
especially acute for beginning researchers who are tasked with
proving their credibility and skill as researchers. In her chapter,
Kathy Radoslovich explores her evolving researcher identity and
her concerns to ensure that the research (informed by a feminist
standpoint perspective) listens to the voices of older people.
She talks honestly about her own embarrassment and difficulty
in talking about sexuality, the mistaken attempts she makes
to communicate indirectly about sex, and her (unsuccessful)
attempts to create 'common ground' by making claims to a
shared marital status. Of course, this is not unique to beginning
researchers (nor should it be read as only an issue of biography
in isolation from the power dynamics which make meaning of

this biography – see below): in her chapter Anna Madill, who is an experienced researcher entering the study of sexually explicit material (homoerotic manga and anime) for the first time, explores her own awkwardness with asking questions about sexuality directly, her embarrassment during some of the interviews and her discomfort with topics which are omitted from the interviews (arousal, masturbation and fantasies). Madill explores the complexities of her identification as an acafan (an academic and a fan), which may be viewed as being too subjective or invested by the academic community, but as not invested enough for other fans who were more embedded into the subcultural scene. While Radoslovich leads with her researcher identity, and Madill identifies as an acafan, in her chapter Nicoletta Landi leads with herself as a sexualised person and explores how this opens up ways of speaking about sexuality which differ from the sex educators she works with, and challenges their narrow vision of sexuality and the heteronormativity which this perpetuates. Being positioned as 'too Dutch' (too open-minded about sex), Landi uses her knowledge of queer communities, her long-term involvement in LGBT activism and her experience as a sex educator to claim expertise in challenging the professionals she worked with. Moreover, she utilises their curiosity about her own experiences and identity as critical moments for raising awareness of the heterosexism and cultural relativism embedded in the sex education programmes being delivered, generating a more personal (erotic) involvement in the research. Morris explores the complexities of class in talking as a single mother with other single mothers about intimacies and sexuality, recognising the interview context and her own positionality as a 'white, educated, mostly heterosexual, mostly middle-class woman' as sometimes opening up opportunities for sexual stories to emerge, but being mindful of the silences. Whilst doing her best to be a 'good researcher' by providing an appropriately private and safe environment for intimate stories to be told, Morris sits this alongside a recognition of the differing 'narrative capital' available to participants and the social and discursive conditions which render some stories untellable. As Rose (1997) argues, being reflexive is not simply about ticking off a checklist (ethnicity, gender, sexuality, class, age, motherhood or marital status), rather it is an on-going attempt to think through some of the relational dynamics that influence the co-creation of knowledge. The chapters in this part reveal the complexities of shifting notions of distance/intimacy and sameness/difference which are most productive for understanding our positionality as embodied and sexualised researchers.

The desiring researcher

Recently, Thomas and Williams (2016) have called for 'more disclosure' arguing that 'sex research of all kinds would benefit if sex researchers would be more willing to consider and discuss their sexual desires' (Thomas and Williams, 2016, p. 86). They suggest four ways in which the sexual desires of the researcher can influence the research: (1) the choice of research topics which are 'sexy, erotic and even arousing' (2016, p. 87); (2) the choice of methods which get 'close to the action' (2016, p. 88); (3) research interactions which 'blur the boundaries between the personal and professional' (2016, p. 89); and (4) findings and conclusions which serve to demarginalise and depathologise sexual minorities. Critical reflexivity puts power at the heart of understanding research dynamics, so whilst the framework offered by Thomas and Williams is useful, disclosing sexual desire and interests is only useful insomuch as these are explored in relation to interactions of power. Without this there is a danger that we will reinforce neoliberal imperatives to be 'sexual adventurers' ever willing to push against societally imposed boundaries around sexuality in the pursuit of pleasure and desire. This risks idolising a kind of macho disclosure. Admissions of discomfort and insecurity become more difficult (but just as insightful) when the pursuit of sexual perfection/pleasurable nirvana is perpetuated as an individual responsibility towards sexual self-actualisation. Insecurities can easily be read as individual hang ups/failures, but often offer deep learning as the chapters by Madill and Radoslovich attest (see also Carter, 2016; Bain and Nash, 2006).

Nor should the presence or absence of desire be taken as simply a matter of personal taste, but should be understood and examined within the broader context in which they are experienced. Cupples (2002) illustrates the importance of this in her discussion of being a *Chela* (foreigner) sexually attracted to 'Latin' men during her fieldwork (and previous visits) in Nicaragua, and the ways in which colonial and racist discourses play a role in this desire. Landi, in her chapter, discusses how being 'seduced' by BDSM during a research project changed the way she approaches sex and sexuality as both a person and a scholar. Her altered understanding of the experience of pain, for example, and her understanding of the 'safe, sane and consensual' code for negotiating consent unites her 'sex positive' approach across different research contexts which enables the deconstruction of sexual normativity. In contrast, there is no mention of sexual desire in Radoslovich's chapter but we should be wary of reading this only as indicative of her (unstated) personal preferences. The context of the research (a residential care home), the coupled status of the research participants (where participants are coded as sexually monogamous and 'unavailable'), and the construction of older people as asexual or undesirable, may work as much against the feeling of desire as against critical reflection on the presence or absence of this desire. Likewise, Madill's hesitation in making her own interest in homoerotic manga and anime public needs to be understood both in relation to the shame experienced in relation to marginalised sexualities, but also the legal context in the UK, which prohibits the circulation of images of children. Indeed, Madill draws an important distinction between finding material arousing (not least because it transgresses personal or cultural norms), and finding it morally acceptable. Desires need to be critically interrogated rather than being taken as some personal essence of sexuality.

Seductive spaces

Ethnographers and anthropologists have referred to the 'seduction of the field' as a way of talking about the erotic enticements of particular research environments and the ways in which these interact with the desire and arousal of the researcher (e.g. Carter, 2016; Cupples, 2002). Some spaces and places are more eroticised and deliberately 'sexy' than others – as touched on in Part III on negotiating contexts – and these spaces bring sexualised identities to the fore more readily than others. The chapters in this part explore how researchers navigate a range of difference spaces – from residential care homes for the elderly, to sex education classes, to fan conventions, to participant homes, to online spaces and BDSM communities. Such spaces call to researchers in different ways. Morris acknowledges the tensions for single mothers of the 'home space' as a place which is ripe with potential for sexual intimacy, but is often also overlain with demands for maternal care. Guilt about being a mother and a sexual, sexually available (single) being, concern about being an appropriate sexual role model for daughters, the cultural privileging of the maternal role, and more immediate financial/ emotional concerns, make it difficult for some to carve out space for sexuality. The messiness of the home space as a place for having intimate conversations about sex in a research interview, bringing with it multiple demands/interruptions from children, brought to the fore the tensions in attempting to reclaim this as a sexual space. Other spaces are more unequivocally sexual. In discussing their approach to researching in the highly-sexualised space of the Pussy Palace, a queer women's bathhouse in Toronto, Bain and Nash (2006) give a thoughtful and provocative account of their own decision-making about how to present their bodies, and how this sometimes broke the codes of interacting in this environment. Their decisions to keep their distance respected their own personal code of ethics, as well as meeting those of institutional review bodies. The same kinds of decision-making and struggles with ethical boundaries and personal psychological comfort can be seen in these chapters as authors negotiate their way through different spaces. Madill, for example, reflects on the ways in which she can sometimes de-eroticise the sexually explicit material – or fans' engagement with this material – as a result of her own 'rather cerebral' approach and her identification of her interest in the material as feminist. Moreover, as she notes, the choice of email and the apparently body-less environment of cyberspace, provides what she experiences as a 'reassuring distance' for the discussion of intimate topics.

Taken together, then, these chapters pick up the dirty work of critically reflecting on the messy, complex, ambiguous, awkward, intimate, arousing, disgusting and tricky work of exploring sexual stories as embodied researchers with our own, often complicated relationship with sex and sexuality.

References

Attwood, F. (2010) 'Dirty Work Researching Women and Sexual Representation' in Ryan-Flood, R. and Gill, R. (2010) *Secrecy and Silence in the Research Process: Feminist Reflections*, Oxford: Taylor and Francis.

Bain, A.L. and Nash, C.J. (2006) 'Undressing the Researcher: Feminism, Embodiment and Sexuality at a Queer Bathhouse Event', *Area*, 38(1), pp. 99–106.

Carter, C. (2016) 'A Way to Meet Queer Women? Reflections on Sexuality and Desire in Research', *Sexualities*, 19(1–2), pp. 119–137.

Cupples, J. (2002) 'The Field as a Landscape of Desire: Sex and Sexuality in Geographical Fieldwork', *Area*, 34(4), pp. 382–390.

Diprose, G., Thomas, A.C. and Rushton, R. (2013) 'Desiring More: Complicating Understandings of Sexuality in Research Processes', *Area*, 45(3), pp. 292–298.

Elliston, D. (2005) 'Critical Reflexivity and Sexuality Studies in Anthropology: Siting Sexuality in Research, Theory, Ethnography, and Pedagogy', *Reviews in Anthropology*, 34(1), pp. 21–47.

Hammond, N. and Kingston, S. (2014) 'Experiencing Stigma as Sex Work Researchers in Professional and Personal Lives', *Sexualities*, 17(3), pp. 329–347.

Irvine, J.M. (2014) 'Is Sexuality Research "Dirty Work"? Institutionalized Stigma in the Production of Sexual Knowledge', *Sexualities*, 17(5–6), pp. 632–656.

Plummer, K. (2008) 'Studying Sexualities for a Better World? Ten Years of *Sexualities*', *Sexualities*, 11(1/2), pp. 7–22.

Rooke, A. (2009) 'Queer in the Field: On Emotions, Temporality, and

Performativity in Ethnography', *Journal of Lesbian Studies*, 13(2), pp. 149–160.

Rose, G. (1997) 'Situating Knowledges: Positionality, Reflexivities and Other Tactics', *Progress in Human Geography*, 21, pp. 305–320.

Thomas, J.N. and Williams, D.J. (2016) 'Getting Off on Sex Research: A Methodological Commentary on the Sexual Desires of Sex Researchers', *Sexualities*, 19(1–2), pp. 83–97.

13 | ROTTEN GIRL ON ROTTEN GIRL: BOYS' LOVE 'RESEARCH'

Anna Madill

Abstract

'Fujoshi' (rotten girl) is a derogatory Japanese term for female fans of homoerotic manga and anime in the genre know as Boys' Love (BL). BL is a global phenomenon and one of the largest, female-oriented, erotic subcultures. I have underway, what is already, the biggest survey of the Anglophone fandom (https://leeds.onlinesurveys.ac.uk/blfandomsurvey) and have, so far, completed 14 face-to-face and around 100 e-mail interviews. This is the first project I have conducted on sexually explicit material and, although I consider myself to be a *fujoshi*, I am not, otherwise, a user of pornography/sexually explicit material. In fact, this research has presented a huge challenge to me in terms of becoming more comfortable discussing sexual topics and, even more personally, in making my own investment in male–male sexuality public. This has meant dealing with feelings of embarrassment and shame, but also of relief in finding and communicating with other women who have a similar erotic fantasy life. However, the project has also made me feel, at times, quite anxious given recent UK prohibited images of children legislation. What does BL represent for me that I am willing to put myself through this, spend most of my spare time on it, and is it really 'research'?

Rotten girl on rotten girl: Boys' Love 'research'

I am really drawn to the idea of one soul loving another regardless of the outside packaging. As for the erotic aspect,

seeing a naked woman having sex with an attractive man was
not something I was interested in reading, but seeing images
of well drawn men being passionately attracted to other well
drawn men ... that interests me. :) (woman, heterosexual, 42,
USA)

'Fujoshi'[1] (literally, 'rotten girl') is a derogatory Japanese
term for female fans of homoerotic manga and anime in the
genre know as Boys' Love.[2] The term, however, can be used
within fandom as a positive playfully-transgressive identity. BL
originated in 1970s Japan and from the mid-1990s it has become
a global phenomenon overlapping with, and in many ways similar
to, Western male–male slash fiction. 'MxM' is now one of the
largest, female-oriented, erotic subcultures, its growth immensely
facilitated and supported by mass access to the internet. In this
chapter, I reflect on three areas of intertwining personal and
methodological relevance to me as a 'sex researcher' in the field
of BL: being an 'acafan';[3] cultural and legal issues; the design
of my online BL fandom survey and experience of conducting
interviews.

Reflections on being a BL acafan

If you don't think I answered this question to your
satisfaction, can you clarify what you meant? (This can be off
the record if you want, but it seems like you're searching for
some kind of answer yourself, here.) (transman, homosexual,
26, USA)

Pornography researchers, when they have commented, tend to
express reservations about personalising their research (Attwood
and Hunter, 2009; Williams, 1993). Erotic material by its very
nature is evocative and pornography is designed to have an
arousing effect. It is not always possible to anticipate what one
will find stimulating or to control this even when material is at

the same time experienced as distasteful, or even repulsive. In fact, the effectiveness of some pornography is probably linked to its transgression of personal and/or cultural proprieties. Hence, in researching erotica it seems important to be aware consciously that finding 'data' arousing is distinct from accepting it morally and from seeking it out for recreational purposes. However, I am in the position of being both a fan and a researcher of BL and have decided, for reasons, some of which are explored in this piece, to make my liking for this material public. Many BL researchers imply their fandom through reporting that they recruited participants from their own personal networks (e.g. Li, 2009) and others are explicit with regard to their status as fans and the influence that BL has had on them personally (e.g. Mizoguchi, 2008). Similarly, a central motivation in undertaking my research on this topic is to try to understand its appeal for me as well as for a sizable population of girls and women – and people of non-binary and trans-gendered identity – around the world.[4]

This is the first project I have conducted on sexually explicit material[5] and, although I consider myself to be a *fujoshi*, and hence identify as a member of an erotic subculture, I am not, otherwise, a user of pornography.[6] In fact, this research has presented a challenge to me in terms of becoming more comfortable engaging with erotica, and discussing sexual topics, and has meant dealing with feelings of embarrassment and shame. This has not been because I am anti-pornography (in general) or feel that sexuality should not be discussed – in fact I consider myself rather liberal. I am learning that my discomfort has been linked to the kinds of explicit materials usually on offer and I find myself relieved to discover through BL a relatively large, female-oriented community with a similar, 'unusual', erotic fantasy life.

I do have one question, which might be several in one, as to what is the reason for your study of this topic and what kind of connections or findings you are hoping to uncover? I have seen so many terrible generalizations and fetishizations of Japanese and East Asian subculture content by western sources, so I'm curious how your study differs and what it aims to achieve. (woman, USA)

Similarly to being a 'fujoshi', being an 'acafan' can be a disparaged identity. It invites a perception within the academy that one is too subjective and invested in a topic to research it properly (Bogost, 2010). Acafandom can also be viewed with suspicion by the community studied. Attending an anime and manga convention, and approaching attendees for interview, clearly revealed to me these tensions. The information sheet about the research, which was approved by my school ethics committee, takes a neutral stance to BL, hence stressing the 'aca' part of my identity. Therefore I felt it was important, given the stigma erotic subcultures can attract and their history of pathologisation, to tell potential participants that I was also a BL fan. However, the convention made me question my identity as a *fujoshi* in that, as a middle-aged academic coming late to BL, the community has, for me, many unfamiliar aspects. For example, attendees seemed able to refer to products by their original Japanese title, BL fans asked each other, and were able to respond to questions, about favourite fantasy pairings in non-BL texts, and many people cosplayed[7] throughout the convention. I also attended my first 'yaoi panel' ...

The yaoi panel was hosted by two cross/cosplaying women, and with a predominantly female audience, there was a lot of (affectionate?) laughter, particularly in relation to anime clips of over-melodramatic scenarios and embarrassingly bad sex scenes. Laughter, particularly in relation to sexually explicit material, can point to underlying anxieties but can offer a productive way to diffuse, and maybe begin to explore, these feelings. However, it may also be viewed as a way of reframing as innocuous what might otherwise be considered problematic. Similarly, many BL texts are also romantic comedies (McLelland, 2000). Informally, one BL fan I spoke to at the convention stressed the fun and community-feeling she enjoyed attending *yaoi* panels. However, another told me that she sometimes found them off-putting and she and her friends had avoided entering one when they heard the audience chanting 'rape, rape, rape!' And, at the *yaoi* panel I attended, at one point a young women behind me exclaimed 'That's *shota*',[8] implying concern about the acceptability of the particular anime clip being presented.

Attending the anime convention, and conducting interviews, has helped me understand some of the tensions in identifying with, while at the same time researching, an erotic subculture – particularly the challenges of negotiating credibility with both the academy and the community. It also allowed me to experience first-hand tensions within the community itself with regard to, what appears to be, a central ideological dilemma (Billig et al., 1988) between the framing of BL as 'harmless fun' and as, in certain respects, 'morally dubious'.

Reflections on cultural and legal issues

> That is not to say that I want to sleep with young boys in reality! In Japan and even Iran, the age consent is not that big of a deal and I can't help finding pederasty interesting! (genderqueer 'woman',[9] heterosexual, 24, Iran)

Most pornography research is on the mainstream heterosexual product for men, who are by far the largest target audience for sexually explicit material, and critical commentary has tended to focus on the detrimental consequences for women of pornography although alongside, and in tension with, a strong anti-censorship feminist literature. The terms of this debate are, however, being challenged as novel forms of pornography are being created by women and distributed by them on the internet (e.g. Ciclitira, 2004). Female authored, and targeted, male–male homoeroticism also, per se, challenges some pro-censorship feminist assumptions about pornography as misogyny (see also Stychin, 1991–1992). Interestingly, the Japanese word 'tojisha' ('the person directly involved and for whom something is at stake', Mizoguchi, 2008, p.194) may capture fans' investment in BL as more than just pornographic representation, and a growing research literature argues that BL is a site in and through which there is a creative reworking of the sex/gender system (McLelland, 2000; Rubin, 1975/2011).

Given this context, of central interest to me are the implications that BL is produced and consumed predominantly by young women, and people who are broadly gender queer, and this helps me to make sense of my identification as a *fujoshi* as a feminist one. However, it is important to avoid the prima facie assumption that female-oriented pornography is inherently more 'worthy' than that produced by and/or targeted at men. For example, I gained some insight into the way I can inadvertently de-eroticise BL through focusing on the feminist potential of its gender parody (e.g. Ogi, 2009), when, after I presented at a departmental seminar, a young man asked me if some women might just read BL to become sexually aroused (counter-argument presented in McLelland, 2000). Moreover, following my first public presentation on BL (Madill, 2010), a female audience member suggested that I might have rather sanitised (her word) the material. Paasonen reminds us that providing reparative readings of an erotica 'should not assume love for the text, or pleasure derived from it' (2007, p. 53). However, stressing the feminist potential of BL does not negate my responsibility as a researcher to consider also the ways in which BL can transgress fundamental cultural values and stray into legally problematic territory. This is particularly so with regard to the potential of some BL to appear to sexualise children.

I have been troubled by stories and, more often, individual BL manga panels in which young(-looking) characters are sexualised. Part of what makes this, for me, troubling (as opposed to a stronger feeling such a shock), is that the sexual activity is usually narratively coherent (i.e. not gratuitous), relationship-based and within overarching genres such as romance, romantic-comedy or (melo)drama. Hence, while to me as a Westerner, such visuals and subject matter privilege a child pornography frame, the way the stories are presented pulls toward other, less problematic, readings. This apparent juxtaposition of content and form can be very disconcerting. On the other hand, although BL is diverse, as I have come to recognise its central tropes and formulas, I find it increasingly familiar, even routine. This makes it very important for me to stay in touch with, and continue to reflect upon, the reaction of my colleagues and audiences as barometers of the current landscape around childhood, sexuality and sexualisation in which I am working.

My current work is on BL sold through commercial channels to UK readers. I would like to extend my research to 'shotacon' which focuses on pre- and pubescent boys, the MxM version sometimes considered a BL subgenre. There appears to be little research on *shotacon*, even in Japanese, and only passing comments on the genre in English language sources (e.g. McLelland, 2000; Zanghellini, 2009). However, unlike BL, Saitō (2007) indicates that *shotacon* is consumed by men and women in about equal proportion. Manga is referred to explicitly in recent Prohibited Images of Children legislation (Coroners and Justice Act 2009), in which the age and gender of producers, or of the majority or target audience is deemed irrelevant.[10] These factors may, however, impact the nature of the material and – most importantly to me – the way it is received, and a distinction is made in the manga community between male-oriented and female-oriented *shotacon*. Saitō (2007) suggests the former to be more conventionally 'pornographic' and the latter to be very similar to BL. The implication is that female-oriented *shotacon* are essentially romantic and dramatic narratives, although detailed analysis does not seem to be available.

The lacuna of research on the content and reception of free-hand, erotic, sequential art of young-looking, fantasy beings which may, or may not, meet prohibitive status within English law (and elsewhere) makes the BL community a hostage to fortune (Madill 2015). I am particularly interested in the potential of female-oriented MxM *shotacon* to have feminist readings (Madill, 2012b). Extending my research to *shotacon* proper would require obtaining immunity from prosecution under Section 64 of the Coroners and Justice Act 2009 (see also Section 160 of the Criminal Justice Act 1988) which sets out the defence of possession for legitimate work reasons. However, as Jones and Mowlabocus (2009) discuss, Act-defined legitimate uses pertain to law enforcement (that is, prosecuting authorities handling the material in the course of their employment) and not to academics independent of government agencies. Moreover, the ethical and legal barriers to researching *shotacon* are magnified because virtually all that is available in English are copyright-contravening scanlations.[11]

Although, in the main, in undertaking my research on BL, I have received encouragement from others, this has been mixed with advice to be cautious and some male colleagues have commented that BL is not a topic that they, themselves, would risk researching. When researchers have a choice, there are many reasons for focusing on a particular area but it would be strange for a researcher to pick a field in which she or he had no interest. However, when the research is on sexually explicit material, the researcher – particularly the self-identified acafan, maybe – is vulnerable to accusations that this interest is prurient. This undermines the worth and legitimacy of the work as well as the researcher's character. For men, the risk of being viewed as merely salacious is exaggerated by the fact that commercial sexual recreation is overwhelming a male-dominated market and that the vast majority of sexual offenders are men (Cortoni et al., 2010). Such anxieties appear well-founded given the extreme public antipathy to publications such as *Child-Loving: The Erotic Child and Victorian Culture* by James Kincaid (1992) which included speculation that the author is, himself, a paedophile (for critique see Bruhm and Hurley, 2004). Although being a female researcher may not lend so easily to such stigmatising stereotypes, it would be naïve to think that I was immune from similar kinds of attack and it is probably wise to anticipate the ways in which I may be positioned by others in relation to this research within different contexts.

Reflections on my BL fandom survey and interviews

> Found your survey via the MangaBookshelf.com. It was interesting, but very frustrating to me in the way the questions were framed: e.g. in most discussions of m/m manga that I participate in, the distinction is drawn between BL (or shounen ai) and yaoi ... (woman, heterosexual (?), USA)

I have underway, what is already, the largest survey of the Anglophone[12] BL fandom (https://leeds.onlinesurveys.ac.uk/ blfandomsurvey). Although going through several stages of piloting, as the above quote suggests, the material is complex and involves sometimes contended terminology which makes it difficult to always be clear. It has five sections: demographics, BL materials, feelings about BL, social relationships and other erotic materials. The seven questions in the final section are all optional under the assumption that, as they are not about BL, they may be experienced as intrusive. However, only a few people have not completed these questions.

Although Japanese researchers suggest that the BL fandom is almost exclusively female and heterosexual (e.g. Mizoguchi, 2008), the few surveys that have been conducted of the global fandom demonstrate a 'queerer' community. The sexual identity categories provided in my survey are 'heterosexual', 'homosexual/ lesbian/gay', 'bisexual', 'polysexual/pansexual',[13] 'not sure' and 'other'. Piloting led to the inclusion of the latter as an option and the biggest single category of self-specified 'other' is 'asexual'. Providing labelled options for less well known sexualities may highlight and, hence, slightly increase their likelihood of selection. Similarly, 'asexuality' may be under-reported and, informally, a respondent told me that, although she considers herself to be asexual, she had selected 'heterosexual' in the survey. Gender categories provided are 'male', 'female' and 'other'. Open-ended responses to 'other' include an interesting and wide range of identifications such as genderqueer, non-binary, agender and transgender. The first and last pages of the online survey include an invitation to take part in an interview and my contact details.

So far, I have completed 14 face-to-face/telephone interviews and completed or started almost 100 interviews via e-mail. E-mail interviews have worked well given the wide geographical location of the BL fandom but also because many participants pursue their activities on-line, are often experienced writers and can fit e-mails around busy lives. E-mails can also provide a reassuring distance in the discussion of intimate topics but, admittedly, this may be a particular benefit for me as the researcher. For example, the survey is collecting information on engagement with a range of erotic materials and I explored this topic in some of the early face-to-face interviews. Most participants had little to say about this, but one discussed a fairly extensive interest in pornography which, for some reason, I found embarrassing. On reflection, her apparent confidence may have triggered in me feelings of exposure in that, although I am a middle-aged researcher conducting interviews about sexuality explicit material, my experience is limited to a very specific genre.

Do you mind if I ask about how old you are? It just helps me with a bit of context.
Haha I don't mind at all! I am 27 years old. It seems silly to be free when talking about my sexuality but get offended when it comes to you asking my age. It's all anonymous anyway! Though I do appreciate you being so polite. :) (genderqueer 'woman', 27, North America)

At first, I made the decision not to ask about gender and sexual identity in the face-to-face interviews, in part due to the rationale that if it was important participants would raise it. However, I was also anxious that questions on this topic would interrupt rapport and, although some participants talked about their gender and sexual identity spontaneously, others chose not to and one appeared very uncomfortable when I approached the subject. The fact that I am usually asking about gender and sexual identity in the e-mail interviews indicates my growing experience and confidence, but also the benefits, to me at least, of the medium. Some participants offer information about their gender and sexual identity in their first e-mail to me, some mention it spontaneously in the course of their replies, and all have answered my questions on the topic. I have also felt skilled enough to ask about gender and sexual identity in more recent audio-recorded interviews.

> Would it be possible for you to give me some commercial yaoi titles in which there are some examples of uncircumcised penises? This must go to the top of my weird request list – so sorry – I hope this does not sound too creepy :((question from Anna, the researcher)

It is interesting to reflect on unplanned omissions in my data collection and it has occurred to me that I am not asking – in the survey or in any of the interviews – about sexual arousal or masturbation in relation to BL materials. This may reflect my own rather cerebral approach to BL. It may also reflect an underlying fear of appearing prurient. Having completed 15 or so e-mail interviews, I was agonising over finding the right words to ask a participant to expand on what she had mentioned about her sexual fantasies. I was mitigating and hedging and apologising, and then thinking that I should just ask pretty directly – after all it was a research interview – and then I realised that I was struggling with a felt sense that if I did ask directly it could seem a bit 'creepy'. So, in the end, I decided that it was still best to 'go round the houses'. However, I now have a better insight into my/ the need to sometimes be a little indirect and/or to acknowledge my own discomfort and have been better able to articulate this fear in later interviews, as exampled above.

> So far the documents make sense … actually I'll feel more comfortable if the interview is a bit informal? I'm used talking about BL as a fan and not someone being interviewed so you will have to excuse me hahahaha … (woman, Philippines)

I have conducted research into the process of research interviewing and am convinced that it is usually good practice to avoid the potential of influencing participants through evaluative comments or discussing one's own opinion within the interview (Madill, 2012a). However, I have learned that such formality can be a drawback in e-mail interviews on intimate topics. My e-mail interviews are being conducted over many exchanges and over, sometimes, several weeks so my personal relationship with interviewees is very important. Moreover, it is essential that people feel safe telling me about highly personal aspects of their life, such as their sexual fantasies. Creating and maintaining the interview as a safe space requires a careful balance between openness on my part, which sets out a sense of, at least, a shared starting point – BL fandom – and of acceptance, while keeping the focus very much on the participant. Hence, I have, at times, commented on my own personal tastes during interviews where it has felt relevant and appropriate, and followed the lead of the participant in terms of formality level, while at all times being highly respectful and expressing my sincere gratitude for their contribution.

Concluding reflections

> You'll never openly tell you like BL manga. If you do, you're a promiscuous child that cannot grow up (because manga is for kids), lewd (because it's porn) and only like it because

you're unsuccessful and don't have a boyfriend (as if a penis is all that need to a woman be successful and happy). I had to heard a lot of times my boyfriend telling me to stop reading this "disgusting thing" and that I had to read hentai,[14] ecchi,[15] etc ... Every time I have to tell him to "fuck off, I'll keep reading it because I like it" ... Answering your questions made me think a lot more about my beliefs and the things I can or cannot accept. (woman, heterosexual, 24, Brazil)

This piece has explored a little of what BL represents for me – as a *fujoshi*, a feminist and, in this context, a *tojisha* – and some of the possible stakes, particularly as an acafan, researching an erotic subculture, aspects of which may be perceived as contrary to fundamental hegemonic values and which, in the UK, currently occupies a legislative grey area. The BL fandom is a way of accessing an otherwise invisible and marginalised counter-public (Wood, 2006) which is, arguably, creatively reworking the patriarchal sex/gender system in their own terms and risking sanctions in so doing. Is my work in this area properly research? I believe so because I believe that the process of discovery – and what we find – is always framed by our personal commitments and social contexts. In this project, I may be a little on the far-side of this for my own comfort ...

Notes

1. A visual pun – 腐女子 – pronounced identically for the term 'girls and women' but where the *first kanji* – 'fu' – has been changed to that indicating 'rotten', so changing the meaning to 'rotten girl'.

2. Variously called, with subtle differentiation, Boys' Love (BL), *yaoi* and *shonen-ai/shonen'ai/shonen ai* (and '*shounen*' variant spellings).

3. Self-designation available to professional academics when researching a topic, usually related to popular culture, with regard to which they are also a professed fan.

4. This is not to deny or under-value the (non-trans)men audience of BL, just to acknowledge a personal motivation.

5. Although I have been involved in research on gender and sexuality including on the intersex condition Androgen Insensitivity Syndrome (Alderson et al., 2004) and on

therapists' experience of sexual boundaries in psychotherapy (Martin et al., 2011).

6. An uncomfortable dabbler more recently, maybe, out of curiosity.

7. Costume play in which people dress and present themselves as characters from fiction.

8. Short for '*shotacon*' which portrays MxM and MxF sexuality involving pre- and pubescent boys.

9. When a participant identifies as genderqueer I have made the decision to place 'woman' [or 'man'] also in inverted commas if this seems appropriate given the manner in which the individual is likely positioned within their larger social context. I do this because I consider it important to acknowledge in terms of understanding their stance towards BL.

10. To reach prohibited status a non-photographic/non-computer-computer-generated-image must be: (1) of a personage who looks to be under 18 years old; (2) pornographic; AND (3) obscene. I contend that BL images are, in context, unlikely to be considered obscene, even if meeting the other two criteria (Madill, 2015).

11. 'Scan-and-translate' fan translated versions uploaded to the internet.

12. The survey is in English and 64 per cent of respondents indicate that English is their first language.

13. Combined to avoid too much fracturing of the categories, although it is debatable if this was the best decision.

14. Sexually explicit manga and anime.

15. Softcore *hentai*.

References

Alderson, J., Madill, A. and Balen, A. (2004) 'Fear of Devaluation: Understanding the Experience of Intersex Women with Androgen Insensitivity Syndrome', *British Journal of Health Psychology*, 9, pp. 81–100.

Attwood, F. and Hunter, I.Q. (2009) 'Not Safe for Work? Teaching and Researching the Sexually Explicit', *Sexualities*, 12, pp. 547–557.

Billig, M., Condor, S., Edwards, D. and Gane, M. (1988) *Ideological Dilemmas: A Social Psychology of Everyday Thinking*, London: Sage.

Bogost, I. (2010, 29 July) 'Against Aca-Fandom: On Jason Mittell on Mad Men'. Available at http://bogost.com/writing/blog/against_aca-fandom/.

Bruhm, S. and Hurley, N. (2004) 'Introduction. Curiouser: On the Queerness of Children' in Bruhm, S. and Hurley, N. (eds) *Curiouser: On the Queerness of Children*, Minneapolis, MN: University of Minnesota Press, pp. ix–xxxviii.

Ciclitira, K. (2004) 'Pornography, Women and Feminism: Between Pleasure and Politics', *Sexualities*, 7, pp. 281–301.

Cortoni, F., Hanson, R.K. and Coache, M.E. (2010) 'The Recidivism Rates of Female Sexual Offenders Are Low: A Meta-analysis', *Sexual Abuse: A Journal of Research and Treatment*, 22, pp. 387–401.

Jones, S. and Mowlabocus, S. (2009) 'Hard Times and Rough Rides: The Legal and Ethical Impossibilities of Researching "Shock" Pornographies', *Sexualities*, 12, pp. 613–628.

Kincaid, J.R. (1992) *Child-Loving: The Erotic Child and Victorian Culture*, New York: Routledge.

Li, Y. (2009) *Japanese Boy-Love Manga and the Global Fandom: A Case Study of Chinese Female Readers*. MA Thesis, Bloomington, IN: Department of Communication Studies, Indiana University.

McLelland, M. (2000) 'No Climax, No Point, No Meaning? Japanese Women's Boy-Love Sites on the Internet', *Journal of Communication Inquiry*, 24, pp. 274–291.

Madill, A. (2010) Opening Keynote: 'Girls Love "Boy's Love": Exploring Sexuality and Gender in Japanese Manga', British Psychological Society Qualitative Methods in Psychology Section Conference, 23–25 August 2010.

Madill, A. (2012a) 'Interviews and Interviewing Techniques' in Cooper, H., Camic, P.M., Long, D.L., Panter, A.T., Rindskopf, D. and Sher, K.J. (eds) *American Psychological Association Handbook of Research Methods in Psychology*, vols 1–3, Washington, DC: American Psychological Association.

Madill, A. (2012b) 'Is Japanese "Homosexual Child Pornography" a Site of Feminist Activism?', Forthcoming Feminisms: Gender Activism, Politics and Theories, BSA Gender Study Group and the Centre for Interdisciplinary Gender Studies, University of Leeds, 26 October 2012.

Madill, A. (2015) 'Boys' Love Manga for Girls: Paedophilic, Satirical, Queer Readings and English Law' in Renold, E., Ringrose, J. and Egan, R.D. (eds) *Children, Sexuality and Sexualisation*, London: Palgrave, pp. 273–288.

Martin, C., Godfrey, M., Meekums, B., and Madill, A. (2011) 'Managing Boundaries under Pressure: A Qualitative Study of Therapists' Experiences of Sexual Attraction in Therapy', *Counselling and Psychotherapy Research*, 11, pp. 248–256.

Mizoguchi, A. (2008) *Reading and Living Yaoi: Male-Male Fantasy Narratives as Women's Sexual Subculture in Japan*. Doctoral Thesis, Rochester, NY: University of Rochester.

Ogi, F. (2009) 'Beyond Shoujo, Blending Gender' in Heer, J. and Worcester, K (eds) *A Comics Studies Reader*, Jackson, MS: University Press of Mississippi, pp. 244–251.

Paasonen, S. (2007) 'Strange Bedfellows: Pornography, Affect and Feminist Reading', *Feminist Theory*, 8, pp. 43–57.

Rubin, G. (1975/2011) 'The Traffic in Women: Notes on the "Political Economy" of Sex', *Deviations: A Gayle Rubin Reader*, Durham, NC: Duke University Press.

Saitō, T. (2007) 'Otaku Sexuality' in Bolton, C.I., Csicsery Jr., I. and Tatsumi, T (eds) *Robot Ghosts and Wired Dreams: Japanese Science Fiction from Origins to Anime*, Minneapolis, MN: University of Minnesota Press, pp. 222–249.

Stychin, C.F. (1991–1992) 'Exploring the Limits: Feminism and the Legal Regulation of Gay Male Pornography', *Vermont Law Review*, 16, pp. 857–900.

Williams, L. (1993) 'Second Thoughts on Hard Core: American Obscenity Law and the Scapegoating of Deviance' in Gibson, P.C. and Gibson, R. (eds) *Dirty Looks: Women, Pornography,*

Power, London: BFI Publishing, pp. 46–61.

Wood, A. (2006) '"Straight" Women, Queer Texts: Boy-Love Manga and the Rise of a Global Counterpublic', *Women's Studies Quarterly*, 34, pp. 394–414.

Zanghellini, A. (2009) 'Underage Sex and Romance in Japanese Homoerotic Manga and Anime', *Social and Legal Studies*, 18, pp. 159–177.

14 | DIARY OF A SEX RESEARCHER: A REFLEXIVE LOOK AT CONDUCTING SEXUALITY RESEARCH IN RESIDENTIAL AGED CARE

Katherine Radoslovich

Abstract

Establishing yourself as a sexuality researcher is a challenging process, and the researcher must also be mindful of how their identity impacts on their research. This chapter undertakes reflexive exploration of a young female researcher's first experience of conducting sexuality research. It explores the relationship between sexuality research, the researcher and being in the field. Firstly, this chapter overviews reflexivity and its utility in exploring processes of knowledge creation. Then, it applies these techniques to a case study undertaken in an aged care field site. Residential aged care presents a special environment for sexuality research, with its particular blend of contested space and home-like environments, and dominant social assumptions that older people are asexual or non-sexual beings. Couples wanting to maintain relationships where one or both partners are living in residential aged care negotiate these elements, as well as managing various disabilities and communication challenges. Conducting sexuality research in this field requires awareness of the researcher's place in institutional dynamics, and of the impacts of being a sexuality researcher specifically. This case study demonstrates the value of adopting reflexive practice to review the interaction of research conduct and researcher identity in order to produce the highest quality research possible.

Introduction

Sexuality studies is a field where adopting and presenting a research identity can prove challenging for the emerging or the established researcher. Sexuality researchers have faced marginalisation within academia, and a diverse range of reactions from the public. The challenges associated with so-called 'sensitive' research, including sexuality studies, have been discussed by a number of authors. Lee (1999, p. 3) discusses the misplaced fears many have over researching the sensitive, while Kulick (1995) has looked into the particular fears and challenges that face early career researchers undertaking sexuality research. Lee has noted that there are high levels of self-censorship around sensitive research, while Kulick argues there is resistance to the publication of such research. Elliston has specifically called for 'critically reflexive approaches to sexuality' and argues that doing so provides the sexuality researcher significant methodological insights (Elliston, 2005, p. 21). Critical discussion about the nature and challenges of the sexuality studies field and the researcher's identification with it has the potential to assist in legitimising the field and producing more confident researchers.

As part of a critical review of sexuality studies, a number of researchers have engaged with the issues surrounding sexualisation of both the researcher and the research subject, and the ethical and practical issues that impact the research process. Pini (2009) and Kulick have looked at the sexualisation of the researcher, particularly during the interview process while Dubisch (1995), Altork (1995) and Willson (1995), among others, have looked at the dimensions and dilemmas of sexual relationships in the field and the sexualisation of research participants. My research takes a different approach to the sexualisation dynamic in the field, looking at the sexual and intimate experiences of a population often assumed to be asexual or non-sexual by social and professional discourses.

In this chapter I will critically review the reflexive process of conducting my doctoral research. This was my first foray into sexuality studies, and the experience has been a formative one. Reflexivity is a useful tool for critiquing sexuality research and the development of researcher identity, as it highlights power dynamics and contextual factors that impact the collection of data and is effective where topics might be considered controversial, sensitive or deviant. The research featured here was undertaken within the context of a residential aged care site. The residential aged care site is a complex environment, at once a total institution and a home-like environment, a workplace and a communal residence. Researching in this environment involves numerous practical considerations in response to the high prevalence of disability among the resident population. It also requires the negotiation of institutional structures that affect both the lives of its inhabitants and how the researcher must situate themselves in the field. In this chapter, I look specifically at the experiences of couples maintaining intimate and sexual relationships within the residential aged care environment. I demonstrate how reflexivity was significant in navigating relationships and space within this field site, and hence contributed to producing the high-quality qualitative sexuality research.

Reflexivity

Emerging during the 'reflexive turn' of the 1970s, reflexivity is a technique widely used throughout the social sciences, particularly in relation to qualitative research. Researchers generally agree that reflexivity is the process of turning one's gaze back upon one's self, 'an explicit, self-aware meta-analysis of the research process' and the researcher's impact therein (Finlay, 2002, p. 531). For the purposes of this discussion, the following definition is adopted:

> Reflexivity in research can be defined as (a) the acknowledgement and identification of one's place and presence in the research and (b) the process of using these insights to critically examine the entire research process. (Underwood et al., 2010, p. 1585)

A number of authors have emphasised the importance of incorporating reflexivity into all stages of the research process, and have critiqued what they perceive as a shallow application of reflexivity by many researchers. Randall et al. (2006) and Coffey (1999) have raised concerns that many researchers acknowledge that they influence the process of gathering data, but have failed to critically examine the nature of this impact. Other critiques, such as those by Ackerly and True (2008) and Sanderson et al. (2013) have focused on the role of reflexivity in analysing and disrupting power relations within research frameworks, and as such reflexivity has become an important part of critical analytical frameworks, such as feminist, queer and sexuality studies. Feminist authors such as Pini (2009) have emphasised the importance of introspection, and give particular focus to the generation of knowledge and the power around it. Reflexivity can specifically address power dynamics by helping to reflect critically on the relationship between researcher and participant. Walby (2010), Underwood et al. (2010) and Holstein and Gubrium (1997) have utilised these approaches to argue that research is multi-directional, with both the researcher and the research participant actively involved in the construction and generation of knowledge. Acknowledging the variety of power influences at play in an interview is important for improving the quality of analysis, shaping methodological choices, and protection of the participant and the researcher. Heeding this advice, this chapter specifically examines my relationships to my field site and its inhabitants, as well as to the research process itself.

Methodology

This research investigated the experiences of couples where one or both partners were living in residential aged care, focusing on the lived realities of love, intimacy, sexuality and the maintenance of relationships under these conditions, and best practice care models for supporting couples in care. Residential aged care facilities (colloquially known as 'nursing homes') provide live-in high or low care services for older people who can no longer live at home, and in the Australian context are run by private companies, not-for-profit organisations and government providers with significant levels of government funding and regulation.

When designing this research project, one of the overwhelming imperatives was to get older people's voices heard in discussions around aged care and sexuality. There have been a number of studies looking into nursing and other care staff's responses to sexualised behaviours from residents in residential aged care settings (Elias and Ryan, 2011; Glimer et al., 2010; Mahieu et al., 2011; Shuttleworth et al., 2010), but the voice of older people, expressed in their own words, is largely missing from discourses on sexuality in care. As the research progressed, it became evident that there are a range of institutional, power and capacity dynamics that shape the ability of older people to tell their stories and for these voices to be heard by aged care providers and by society at large. For this reason, feminist standpoint theory was utilised to provide effective strategies for engaging older people's knowledges and experiences. Feminist standpoint theory provides a methodological framework which privileges the knowledges of oppressed people and actively seeks ways of transforming repressive power structures.

This project utilised a qualitative multiple methods approach, combining in-depth interviews and participant observation techniques to gain a rounded insight into the experiences of couples in residential aged care. Research was conducted between May 2014 and October 2015 at three residential aged care sites run by Helping Hand Aged Care, a South Australian medium-to-large-scale, high-quality, not-for-profit aged care provider. Interviews were conducted with couples where one or both partners lived in residential aged care, and with staff members. Observation research was conducted at the residential aged care sites, including joining the 'Lifestyles' staff team on daily activities, accompanying couples on recreational activities and daily routines, and attending recreational activities as an observer. I also attended numerous industry-run sexuality training workshops for staff. Analysis was conducted using feminist standpoint theory and thematic analysis.

Thirteen couples were interviewed for this research. Of these couples, three lived in care together while ten were separated with one partner living in the community and the other in care. From here individuals living in residential aged care are described as 'residents', while individuals living in the community are described as 'partners'. All couples involved were married and heterosexual, and with the exception of two couples (one couple married on site and one couple who had been married for ten years), all had been married for a minimum of 30 years. These participants were aged between 62 and 94.

Seven staff were also interviewed, to gain insight into staff understandings of the needs and experiences of couples in their care, and to examine the policies and practices that the aged care organisation utilises in their care models. These staff members included nursing staff with direct care responsibilities, site managers, a lifestyles coordinator and executive directors with responsibilities for research and development, staff training, care design and living environments. All staff members interviewed were female, and aged between 40 and 60 years old. This is typical of the Australian residential aged care workforce, where 89 per cent of direct care staff are female (ACSA, 2016), and the median age for all direct care positions is 48 years (King et al., 2012, Table 3.6).

All interviews with staff and couples were recorded and transcribed, except for two interviews where the participants refused permission to record and notes were taken by hand by the researcher during the interview. All participants have been assigned pseudonyms and job titles for staff have not been included to protect their privacy. The research was conducted with approval from the University of Adelaide's Human Research Ethics Committee.

Sexuality and intimacy in care

The intersections of ageing and sexuality within the residential aged care environment are an under-acknowledged and under-researched aspect of later life. Older people's sexual and intimate realities are often rendered socially invisible by prejudices and assumptions around ageing and sexuality. There exists a pervasive social norm that sees older people as non-sexual or asexual beings as a result of the ageing process. In a society where 'dominant images of sexuality revolve around the youthful, healthy, beautiful body and represent a marked contrast with those associated with old age, invoking as they do physical decline, decrepitude and sickness', these prejudices and social assumptions have impacted on both research and policy decisions made in relation to ageing sexuality (Gott et al., 2004, p. 2093). As Marshall and Katz (2002) put it, 'most academic and professional fields, critical and otherwise ... accept the biological tradition, claiming that sexual decline is a natural consequence of the ageing process' (p. 43). As an 'outsider', it is easy to be swayed by social perceptions and prejudices of the residential aged care site. The colloquial 'nursing home' is a source of anxiety for older people who fear entering in such an institution, and is seen as a place of broader social exclusion, often derided in popular culture as 'God's waiting room'. As such, the idea of maintaining a sexual, intimate and engaged relationship in care may be surprising to many. However, it is exactly these prejudices and assumptions that this research sought to challenge. By speaking directly to older people about their intimate and sexual relationships in care, this research presents alternative storylines of the older person. It also looks at the systemic and structural aspects of residential aged care that hinder the expression and fulfilment of these relationships.

Understanding sexuality and intimacy

Within sociological discourses, sexuality and intimacy can be understood as distinct yet interconnected concepts. Sexuality involves a wide aspect of human experiences, including sexual and gender identities and roles, sexual orientation, intimacy, pleasure, eroticism, desires, beliefs, attitudes and values, and reproduction (World Health Organization, 2010). Intimacy, meanwhile, can be defined as 'a sharing of innermost qualities' (Kasulis, 2001, p. 28). Intimacy is colloquially used as a euphemism for sexual intercourse, but more accurately refers to the closeness of two people. It involves trust and empathy, and is often based 'on years of sharing and caring' (Kasulis, 2001, p. 29).

In looking at older people's experiences of relationships in care, I explored themes of both intimacy and sexuality. Paths of questioning examined how older people's relationships were maintained and how they changed in the face of institutional structures and changed personal circumstances. This included physical and emotional expressions of closeness, as well as aspects of sexual intimacies and practices. In illuminating these people's experiences, I also sought to assess the impacts that institutional structures have on these experiences. This reflexive analysis will overview some of these findings.

Intimacy and sexuality in residential aged care

The experience of intimacy and sexuality by couples in this study was shaped by the institutional environment of residential aged care, and the life-stage factors associated with ageing and illness. Residential aged care has both similarities and differences to that of other institutional environments. The residential aged care site is part of the broader ageing health care system, but it is different from other heath sites in that it is at once a care site, a home-like environment and a palliative care location. Although a small number of people transit through the respite services of residential care sites, the majority of residents enter residential aged care with the knowledge that they will likely be in care until their death. Indeed, the sense of finality, that their spouse was never coming back, was a common theme in a number of partners' statements. Jenny (partner, aged 62), whose husband went into residential care with mental health problems and co-morbidities including diabetes and kidney problems, said: 'I know there is a possibility that he could probably come out but, you know at some stage, I don't know, but, you know, it is final when they come in here.'

Meanwhile, James (partner, aged 75) talked about negotiating grief and the sense of loss and ending of their relationship after his wife, Evie (resident, aged 76), moved into care:

> So she'd been in there ever since ... And I've been on my own since, you know, because she never did come home again. I think it was [staff member] said to me – you know, because I think she realised I was having a fair bit of trouble just accommodating this – she said to me, 'The trouble with it is, when you have dementia you lose the person to the dementia first. Then you lose them to a nursing home and then you lose them when they die'. So you lose them three ways, so she said, 'This will be your second way'.

Residential aged care is an environment where death and grief are a constant presence, juxtaposed against 'lifestyles' and health activities aimed at giving life meaning or at least maintaining the body. For older people, intimacy, sexuality, relationships and anticipated or experienced grief become intertwined. Conducting sexuality research in this context required the negotiation of grief while providing outlets for the discussion of sexual expression and intimacy.

Intimacy, in the sense of 'a sharing of innermost qualities', was important for all couples, and its loss keenly felt for those couples who felt unable to maintain this connection. In residential aged care, quality, uninterrupted time together emerged as a common theme in maintaining intimacy. All couples expressed a desire to spend time together, and this was a central part of maintaining their relationships and closeness. Jenny stated that one of the most distressing things about her husband's move into care was that they did not get to spend as much time together and did not have the same level of privacy as they did at home. As she put it, 'You think retirement you're going to sit and have long chats and go on holidays and things like that'. Instead, Jenny found herself commuting for up to two hours per visit to her husband. Other couples found they had more time together due to shorter commutes, but still experienced challenges around privacy. Couples like Stanley (partner, aged 75) and Olive (resident, aged 73) had developed a daily routine of activities together, including watching favourite television shows, having a morning tea of hot chocolate and scones on site, and attending craft activities together. They also made regular outings offsite to have private and uninterrupted time together. Oscar (partner, aged 72) took his wife Martina (resident, aged 67) on daily drives and outings, spending hours together. Ada (partner, aged 77) made a point of visiting her husband Alfie (resident, aged 78) every day for the 18 months he was in care, with their time together remaining significant to both even as Alfie lost the ability to speak. These couples' routines developed consciously in response to the realities of residential aged care life, in particular issues related to privacy and to the impact of health changes, with multiple layers of intention and meaning attached to each activity.

For example, couples where one partner had dementia sometimes experienced the routines around intimacy differently. This was the case for James and Oscar, whose wives Evie and Martina had developed dementia. James describes how his visits remain significant to him, but feels that Evie gets less out of the visits. He visits regularly, but for short periods of time.

James: These days I go visiting Evie and I like doing that, I get a lot out of it. She doesn't get much, she sort of – 'See you later …' type thing, you know, and I go …

Facilitator: What do you do when you visit?

James: Oh, just sit and talk to her. You can't get much answer. I tell her everything that happens in great detail, which I'm good at, because that's a way of keeping her occupied. And she sits there and she laughs and all that, and I enjoy the visits.

Oscar similarly describes how he finds spending time with his wife rewarding, even if she struggles with maintaining connections to his broader life. For them, spending time together in silence is enough to maintain their connection and intimacy. Hence their long car trips together provided an opportunity for closeness and engagement, without the need for words.

In a number of cases, these routines were structured to incorporate aspects of care. The giving of care for many couples represented an intersection between intimacy and sexuality, providing opportunities for touch, affection, love and connection. For Ada, helping Alfie eat dinner, and eventually feeding him, was an important part of their intimacy, while routines such as goodbye kisses and casual touches were important to maintaining their connection and sexual intimacy. For Mabel (partner, aged 76) and Clarence (resident, aged 76), activities like Mabel assisting Clarence to move in and out of his wheelchair were a chance for cuddles and a kiss. These moments were particularly valued by the couple, particularly after sexual activities, such as intercourse and manual stimulation, became too challenging in their room on site. Mabel explained that the en suite bathroom in Clarence's room was the only place they felt guaranteed privacy for sexual activities, and over time Clarence's physical condition deteriorated, making it too difficult to engage in such activities in the bathroom.

Overall, the couples I spoke to had developed a range of strategies for reshaping and maintaining intimate and sexual aspects of their relationships in the face of physical and emotional challenges brought about by the necessity for residential aged care support. They were also highly adaptive to the institutional constraints they faced, which will be outlined below. It was in relation to institutional constraints that reflexivity became particularly significant for the research process.

Privacy, institutional care and maintaining intimate relationships

Similar to other health institutions where staff presence gives a sense of continuous surveillance, ideas around ownership of space and privacy are problematic in residential aged care. Privacy dynamics vary significantly from what couples may experience in their own homes, and utilising these services required the restructuring of their time together. During my fieldwork, I observed numerous instances where, from my perspective, privacy seemed to have been violated. For example, in one interview in a resident's room there were five interruptions from staff, for tasks including wound management and cleaning. This was reflective of realities of life in this environment, described in another interview:

> There's always somebody in and out because, you know, they
> bring in morning tea and they come and get him for lunch
> and medication and things, so yeah, it's good, but you know,
> you don't get total privacy. You don't get two hours to sit and
> chat. (Jenny, partner, aged 62)

The residential care site is an example of a total institution. Scott (2011) describes the total institution as 'one in which members are immersed and enclosed – physically and sym-bolically – for a long period of time, to the exclusion of other attachments, and which aims fundamentally to change their identities' (2011, p. 1). The residential aged care environment is an all-encompassing one, where people live, eat, sleep, bathe and socialise to a schedule, where there is an expectation of a level of conformity to an imposed routine, and a residents can become isolated from the broader community. One of the senior staff members I interviewed described residential aged care as an example of 'contested space', referring to the tension inherent in this institutional environment over ownership of space, where residents live as well as receive a service.

> There is a term also called contested space … there's lots
> of issues within residential care. You know, whose space is
> it? Is it a space that's owned by the resident where they live,
> and we knock and request permission to enter? I believe it
> is. Having said that, it is also a place where people work and
> provide support. But the need to go in and out happens at
> different times of the day, so I think clients will probably feel
> more in control of their space at some times of the day than
> others. (Linda, staff)

Through reflexive analysis on my role as a sexuality researcher, I have had to reconsider my own place in the privacy dynamic. Initially, I saw myself as a private visitor attending residents in their own space, and saw myself as independent from the site management. From this perspective, therefore, it appeared that staff who entered resident rooms during multiple interviews were ignoring or disrespectful of the fact that residents had visitors. Where I was interviewing couples in public locations, rather than in their rooms, this seemed less intrusive, as residents were generally happy to talk to people they knew. However, where these interruptions occurred in the resident's own room, I was surprised by their tolerance of the intrusion. It later occurred to me that I may have misinterpreted the way I was perceived. While staff visiting their rooms may not have been aware I was a researcher (I had a badge identifying me as such, but was not wearing university logo clothing as other student placements typically do around the site), residents were certainly aware that I was. It is possible that I was seen as associated with the site itself, rather than as an independent outsider, and thus they may have felt no need to turn staff away. However, my observations also suggested that residents rarely decline staff requests for entry. It is a challenging dynamic to interpret, but it is important for the sexuality researcher to be aware of how their presence and how they are perceived by participants impacts the research process.

As a researcher, I also had to be conscious of the impact of the location of interviews on the information participants were prepared to share. Couples were given the opportunity to nominate a location for their interview, including the resident's room, the on-site café, meeting rooms onsite, at the partner's home or another nominated location. Five couples actually chose to have their interviews in the site café or in sitting areas in communal corridors. Five couples chose to be interviewed in their rooms. Only three chose locations that could be considered fully private, in the sense that they avoided observation, those being their own home or a private onsite meeting room. This suggested to me that sensitivities and expectations around privacy actually differed for me compared to my participants. For the most part, participants were comfortable discussing their relationship in the location chosen, with one couple encouraging me to continue interviewing them while a staff member was in the room changing a wound dressing. One partner expressed some discomfort over the course of questioning related to intimacy, but it is unclear whether the discomfort was over discussing sexuality and intimacy itself, or over discussing it in a semi-public location (walking around the site without anyone immediately present). While most participants were comfortable discussing their relationships, discussing sexual practices was something that I, as a researcher, was less comfortable doing in more public locations. It felt uncomfortable asking older people about issues of sexuality in more public places. I identified this feeling as connected to my awareness of social expectations of older people as uncomfortable talking about sexuality. While my research directly challenged notions of the asexual or non-sexual older person, it took experience to learn how and when participants were actually comfortable talking about their sexuality.

Interviewing about intimacy and sexuality

As an emerging sexuality researcher, building the courage to ask sexual questions of participants was a significant personal challenge. I say courage, as confronting ageist stereotypes was a significant concern for me beginning this research and undertaking this research directly challenged social assumptions around ageing that I had grown up with. This personal experience was further complicated by growing up in familial and social circles where discussion of sexuality was minimal. In undertaking sexuality research, I was entering a field I had academic knowledge of, but for which I lacked conversational experiences. I was also concerned about how this research, and myself as the researcher, might be perceived or received when made public that I was studying sexuality. In practice, I found that I was significantly more comfortable talking to staff about sexuality, compared to older people. Asking staff about the clinical and social support aspects of their role was more comfortable than asking older people about their own expressions of sexuality and intimacy. As researchers, we have to learn to manage our own sensitivities, while being conscious of our participants. There can also be generational differences in talking about specific experiences.

Underwood et al. (2010) argue that age can influence the research process. In their research, they found that generational experiences impacted the way different age cohorts interacted with the research process and discussed sexuality. For my research project, I found my own expectations around ways for approaching sexuality were ineffective. Initially, I thought that approaching sexual topics indirectly would make older people more comfortable talking to me, and that I could use common experience to discuss the issue. To this end, I would reference my own status as a married woman in the expectation that wives in particular would feel more comfortable opening up to me. Instead, I found that referencing my marital status made no impact on what people shared, and referring to sexual matters indirectly saw participants also speak indirectly. For example, the conversation below saw Mabel talking indirectly on sexual activities:

Mabel: I'm not saying intercourse because that was too difficult but you know, there's other things apart from that.

Researcher: I'm getting married, I know what you're talking about.

Mabel: Yeah and so when he first came here we'd go in the bathroom, we shut the door and do whatever you're doing, and that has become more difficult.

(Interview with Mabel, partner, aged 75)

After three interviews where this approach had limited success, I changed tack and began asking questions directly. This proved far more effective. For example, this conversation with Oscar demonstrates how forthcoming participants could be when asked directly about sexuality:

Researcher: Do you still have the physical aspect of your relationship?

Oscar: No, you want me to tell you why?

Researcher: Yeah, if you are comfortable telling me.

Oscar: As long as it doesn't go on Facebook or anything.

Researcher: No it won't.

Oscar: And as long as the people here don't know.

Researcher: Yep.

Oscar: I'm a diabetic, so that's knocked me around as far as my functions go and 18 months ago, June not last year, the year before, I was diagnosed with prostate cancer. And I've never had Martina over here overnight, I can't lock the door here. And physically I'm not able to … But it's not all about physical sex. And with Martina the way she is, I wouldn't want to have sex with her, perhaps not knowing what's going on for my own self-satisfaction, you know? When I have sex my partner, my wife, has got to enjoy it as much as I do. So hence, I could become a priest now! [Laughs]

(Oscar, partner, aged 72)

The research process quickly revised my expectations and practice around the most effective ways of broaching sexuality in this context.

Conclusion

Conducting sexuality research can be a confronting process for the first-time researcher. It challenges stereotypes and expectations around different population groups, and requires introspection and reflexivity from the researcher, to adapt to the particular needs of the research participant. The research site also impacts this process, with power dynamics and environments impacting the experience. In the case of the residential aged care site, communication, disability and ageism are particularly significant factors to be negotiated. The researcher must also be aware of their own place in the research process. It is therefore vital to reflexively analyse the interaction of research and researcher identity, to produce the highest quality research that can be achieved.

In this chapter, I have done a thematic-based reflexive analysis of a doctoral research project conducted in a specific field environment. I have demonstrated how this environment shapes the researcher's relationships with participants, and how reflexive insights helped to better engage with participants. I have shown how the institutional and physical spaces of the residential aged care site can impact on the research process, and how a reflexive eye can shape more effective strategies for engaging with these realities. Overall, the reflexive research process was effective in illuminating my own expectations around working with older people, and in assisting to overhaul ineffective approaches to sexuality research with this population. The result is a more rigorous and effective research outcome.

References

Ackerly, B. and True, J. (2008) 'Reflexivity in Practice: Power and Ethics in Feminist Research on International Relations', *International Studies Review*, 10, pp. 693–707.

Aged and Community Services Australia (ACSA) (2016) *Senate Inquiry on the Future of Australia's Aged Care Sector Workforce*, Submission, ACSA, Deakin.

Altork, K. (1995) 'Walking the Fine Line: The Erotic Dimension of Fieldwork Experience' in Kulick, D. and Wilson, M. (eds) *Taboo: Sex, Identity and Erotic Subjectivity in Anthropological Fieldwork*, London: Routledge, pp. 81–105.

Coffey, Amanda (1999) *The Ethnographic Self*, London: Sage.

Dubish, J. (1995) 'Lovers in the Field: Sex, Dominance and the Female Anthropologist' in Kulick, D. and Wilson, M. (eds) *Taboo: Sex, Identity and Erotic Subjectivity in Anthropological Fieldwork*, London: Routledge, pp. 22–38.

Elias, J. and Ryan, A. (2011) 'A Review and Commentary on the Factors That Influence Expressions of Sexuality by Older People in Care Homes', *Journal of Clinical Nursing*, 20, pp. 1668–1676.

Elliston, D. (2005) 'Critical Reflexivity and Sexuality Studies in Anthropology: Siting Sexuality in Research, Theory, Ethnography and Pedagogy', *Reviews in Anthropology*, 34, pp. 21–47.

Finlay, L. (2002) '"Outing" the Researcher: The Provenance, Process, and Practice of Reflexivity', *Qualitative Health Research*, 12(4), pp. 531–545.

Glimer, M., Meyer, A., Davidson, J. and Koziol-McLain, J. (2010) 'Staff Beliefs about Sexuality in Aged Residential Care', *Nursing Praxis in New Zealand*, 26(3), pp. 17–24.

Gott, M., Hinchliff, S. and Galena, E. (2004) 'General Practitioner Attitudes to Discussing Sexual Health Issues with Older People', *Social Science and Medicine*, 58, pp. 2093–2103.

Holstein, J. and Gubrium, J. (1997) 'Active Interviewing' in Silverman, D. (ed.) *Qualitative Research: Theory, Method and Practice*, London: Sage, pp. 113–129.

Kasulis, T. (2011) *Intimacy and Integrity*, Honolulu, HI: University of Hawai'i Press.

King, D., Mayromaras, K., Wei, Z., He, B., Healy, J., Macaitis, K., Moskos, M. and Smith, L. (2012) *The Aged Care Workforce, 2012: Final Report*, Bedford, SA: National Institute of Labour Studies.

Kulick, D. (1995) 'The Sexual Life of Anthropologists: Erotic Subjectivity and Ethnographic Work' in Kulick, D. and Wilson, M. (eds) *Taboo: Sex, Identity and Erotic Subjectivity in Anthropological Fieldwork*, London: Routledge, pp. 1–21.

Lee, R. (1993) *Doing Research on Sensitive Topics*, London: Sage.

Mahieu, L., Van Elssen, K. and Gastmans, C. (2011) 'Nurses' Perceptions of Sexuality in Institutionalised Elderly: A Literature Review', *International Journal of Nursing Studies*, 48, pp. 1140–1154.

Marshall, B. and Katz, S. (2002) 'Forever Functional: Sexual Fitness and the Ageing Male Body', *Body and Society*, 8(4), pp. 43–70.

Pini, B. (2009) 'Interviewing Men: Reading More Than the Transcripts' in Townsend, K. and Burgess, J. (eds) *Method in the Madness: Research Stories You Won't Read in Textbooks*, Oxford: Chandos Publishing, pp. 95–106.

Randall, W., Prior, S. and Skarborn, M. (2006) 'How Listeners Shape What Tellers Tell: Patterns of Interaction in Life History Interviews and Their Impact on Reminiscence by Elderly Interviewees', *Journal of Aging Studies*, 20, pp. 381–396.

Sanderson, T., Kumar, K. and Serrant-Green, L. (2013) '"Would You Decide to Keep the Power?": Reflexivity on the Interviewer–Interpreter–Interviewee Triad in Interviews with Female Punjabi Rheumatoid Arthritis Patients', *International Journal of Qualitative Methods*, 12, pp. 511–528.

Scott, S. (2011) *Total Institutions and Reinvented Identities*, New York: Palgrave Macmillan.

Shuttleworth, R., Russell, C. and Weerakoon, P. (2010) 'Sexuality in Residential Aged Care: A Survey of Perceptions and Policies in Australian Nursing Homes', *Sexuality and Disability*, 28, pp. 187–194.

Underwood, M., Satterthwait, L. and Bartlett, H. (2010) 'Reflexivity and Minimization of the Impact of Age-Cohort Differences between Researcher and Research Participants', *Qualitative Health Research*, 20(11), pp. 1585–1595.

Walby, K. (2010) 'Interviews as Encounters: Issues of Sexuality and Reflexivity When Men Interview Men about Commercial Same Sex Relations', *Qualitative Research*, 10(6), pp. 639–657.

Willson, M. (1995) 'Perspective and Difference: Sexualisation, the Field, and the Ethnographer' in Kulick, D. and Willson, M. (eds) *Taboo: Sex, Identity and Erotic Subjectivity in Anthropological Fieldwork*, London: Routledge, pp. 190–208.

World Health Organization (2010) *Developing Sexual Health Programmes: A Framework for Action*, Geneva: World Health Organization.

15 | MUM'S THE WORD: HETEROSEXUAL SINGLE MOTHERS TALKING (OR NOT) ABOUT SEX

Charlotte Morris

Abstract

'Mum's the word' is an English expression which loosely translates as 'you need to remain silent'. This chapter reflects on the experience of conducting research into the intimate lives and narratives of heterosexual single mothers. Within these research encounters, what sexual stories were and were not being told? It explores factors involved in enabling participants to talk about sex within the wider context of their intimate lives and also attends to the silences and omissions in their narratives. While narrative researchers are often exhorted to attend to silences, what does this mean in practice? The paper reflects on the sexual stories being told (or not) whereby sex emerged alternately as a site of pleasure, liberation, risk, uncertainty, necessity and absence (welcome or unwelcome), identifying moments of silence within them. In so doing, it discusses contingencies of the research interview, including access to 'narrative capital' more broadly, alongside a consideration of specific complexities around gender, class and motherhood.

This starts with the importance of the story not told. But this area, of all areas, is the least researched or understood. We are trying to grasp a story before it becomes a story! This is the shadow ghost land of "no stories", an "uncertain, shadowy kind of existence" that Arendt talks about (1958, p. 50). Here are murmurings and ambiguities floundering to be made sense of. In the sexual world such muddles can be enormous –

a widespread dimly articulated world of sexual fantasy, passion, love and hate – that is rarely understood at all. (Plummer, 2017 on 'Narrative Power, Sexual Stories and the Politics of Story Telling')

Introduction

This research was originally conceived as a feminist piece of work with the goal of 'giving voice' to single mothers and the intimate realm of their lives, a previously neglected area of research. It stemmed from my own experiences as a single mother, the fascinating conversations I had with other women in similar situations, and the sense that there were a wealth of stories of intimate lives to be told. Working within the sociological field of intimacy, I set out to capture broad narratives of intimacy, conceiving intimacy as encompassing a range of physical and emotional connections with others, including current and ex-partners, lovers, friends, extended family and children. My overarching concern, from a feminist standpoint, was highlighting experiences which were largely invisible; aiming to highlight the multi-faceted complexity of single mothers' lives and to attend to intimate dimensions which were largely absent from the main body of sociological research on lone parenthood. Recognising the limitations as well as the possibilities of the notion of 'voice' in research, this chapter sets out to explore some key questions: What stories are enabled or disabled in the research encounter and what silences remain? To what extent do gender- and class-inflected silences around sexual and intimate experiences come into play in the research encounter? How possible is it to speak about experiences as a sexual being as well as being a mother?

The study specifically set out to examine the experiences of heterosexual single mothers – heterosexuality typically deemed to be normative, taken-for-granted and unproblematic (Jackson, 2005; Hockey et al., 2007; Van Every, 1996). An underlying intention was to explore and visibilise heterosexuality as an institution which contains its own norms, practices and hierarchies

(Van Every, 1996). It is recognised that heterosexuality is not clear-cut as a category, encompassing diverse experiences and blurred boundaries; some participants disclosed bisexual and lesbian experiences in the course of the interviews and one, it transpired, now identified as gay although the majority of her intimate experiences had been lived out as a heterosexual woman and so she contributed valuable narrations of her experiences as both a heterosexual and gay identifying woman to the research. The sample of 24 heterosexual single mothers in the southeast of England was comprised of women in a range of working and family situations and diverse in terms of age and social background but not ethnicity, being mainly White. Some identified unproblematically as middle or working class while others held an uncertain position, stating they were originally from a working-class background were now in full-time and/or professional roles while others had grown up in relatively affluent settings but were now unemployed or in low-paid work and living in social housing. In several cases there was a suspicion and/or rejection of the concept of class, possibly through fear of being labelled or judged.

As Plummer (1995) maintains, the telling of sexual stories only becomes possible within certain historical contexts. For single mothers living in Britain, the political and cultural context has been particularly challenging over the past two decades, with the popular press often providing a platform for 'new right' or neoconservative discourses stressing the importance of 'traditional' family values while decrying so-called welfare dependency. Consequently, single mothers have tended to be spoken *about* rather than having opportunities to tell their stories, sexual or otherwise. Indeed, they have often been discursively linked to a perceived decline in 'family values'; following a moral panic in the late 1980s and 1990s in the British media which blamed single mothers for a host of social issues including a lack of male role models, crime, housing and poor educational outcomes as well as declining marriage rates; such concerns re-emerged in discourses around 'troubled families' (McCarthy et al., 2014) following inner-city riots in the earlier part of this decade. Land and Lewis (1998) note that such 'moral panics' about single mothers are specific to Anglo-American societies. Yet the average span of lone parenthood is five years (Skew, 2009) with the majority re-partnering and so it is not usually a permanent situation. While media representations focus on perceived problems of young mothers (Tyler, 2008), the average age of single mothers is 38^1 and while single mothers' choices are seen negatively, women seldom choose to parent alone (Gillies, 2007). Rather, they are most likely to become a single parent through separation or divorce. Outrage in the popular press at perceived disproportionate access to resources through the welfare state belies the fact that single parent families are likely to live in poverty,[2] particularly in a climate of austerity (De Agostini et al., 2014; Browne and Elming, 2015).

Theorists have linked such negative depictions of single mothers as part of a broader backlash against feminism and the demise of the male breadwinner male-headed family with women in the role of dependent domestic service provider and primary carer (Lewis, 2001). They have also come to epitomise the figure of 'the chav' – represented as a member of an underclass selfishly having children and claiming welfare benefits at the expense of tax payers (Tyler, 2008). 'Family values' commentaries blame women for selfishly pursuing self-fulfilment at the expense of families while emasculating men and stripping them of their traditional breadwinning role (Lewis, 2001). The control of women's sexuality is an implicit aspect of such narratives, with sexuality as ideally confined to the permanent married heterosexual unit (Fox Harding, 1996). Single mothers then, operating outside the authority of a male head of household, are frequently positioned as a threat to the social order; labelled as irresponsible, promiscuous and exhibiting a desire for unrestrained procreation, along with a refusal to provide a 'civilizing force' for men through conventional domesticity (Mann and Roseneil, 1999). Such underlying cultural assumptions affected most of the participants in my study in terms of how they viewed themselves and how others viewed them; this may have had some impact on what they felt they could say.

Sexual stories

The overarching doctoral research study (Morris, 2014) focused on a holistic understanding of intimacy, including a wide spectrum of personal relationships as experienced over a lifetime. The transition to single motherhood often disrupted previous intimate lives as lived and understood, entailing a reflection and re-evaluation of current and hoped for intimate relationships. Narratives often foregrounded children and friends rather than lovers, reflecting shifting realities and priorities. For some, there were more urgent or pressing stories to tell – recovery from domestic abuse and unequal relationships (Morris, 2015); the trauma of relationship breakdown and transition to single motherhood; stories of everyday coping and survival, alongside more redemptive stories of successful parenting, developing positive relationships and educational achievements. Interwoven among these broader narratives of intimacy were sexual stories, encompassing themes of recovery, survival, pain, pleasure, absence and possibility. In some cases, sex was central to the main narrative, conveyed as a liberating, empowering force. Sex was often depicted as one aspect of a 'dating' phase en route to (re)partnering; at other times, it was viewed as risky and/or in conflict with the mothering role; as unnecessary, disappointing, associated with emotional pain, unattainable in current circumstances or simply as an absence. Several participants described sexual journeys, characterised as reawakening of sexual desire and pleasures, liberation from a restrictive motherhood identity or simply exploring new possibilities following relationship breakdown.

For those with the social and financial resources to do so (in terms of accessing childcare, the internet and the expenses associated with dating), becoming single represented an opportunity to experiment with romantic and sexual relationships and to engage with 'everyday experiments in living' (Giddens,

1991; Weeks et al., 2001). Whether through choice or necessity, intimate lives shifted in significant ways. At times experimentation was connected to wanting to experience sexual pleasure and other forms of fulfilment missing in previous partnerships. For a number of participants, becoming a single mother represented an opportunity to seek sexual pleasure and excitement, to take 'positive risks', through experimenting with casual relationships, pushing the boundaries and discovering what they ideally wanted from lovers and relationships. This shift signifies a transcendence of the 'asexual mother' role (Rich, 1977), providing an antidote to the everyday rigours of survival and coping with immediate financial, practical and emotional pressures. Sexual exploration links to Giddens's (1991) notion of 'plastic sexuality' and recent cultural emphases on sex primarily for pleasure (rather than procreation). However, the reality was rather more complex and shaped in part by entrenched heteronormative understandings of romantic coupledom and the ultimate objective of re-partnering.

For Sandra (a working-class mother of two, aged 50), rediscovering her sexual and feminine side was part of a recovery process during the difficult period after her husband left her and their children for another woman. She experienced a particularly difficult period of adjustment in terms of emotions, parenting, finances, housing, legal battles and resulting stress and mental health challenges. However, as described in the extended extract below, her children encouraged her to begin to enjoy her femininity (becoming a sexual being) again and she gradually started dating. She dated casually for two years before settling with two long-term lovers (at the time of the interview she had chosen to remain with one of these lovers). While her sexual life with her husband had not been satisfying, she had been willing to renounce that aspect of herself within the marriage but began to rediscover the pleasures of sex again – exemplified in her discovery that some men (in contrast to her husband) enjoyed giving oral sex:

I sacrificed that part of myself, the sex life, for the children and the family. So ... I was OK with that – for instance he didn't give me oral sex in all the time we were together. I was OK with that 'cos what you don't get you don't miss. So when I started dating afterwards and discovered men like giving oral sex it was great – yeah!

Anna similarly wanted to rediscover her sexuality when her marriage of 22 years ended and so she initiated a sexual relationship with the friend of a friend specifically for this purpose, which she termed a 'fuck buddy' relationship. This was not experienced unambiguously as liberating or empowering. While the arrangement served its purpose of experimentation and sexual discovery, in the event she found it difficult to separate sex and emotions:

I thought I'd lost my libido and I didn't realise I was a sexual being and so that was about sex and it was a good lesson because it made me think a lot about the relationship between sex and intimacy ... because I thought I didn't want to be emotionally close to anybody I was interested in just having a fuck buddy relationship and that was basically what was set up but I realise that um ... that it was very difficult for me to separate my emotions from just sex.

Anna initially dated a variety of men – usually met through internet dating sites – and engaged in casual sexual relationships. Eventually she developed the confidence to explore her sexuality and embarked on an open relationship with another woman with whom she had developed a close friendship. For her, the transition to single motherhood represented an opportunity to reshape her sexual identity and life. Karen likewise found that becoming single entailed the beginning of a new phase in her intimate life. This involved experimenting with relationships: 'Trying different situations of going out and being with people and seeing how I felt'. Having been in a marriage where she experienced severe emotional abuse, she was initially anxious about physical contact with men so turned to internet dating sites. Having begun by talking to different people online she eventually started dating and building up her sexual confidence. The internet was key to enabling her experiences, providing an opportunity to date men from a range of backgrounds; like other women in her situation dating websites opened up a new world of possibilities and provided an important learning experience. For Steph, internet dating similarly enabled her to learn more, as she described it, about men and about herself and what she wanted, which was her primary intention alongside having fun. Internet dating in some ways proved emancipatory for participants who had been in long-term, unfulfilling relationships. Steph related that the experience had a positive outcome for her, whereby she eventually met her current partner with whom she developed a fulfilling long-distance 'living apart together' relationship (Duncan and Phillips, 2010). Contrastingly, Karen explained that she had developed a certain amount of cynicism after negative experiences with internet communication, especially with men she described as 'players', those who persuade vulnerable women to have sexual relations with them through romantic overtures but then disappear or who seduce a number of women simultaneously.

Silences: speaking and not speaking about sex

I now turn to reflect on moments within the narratives where there may have been silences or gaps around the telling of sexual stories. In the previous section I highlighted examples where participants were very open, confident and articulate in depicting and discussing their intimate and sexual lives. However, this was not always the case and the business of approaching and attempting to interpret silences and gaps in narrative telling is precarious as story-telling is overlaid by many complex variables. As discussed, narratives are fluid, ever shifting and contingent, especially when in a research interview context (Plummer, 1995).

Nevertheless, I have found that reflecting on possible silences is an important part of the process, opening out the different dimensions, possibilities and limitations of narrative telling and enabling further attention to context.

It has been posited that we live in a highly confessional era (Foucault, 1976) where we are constantly encouraged to disclose experiences, indeed such disclosures are often celebrated. Sex is constantly being spoken about across ever burgeoning social mediums, including TV and social media and a widespread sexualisation of society is frequently referred to (Attwood, 2006). Yet there may still be some sexual stories which are felt to be too personal, embarrassing and obscene – stories which are simply untellable (Phoenix, 2010). Silences may be brought about by a need for self-censorship and/or self-protection in a climate of judgement: 'Despite a belief that in late modern societies we are incited to speak about sex, tension and silences still persist and some types of speech and speakers are strongly discouraged' (Attwood, 2010, p. 177). Moreover, such silences tend to be gendered due to a context in which women have historically rarely been given the opportunity to speak authoritatively about sex, despite often being the object of sex talk, where they are frequently disbelieved and yet where 'their own speech continues to excite considerable disquiet and suspicion' (Attwood, 2010, p. 184). Indeed several participants spoke of hiding or playing down their status as single mothers due to fear of judgement from relatives or colleagues, especially those from a Catholic background who felt that being divorced was stigmatised within their extended families, and certainly participants spoke of hiding as far as possible the fact that they were dating and/or having sex from families, neighbours and others and this is likely to be connected with wanting to maintain their feminine respectability (Skeggs, 1997) – an insight to which I will return.

In some cases, the absence of sex within the intimacy narratives was simply a reflection of reality; this absence was not unsurprising, in cases where participants were struggling with everyday financial survival alongside care and management of their young families. For some, 'not having sex' was an important aspect of their narrative and acknowledged as one aspect of their circumstances – whether missed or indeed celebrated; in some cases not having sex became a choice. Sofia felt that there was simply no room in her life for sex, quite literally, as she slept with her two young children for mutual comfort and to ensure they all slept at night. Her everyday life was fully caught up with their care and managing acute financial constraints without any practical support: In this scenario, she felt sex was not a possibility, comparing herself to a friend, another single mother who did find the time and resources to date and have sex; in this case not having sex was a *meaningful* absence, something that was felt to be missing from her life. Susan, in contrast to Sandra (introduced earlier) found it a relief not to have to undertake what might be termed 'femininity work', seen as a necessity for being sexually attractive but a time consuming, inconvenient aspect of dating. Once her daughter became older and her life was not focused exclusively on parenting she chose to spend her time on creative pursuits and career advancement. Susan felt that she had developed a fulfilling intimate life through friendships and that having a romantic/sexual partner would not necessarily enrich her life further and the content of her narrative reflected these choices.

Narrative capital (Goodson, 2013) refers to people's opportunities to tell, develop and practise stories – Karen as an example, had stories which were well rehearsed in her community and family, where relating experiences was the norm and in her case there were plenty of interesting experiences to relate. In Sandra's case, openness about sex was evidently an important part of her identity, although the reasons for this were not discussed. She stressed that with her children she was open about sex and planned to forge a career in sex advice for young people. She communicated that talking was important for her; she spoke about coming from a close-knit community where women continually shared experiences in contrast to her current inner-city area where social life was more fragmented. For other participants, the interview was the first opportunity to tell about their experiences and in particular, their experiences of sex as a single mother. A lack of narrative capital is therefore likely to have influenced the telling (or not) of sexual stories in some cases.

There are potentially multiple factors within the research process which may have enabled or inhibited the process of telling, of disclosing, including the research setting, the contrasting social location and set of experiences of interviewer and interviewee and resulting impression and interactions, down to the minutiae of time of day, where the interview fitted into the daily routine and what the researcher was wearing. In terms of the interview setting, I gave participants the option of being interviewed in their own homes where they might feel more safe and comfortable. I was also aware that it might be difficult for single mothers to travel, given their childcare responsibilities and numerous time demands. Approximately one-third of participants chose this option while others chose to travel to my home which was a more neutral setting for them, away from other family members and distractions. In a few cases it was necessary to meet somewhere neutral such as a quiet café. Interviews which took place in a home setting tended to be longer and enabled more disclosure, detailed story-telling or 'opening up' about experiences. The home setting lent an informal, friendly tone to the interviews, refreshments were provided and the interviews usually began with informal chatting about our children, work and lives in general. This often felt close to a situation where I would normally talk with other parents, in a home setting and in a spirit of openness and sharing of experience. Indeed, where interviews took place in a home environment they tended to be more intimate and in-depth. This is likely to be due to a better opportunity to build genuine rapport and less time pressure – alternative settings were usually chosen to fit around work and childcare responsibilities and so were more time-bound.

The main drawbacks of interviewing in a home setting were the chances of interruption from younger children and the risk of being overheard by family members. Usually it was possible to organise interviews when single mothers were alone but where, for example, one single mother (Natasha) who was working full-time could only meet at her home in the evening and her children were struggling to sleep and disturbed us on several occasions, curious about the stranger in their home. This challenge prompted reflection, partly based on experience, of the difficulty in finding space and time to develop intimacy and indeed to have sex, with children in the vicinity and the cultural emphasis on protecting children. Natasha's interview had to be paused several times while the participant settled her children. On another occasion a young child was in the same room and frequently wanted attention so the recorder was paused while the participant, Chloe, attended to her child's needs. While this inevitably had some impact on the flow of narratives, it also helped to build rapport – having been in the situation of caring for young children I was sympathetic to the continual need to parent. There was humour in the recognition of attempting to discuss intimacy, particularly sexual intimacy, in family environments. It also replicated numerous occasions where I and my friends would attempt to share and discuss experiences while tending to children and so this did not feel as awkward as it might have for another researcher who did not have such experiences. Opportunities to share experiences can take on a sense of urgency, particularly for single mothers who seldom have this opportunity and so overall, these conditions were not detrimental to the quality of the data. There was an instance in which a participant's older child was in the house and on a few occasions, the participant lowered their voice. It is conceivable that certain elements of their story were omitted or diluted. Some participants revealed that their children did not know the details of their parents' relationship breakdown, especially in cases of abuse. At times participants wanted to keep their sexual lives separate from their parenting lives so there was much sensitivity surrounding various topics. A parallel can be drawn here in terms of the difficulty of finding appropriate spaces in which to discuss intimate lives with finding child-free space and time for sexual relationships, especially for those lacking in resources and support.

There were moments where I almost forgot I was interviewing and felt like a 'girlfriend' (close female friend), sitting on sofa drinking wine after kids had gone to bed and disclosing sexual experiences. Sometimes the conversations triggered by the interview continued after the recorder was switched off (and in a few cases ongoing conversation enabled friendships to develop). 'Neutral' (although this term is contestable) and public settings, understandably, were not quite so conducive to the telling of sexual stories, however, being at home could also create barriers to telling, especially when children were in the vicinity. It was hard for participants to focus when in 'mother mode' – for example, answering the phone to a teenage daughter, being concerned about picking a child up on time and in several cases being interrupted by children. The age of children is relevant here – while very young children could be disruptive there was often less chance of them understanding what was being said; conversely, it was problematic when one participant's adolescent child frequently came downstairs after bedtime. The participant lowered her voice when speaking about the children's father and it wasn't until she was confident her children were asleep that she fully relaxed and opened up about her intimate life. Nevertheless, many of the interviews felt intimate in their own right. There is also much scope for reflecting on my own identity and the myriad ways in which I present (or perform) my own sexual identity in research encounters, my positionality as a white, educated, mostly heterosexual, mostly middle-class woman in relation to participants and this is a complex area with no easy or obvious answers. Indeed, as Rose (1997) states, we cannot really know what is going on in any given research encounter. It should also be recognised here that the telling (or not) of sexual stories is classed as well as gendered and, as previously touched on, for women, is bound up with the performance of appropriate femininity and 'respectability' (Skeggs, 1997).

Appropriate femininities are inextricably bound up with gendered and classed notions of motherhood: participants frequently reported experiencing guilt around being a mother and a sexual, sexually available (single) being. For those with daughters, the management of their sex lives in line with culturally acceptable notions, was especially important as there was a perceived need to model appropriate sexual behaviour. The cultural emphasis on the centrality of motherhood (Hays, 1996) may also reflect that single mothers feel more confident in portraying their 'mother' and 'carer' identities as these are socially and culturally approved (Skeggs, 1997). Privileging motherhood identities over sexual identities may be one way in which some participants maintain feminine 'respectability', especially in the face of moral judgements about single mothers. There were certain participants with whom I had a particularly high level of reciprocity and well worked through sexual stories; in several cases these were women from a similar middle-class background to me who perhaps sensed we shared a level of 'worldliness' and willingness to openly talk about sex alongside the social and cultural capitals to be able to engage in these discussions. There were also working-class women such as Sandra for whom being open about sex was very important. Karen likewise clearly enjoyed talking about her sex life and had plenty of stories to relate about her experimentations. Both women described coming from traditional working-class communities and remaining close to their families with high levels of self-disclosure. To some degree this may reflect a shifting socio-cultural milieu, in which sexual openness is deemed attractive, even aspirational. Nevertheless, I would maintain that narrative capital is a key concept to understanding the ability to narrativise experiences. In terms of social status, many participants had somewhat precarious identities – some having gained in status through the accumulation of education and professional experiences – and the cohort included several who described themselves as coming from working-class backgrounds but now working in professional roles. While conversely, some of the mothers portrayed themselves as having lost status through lack of money, poor job security or having to work part-time because of caring responsibilities, sometimes having had to leave well paid jobs and homes. Many had experienced personal and health issues which were detrimental to their career prospects and now lived in social housing where they viewed themselves as out of place. It was in these cases specifically, where participants felt their previous identities and social status to be under threat, where there was certainly more judgement about the sexual behaviour of other single mothers and where I perceived more reticence about talking about sex.

It should also be noted that disclosing details about a sexual relationship while being recorded by an interviewer could have some very real and detrimental material implications: one homeless participant, Anita, was currently staying with a male friend and she spoke very warmly about some of the day to day intimate moments they shared but I noticed that she drew back from opening up further about their relationship at certain points in the interview. Afterwards I realised of course that if she mentioned any sexual relationship or gave an impression (or it could be interpreted) that they were a couple in any way, there was a chance of her being reported and her social security benefits being withdrawn and also possible implications for any benefits he was receiving. The point here is not to speculate about their relationship but to recognise the gravity and potential implications of disclosures about sexual lives within specific socio-economic domains.

Overall, despite the potential pitfalls of opening up about sexual relationships and the differences between myself and participants, they were aware they were speaking to another single mother who was likely to empathise with the kinds of story being told. This is likely to have enabled to some extent the level of disclosure and the quality and detail of responses. However, at times there was a sense that participants were speaking to a wider audience, especially for example, when giving opinions about domestic violence or negative representations of single mothers. There was a sense in which participants wanted to convey the realities of the experience, the everyday lived experience, material struggles and lack of choice as opposed to popular representations. This may have stemmed from awareness that this research data might reach the public domain and so was a potential vehicle for enabling a political voice as well as an opportunity to tell their unique personal story to an empathetic listener.

Conclusions

Attending to the silences and the sexual stories which remained untold, has enabled an opening out of further dimensions of analysis, especially when situating the stories and silences within the wider social, cultural, political and economic milieu. It has highlighted the following aspects of sexual story-telling: the resources and types of capital, including narrative capital, on which participants are able to draw and which are necessary in order for such stories to be told; the performance of appropriate gendered and classed identities and conversely, presentations of spoiled identities (Goffman, 1963), stigma, shame and embarrassment; the (classed) power dynamics of the interview encounter; silencing spaces and enabling spaces which can facilitate or constrain talking about sex; the presence of hidden aspects of lives or secrets (Smart, 2011); absences which are chosen or otherwise and meaningful absences which nevertheless form part of the story; fear of exposure and judgement and the wider context which shapes such responses. Indeed it enables further consideration of the policing of boundaries of what intimacies are and are not possible and under what circumstances and following on from this, what it is possible to speak about and what sexual stories are unspeakable, linking to Plummer's (2003) concept of 'intimate citizenship'. I maintain the importance of attending to voice and of conducting research that enables marginalised voices to be heard and to be taken seriously as knowledge. Single mothers' stories are rarely heard in public or academic domains and so this imbalance needs to be redressed to enable better understanding of their lives. However, it is also important to acknowledge moments of silence in research, layers of experience which may go unacknowledged and unvoiced. As Plummer (1995) contends, the telling of certain sexual stories only becomes possible at certain moments: in extension to this, I understand voicing experiences as a highly contextualised, nuanced process which is strongly inflected by social and cultural status and intersections of gender, class, sexuality and other factors. Material situations and wider policy contexts also shape people's ability to tell (Squire, 2008) and Anita's case here, with constraints around receipt of welfare benefits, provides an example of this. A person's 'narrative capital' (Goodson, 2013) is also key here: some people are in contexts which are rich in social resources and the opportunity to tell, develop and rehearse their stories, even while they may be living in circumstances of relative material deprivation. As researchers, we do our best to coax (Plummer, 1995) or enable the telling of stories through facilitating settings and situations to be conducive to disclosure, finding common ground and establishing reciprocity with participants. Maintaining reflexivity and recognising ways in which our own positionality impacts on what is told and what is not told is an important aspect of the research process. Attending to silences has enabled a deeper reflection on the process, particularly in terms of the underlying power dynamics. Nonetheless, while differences between the researcher and researched (including race, gender and socio-economic background) enter interviews this is never entirely predictable – identities and power relations are shifting and complex. Complexities around gendered, classed identities were especially pertinent here, in a context where single mothers are so often judged, labelled and stigmatised. Here, the commonality between researcher and participants in being single mothers may have mitigated against this but undoubtedly other factors came into play. It is important to acknowledge such limitations as well as the possibilities and value of bringing previously untold stories into public and academic domains.

The interviews were an intense experience for myself and the participants: participants had often not told their story to anyone previously and so they were often disclosing and relating extremely difficult experiences for the first time. This meant that it could be challenging to listen and at certain points the interviews felt emotionally charged. Indeed, some aspects of stories were difficult to hear – containing as they did accounts of domestic abuse, poverty, mental ill-health, thoughts of suicide and homelessness. At the same time there was a strong sense of it being a privilege to have the opportunity to listen to these stories, to gain unique insights into participants' experiences and how they made sense of these. Participants responded positively to the experience of taking part in the research as it gave them a chance for their voices, their stories, to be heard and valued. Stories await their moment to be told (Plummer, 1995) and it is imperative, in order to counter historical and continuing negative depictions, misconceptions and judgements of single mothers in UK society, that the wealth of stories they have to tell about their lives – including experiences of sex and intimacy – are heard.

Notes

1. Gingerbread analysis of Labour Force Survey (April–June 2015). Aged 16–19 years.

2. DWP (2017) Households below Average Income, 1994/95–2015/16, Table 4.

References

Attwood, F. (2006) 'Sexed Up: Theorising the Sexualisation of Culture', *Sexualities*, 9(1), pp. 77–94.

Attwood, F. (2010) 'Dirty Work: Researching Women and Sexual Representation' in Ryan-Flood, R. and Gill, R. (eds) *Secrecy and Silence in the Research Process: Feminist Reflections*, Oxon and New York: Routledge.

Browne, J. and Elming, W. (2015) *The Effect of the Coalition's Tax and Benefit Changes on Household Incomes and Work Incentives*, IFS Briefing Note no. 159, London: Institute for Fiscal Studies. Available at www.ifs.org.uk/uploads/publications/bns/BN159.pdf.

De Agostini, P., Hills, J. and Sutherland, H. (2014) *Were We*

Really All in It Together? The Distributional Effects of the UK Coalition Government's Tax-Benefit Policy Changes, Working Paper no. 10, London: Centre for the Analysis of Social Exclusion, London School of Economics. Available at http://sticerd.lse.ac.uk/dps/case/spcc/wp10.pdf.

Duncan, S. and Phillips, M. (2010) 'People Who Live Apart Together (LATs): How Different Are They?', *The Sociological Review*, 58(1), pp. 112–134.

Foucault, M. (1998 [1976]) *The Will to Knowledge: The History of Sexuality, Volume 1*, London: Penguin.

Fox Harding, L. (1996) 'Parental Responsibility: The Reassertion of Private Patriarchy?' in Silva, E.B. (ed.) *Good Enough Mothering? Feminist Perspectives on Lone Motherhood*, London: Routledge.

Giddens, A. (1991) *Modernity and Identity: Self and Society in the Late Modern Age*, Cambridge: Polity Press.

Gillies, V. (2007) *Marginalised Mothers: Exploring Working-class Experiences of Parenting*, London: Routledge.

Goffman, E. (1990 [1963]) *Stigma: Notes on the Management of a Spoiled Identity*, London: Penguin.

Goodson, I. (2013) *Developing Narrative Theory: Life Histories and Personal Representation*, London and New York: Routledge.

Hays, S. (1996) *The Cultural Contradictions of Motherhood*, London: Yale University Press.

Hockey, J.L., Meah, A. and Robinson, V. (2010) *Mundane*

Heterosexualities: From Theory to Practices, Basingstoke: Palgrave Macmillan.

Jackson, S. (2005) 'Sexuality, Heterosexuality and Gender Hierarchy: Getting Our Priorities Straight' in Ingraham, C. (ed.) *Thinking Straight: New Work in Critical Heterosexuality Studies*, New York: Routledge.

Land, H. and Lewis, J. (1998) 'The Problem of Lone Motherhood in the British Context' in Ford, R. and Millar, J. (eds) *Private Lives and Public Responses*, London: PSI.

Lewis, J. (2001) *The End of Marriage? Individualism and Intimate Relations*, Cheltenham: Edward Elgar.

McCarthy, J., Hooper, C.A. and Gillies, V. (eds) (2014) *Family Troubles? Exploring Changes and Challenges in the Family Lives of Children and Young People*, Bristol: Policy Press.

Mann, K. and Roseneil, S. (1999) 'Gender, Agency and the Underclass' in Jagger, J. and Wright, C. (eds) *Changing Family Values*, London: Routledge.

Morris, C. (2014) *Unsettled Scripts: Intimacy Narratives of Heterosexual Single Mothers*, DPhil Thesis, Brighton: University of Sussex. Available at http://sro.sussex.ac.uk/48918/.

Morris, C. (2015) 'Considerations of Equality in Heterosexual Single Mothers' Intimacy Narratives' *Sociological Research Online*, Special Issue on *Intimacy and Equality*, 20(4), 6. Available at www.socresonline.org.uk/20/4/6.html.

Phoenix, A. (2010) 'Supressing Intertextual Understandings: Negotiating Interviews and Analysis' in Ryan-Flood, R. and Gill, R. (eds) *Secrecy and Silence in the Research Process: Feminist Reflections*, Oxon and New York: Routledge.

Plummer, K. (1995) *Telling Sexual Stories: Power, Change, and Social Worlds*, New York: Routledge.

Plummer, K. (2003) *Intimate Citizenship: Personal Decisions and Public Dialogues*, Seattle, WA: University of Washington Press.

Plummer, K. (2017) 'Narrative Power, Sexual Stories and the Politics of Storytelling' in Goodson, I., Antikainen, A., Sikes, P. and Andrews, M. (2017) *The International Handbook on Life History and Narratives*, Oxon and New York: Routledge. Available at https://kenplummer. com/publications/articles-since-2000/2016-narrative-power-sexual-stories-and-the-politics-of-story-telling/.

Rich, A. (1977) *Of Woman Born: Motherhood as Experience and Institution*, London: Virago.

Rose, G. (1997) 'Situating Knowledges: Positionality, Reflexivities and Other Tactics', *Progress in Human Geography*, 21, pp. 305–320.

Skeggs, B. (2002 [1997]). *Formations of Class and Gender: Becoming Respectable*, London: Sage.

Skew, A.J. (2009) *Leaving Lone Parenthood: Analysis of the Repartnering Patterns of Lone Mothers in the UK*, PhD Thesis, Southampton: University of Southampton. Available at https://eprints.soton. ac.uk/72373/.

Smart, C. (2011) 'Families, Secrets and Memories', *Sociology*, 45(4), pp. 539–553.

Squire, C. (2008) 'Analysing Narrative Contexts' in Andrews, M., Squire, C. and Tamboukou, M. (eds) *Doing Narrative Research*, London: Sage.

Tyler, I. (2008) 'Chav Mum Chav Scum', *Feminist Media Studies Online*, 8(1), pp. 17–24.

Van Every, J. (1996) 'Heterosexuality and Domestic Life' in Richardson, D. (ed.) *Theorising Heterosexuality*, Buckingham and Philadelphia, PA: Open University Press, pp. 39–54.

Weeks, J., Heaphy, B. and Donovan, C. (2001) *Same Sex Intimacies: Families of Choice and Other Life Experiments*, London: Routledge.

16 | SEX AND THE ANTHROPOLOGIST: FROM BDSM TO SEX EDUCATION, AN EMBODIED EXPERIENCE

Nicoletta Landi

Abstract

In this contribution my aim is to analyse the topic of doing research on sex and sexualities starting from my personal experience as a sexualised person and as an anthropologist in order to reflect on the researcher's identity's role while analysing sex and sexualities. Investigating such topics is a complex challenge since it implies a reflection on social and personal values, experiences and desires concerning (the scholar's) sexuality while highlighting sexual plurality and its complexity. Throughout two ethnographic case studies, one about BDSM (bondage, domination, sado-masochism) and the other about sex education for teenagers – both led in the contemporary Italian context – I present the methodological, theoretical and empirical implications and challenges of researching sex and sexualities throughout an engaged and reflexive approach. I claim that (sexual) reflexivity can contribute both to a deeper comprehension of the topics being analysed and, at the same time, stimulate wider reflections of the scholar's role while investigating intricate topics such as sex and sexualities.

Sex is not the answer, sex is the question, yes is the answer. (Howard Hoffman, quoted in Hastings and Magowan, 2010, p. 1)

Introduction

In this chapter, I discuss the theme of researching sex and sexualities starting from my experience as anthropologist and sexualised person currently working on teenage sexual health promotion and sex education mainly in Italy. My personal and academic skills cover anthropology and education considering that I am trained as a qualitative researcher and as a freelance sex educator.[1] I cooperate with the Italian academy, local associations (especially LGBT[2] ones) and public institutions – such as the Municipal Health Service – promoting sexual health and gender equality.

My background lies in the field of social sciences and humanities and I consider myself a 'sex researcher': as someone particularly focusing on topics related to sex, and a number of different subjects related to sexualities such as gender, sexual orientation and sexual plurality. Considering sex and sexualities as a complexity of social, cultural, political and economic factors – as Scheper-Hughes and Lock (1987) suggest – I claim they should be analysed as social constructs beyond any reductionism or essentialism and, according to my experience within the Italian academic context where sex and sexualities are still uncovered topics, it is important to stress their specificity in order to enlarge its visibility as a subject to be investigated. At the same time though, I agree with Kath Weston (1998) when she affirms that scholars cannot just study sexualities as a topic per se since it is integral to many other subjects analysed by social scientists.

Referring to these themes, then, my position is to consider sex and sexualities as topics needing their specificity to be recognised and at the same time to be connected to a deeper analysis of those socio-political factors influencing them.

In this sense, for what concerns methodology, reflexivity within qualitative research (Stanley and Wise, 1990) and an engaged approach to researching can be useful to deconstruct sex and sexualities in their intricacy, and to stress their importance as both topics per se and, at the same time, as specific themes needing to be further investigated inside and outside the academy.

I will unpack these questions by presenting two different (but connected, one to the other) case studies, in order to stress that investigating sex and sexualities often implies a personal engagement of the researcher since it involves his/her identity and experiences (Piasere, 2009) and that his/her sexuality can be part of methodological and theoretical reflections.

Since research is a dynamic process, reflexivity 'involves an awareness that the researcher and the object affect each other mutually and continually in the research process' (Alvesson and Skoldberg, 2000 in Haynes, 2012, p. 73). Especially within action-research activities (Barbier, 1997), as I will indicate through some vignettes taken from my fieldwork, reflexivity becomes an important methodological tool: it can firstly stimulate a deeper understanding of the scholar's (sexual) positioning on the field; secondly it can lead to a deeper understanding of the topics being analysed and, last but not least, it can stimulate a more proactive and engaged attitude towards researching. I refer to Norma González's idea of engagement, especially within educative settings, according to whom anthropology can be 'effective in interrogating the structural inequities of educational policy and practice' (2010, p. 249). I also claim anthropology can address social issues as a public discipline (Borofsky, 2000) and, especially in relation to action-research, it can impact the stakeholders' lives (including the researcher's) by suggesting to them resources to empower themselves.

Then, giving value and visibility to the (sex) researcher's personhood – in addition to his/her analytical expertise – could help unpack sex and sexualities' complexity, making action-research more effective and, finally, innovating social sciences' methodological references, eventually including researchers' sexual identity as part of the investigation process, as both methodological and epistemological resources.

The first case study is an investigation among those, mainly in northern Italy, who practise BDSM (bondage, domination and sado-masochism) as – according to my analysis – an *ars erotica* (Landi, 2014). Throughout interviews and a wider participation in these persons' lives, I have been exploring the performative ways individuals, couples and groups share an aesthetic sense, embody and perform their sexualities involving specific physical stimulation, and role-play.

As I will show in this paper, analysing BDSM between 2008 and 2009 helped me in developing an open-minded approach to sex and sexualities that I could use while being either a sex educator myself or also while analysing sex education for teenagers as a PhD student and an anthropologist. The second case study, in fact, concerns action-research I carried out between 2012 and 2015 within an Italian counselling centre aimed at teenagers. It is part of the national health care system; it is called Spazio Giovani (Youth's Space) and is located in Bologna (northern Italy). Together with its professionals, I worked on the trial of a sex education programme named *W l'amore* (Long Live Love) addressed to preadolescents, their schoolteachers and families.

In both surveys, I realised researching sex and sexualities involves the researcher's identity, his/her experiences, desires and perspectives on gender, sexualities, relationships and research itself that can't be ignored. I assume an engaged and reflexive positioning – I experienced firstly studying BDSM and afterwards working on sex education – can represent an important resource for those who mean to dive into sexualities' complexity, its challenges, contradictions and ambivalences both as scholars and as persons.

BDSM

'How does it feel to be tied up?'
'Well, you should give it a try!'[3]

I started researching sexualities by studying those who practise BDSM (bondage, domination, sado-masochism) in Bologna and Milan, for my Master's Degree at the University of Bologna, between 2008 and 2009. Even though it was long time ago, I think – as the first survey I carried out about eroticism – the study of BDSM as a consensual erotic role-play deeply influenced (and still does) the way I approach sex and sexualities both as a person and as a scholar.

Paying attention to and processing the emotions I experienced in the field – excitement, curiosity and sometimes disappointment – throughout a reflexive attitude turned out to be useful to understand both the connections between physical pain and sexual pleasure, and sexualities' complexity. The scholar's desiring body – together with lust and pleasure – should be part of the research in order to produce a knowledge concerning sex and sexualities that is not deficient (Spronk, 2011).

Doing BDSM[4] – as the people I interacted with used to say – is a specific way to intend eroticism and to experience bodies and sexualities, and it is also part of a personal and social construction (Langdridge and Butt, 2004).

In A.'s words, 'advanced sexualities are not better then others, they're just more advanced and help you develop a more critical approach to what you are doing'.[5]

Also, according to S., '[d]oing BDSM is part of a wider development of your relationship with yourself and your body. I have a good relationship with myself in general'.[6]

Identities are social constructs, being embodied and performed (also) throughout sexual practices, which can imply (also) physical pain or power imbalances. Even if in contemporary society pain and pleasure are mostly represented as antithetical (Scarry, 1985), eroticism for some persons and groups can be connected to intense body stimulation. A slap, during a negotiated sexual play, is part of a meaningful relationship between subjectivities and it can also be a specific way to experiment with intimacy and agency. Doing BDSM is about personal and negotiated choices, and it is a ritualised expression of embodiment processes (Csordas, 1990). Meanings, values, intentions and fantasies are negotiated and lived within an intimate human exchange where personal and relational agency is fundamental: in such settings pain doesn't have to be overcome but, instead, it can be expressed throughout (sexually enjoying) negotiated options. Pain can be understood, managed and experienced: whiplashes, hot wax dripping, bodies tied in uncomfortable but charming positions – such as in *Shibari*[7] practices – are ways to express sexual preferences. As E. suggests, '[t]he rope creates a physical connection that stimulates expectations and, consequentially, erotic desire'.[8]

For those who are into BDSM, sex doesn't follow any conventional rule even if normativity is part of the game: power can be something to play with within the constant tension between the will to be 'normal' and experiencing, at the same time, a peculiar way to define and live sex, sexualities and relationships. 'It's a weird activity, but it is normal. Even *vanilla* couples, while they have sex, they scratch backs or hit butts', A. suggests.[9] While analysing BDSM, talking to the people involved in the community, experiencing an aroused curiosity concerning the practices I was observing and sometimes participating in, I felt overwhelmed by all those feelings as a scholar but also as a woman and a sexualised person.

I think I developed a 'sex positive approach' – which I currently use while working on sex education – exactly while letting myself be seduced by BDSM. By the expression 'sex positive approach' I mean a non-judgemental and curious attitude to sex and sexualities, enabling me to empathise with the stakeholders I live and work with today: families, social and health workers, teachers and especially teenagers. I think the SSC code,[10] used by those who do BDSM to define their play, can represent a valid reference for sex education, too: an open-minded and negotiation-based attitude to sex and sexualities can unite two very different fields under the same idea of sexual awareness, relational negotiation and lust.

Working on themes related to sex and sexualities, though, is challenging for the person and the anthropologist especially because an interest for these topics has become only recently explicit for qualitative researchers. As Hastings and Magowan (2010) indicate, for a long time sex – as a research topic and especially as a part of the field experience – has been denied or neglected because anthropologists needed to legitimate their discipline and its credibility. Anthropologists used to abstract sexuality from empirical experiences, especially their own, insisting on the differences between the researcher and the 'natives'. Today researching sex and sexualities – according to my perspective – can't be carried out without a reflexive approach involving the researcher and, eventually, the stakeholders with whom he/she is dealing. Analysing sex and sexualities should be connected to a more theoretical analysis of the empirical sexual experiences in order to deconstruct sexual normativity (Foucault, 1976) concerning behaviours, identities and representations (also the scholar's): lust and the body should be brought back into sex and sexualities studies (Plummer, 2008) for both the researcher and his/her informants.

Researching in general in fact, as Van der Geest et al. suggest (2012), generates important insights on the self/other relationship, and, in the specific case of investigating eroticism and sexual practices, researching also becomes an inter-subjective process made of erotic subjectivities dealing one with the other, addressing topics such as desire and identity – questions that 'lie at the heart of anthropological knowledge' (Kulick and Willson, 1995, p. 5).

Spazio Giovani and *W l'amore*

'Pleasure is not in the science syllabus!'[11]

After having disclosed sex and sexualities' complexity during my experience within northern Italy's BDSM community, and after having developed analytical and educative skills as a sex educator myself, my focused turned to action-research on sex education, which I carried out for my PhD at the University of Bologna. I took part in the activities of Spazio Giovani, which is a free-access counselling centre – part of the Italian public health care system and managed by the regions' network[12] – addressed to youth: its psychologists, gynaecologists, obstetricians and social workers offer medical, educative and psychological advice to teenagers aged between 13 and 19. According to Italian law[13] minors can have free access to educative and medical public services concerning the prevention of STIs,[14] contraception, and sexual and relational wellbeing. Spazio Giovani professionals cooperate with many public schools through sexual health promotion programmes – mainly set up by Spazio Giovani professionals themselves – involving teachers, tutors and parents. Although Italy hasn't unitary national policies regulating and implementing sex education[15] in fact, many public institutions and associations promote gender equality, gender-based violence prevention and sexual/relational wellness through specific local and national projects and services taking place in school settings.

During the time I spent within Spazio Giovani, dealing with its professionals, my aim was to unpack the institutional ways teenage sexualities are defined and handled by public policies and educative practices, and to trial anthropology's contribution within (teenage) sexual health promotion. I articulated the questions through a (sexually) reflexive and engaged approach by firstly observing Spazio Giovani professionals doing *edutainment*[16] activities with secondary school classes at the centre and, afterwards, by participating in *W l'amore*'s trial.

W l'amore is inspired by the Dutch evidence-based[17] project *Lang leve de liefde* (Long live love), developed by SOA Aids Nederland and Rutgers, in cooperation with the national Dutch health care system, and addressed to adolescents, their secondary school teachers and families and with a focus on the use of educative material (a handbook, a magazine and a website).[18]

During the action-research intended to adapt *Lang leve de liefde* to the Italian context, I worked together with psychologists and health professionals from some of Emilia-Romagna's (the region where Bologna is located) Spazio Giovani in order to create a project that could answer the youths', the families' and the teachers' needs concerning sexual health. Regarding methodology and my positioning, first of all I tried to consider personal engagement as an essential part of my fieldwork and, secondly, I used it as a stimulus to be more present and proactive in the field.

While observing Spazio Giovani professionals' educative work with the students and while participating in *W l'amore* experimentation, the topics that touched me the most were: cultural relativism, heteronormativity, sexual plurality and (female) pleasure. I also noticed a general lack of reflection – among the stakeholders – on how gender roles influence (teenagers') sexual behaviour. These issues turned out to be complicated, needing to be addressed by all the action-research participants, including me: they stimulated me, in fact, both as a person and as a scholar.

Regarding the first issue, I witnessed Spazio Giovani's workers' professional habitus (Tarabusi, 2010) often being unable to handle teenagers' biographies and what Ruba Salih (2005) stresses are (teens') multiple subjectivities: 'Arab boys are homophobic and they don't usually respect women's rights. It's part of their culture', asserted a psychologist while telling me how difficult is to deal with teenagers having different socio-cultural backgrounds.[19]

With their focus on heteronormativity, I observed that when teenagers asked Spazio Giovani professionals when is the right moment to have sex, how sex works or how it is possible to avoid unwanted pregnancies and STIs, the most recurrent answers were: 'When a boy and a girl think it's the right moment to have sex, they should think about safe sex' or 'sexual intercourse is when a penis penetrates a vagina'.[20]

In order to avoid heterosexism, I asked them: 'Why do you always talk about sex in terms of heterosexual genital intercourse? Why don't you talk about anal penetration too, or about the use of sex toys among girls for example?' One of Spazio Giovani's psychologists answered: 'Oh, c'mon. You are too Dutch! We can't talk like this to the kids otherwise it's going to be a mess!'[21] In the same way, they mentioned homosexuality only if asked about it:

'It's true, we only talk about it when the kids ask questions about it. We always take for granted their heterosexuality, but you are right, maybe they're not straight'.[22]

My suggestion was: 'We should consider that we may be talking to those who don't conform to gender norms, or homosexuals, or queer boys or girls. Sex education should not be just about the prevention of sexually transmitted infections or undesired pregnancies but about general wellbeing'. A surprised psychologist answered: 'Queer what? I don't even know who these queers are!'[23]

When I provocatively used my academic and personal competences concerning sexual plurality – using, for example, the word 'queer' – the first reaction of Spazio Giovani workers was mostly annoyance but, little by little, they admitted they learned something from 'the anthropologist':[24] 'When we started meetings with the students or with the teachers we always greeted them using heterosexist language, now we have learned how to include women too'.[25]

Learning together – the stakeholders and I – not to take teenagers' heterosexuality for granted and to enhance sexual plurality represented a crucial challenge during the whole of *W l'amore*'s trial. I believe, though, that homosexuality remains one of the most complicated topics to address, especially for adults: 'Will participating in sex education make my daughter *become* gay?' asked a frightened father during a meeting intended to present the project to a group of parents.[26]

The intricacy of the Italian socio-political context – closely related to Catholicism's role – has a fundamental part to play in the way homophobia is still widespread in school settings. Furthermore teenage sexual health is not handled comprehensively by either the school system or other public services,[27] and public policies and health/educative practices mainly promote an emergency-based and medicalised approach. Although such services and practices are supposed to reduce risky sexual behaviours, what they don't consider important are aspects of sexuality such as sexual plurality, consent and pleasure. As Allen suggests (Allen, 2006; 2013) and as my fieldwork has shown, pleasure is at the same time one of the most difficult and crucial topics to be discussed within sex education programmes. During the *W l'amore* trial, in fact, an illustrated representation of female external genitals, that included the clitoris, was described as 'violent and pornographic'[28] by many teachers (mostly women in their forties and fifties). A headmaster even asked if we – as the lead team monitoring the project trial – could remove the word 'anus' from the image.[29] Even in the adolescents' words, pleasure still seems to be problematic. Girls often ask if they can also experience orgasm such as boys do,[30] or claim: 'If you like sex, you are an escort!'[31]

In this scenario, I felt adolescents' sexualities and agency were minimised: this is why I decided to express my discomfort as a 'sex researcher' and as a woman in order to stimulate Spazio Giovani professionals to develop a more inclusive approach to sexual plurality, gender identities and social factors influencing sexualities. I tried to motivate the group of professionals (social workers, psychologists and schoolteachers) I was working with to think about and, consequentially, to handle (teenage) sexual health beyond physical well-being itself in order to consider sex, sexualities and sexual health in a more comprehensive way, as suggested by the most internationally recognised documents concerning sex education implementation such as the WHO's *Standards for Sexuality Education* (WHO, 2010).

Performing the role Spazio Giovani professionals gave me – the open-minded (too Dutch!) 'sex researcher' and the sex education expert with long-term experience within LGBT activism – I decided to get involved as a scholar and as a woman, and to use my experience inside queer[32] communities (such as the LGBT and the BDSM ones, about which I was frequently asked) in order to take advantage of the curiosity Spazio Giovani professionals showed about my experiences and my approach to sexualities in general.

Among Spazio Giovani professionals, together with a widespread curious appreciation of my expertise, I sometimes experienced the stigma concerning dirty work (Irvine, 2014) that 'sex researchers' can face inside and outside the Academy. In this case, the 'too Dutch' definition seemed to be meant to describe me as a too liberal (and bizarre) sex expert. Even if I sometimes felt discomfort in being so stereotypically perceived, I tried actively to use such a sex-related connotation in order to step outside the conservative Italian context and to give my insights some kind of legitimacy and visibility instead.

Introducing 'too Dutch' perspectives on teenage sexualities was my personal and methodological strategy to be part of this specific case study and to trial anthropology's contribution within sex education provided by public health services. In fact, I performed this 'too Dutch' connotation in order to make the stakeholders involved in the experimentation aware of the risks of heterosexism and the cultural relativism embedded in sex education, and at the same time I tried to stress the importance of developing a comprehensive and inclusive approach to teenage sexualities, not only to avoid heterosexism, but also in order to consider (female) sexual pleasure as an important topic (Allen, 2006; Lamb, 2008) and, more generally, to re-think adolescence beyond any biomedical reductionism.

Analysing sex education as an anthropologist and a sex educator myself made me highlight how sex education concerns many crucial topics related to socio-political representations and experiences regarding (teenage) sexualities (Allen, 2011), and how policies and practices related to sex education often generate stereotypical and normative insights concerning teenage sexuality. Moreover, the perspectives of the stakeholders involved in this field (policy makers, social workers, schoolteachers, families and adolescents) can be ambiguous, contradictory and discordant.

In this intricate scenario, anthropology can have the double role of being an analysis tool and, more practically, being part of an intervention strategy by suggesting points of view and operative plans in order to, first, stress the complexity of (teenage) sexualities and, secondly and more practically, improve teenagers' access to resources that can empower them in relation to their sexual health.

Actively engaging within this field can imply questioning the researcher's experiences and identity even with regard to what concerns his/her own sexuality. Even it is not a universal methodological suggestion, during my research experiences I have been noticing – and this is my personal perception – the impossibility of not willing to be touched by the topics being investigated. This (erotic) involvement can complicate the investigation and data processing processes but, at the same time, it can be an important resource to get to the core of the subjects and the (sexual) experiences being studied.

Starting from my experience in the field, I claim sex and sexualities (especially teenagers') are still huge taboos in the Italian school system (Batini and Santoni, 2009; Carnassale, 2014; Allen et al., 2014). Moreover, sex education should not only be about sharing information about the prevention of STIs through an emergency-based approach meant to reduce sexual risky behaviour, but it should also consider consent and pleasure in order to eroticise safe sex (Plummer, 1995). Sexual health promotion, in fact, should not only be based on a dominant medical discourse but be challenged by a critical socio-cultural reflection on what is healthy and what is not in a wider sense (Claes and Reynolds, 2013).

Together with offering an interesting perspective to reflect on wider conceptions and representations of (teenage) sex and sexualities, sex education represents an occasion for the stakeholders to get involved in a process of negotiating opinions and goals about sexual orientation, gender stereotypes, personal values and many other issues connected to sexualities and health more generally (Allen, 2011). Even if the main goal of sex education should be to catch the emic perspective of teenagers on sex in order to understand youths' needs without being judgemental or moralising, another aim can be to stimulate a confrontation among stakeholders with different perspectives. Sex education, in fact, can represent a crucial empowering tool for all those involved – teenagers and adults – but, as emerged from my experience, there's still a long way to go, at least in contemporary Italy.

As a researcher working on such topics through an engaged approach, I claim that a reflexive attitude – preferably shared by all the stakeholders – can improve the (action-) research course itself but also wider scientific processes about crucial topics such as intimate citizenship (Plummer, 2003, 2005a, 2005b; Richardson, 2015) and personal, socio-political and sexual empowerment.

With regard to methodological research strategies, considering the stakeholders' personal values and experiences and focusing subjectivities and points of view can all highlight how research is a deeply inter-subjective process where every perspective can contribute to a proper consideration of sex and sexualities as a scientific and social topic.

Conclusions

As I tried to show throughout the presentation of the case studies of BDSM and sex education – according to my perspective – the researcher's experience and his/her identity can be touched by the topics being analysed and, consequently, be part of the whole research process. As Olivier De Sardan (2009) claims, the scholar is a co-actor in the field he/she is investigating and researching is not a neutral process.

From the survey I carried out within the community of those who are into BDSM in northern Italy, I learned that as scholars, we often share with our informants the same sexual fluidity and complexity, and that doing research is an inter-subjective process. During the action-research on sex education I felt involved within this field both as a researcher/sex educator and as a woman. During the survey, in fact, I realised that the heterosexist, cultural relativist and stereotypical processes Spazio Giovani professionals were often defining in handling teenagers' sexualities and health moved me. Especially as a woman, I noticed how (young) females' sexualities are socially stigmatised (Lamb, 2008) and how teenagers' (sexualised) bodies are defined and managed through normative power relations (Foucault, 1976), embodied in public policies and educative practices or, as it happens in Italy, their lack or fragmentation.

Normativity embedded within (sex) education needs to be deconstructed in order to highlight how (sex) education is a social responsibility that needs to be innovated, implemented and related to all the shades of which human – and sexual – identities are made. Sexual health promotion should let the stakeholders – especially the younger ones – access resources about sexual health in order to help them empower themselves, and to be able to experience consensual, satisfying and plural (sexual and relational) experiences.

As a scholar, deconstructing sex and sexualities through a critical approach in order to co-construct an innovative and more inclusive way to handle teenage sexualities means (also) analysing one's own experiences, representations, values, needs and desires. I claim that working as 'sex researchers' inevitably engages the scholar's intimacy, in his/her 'flesh and blood' (Lyons and Lyons, 2004, p. 10; Spronk, 2011) and, in this sense, researching sex and sexualities means renewing the sense of engagement and scientificity, and giving visibility, social recognition and legitimacy to those who analyse sex and sexualities.

At the same time, sexual reflexivity and positioning awareness – in the field but also while processing and presenting research data – stimulate questions about methodologies and interdisciplinarity. According to my experience, in this scenario, anthropology's tools can be useful to deconstruct sexual normativity and to highlight sexual complexity, but it is in working with professionals from other branches of knowledge that this process can be articulated more effectively. Besides being an intimate process, researching sex and sexualities can also be a plural one: an interdisciplinary approach and plastic methodologies stimulate fertile reflections on identities, lust, relationships, health and, last but not least, researching itself. Professionals and scholars from different personal and disciplinary backgrounds can contribute to a more exhaustive analysis of sex and sexualities. Moreover, sexualities should not be normalised by intellectual and academic convention, neutralising the erotic side of studying sexualities (Claes and Reynolds, 2013), since this erotic aspect of researching is about everyone's selfhood, including the researcher's, and it represents one of the most intriguing ones. Researchers using qualitative methodologies should be aware of this complexity: according to my experiences – within a BDSM community and among those involved in *W l'amore*'s trial – the erotic implications of researching are complicated to handle but also fascinating and epistemologically useful.

They can help us all – scholars and people in general – dive into the complexity of eroticism and, at the same time, generate knowledge (and eventually educative practices) about health and lust while respecting plural identities and experiences, promoting intimate citizenship (Plummer, 2003, 2005a, 2005b; Richardson, 2015) and contributing to co-create a more inclusive society.

Notes

1. I was trained as an anthropologist at the University of Bologna (between 2002 and 2016) and as a sex educator at CIS, Centro Italiano di Sessuologia (Italian Centre for Sexology) based in Bologna (between 2010 and 2011).

2. Lesbian, gay, bisexual, trans.

3. Bologna, October 2008. This is an extract from a conversation I had with E., a self-defined bisexual dominant rigger. I met her very often during the investigation process since she introduced me to bondage practice and to a professional photographer for whom I posed as a model during a bondage setting. The pictures were part of the exhibition 'Mother Earth' within the 2009 edition of Bologna's Bizzarro Film Festival. Since I am writing this essay many years after my fieldwork within the BDSM community, without the chance to re-negotiate its members' participation in the study, I decided to leave their identity as anonymous. All the quotes included within the text are my translations from Italian into English.

4. 'Fare BDSM' in Italian.

5. Milan, September 2008. A. was a self-defined dominant heterosexual male I often talked with at both public and private events.

6. Milan, January 2009. S. was also a self-defined dominant heterosexual male.

7. *Shibari, Kinbaku,* bondage are the most used words to indicate specific techniques to tie the body up during erotic or performative plays in both private and public settings such as parties and exhibitions.

8. Bologna, October 2008. E. was a self-defined bisexual dominant rigger.

9. Milan, October 2008. The expression 'vanilla' – commonly used by those into BDSM – is used to define those who are not into role-plays and sexual experimentation. Through a metaphor, it refers to the fact vanilla is the most ordinary taste within a wider number of more tasty possibilities.

10. Sane, safe and consensual. The SSC code is widely used by those who are into BDSM plays in order to emphasise the consensuality and normality of their sexual preferences. The word 'normal' was one of the most recurrent words used during the discussions I had with either dominant, submissive or even switch players. Switch players are those who switch between being dominant and submissive.

11. Bologna, October 2013. This is a schoolteacher involved in *W l'amore* trial speaking: she was showing her discomfort regarding being committed to talk about sexual pleasure with her students. Even if I could understand her embarrassment (Italian schoolteachers are not trained to talk about sexuality in their classes), I felt disappointed and discouraged seeing how – within the Italian school system – sex and sexualities are often reductively considered as just biomedical issues and, still, a wider taboo.

12. In Italy the regional government controls the organisational and financial management of local health services such as Spazio Giovani.

13. *Legge per l'istituzione dei consultori familiari* (Law for the institution of family planning clinics), 27 August 1975 n. 405. Available at www.salute.gov.it/imgs/C_17_ normativa_1545_allegato.pdf (accessed July 2016).

14. Sexually transmitted infections, which are infections that are commonly spread by sex, especially vaginal intercourse, anal sex and oral sex. Their causes are bacteria, viruses and parasites.

15. The only national law that regulates public services delivering sex education is the Law n. 405/1975 (see note 13, above).

16. 'Edutainment' is shorthand for educational entertainment. Activities such as watching videos or doing role-plays are meant to give teenagers basic information about undesired pregnancies and the prevention of STIs. For research and privacy-related reasons, I observed and took part only in group activities such as the edutainment ones or *W l'amore* experimentation. I did not analyse those activities that addressed individuals such as psychotherapy addressed to teens.

17. Even if inspired by an evidence-based project such as *Lang leve de liefde* (Long live love), the *W l'amore* trial implied both a mainly qualitative investigation (interviews, focus groups and questionnaires) of the Italian stakeholders' (schoolteachers, families, social workers and teenagers) opinions and requests concerning sex education in general and *W l'amore* in particular, and an adaptation of the Dutch material to the Italian context. For further information about *Lang leve de lifede*, see www.langlevedeliefde. nl (accessed July 2016). To know more about evidence-based approaches, especially within sex education, and their implementation in the Netherlands, see Hofsetter et al. (1996); Schaalma et al. (1996); Schutte et al. (2014); Fergusona et al. (2008).

18. *W l'amore* was funded by Regione Emilia-Romagna inside the *XV Programma Prevenzione e lotta AIDS* (XV programme for AIDS prevention), promoted by the Regional Law n. 135/90 of June 2013.

19. Bologna, April 2013.

20. Bologna, November 2012.

21. Bologna, October 2012. The expression 'too Dutch' referred to the fact that I have been living for personal and study-related reasons in the Netherlands. The psychologist thought I had developed there a progressive and liberal approach to sexualities she felt to be 'too much' for the conservative Italian context.

22. Bologna, January 2013.

23. Bologna, May 2014.

24. This is how Spazio Giovani workers used to refer to me during the time I spent at the youth centre.

I am not sure what they meant by that, or if they completely understood – at least during the first phases of my research – my competences or research goals.

25. Spazio Giovani psychologist. Bologna, June 2015. She referred to the fact that, given that in Italian plural words are always characterised as masculine, they learned to use the expression 'Ciao a tutti e tutte' ('Hi everyone' including the feminine) instead of 'Ciao a tutti' ('Hi everyone').

26. Bologna, September 2013. The social stigma of homosexuality, especially within schools, is a topic needing further analysis that can't be articulated in this context. *W l'amore* has been strongly attacked by associations like Sentinelle in Piedi (Standing Watchers), Giuristi per la Vita (Lawyers for Life), Movimento per la Vita (Pro-Life Movement) and a number of other small, informal parent groups that were creating a huge debate about sex and gender education during 2015 and 2016 in Italy. To know more about these themes see Batini and Santoni (2009); Graglia (2012) and Carnassale (2014).

27. In Italy, sex education is often accused (as were *W l'amore*) by (more or less formal) groups of citizens, political parties and politicians (whether religious or not) of destroying traditional family values, promoting homosexuality and 'gender ideology' and prematurely sexualising childhood. To know more about this topic, see Garbagnoli (2014); Crivellaro (2015).

28. Bologna, October 2013.

29. Bologna, September 2013.

30. Bologna, April 2014.

31. Bologna, April 2013. On the *slut-shaming* theme, see Lamb (2008); Ringrose and Reynold (2011).

32. The term 'queer' is used to indicate sexual and gender groups or individuals that are not heterosexual or do not conform to commonly accepted gender roles concerning masculinity and femininity. Originally having a negative connotation (meaning 'strange'), 'queer' became, between the late 1980s and the 1990s, a word – for both scholars and activists – through which to affirm a politicised identity. Queer identities are often adopted by those who reject traditional gender identities and related binaries and look for a less conformist and normative way to identify and perform their existences.

References

Allen, L. (2006) 'Beyond the Birds and the Bees: Constituting a Discourse of Erotics in Sexuality Education', *Gender and Education*, 16(2), pp. 180–220.

Allen, L. (2011) *Young People and Sexuality Education: Rethinking Key Debates*, New York: Palgrave Macmillan.

Allen, L. (2013) 'Girls' Portraits of Desire: Picturing a Missing Discourse', *Gender and Education*, 25(3), pp. 295–310.

Allen, L., Rasmussen, M.L., Quinlivan, K., Aspin, C., Sanjakdar, F. and Bromdal, A. (2014) 'Who's Afraid of Sex at School? The Politics of Researching Culture, Religion and Sexuality at School', *International Journal of Research and Method in Education*, 37(1), pp. 1–13.

Barbier, R. (1977) *La recherche-action dans l'instituition educative*, Paris: Gauthier-Villars.

Batini, F. and Santoni, B. (2009) *L'identità sessuale a scuola: educare alla diversità e prevenire l'omofobia*, Napoli: Liguori.

Borofsky, R. (2000) 'Public Anthropology: Where to What Next?', *Anthropology News*, 41(5), pp. 9–10.

Carnassale, D. (2014) 'Le ragioni di un'assenza. Educazione alle tematiche relative al genere e alla sessualità nei contesti scolastici' in Bonetti, R. (ed.) *La trappola della normalità. Antropologia e etnografia nei mondi della scuola*, Firenze: SEID, pp. 159–190.

Claes, T. and Reynolds, P. (2013) 'Why Sexual Ethics and Politics? Why Now? An Introduction to the Journal', *Journal of the International Network of Sexual Ethics and Politics*, 1(1), pp. 5–18.

Crivellaro, F. (2015) 'Contro il genere', *Rivista Il Mulino*, 14 May. Available at www.rivistailmulino.it/news/newsitem/index/Item/News:NEWS_ITEM:2819.

Csordas, T. (1990) 'Embodiment as a Paradigm for Anthropology', *Ethos: Journal of the Society of Psychological Anthropology*, 18(1), pp. 5–47.

Fergusona, R., Vanwesenbeecka, I. and Knijnb, T. (2008) 'A Matter of Facts … and More: An Exploratory Analysis of the Content of Sexuality Education in the Netherlands', *Sex Education*, 8(1), pp. 93–106.

Foucault, M. (1976) *Histoire de la sexualité*, Volume 1: *La volonté de savoir*, Paris : Gallimard.

Garbagnoli, S. (2014) '"L'ideologia del genere": l'irresistibile ascesa di un'invenzione retorica vaticana contro la denaturalizzazione dell'ordine sessuale', *AG. About Gender, Rivista internazionale di studi di genere*, 3(6), pp. 250–263.

González, N. (2010) 'Advocacy Anthropology and Education: Working through the Binaries', *Current Anthropology*, 51(S2), pp. S249–S258.

Graglia, M. (2012) *Omofobia: strumenti di analisi e di intervento*, Roma: Carocci Faber.

Hastings, D. and Magowan, F. (2010) *The Anthropology of Sex*, Oxford: Berg.

Haynes, K. (2012) 'Reflexivity in Qualitative Research' in Symon, G. and Cassel C. (eds) *Qualitative Organizational Research: Core Methods and Current Challenges*, Thousand Oaks, CA: Sage, pp. 72–89.

Hofsetter, H., Peters, L.W.H., Meijer, S., Van Keulen, H.M., Schutte, L. and Van Empelen, P. (1996) 'Evaluation of the Effectiveness and Implementation of the Sexual Health Program Long Live Love', *Bulletin of the European Health Psychology Society*, 29(4), pp. 583–597.

Irvine, J. (2014) 'Is Sexuality Research "Dirty Work"? Institutionalized Stigma in the Production of Sexual Knowledge', *Sexualities*, 17(5/6), pp. 632–656.

Kulick, D. and Willson, M. (eds) (1995) *Taboo: Sex, Identity, and Subjectivity in Anthropological Fieldwork*, London and New York: Routledge.

Lamb, S. (2008) 'The "Right" Sexuality for Girls', *Chronicle of Higher Education*, 54(42), pp. B14–B15.

Landi, N. (2014) 'BDSM: Ars Erotica between Pain and Pleasure' in Fox, R.F., Monteiro, N.M. (eds) *Pain without Boundaries: Inquiries across Cultures*, Oxford: Interdisciplinary Press.

Langdridge, D. and Butt, T. (2004) 'A Hermeneutic Phenomenological Investigation of the Construction of Sadomasochistic Identity', *Sexualities* 7(1), pp. 31–53.

Lyons, A.P. and Lyons, H.D. (2004) *Irregular Connections: A History of Anthropology and Sexuality*, Lincoln, NE: University of Nebraska Press.

Olivier De Sardan, J.P. (2009) 'La politica del campo. Sulla produzione di dati in antropologia' in Cappelletto, F. (ed.) *Vivere l'etnografia*, Firenze: SEID, pp. 27–63.

Piasere, Leonardo (2009) 'L'etnografia come esperienza' in Cappelletto, F. (ed.) *Vivere l'etnografia*, Firenze: SEID, pp. 65–95.

Plummer, K. (1995) *Telling Sexual Stories: Power, Change and Social Worlds*, Hove: Psychology Press.

Plummer, K. (2003) *Intimate Citizenship: Private Decisions and Public Dialogues*, Seattle, WA: University of Washington Press.

Plummer, K. (2005a) 'Intimate Citizenship in an Unjust World' in Romero, M. and Margolis, E. (eds) *The Blackwell Companion to Social Inequality*, Oxford: Blackwell, pp. 75–100.

Plummer, K. (2005b) 'The Square of Intimate Citizenship: Some Preliminary Proposals', *Citizenship Studies*, 5(3), pp. 237–253.

Plummer K. (2008) 'Studying Sexualities for a Better World? Ten Years of Sexualities', *Sexualities*, 11(1/2), pp. 7–22.

Richardson, D. (2015) *Rethinking Sexual Citizenship*, London: Sage.

Ringrose, J. and Renold, E. (2011) 'Slut-shaming, Girl Power and "Sexualisation": Thinking through the Politics of the International SlutWalks with Teen Girls', *Gender and Education*, 24(3), pp. 333–343.

Salih, R. (2005) *Attraversare confini: soggettività emergenti e nuove dimensioni della cittadinanza. Quale Storia per una società Multietnica. Rappresentazioni, timori e aspettative degli studenti italiani e non italiani. Un percorso di ricerca*, London: SOAS Research on-line.

Scarry, E. (1985) *The Body in Pain: The Making and Unmaking of the World*, Oxford: Oxford University Press.

Schaalma, H.P., Kok, G., Bosker, R.J., Parcel, G.S., Peters, L., Poelman, J. and Reinders, J. (1996) 'Planned Development and Evaluation of AIDS/STD Education for Secondary School Students in the Netherlands: Short-term Effects', *Health Education Research*, 29(4), pp. 583–597.

Scheper-Hughes, N. and Lock, M. (1987) 'The Mindful Body: A Prolegomenon to Future Work in Medical Anthropology', *Medical Anthropology Quarterly New Series*, 1(1), pp. 6–41.

Schutte, L., Meertens, R.M., Mevissen, F., Schaalma, H., Meijer, S. and Kok, G. (2014) 'Long Live Love: The Implementation of a School-based Sex-education Program in the Netherlands', *Health Education Research*, 29(4), pp. 583–597.

Spronk, R. (2011) 'Beyond Pain, towards Pleasure in the Study of Sexuality in Africa' in Lyons, A.P. (ed.) *Sexualities in Anthropology: A Reader*, Chichester: Wiley-Blackwell, pp. 375–381.

Stanley, L. and Wise, S. (1990) 'Method, Methodology and Epistemology in Feminist Research Processes' in Stanley, L. (ed.) *Feminist Praxis*, London: Routledge, pp. 20–62.

Tarabusi, F. (2010) *Dentro le politiche. Servizi, progetti, educatori: sguardi antropologici*, Rimini: Guaraldi.

Van Der Geest, S., Gerrits, T. and Singer Aaslid, F. (2012) 'Ethnography and Self-exploration', *Medische Antropologie*, 24(1), pp. 5–21.

Weston, K. (1998) *Long Slow Burn: Sexualities and Social Science*, New York: Routledge.

World Health Organization (WHO) Federal Centre for Health Education (2010) *Standards for Sexuality Education in Europe: A Framework for Policy Makers, Educational and Health Authorities and Specialists*, Cologne: World Health Organization.

APPENDIX

AN INTERVIEW WITH KEN PLUMMER

Charlotte Morris

Ken Plummer is a UK sociologist who has researched widely and published some 15 books and over 140 articles on life stories, narratives, symbolic interactionism, humanism, rights, intimacies, global inequalities, queer theory, sexualities, masculinity and the body. Amongst the most prominent of his 'early' books were *Sexual Stigma* (1975), *The Making of the Modern Homosexual* (edited, 1981), *Documents of Life* (1983, 2nd edition 2001), *Modern Homosexualities* (1993), *Telling Sexual Stories* (1995) and *Intimate Citizenship* (2003). He also edited *Symbolic Interactionism* (2 volumes, 1988), *The Chicago School: Critical Assessments* (4 volumes, 1997) and *Sexualities: Critical Concepts in Sociology* (4 volumes, 2001). In 1996, he became the founder editor of the journal *Sexualities*, and edited it for 16 years. Between 1996 and 2012 he published five editions of the textbook *Sociology: A Global Introduction* with John Macionis.

He retired in 2006, due to illness; and a successful liver transplant saved his life. After retirement he continued to write. His post-transplant books have included: *Cosmopolitan Sexualities: Hope and the Humanist Imagination* (2015); *Imaginations: Fifty Years of Essex Sociology* (2014); *Sociology: The Basics* (2010) (also published in Indonesian, Portuguese, Chinese and Spanish) (2nd edition in 2016); and a fifth edition of *Sociology: A Global Introduction* (with Macionis) (2012). At the time of writing this, he has two books under contract: *Narrative Powers: Making Critical Stories for a Better World* and *Flourishing Lives: A Manifesto*

for Critical Humanism. He, rather casually, maintains a website at:
http://kenplummer.com/.

In this interview he talks to Charlotte Morris about his life,
work and values and reflects on the development of research in
the field of sexualities over the course of his career.

*To begin, what first drew you into researching in the field of
sexualities?*

Well I guess it's been 50 years since I started doing sociology – a
long time. So there could be a lot we could talk about ... It starts
really in 1966, I'm doing my first degree in sociology in what was
then called Enfield College and became known as Middlesex and
I was doing the London degree in sociology which included social
psychology. My tutor was Stan Cohen; it was his first teaching
post and I was in awe of the man. He taught me symbolic
interactionism and the following year he taught me criminology –
and he let me write an essay on homosexuality. And that's the key
to it. I knew since I was a little boy that I was something like 'gay'
– certainly as a very young boy I can remember being attracted
to men and it goes all the way through but it was at that age
– about 19, 20 – that I was really trying to sort it all out. You have
to remember it was still against the law, it was still considered
a 'sickness', and it was still a sin – and all the rest of it. And so
suddenly sociology became more than a discipline of study, it
became something that I could use to make sense of my life and
my environment, through symbolic interactionism and deviancy
theory, and labelling theory in particular. So I wrote this essay
on sociological aspects of homosexuality for Stan Cohen and he
was really very positive and encouraging about it. And it led me
to think, 'I'm enjoying this!' I enjoy studying. My family had not
been bookish but I now liked books – so to cut a long story short,
what drew me to this field of study were very personal reasons
about being gay and wanting to understand it and wanting to
apply this theory I'd learned about to my life and the world. It

was at the moment that the law was changing and I thought I could see how I could bring all these things together. So it was a very exciting moment in my life.

1966 was also the year I came out as gay, hung about in the gay bars of London – I didn't realise then and that I was going to do this research; that came a year later in 1967. And a little later, in 1970, was backed up by the Gay Liberation Front, which I was active in. These things changed my life. And all these things coalesced and before I knew where I was I was embarking on a career of being an academic homosexual!

And can you relate any stories about your earliest research encounters?

Yes, well I get my first degree. And I have an undecided year where I am not sure what I'm going to do. Initially I was going to be an Employment Officer, I did that for about four months; then I was a Community Service Volunteer. And then I decided to go for a PhD. My PhD was to look at – this was very early days – the impact of the changing laws, and focus on gay men and how they responded to being stigmatised and so forth. Every single interview is a story and they are all more or less interesting so I have lots of stories about it. I can tell some good stories but they do tend to be the slightly atypical ones ... so for example, in those days to do an interview I would hire a room in the LSE, it was a small boxy office. In one of the interviews a curious, tall, bearded Eastern Orthodox priest in full mufti came in – and you have to remember I was 21 and not entirely ugly – and he just went for me! There were a whole series of interviews that were very risky; I mean these days with ethics committees people would want to know what I was going to do ... this particular man pursued me for several months and he was nice enough but he didn't want the same thing that I wanted; so there was that going on but that was exceptional ... there was also one time when I thought I was falling in love with the person I was interviewing and had to restrain myself so it also happened the other way round! This is all very early days, I'm still very young and I don't know much about what I'm doing quite honestly. In those days there were few methodological handbooks, nothing on self-reflexivity, discussions of personal problems were an indulgent taboo.

So what were some of your big learning curves in terms of doing research?

Everything! Absolutely everything was a learning curve. If you look back to the mid-1960s on the history of sexualities research, there's obviously not much going on! There is a history going back to the nineteenth century at least – people doing sexology, interviews and so forth but in the main it involved a clinical, medical, biological tradition. There really were not many people doing social research – I could probably list them all now – Michael Schofield (who had published under the name Gordon Westwood), Evelyn Hooker, Mary McIntosh ... there weren't many people in the field and so there wasn't a lot going on. That of course was a very exciting thing because you're at the forefront of something for a little while; but you're not getting much guidance – deep learning curves about everything!

Were there any colleagues who helped you to develop?

Well, Stan Cohen inspired me theoretically and encouraged me; Paul Rock was at the LSE and he was a wonderful supervisor. He commented on my PhD, saw me about once a term and he infused me with the subtlety of symbolic interactionism – he helped me become a symbolic interactionist. He just understood deeply the ideas of complexity and ambiguity, the contingency and the flux of it all – he spoke like that, wrote like that and slowly over the five years I was doing my PhD part-time it soaked into me. When I was teaching I had an inspirational colleague called Jock Young who broke the rules really, he didn't read from a text, he sort of stomped up and down the room and shrieked and I realised in retrospect that it was terribly influential on my lecturing style: I have rarely followed a text really, a written text is not a spoken word. So he was a great influence and then of course there was the great Mary McIntosh. I wrote to her in 1967 when she was at Leicester University and she replied – she was just on the verge of writing the famous 'The Homosexual Role' article which I read; and subsequently in the 1970s we became colleagues and lifelong friends so she was influential ... Michael Schofield was another very important person in my life. Never an academic, he wrote four books on homosexuality and a book on sexuality and young people in two volumes. From the 1940s to the 1970s he was quite a prominent name – and then I went to his house in Hampstead and we actually became lifelong friends. He died a few years ago and he inspired me as he was a kind of pioneer in what were actually very dangerous times to write about homosexuality. He had to write under another name – Gordon Westwood – these were very different times. He was very involved with the Homosexual Law Reform Society, with changing the law, and of course it did eventually change in 1967 – just when I was starting out. Exciting times. That's why I'm saying 50 years – half a century ago it was not the same world ...

And what was it that prompted you to start writing on research methodologies?

Well, when I was doing my PhD I wrote a paper called 'Forty Problems with Participant Observation': it guided me in what I was doing in the London clubs where I was both doing participant observation and interviewing people at the same times as I was coming out! I was very young and foolish! But I was also reading books like T.S. Bryun's *The Human Perspective in Sociology* (no-one talks about it much anymore, but it turned me on) and Norman Denzin's important text *The Research Act* as I struggled along trying my best to do fieldwork properly. So that's when I started to become interested in method. I just wanted to know how to do it much better than I was doing it. I wrote the first edition of *Documents of Life* in the early 1980s in a kind of exasperation with methods! In truth much of what I was doing really wasn't very good. In the end I dropped the methodology and the research – if you read my PhD (which was basically *Sexual Stigma*), it shifts into the theoretical!

So I don't do really 'do' methods, though I have often been tagged as such. I did theory all the way and actually that's what I've done for most of my life. One of the problems I have – and maybe I shouldn't be saying this – is that I have enormous trouble with data and I think everybody does. Data is profoundly problematic. All data. Another big book that was around at that time was *Method and Measurement in Sociology* by Aaron Cicourel – everyone was reading it; but that also made data very problematic, there was nothing straightforward about it at all ... this was 50 years ago. I don't necessarily believe everything someone is telling me. I know as an interactionist that people will say different things at different times and I know the complexity of a life is that whatever you say at one moment can only be scraping the surface of that moment. There will be lots and lots of other things going on which you're not touching. And so I became more and more interested in the complexity of doing research. I think that what's happened is a huge and largely fake methodological apparatus driven by methodological protocol whereby you've got to do this or that and everything's laid out – you've got to have your beginning, your middle and your end before you've even started! And I think that's very damaging. If PhD students are told 'you've got to follow this protocol' it's a disservice to intellectual life – a really serious problem and unfortunately I feel it has gone that way ... In one of my earliest papers I invented a methodology, I used to joke about it, I called it AHFA – Ad Hoc Fumbling Around! And that was my methodology. By the mid-1970s I was referring to AHFA. It is dangerous to be too mechanistic about it.

Do you have any advice about working with some of those imposed constraints?

This is a very difficult time for universities – markets, management and metrics dominate them and they're ruining universities. That's my very strong view. That's not to say that when I see students they're not as wonderful as ever, they're just as vibrant and interesting and curious but they're being sat on by all this absurd bureaucracy and administration; by people who have little interest in intellectual life. It is taking over so I stay away from universities as much as possible. What surprises me is that there hasn't been massive resistance to this – it started in 1984 when the first research assessment exercises were done. That was a one off, it was not supposed to dominate the whole of university life subsequently but it has. I gather now there's a teaching assessment coming up too; which is also dominating university life – it's all dangerous rubbish – expensive, damaging, dangerous rubbish!

This leads quite nicely into the next question, which is about your personal and political values – what they are and how they've underpinned your research.

Well I can't say that I had strong values clearly sorted out at an early stage – you know, the whole of life is a fumbling around – now I've got that phrase back in my mind – but it is. I mean there are people who have a passionate set of beliefs and commitments – Marxism or Christianity or whatever – and they follow them through for the whole of their lives; but not many people I suspect. I think people have doubts, they change, even within their own frameworks. I was a Christian once but being gay and being Christian in the 1960s wasn't at all compatible: the Church was very hostile – it's less so now but it was horrendous then; and many religions are vile and hostile to gays today still. I decided on the side of gayness rather than Christianity; so there were big issues around that to get sorted out. But I suppose it's only in the latter years (by which I mean in the last 25 years) that

I've started to seriously think ethically and realise that you need to be clear about your value baselines in your research – I was clear in the early stage that ethics came into research and that values came into participant observation and I read Weber on value baselines. I was always aware that there were issues. But I had never articulated my values. I think that instead of having [often ridiculous] research methods training sessions that get you to think about all sorts of rigorous things that don't make much sense once you're in the field, training should really talk about the ethics – the principles and values that shape you and your life and why you want to do this research – what's the purpose of it? What's the point of it? Where are you coming from – are you doing it just for the sake of it? Surely not – you've got to have some view of what the ethical life should be like. So in the latter years in my writings I constantly harp on about ethics and values. I call my values loosely humanist: about care, dignity, justice, rights, human flourishing. But I have to be careful with that as the secular humanists have also co-opted that word. So I call it critical humanism to differentiate it in a number of ways – one of which is that critical humanism recognises the importance of diverse religions in the lives of people.

How to put these values in a nutshell?

Basically humans are ethical creatures and from the moment of birth – at the moment of birth when you are drawn into a bond which is a caring bond with your parents; and from that moment on there is a role taking and playing and pleasing with the caretaker – usually the mother looking after you; and the creation of that bond is around empathy and caring so all that is established. Other people matter. There is the start of the social bond. I'm not a mother but I think you are – it's not just the empathy and the caring for the child that the child picks up on but it's also the dignity and respect of the child as a person growing; and you put these things together and you begin to respect the basic human right of the dignity of a person and so much comes from that: justice, treating people fairly ... I've recently watched *I Daniel Blake* and it divides the world into two types of people really: there are those who have care, respect and dignity for other people and there are those who simply don't; and it's horrifying to see when people don't. Many powerful people fail on this count. And in terms of research you can just go and do your research and not look after the people you're interviewing: and I guess I did that to some extent in my earliest days – I wanted to get my PhD! They had little regard for me (because sometimes they were pursuing me quite dangerously) and I had little regard for them because I was just using them to tick the right research boxes. But ideally from that sense of care for the other and their dignity, other values such as the importance of human flourishing and justice appear – so all those things hang around together. But it takes a while to get there and that's where I've got to now 50 years on. I wasn't told that at the beginning! In some ways I think I've always had those values, I think a lot of people have them; but I've only later articulated them and I ground them in being human.

For you personally, what have been the highlights of your career?

That is a difficult one! Let's put it like this ... there's a sense in which my whole life has been one long drift! I had no idea I would have done any of this when I was young. If you'd asked me at school, I had no idea I would go to university. I had no idea when I was at university I was going to go on to do a PhD. I had no idea when I finished my PhD that I was going to go on and teach and then teaching all those years – I was teaching for over 25 years before I became a professor. I had no idea I was going to be a professor – professors in those days were extremely rare so it wasn't for me to become a professor! So none of these things were sort of planned, they just happened, which made them all very exciting at the time. I have the impression that these days people are much more driven – I mean it was a better time, an easier time – you could drift in and out of things. When I got my first job eight other people were appointed sociology jobs on the same day – you don't have that now! So it's a totally different environment.

So the highlights flowing from that would be – there are so many rewarding moments – the simple things would be the students' 'thank you', that's very nice because most of life, you just do it and nowadays I deal with a lot of professionals – medical people – and I make sure I thank them because they're doing their job and they do it well. And it's important to thank them and say how they are appreciated. And these are very nice moments for me too. There are also critical big turning point moments: so I would say a moment would be when I got the job at Essex because that completely transformed my life. I felt that I was in a really serious sociology department where people were doing really serious things. I was just in awe of almost everyone around me when I arrived and I couldn't believe my luck; I also thought, 'I shouldn't really be here – little dim me amongst these giants!' And slowly you come to realise that they're just human beings, not monsters at all but very nice people and they've made a very stimulating environment. Another critical moment would be me going to Santa Barbara – that was a big year for me, it was 1976, I'd come to Essex in 1975, I'd set up my first and only research project in the 1970s with an ESRC grant and so I'd started that project and I met someone and went to America and part of the project was a two-month tour of sex research in America so I went to the Kinsey Foundation, Master and Johnson's Sex Research Laboratories and various institutes in San Francisco, so it was a very lively, dynamic moment with a lot happening – going to America, going to Essex, getting established, I'd finished my PhD and got my first book out, getting a grant and going to America – it was extraordinary! And actually I had complicated relationships at that time. I met [my partner] in 1978 and slowly my life became more settled. There was a kind of whirly burly period between 1966 till 1978 where life was very on the go and then I settled down with love ... I don't know if it's the right word to use – love – but anyway, I became much more settled with a good relationship and being at Essex – so that was a big, big moment.

Another big moment would be the AIDS crisis – that was maybe 1982 to about 1987, 1988 and that was just ... it's very hard for people now to realise; this was an epidemic of massive proportions where we actually thought gayness was going to be killed off – everybody was dying, it was constantly in the press and the gay community as we'd seen it in the 1970s was now gone and gay radicals of the 1970s had now become professional AIDS workers – the whole world had changed. And actually, you know, for a long while it looked, a bit like it does with Trump at the moment, like the end of the world – you can't imagine what it's going to be like any longer because it's all getting so bad. So that was a very troubled time and I did do quite a bit of research into HIV and AIDS at that moment but I only published one major article and then I left the whole field. It actually led me for a while to leave the whole field altogether and I did some books on Chicago sociology and symbolic interactionism, all sorts of things to take me away from that field, I didn't want to do it anymore at that time – it reduced me to tears basically, it was all too much and I thought 'I don't have to do this'. I know I should have done it but actually I also noticed out of the corner of my eye, there were thousands of people doing this research, it was a sort of research industry – I simply didn't want to be part of that. So that's another moment.

Another key moment comes to mind – I was head of department for a time and a moment comes in life when you become the bureaucrat you never wanted to be; although I always tried not to be the bureaucrat. But then when that finished and [my partner] finished teaching in around 1995, we went on a world tour – for three months we travelled. We got a thousand-pound ticket to travel the world and see places and we had a great time. While travelling, two major projects entered my life and one was the journal *Sexualities* – I was in Thailand, communicating with Sage and writing a proposal for this journal which – and I thought it needed to be done. There was so much beginnings of work at that stage which needed a publication home. Now of course there are a lot of journals ... but that was a big thing and of course at the same time also I started writing text books, so both of these things happened in 1996. Quietly I'm pleased the journal got going and I'm very pleased about the text books because I really enjoyed doing that – it broadened my perspective very significantly.

One thing I'd like to add in terms of advice ... don't get caught in a rut of doing one thing only because life's too short for that. Having a range of interests prevents boredom creeping in and it just gives you a bit more resilience than if you do just one thing.

Having been the editor of Sexualities for 20 years you must have had such an insight into how the field was developing ...

If you put sexualities research into a 50-year time scale, then it's almost unbelievable how the social study of sexualities has changed. In the 1960s, there were very few of us around – Jeff Weeks, Mary Macintosh ... we did set up a British Sociological Association sexualities strand in the mid 1970s and we did have two or three conferences; but there were very few involved – there wasn't much going on. It got muddled a lot with feminism as gender studies started gradually to appear. I was teaching sexuality studies at both Essex and Santa Barbara by the mid-1980s but it was very rare. There weren't many courses around – the MA in Sexual Dissidence at Sussex was one of the first, a very important course and as far as I can recollect it got going somewhere in the mid-1980s – it was probably the first graduate scheme in the country. A few of us had been working in the field for some 20 years: it was a slow process. It was leading up to Queer Theory in around 1989 and then you start to sense there are a lot of people gravitating towards this field and then by the 1990s it really is taking off – there's a lot of stuff happening. Bookshops were full of sexuality studies and particularly gay and lesbian studies – really a book explosion at that time; and conferences were beginning to appear all over the world. So that's what led me towards *Sexualities*, the journal, in 1996. By then, you could identify critical sexualities studies as a global phenomenon. I was working on a four-volume history of sexualities studies collection which was trying to take stock of this massive growth. So now almost every social sciences department worth its name had to have gender and sexualities which means of course that in terms of support at university, students are not in isolation any longer. So that's all the good news really ... the bad news is that universities have often become marketised, bureaucratised soul destroying places but I don't think they are for students if they can find their own pathways through them – and just, I don't know, resist or ignore or create their own pathways of creativity which is not the way the university will encourage them to go. I mean I might be totally wrong because I'm not in there.

Is there anything else you would like to say about the field?

Life is a series of contingencies and travails and along the way you can see changes taking place – 100 years ago there was very little except pathology; 50 years ago there was very little but laws, though they were beginning to change; now there's this fantastic amount of stuff and it's out there and it's changing the world. And what will it be like in 25 years' time? There'll be more of it – more things have been set up and they will be modified, they will be changed but these ideas are not going to go away.

What is it specifically about studying this topic that is special?

It was special in the 1960s because there was so little of it. What was important in sexualities research then for me was that it wasn't discussed very much; and it needed to be put on the table. At the same time it was very stigmatised and I had to go very carefully as it was potentially quite dangerous. This put it apart from, for example, research in social class or education – they don't have those problems of stigma attached. But now there is such a wide community of scholars doing this kind of research, and the world has moved on in terms of public talk about sexuality – it's just everywhere. It's not any longer really a special issue ... there are problems but they're the problems all research faces. For example, the danger of quantifying things that are not quantifiable. There's such a willingness to rush in and give statistics about things that are not really usefully measured. But that is true of many topics. There is also always the danger of taking at face value what people say when in fact there's a complexity of layers of argument and muddle that lie behind it, you've really got to try and unpack. It's also important to realise that you can change the world as you research it – and quite dangerously so sometimes if you're not careful – you can change people's views on sexuality. Some people were literally coming out in my interviews and articulating for the very first time what it means to be gay; and so the interview was actually changing someone's life. What a responsibility! But, again, this is true of a lot of research.

We've touched a lot on the difficulties facing our universities and the challenges of the current context newer researchers are working in – have you any advice to offer on navigating your way through this?

I think what you're doing is a major thing in itself: holding conferences outside the mainstream. And that's fantastic. Again to go back, in the earliest days when I did research there was a breakaway group, it's now in the annals of history, the National Deviancy Conference but it was based at York, a breakaway group of radical sociologists who thought much of sociology was bourgeois nonsense. It was a breakaway group to let the 'deviants' speak who were not being heard and to listen to others, including women who were silenced groups in the 1960s. It was libertarian and Marxist inspired, set up by people like Jock Young, Stan Cohen, Mary McIntosh and Laurie Taylor and I it ran for about five, six, seven years and there was such a lot of solidarity and support for a range of different fields. What all people had in common I suppose was 'the outsider' – the outsider who was not acceptable in mainstream sociology or criminology and it was a space for these voices to speak. This solidarity in breaking away from conventional academia and giving each other support set me on a path of relative free thinking. And that's one of the things that's needed – solidarity and support in resisting dominant academic orders ... At [some universities] there are a lot of people working in that field but in other places there's nobody so that's one thing and there's the obvious thing of where one has strength in numbers to resist some things people are trying to do to you. I know it's easy to say from afar – in my retirement – but I used to always think that where there's a will, there's a way. There are an awful lot of people just going along with it all – the world doesn't have to be like that you know and, for example, you don't have to get big grants. Virtually my whole life has been lived without hardly any grants at all. I guess I would never get a job in a university now. I don't need money – you talk to people, you read books, you analyse things that are going on, you hang around with people, you think, think and think! There are all sorts of things you can do ... You might need small amounts of money here and there but not much – most qualitative research needs hardly any money at all! But it seems to me you're made to get large sums of funding! Which is a waste of money when research does not really need it. But I guess you won't get a promotion without winning large sums of money now. It is all a mockery and a disgraceful shame.

It would be nice to just talk a little more about your concept of intimate citizenship if you wouldn't mind giving me an outline of that and how you feel it is still relevant.

It's quite an old concept now. It derived from the book I did in the early 1990s called *Modern Homosexualities* and it was a series of studies examining where queer studies were going to go, partly about the global direction and partly about the human rights direction. It was becoming very clear then that arguments from the 1960s through 1980s were actually developing a 'rights' model of sexualities which would begin to become stronger and stronger in the 1990s. I was playing around with the notion of sexual rights. I wasn't happy with the idea of sexual rights because it was too restricted to sexuality. And I wasn't happy with the idea of citizenship because it was too restricted to all the orthodox things that politics is about. It didn't go into the areas I was interested in. And so the word 'intimate', implying the personal life, the closeness of people to the personal life seemed a better word than sexual, although I have noticed people tend to talk about either sexual citizenship or sexual/intimate citizenship, but the people who talk about intimate citizenship tend to take it right out of the field of sexuality into mental health, for example – ageing or all kinds of other things, which is fine because I did mean it to go in that direction. It seemed to me that it ties in with these values I've been talking about, absolutely centrally because if you start appreciating value-based lives of care, of empathy, of dignity of people ... the rights-based argument on its own isn't enough, you need to take it into a wider set of values and intimate citizenship starts to do that, it takes it into emotionality, of looking after the body, of human flourishing really and considering not just citizenship in terms of legal rights or welfare rights but the choices people have in their life about how they can flourish best and I still think it's a good idea, I just haven't put my mind into it much recently and haven't seen much about it but the new book I'm going to be doing after this one is called human flourishing and I will return to it I think.

You were writing quite a lot about hope in your last book and it feels like there is a huge need in the world today for hope ...

This is very important. A lot of people are now talking about hope in these dire times. To tell you the truth in all of my 70 years I can't conceive of more dark times than we are in and I can't stop worrying about it really and I think about where it's all going to lead. Then I think 'well it's always going to be like that, the world is always a troubled place'. Just before I was born there was the holocaust, the First World War, colonialisms, slavery, it just goes on and on, rolling back through the whole of history – rotten governments doing rotten things to ordinary people. But then you'd just go crazy if you always thought like that so you have to think positively.

I've got this story which is from Rebecca Solnit in her wonderful little book *Hope in the Dark*. It's just been revised and reissued in the wake of the horrors of Trump. She draws from one of my favourite films, Frank Capra's *It's a Wonderful Life*. Now this film isn't just a Christmas joke and it isn't just an apology for capitalism. It's a marvellous story of the contingency of little lives, and how little lives are interweaved in the looking after of each other. Through one crisis after another, our hero is brought to the point of suicide, when Clarence the Angel of Alternative History halts his suicide to show what his community would have been like if he hadn't lived his life, the many wonderful things that wouldn't then have happened. The small acts of kindnesses that people do in their everyday lives really make a difference in the way the world is. And maybe this is the secret of how the social world is constituted – through everyday kindness rather than governing brutalities. It is destroyed by all the big monstrous acts of violence but within those little kindness acts, that's what we have to be concerned with, and we have to nurture those and let them flourish and they're everywhere so that's in a sense what we have to study – to move the world forward in those little generous acts. Most people get through their lives treating each other well, looking after each other – bad moments, things happen along the way and these are the things that each generation has to point to and challenge. Our small kindnesses don't matter very much on a big scale but in little ways they all add up to make the world a better place – so there is hope!

An Angel of Alternative History shows us the others ways. It's one way of getting through it – these terrible things, they've always been there but good little things have always been there too. There are people in dire poverty struggling through the world but can still get through it because of the little kindnesses that they give and are given.

In that vein, what would you say to people who said what's the point of doing research on sex and intimacy with all that's going on in the world?

Little lives have to do what little lives have to do ... the world is full of diversities and we all have to do different things. It's important that there are people who want to do sex research and have a passion about it ... they really have a problem and a puzzle and in a small way and they want to, to improve and enhance the way the world works.

You talk a lot in your last book about how a lot of plurality and diversity has opened up – can you say a little bit about that?

The Brexit thing has left me a bit despondent, it's gone the opposite direction of what my last book was about – we did seem to be moving in the direction of more cosmopolitanism, an acceptance of difference and diversities, a reduction in inequalities, a taking care of the Other rather than a stigmatising of the Other; and the recent turns have been in completely the opposite direction to that. But that's for the moment and you have to remember the 48 per cent against Brexit ... but the trouble was that nobody in the Brexit debates spoke of these big issues: of the environment, of caring for the world and each other, of living and loving with difference – they just weren't issues on the agenda. The whole Brexit debate was allowed to be shockingly and badly framed ...

So how do we survive?

I guess these are indeed very dark times. So many things I've struggled for all my life are now under threat. I wake up in the night worrying about what can be done; but we've got to move on. I despair of our governments. I know of course that most people have lived difficult, terrible, tragic lives throughout history and I've been kidding myself through much of my life that things were going to get better. Things won't necessarily ever get better; but there will hopefully be a growing number of people experiencing flourishing lives and there are now more people flourishing than in the past – although populations are so large it's hard to calculate. I have to say my own generation is probably living the most privileged lives of any cohort throughout the whole of history; terrible as things are, there are some signs of potentials for some kind of human advance! We have to, as I like to say, recognise the inevitability of disappointment yet acting with the importance of hope.

So any final words for someone just starting out on their research journey now?

Fantastic. Keep at it. There's so much to be done despite all the terrible and difficult things happening in the world, there are new spaces to create, exciting new projects to do, new stories to be told that can edge the world along to be better. Change the world, make it a better place and don't let the dominant buggers wear you down! It is actually quite simple. Be passionate about your research, your teaching, your work: make sure you have a good reason for doing it, find your values, make sure you know where you stand, not just in terms of why you are doing your research and where you want to take it but also in how you treat people. When I meet great PhD students today, many feel, 'It's not enough just to do a PhD, I have to continue this work, take it on to another higher point, I've got to see how it works in practice, try and get other people to think like this' – all these little avenues are being created all the time, all of these possibilities. It is going back to *It's a Wonderful Life*. Even in bad times, we act in the world, put our energies and ideas out there to make the world a better place, and bit by bit we see the small consequences of change – there is always plenty of scope and so much to be done …! And there will be better days if we work for them.

References

Plummer, K. (1975) *Sexual Stigma: An Interactionist Account*, London: Routledge.

Plummer, K. (1981) *The Making of the Modern Homosexual*, London: Hutchinson.

Plummer, K. (ed.) (1990) *Symbolic Interactionism: Two Volumes of Readings*, Aldershot: Edward Elgar.

Plummer, K. (1992) *Modern Homosexualities: Fragments of Lesbian and Gay Experience*, London: Routledge.

Plummer, K. (1995) *Telling Sexual Stories: Power, Change and Social Worlds*, London: Routledge.

Plummer, K. (ed.) (1997) *The Chicago School: Critical Assessments* (4 volumes), London: Routledge.

Plummer, K. (2001) *Documents of Life 2: An Invitation to a Critical Humanism*, London: Sage.

Plummer, K. (2001) *Sexualities: Critical Concepts in Sociology* (4 volumes), London: Routledge.

Plummer, K. (2003) *Intimate Citizenship: Personal Decisions and Public Dialogues*, Seattle, WA: University of Washington Press.

Plummer, K. (2010, 2016 rpt.) *Sociology: The Basics*, London: Routledge.

Plummer, K. (2014) *Imaginations: Fifty Years of Essex Sociology*, Wivenhoe, Essex: Wivenbooks.

Plummer, K. (2015) *Cosmopolitan Sexualities: Hope and the Humanist Imagination*, Cambridge: Polity.

Plummer, K. and Macionis, J. (2012) *Sociology: A Global Introduction*, 5th edition. Harlow: Pearson Education.

ABOUT THE EDITORS AND CONTRIBUTORS

Editors

Paul Boyce is a senior lecturer in anthropology and international development in the School of Global Studies, University of Sussex. He is co-founder of The European Network for Queer Anthropology (ENQA) and co-editor of the book series *Theorizing Ethnography: Concept, Context and Critique*, with a co-edited book entitled *Queering Knowledge* forthcoming in 2018. Current research explores access to welfare and employment among non-cis-gendered peoples in North East India (funded by the University of Sussex Social Science Impact Fund). He has conducted research on sexualities and HIV ethnographically in India since the mid-1990s, and has worked as a research consultant on sexual rights, health and wellbeing in countries including Kenya, Nepal and Vietnam.

Andrea Cornwall is professor of anthropology and international development, head of the School of Global Studies and deputy pro-vice chancellor (Equalities and Diversity) at the University of Sussex. She is a political anthropologist who specialises in the anthropology of democracy, citizen participation, participatory research, gender and sexuality. She has worked on topics ranging from understanding women's perspectives on family planning, fertility and sexually transmitted infection in Nigeria and Zimbabwe, public engagement in UK regeneration programmes, the quality of democratic deliberation in new democratic spaces in Brazil, the use and abuse of participatory appraisal in Kenya, domestic workers' rights activism in Brazil and sex workers' rights activism in India.

Hannah Frith is a qualitative researcher in the field of sexuality studies at the University of Brighton. Her research interests centre on exploring embodiment and sexuality and in critically deconstructing the discourses, practices and subjectivities of heterosexualities. Her book *Orgasmic Bodies: The Orgasm in Contemporary Western Culture* was published in 2015.

Laura Harvey is a lecturer in sociology at the University of Brighton. Her interests include sexualities, everyday inequalities, research with young people, feminist methodologies and discourse analysis. She is particularly interested in innovative qualitative methods for researching everyday experiences. She is the co-author of *Mediated Intimacy: Sex Advice in Media Culture* (with Meg John Barker and Rosalind Gill) and *Celebrity, Aspiration and Contemporary Youth: Education and Inequality in an Era of Austerity* (with Heather Mendick, Kim Allen and Aisha Ahmad).

Yingying Huang is an associate professor in the Sociology Department and director of the Institute of Sexuality and Gender, Renmin University of China. Her work is based in China and includes research focusing on female sex workers; male clients, women's bodies and sexuality; social aspects of HIV/AIDS, and qualitative methodology, especially relating to marginalised groups. Her recent research projects include: 'The Emerging Grassroots Groups of Female Sex Workers in China', 'The Changing Sexual Discourses and Contexts in China since the 1980s' and 'Sexual Stories and Body Memories in Contemporary China'. She is also one of the key sponsors of a biannual international conference on sexualities in China and the National Workshop on Sexuality Research in China, both of which were inaugurated in 2007 and was a keynote speaker at the University of Sussex Researching Sex and Sexualities conference in 2015.

Charlotte Morris is a teaching fellow in sociology, gender studies and education at the University of Sussex. Her doctoral thesis (2014) was entitled 'Unsettled Scripts: Heterosexual Single Mothers' Narratives of Intimacy' and is available at http://sro.sussex.ac.uk/48918/. Alongside research interests in intimacies, heterosexuality, motherhood and gender, she researches in the field of higher education learning, (in)equities, care and wellbeing and is also currently a research fellow with the Centre for Higher Education and Equity Research. She co-convened the International Researching Sex and Sexualities conference at the University of Sussex in 2015.

Contributors

Alba Barbé i Serra is a doctor in social and cultural anthropology. Her thesis is titled 'Cross-dressing in the Catalan Context of the 21st Century'. As an anthropologist and social educator she specialises in the study of gender violences, homophobia and transphobia, as well as the shaping of public policies and the execution of educational interventions to eradicate them. She is a member of the Research Group on Social Control and Exclusion (GRECS) and the Catalan Anthropology Institute (ICA). She has published in journals such as *Journal of Language and Sexuality* and *Sapiens Research*. Her co-edited books include *Cua de sirena, Pessigolles* and *La construcción de las identidades de género: Una guía para trabajar con jóvenes y adolescentes*. 'EnFemme' is her first feature-length documentary: http://enfemmedoc.com/en/.

Meg-John Barker is a writer, therapist and activist-academic specialising in sex, gender and relationships. Meg-John is a senior lecturer in psychology at the Open University and a UKCP accredited psychotherapist, and has over a decade of experience researching and publishing on these topics including the popular books *Rewriting the Rules*, *The Secrets of Enduring Love*, *Queer: A Graphic History*, *Enjoy Sex*, *How to Understand Your Gender* and *The Psychology of Sex*. Website: www.rewriting-the-rules.com. Twitter: @megjohnbarker.

Catherine Barrett has been addressing older people's sexuality for over 20 years as a clinician, researcher and educator. In 2016 Catherine established the OPAL Institute, an Australia-based programme promoting the sexual rights of older people. Catherine is passionate about challenging ageism, privileging the voices of older people and utilising arts-based approaches to achieve real change.

Fran Carter is a senior lecturer in visual and material culture at Buckinghamshire New University. Her research interests centre on gender, sexuality and consumption, and she has a particular interest in methodology for design research. She completed her PhD, 'Magic Toyshops: Narrative and Meaning in the Women's Sex Shop', at Kingston University in 2014. It focuses on the design of sexual retail spaces and goods, investigating notions of female empowerment achieved through the consumption of goods and spaces dedicated to the pursuit of female erotic pleasure. She contributed to *Love Objects: Emotion, Design and Material Culture*, published in 2014 by Bloomsbury.

Natalie Day recently completed her PhD in sociology at Newcastle University, with a thesis titled 'A Sociological Analysis of the Sexual Learning Processes and Practices of Heterosexual Young Women in Northeast Brazil'. Natalie carried out nine months of fieldwork in a small town in the interior of Bahia, an experience she reflects upon in her contribution to the current volume.

Natalie Edelman is a mixed methods researcher whose work focuses on the use of social epidemiological approaches for the development of community-based sexual health interventions. She is currently a senior research fellow at the University of Brighton, having worked previously as a research fellow at UCL and as a research methodologist for the NIHR Research Design Service – South East for several years. Her interests include complex intervention development, critical epidemiology and patient and public involvement in research.

Vicky Johnson is a principal research fellow focusing on childhood and youth research and social pedagogy in the School of Education at Goldsmiths, University of London. She has over 20 years of experience as an NGO manager, researcher and consultant in social and community development, both in the UK and internationally. Vicky's key focus of research and publication is in the field of children and young people's participation. Research for the International Planned Parenthood Federation

(IPPF) has led to the reconceptualisation of youth programming to realise sexual rights across the Federation using her change-scape framework.

Cara Judea Alhadeff, visiting professor of gender and critical pedagogy at UC Santa Cruz, is a scholar and artist whose work engages feminist embodied theory. She earned her PhD from the European Graduate School. Alhadeff's first transdisciplinary book, *Viscous Expectations: Justice, Vulnerability, the Ob-scene* (2013/2014), scrutinises how racial hygiene, ethnocentrism and anti-intellectualism configure the troubled yet vital concept of equality. Fusing theory and image, *Viscous Expectations* explores vulnerability as a strategy for collaborative justice. As co-founder of 'Occupy Education, Pregnancy, Parenting', she has worked with communities to disentangle the roots of systemic corporeal and social violence – recognising how pregnancy, birth and mothering in the US function as officially sanctioned misogyny. As co-organiser for the San Francisco Bay Area's First International Birth Justice Fair, Alhadeff has collaboratively protested infrastructural racism and sexism in education, healthcare and housing. Alhadeff has exhibited her photographs and performance videos and presented lectures and workshops throughout Asia, Europe and the US.

Nicoletta Landi, who received her PhD from the University of Bologna, is an Italian anthropologist focusing on sexual health, gender equality, sexualities and performativity, BDSM, adolescence, sexual rights and public anthropology. Her theoretical skills are foregrounded in the areas of anthropology and sexualities studies, and she is skilled in ethnographic and action-research methodologies. She works as a freelance sex educator addressing both adults and adolescents in cooperation with Italian and international organisations through an intercultural and inclusive approach to sexual and gender plurality. She is a member of EASA (European Association for Social Anthropology), SIAA (Italian Society for Applied Anthropology) and ANPIA (National Italian Association for Professional Anthropology).

Eva Cheuk-Yin Li is a cultural sociologist, and her research focuses on interdisciplinary inquiry into media, culture, gender and sexualities in transnational and East Asian contexts. She is currently finishing her PhD at the Department of Film Studies, King's College London. Her work has appeared in *Crime Media Culture*, *East Asian Journal of Popular Culture*, *Transformative Works and Cultures* and several edited volumes.

Ester McGeeney is researcher and practitioner currently working for the young people's sexual health charity Brook. Previously Ester worked for the Centre for Innovation and Research in Childhood and Youth at the University of Sussex. Here Ester was co-investigator an ESRC knowledge exchange project working with the young people's sexual health charity Brook entitled 'Good sex?: Building evidence based practice in young people's sexual health' (http://goodsexproject.wordpress.com). This project aimed to use Ester's PhD data and research findings to create resources for practitioners to use in their work with young people on sexual pleasure. The PhD (2013) explored young people's sexual relationships and cultures. Ester is interested in how young people's conceptions of pleasure can be theorised and used to inform the delivery of sexual health services for young people. Her studentship was funded by Brook and The Open University.

P.J. Macleod is a genderqueer academic-activist, passionate about intersectional feminisms, bodies, identities and sexual/reproductive rights. They are currently working on a PhD (Middlesex University) having previously completed a gender studies MA (SOAS) and BA in Arabic and Middle Eastern Studies (Durham University). P.J. works in the charity sector on youth, gender and social justice initiatives. When not lowering the tone of otherwise civilised social events with sex-and-relationships-education trivia, P.J. can be found competing on the queer ballroom dance circuit and is a board member of the European Same-Sex Dance Association. Twitter: @PJaMacleod.

Anna Madill is chair of qualitative inquiry and deputy head of the School of Psychology, University of Leeds, UK and a member of the university Centre for Interdisciplinary Gender Studies. She is a co-founder and former chair (2008–2011) of the British Psychological Society Qualitative Methods in Psychology Section and an external examiner at the Tavistock and Portman NHS Foundation Trust, London. Anna received British Academy funding (2011–2013) for 'Understanding Japanese Boys' Love Manga from a UK Perspective'.

Katherine Radoslovich is in the final stages of completing her Doctor of Philosophy in gender studies and social analysis at the University of Adelaide, South Australia. She holds a Bachelor of International Studies with First Class Honours and a Bachelor of Development Studies. This chapter draws directly on her field experiences while undertaking her doctoral research. Katherine is passionate about sexual and reproductive health and wellbeing across the lifecourse.

Lucy Robinson is professor of collaborative history at the University of Sussex. She writes on popular music, politics and identity, feminism and punk pedagogy. Her book *Gay Men and the Left in Post-war Britain: How the Personal Became Political* is available through Manchester University Press. Since then she has worked on the Falklands War, charity singles, music videos, zine cultures, digital memory, protest and the politics of popular culture. As well as co-ordinating the Subcultures Network, and the open access digital project Observing the 80s, she has recently advised on an exhibition on Jersey in the 1980s and on a new documentary project funded by the BFI, *Queerama*.

Rachel Thomson is a sociologist by discipline whose research interests include the study of the life course and transitions, as well as the interdisciplinary fields of gender and sexuality studies. She is a methodological innovator and is especially interested in capturing lived experience, social processes and the interplay of biographical and historical time. She is a professor of childhood and youth studies, elected member of the Academy of Social Sciences, co-director of Sussex Humanities Lab, member and previously founding director of CIRCY (the Centre for Research and Innovation in Childhood and Youth). She has also been 2015–2017 visiting professor at SFI (Danish National Centre for Social Research).

Pam Thurschwell began teaching at Sussex in 2007 having previously worked or studied at University College London, Cambridge and Cornell University. She is the author of *Literature, Technology and Magical Thinking, 1880–1920* (2001) and *Sigmund Freud* (2000; second edition, 2009) and is the co-editor with Leah Price of *Literary Secretaries/Secretarial Culture* (2005); with Nicola Bown and Carolyn Burdett of *The Victorian Supernatural* (2004), and with Sian White of a special issue of *Textual Practice* on Elizabeth Bowen (2013). She has written on a wide variety of writers and artists including Henry James, Bob Dylan, George Eliot, Elvis Costello, Bruce Springsteen, Morrissey and Daniel Clowes. Her most recent articles are on Carson McCullers and Toni Morrison in *English Studies in Canada* 38(3–4), and Freud and Willa Cather in *A Concise Companion to Psychoanalysis, Literature and Culture* (edited by Laura Marcus and Ankhi Mukherjee, 2014). In July 2014, she organised a one-day symposium on the album and film *Quadrophenia* via the Centre for Modernist Studies at the University of Sussex, and in October 2016, a symposium, *Late and Later James/James at Lamb House*, in conjunction with the National Trust.

Catherine Vulliamy is a final year PhD student in gender studies in the Department of Social Sciences at the University of Hull. Her work focuses on the relationship between love and sexuality, particularly in the context of shifting or fluid desires, orientation and practice. She brings to her current work her prior experience as a researcher with Save the Children (UK), where she was involved in developing and using creative and innovative methodologies in research with children and young people. Prior to returning to education, Catherine had spent 20 years working in the voluntary sector, primarily with young people.

INDEX

Brucks, M., 141
bunan bunü (neither men nor women), 46–7
Butler, J., 33, 48–9, 153, 222

Cahnmann, M., 139, 140, 141
carnal knowledge, 178
Carrefour (Kristeva), 34
casual sex, 49–50
cervical screening, 69
Cesara, M., 221
child sexual abuse, 69
children: images of, 269; *see also* Boys Love (BL) manga
China, *Putonghua* pronouns, 52
Cicourel, A., 344
Cioran, E.M., 27
Coco de Mer (shop), 83
Coffey, A., 282
Cohen, Stan, 340, 342, 352–3
collages, 125–6; musical collages, 125–6, 131, 132–3
Conaway, Mary Ellen, 221–2
confidentiality, 152, 189, 205–6, 210
Connell, R.W., 246
constructivism, 3–4, 12, 50
contraception, 63, 67, 68, 69, 73, 186, 201
cover versions (of songs), 150–1, 159–65, 166–7
creative methods: and artistic abilities, 103, 115, 116, 117, 160–1; enhancement of researcher-participant relations, 129–30; entry points for abstract issues, 130–1; interview objects, 127–8, 129–30, 132; on love and sexuality, 122–5; overview, 99–103, 128–9; reflective potential, 100, 112, 116, 131–2; *see also* body mapping; cultural patchworks; ventriloquism
Crimp, D., 34
critical humanism, 346
critical realism, 66
critical reflexivity, 13, 255, 280
critical sexuality studies, 110–11
critical social epidemiology, 62, 70–6
cross-dressing, 219, 222–4

cultural differences, 174–9
cultural grammar, 203–6
cultural patchworks: collages, 125–6; communication beyond the verbal, 131; creative method, 101, 102, 122–5; dissemination, 133–4; interview objects, 127–8, 129–31, 132; musical collages, 125–6, 131, 132–3; personal journals, 125, 127; reflective potential, 100; varied types, 125
cultural relativism, 257, 326, 329
cultural traditions, and young people, 185, 186–7, 326
Cupples, J., 259

Daniel, E.V., 141
dating, single mothers, 303–5
Deleuze, G., 27, 28, 29–30, 33
dementia, 107
Design Week (magazine), 81
desire *see* sexual desire
Despuentes, V., 39
deterritorialised sexualities, 26, 27, 30–1
devadasi (never-to-be-married-to-a-man) girls, 234
Dezeen (magazine), 81
Dickson-Swift, V., 213
Diprose, G., 256
Disney, 133
Doucet, A., 88–9, 92–3
drug abuse, 67, 68–9
Dubish, J., 280
Duden, B., 28

Easton, D., 203
Eisner, E.W., 141
ejaculation, 20–1, 26–7, 32, 225
El Saadawi, N., 35–6
elderly people *see* older people; residential aged care
Elders, Joycelyn, Surgeon General, 32
Elliston, D., 280
email, as research medium, 261, 273
emotion, 224–7, 304
emotion work, 211–13
emotional ethnography, 178

ZED

Zed is a platform for marginalised voices across the globe.

It is the world's largest publishing collective and a world leading example of alternative, non-hierarchical business practice.

It has no CEO, no MD and no bosses and is owned and managed by its workers who are all on equal pay.

It makes its content available in as many languages as possible.

It publishes content critical of oppressive power structures and regimes.

It publishes content that changes its readers' thinking.

It publishes content that other publishers won't and that the establishment finds threatening.

It has been subject to repeated acts of censorship by states and corporations.

It fights all forms of censorship.

It is financially and ideologically independent of any party, corporation, state or individual.

Its books are shared all over the world.

www.zedbooks.net
@ZedBooks